Reading Popular Narrative

A Source Book

Edited by Bob Ashley

Leicester University Press
London and Washington

Leicester University Press
A Cassell Imprint
Wellington House, 125 Strand, London WC2R 0BB
PO Box 605, Herndon VA, 20172

First published 1989 as *The Study of Popular Fiction: A Source Book*
Revised and expanded edition 1997

British Library Cataloguing in Publication Data
A catalogue record for this book is available from the British Library

ISBN 0 7185 0082 2 (Hardback)
        0 7185 0083 0 (Paperback)

Library of Congress Cataloging-in-Publication Data
Reading popular narrative: a source book/edited by Bob Ashley. –
    Rev. and expanded ed.
        p. cm.
    Includes bibliographical references and index.
    ISBN 0–7185–0082–2 (hard cover). — ISBN 0–7185–0083–0 (paperback)
        1. Popular literature — Great Britain — History and criticism —
Theory, etc. 2. English fiction — History and criticism — Theory,
etc. 3. Authors and readers — Great Britain — History. 4. Reader-
response criticism. I. Ashley, Bob, 1946–   .
PR408.P67R43   1997
820.9—dc20   96–38315
                                                                    CIP

Typeset by Pantek Arts, Maidstone, Kent
Printed and bound in Great Britain by
Creative Print and Design Wales, Ebbw Vale.

CONTENTS

			vii
Preface			ix
Acknowledgements			

Part 1: Introduction: the reading of popular texts: 1
     some initial problems

1	K. Worpole	*Reading by numbers: contemporary publishing and popular fiction* (1984)	5
2	L. Fiedler	'Towards a definition of popular literature' (1975)	9
3	R. Rollin	'Against evaluation: the role of the critic of popular culture' (1975)	13
4	P. O'Flinn	'Production and reproduction: the case of *Frankenstein*' (1983)	18

Part 2: Mass society theory: British 'literary' and   33
     continental 'sociological' approaches

         36

Theory and methodology

         36

5	Q.D. Leavis	*Fiction and the reading public* (1932)	39
6	R. Williams	*The long revolution* (1961)	43
7	T.W. Adorno	'Culture industry reconsidered' (1967)	
8	S. Hall and P. Whannel	*The popular arts* (1964)	49
9	Walter Benjamin	'The storyteller' (n.d.)	52

         56

Applications

| 10 | Q.D. Leavis | 'The case of Miss Dorothy Sayers' (1937) | 56 |
| 11 | T.W. Adorno | 'On popular music' (1941) | 59 |

Part 3: Formula, genre and the structuralist analysis of narrative 67

Theory and methodology 71

12 John G. Cawelti 'The concept of formula in the study of popular literature' (1969) 71
13 Vladimir Propp *Morphology of the folk tale* (1928) 75
14 Roland Barthes 'Introduction to the structural analysis of narratives' (1966) 79
15 Will Wright *Sixguns and society: a structural study of the Western* (1975) 86
16 Stephen Neale *Genre* (1980) 87

Applications 92

17 John G. Cawelti *The six-gun mystique* (n.d.) 92
18 Elizabeth Kwasniewski 'Thrilling structures? science fiction from the early *Amazing* and detective fiction' (1987) 96
19 Umberto Eco 'The narrative structure in Fleming' (1966) 101

Part 4: Ideology, readers, pleasure: post-structuralism, deconstruction, psychoanalysis 111

Theory and methodology 120

20 Louis Althusser 'Ideology and ideological state apparatuses' (1971) 120
21 English Studies Group, CCCS, University of Birmingham 'Recent developments in English Studies at the Centre' (1976) 121
22 Roger Bromley 'Natural boundaries: the social function of popular fiction' (1978) 123

23	Pierre Macherey	*A theory of literary production* (1978)	129
24	Roland Barthes	'The death of the author' (1978)	132
25	Roland Barthes	*The pleasure of the text* (1973)	134
26	Stuart Hall	'A critical survey of the theoretical and practical achievements of the past ten years' (1976)	137
27	Tony Bennett	'Marxism and popular fiction' (1981)	143
28	Sigmund Freud	Classic psychoanalytic texts: 'Anxiety'(1926), 'Totem and taboo' (1912–13), 'The uncanny' (1919), 'Medusa's head' (1922), 'Fetishism' (1927)	152
29	J. Lacan	'The dream of Irma's injection' (1954–55)	162
30	Otto Rank	*The double: a psychoanalytic study* (1914)	164
31	Julia Kristeva	*The powers of horror* (1980)	166

Applications 167

32	Bob Dixon	*Catching them young 2: political ideas in children's fiction* (1977)	167
33	Jerry Palmer	'Thrillers: the deviant behind the consensus' (1973)	170
34	Tom Moylan	*Demand the impossible: science fiction and the Utopian imagination* (1986)	176
35	Joseph Grixti	*Terrors of uncertainty: the cultural contexts of horror fiction* (1989)	180
36	Noel Carroll	*The philosophy of horror* (1990)	182
37	Robin Wood	'An introduction to the modern American horror film' (1984)	189
38	Carol Clover	*Men, women and chain saws: gender in the modern horror film* (1992)	192
39	Mladen Dolar	'"I shall be with you on your wedding night": Lacan and the uncanny' (1991)	198
40	Roger Dadoun	'Fetishism in the horror film' (1989)	202
41	Barbara Creed	*The monstrous-feminine: film, feminism and psychoanalysis* (1993)	204
42	Kaja Silverman	*The acoustic mirror* (1988)	208

43 Cora Kaplan   'An unsuitable genre for a feminist?'
                        (1986)   211
44 Angela   '*Jackie*: an ideology of adolescent
    McRobbie   femininity' (1978)   215
45 Janet Batsleer   'Pulp in the pink' (1981)   217
46 Alison Light   '"Returning to Manderley": romance
                        fiction, female sexuality and class'
                        (1984)   222
47 Elizabeth Frazer   'Teenage girls reading *Jackie*' (1987)   226
48 Catherine Belsey   *Critical practice* (1980)   236

Bibliography   240
Index   245

PREFACE

Since publication in 1989 of *The Study of Popular Fiction*, there have been significant shifts in emphasis in the academic analysis of popular texts. Increasingly, such analysis occurs in the context of media studies or some combination of the categories: media, communication and cultural studies. Increasingly infrequently does textual analysis focus its attention solely on written texts. Much of the material in *The Study of Popular Fiction* addressed visual texts; in this volume, that tendency is endorsed with several additional extracts relating to film and a revised title which underlines the shift towards a range of narrative forms, embracing the cinematic and televisual alongside prose fiction. The other principal change is the enhancement of the coverage of the horror genre and psychoanalytic theory, both of which could arguably have been better represented in the previous title and both of which demand extensive coverage by virtue of their prominence during the 1990s among, respectively, 'popularity ratings' and theoretical interventions.

Beyond this, and the obviously necessary updating of bibliographies, the fundamental aims remain as before. Though some progress has been made since 1989, the reading of popular narrative remains problematic. Unless we confront problems of methodology, our reading of the popular will be constrained within the limits of intelligent 'common sense'. This volume is designed both to heighten awareness of these limitations and to offer assistance to the reader prepared to demand, 'What kinds of questions *should* I ask about popular texts?' The collection is based in the experience of some fifteen years of teaching popular texts to undergraduates on several degree courses in communication studies and media and cultural studies, and the principle of selection is simple enough: I have reprinted those materials which seem to have been most useful to students confronting the theoretical and methodological problems of reading popular narratives. The result is a collection of considerable diversity which commends no particular approach above the rest, and which encourages the reader to sharpen his/her* critical approaches to popular texts by drawing as appropriate on the perspectives represented. The readings will not be uniformly interesting and it is probable that the reader will gain most from the more recent extracts in Section Three. It should be stressed, however, that, though critical engagement is anticipated throughout, no extract is offered simply for rejection. A further point should be made about the sectioning of the volume which may also offer some guidance as to its use. The introductory essays indicate some of the most obvious ways in which certain influential tendencies may contribute to the reading of popular texts. Each section subsequently reprints a range of key statements of 'theory and methodology' followed by 'applications' in which these perspectives are drawn on in readings of particular texts or genres. This volume thus seeks to replicate in its organization something of the processes of

---

* From here on, editorial contributions will employ alternately masculine/feminine forms.

identification of problems, assimilation of theory and application to texts which it commends to its readers.

My thanks are due to the authors who permitted me to edit their work. Though some of the richness of some of the arguments may inevitably have been lost, I trust there have been no fundamental distortions. I am further indebted to Viv Chadder, whose enthusiasm for the horror genre and expertise in psychoanalytic theory have been crucial to the revising of the volume. I am sure that my thanks are echoed by those sensitive students who did not find it easy to deal with some of the horrors she has confronted them with!

ACKNOWLEDGEMENTS

The author and publishers wish to thank the following who have given permission for the use of copyright material:

The estate of the author and Chatto & Windus for extracts from Q.D. Leavis, *Fiction and the Reading Public* (1932) and R. Williams, *The Long Revolution* (1961); the author and Comedia Publishing for extracts from K. Worpole, *Reading by Numbers. Contemporary Publishing and Popular Fiction* (1984); Bowling Green University Popular Press for extracts from L.A. Fiedler, 'Towards a Definition of Popular Literature', in C. Bigsby (ed.), *Superculture* (1975); R.B. Rollin, 'Against Evaluation: the Role of the Critic of Popular Culture', in *Journal of Popular Culture*, Vol. 9, (1975); J.G. Cawelti, 'The Concept of Formula in the Study of Popular Literature', in *Journal of Popular Culture*, vol. 3, (1969), and *The Six-Gun Mystique* (nd); the authors and editors and Methuen & Co. for extracts from T. Bennett, 'Marxism and Popular Fiction', and P. O'Flinn, 'Production and Reproduction: the Case of *Frankenstein*', in P. Humm, P. Stigant and P. Widdowson (eds), *Popular Fictions: Essays in Literature and History* (1986); *New German Critique* for extracts from T.W. Adorno, 'Culture Industry Reconsidered' (1967); Century Hutchinson (Publishing Group Ltd) for extract from S. Hall and P. Whannel, *The Popular Arts* (1964); excerpts from 'The Storyteller' in Walter Benjamin, *Illuminations*, © 1955 Suhrkamp Verlag, Frankfurt a.M., English translation Harry Zohn, © 1968 Harcourt Brace and Company, reprinted by permission of Harcourt Brace and Company; William Collins Sons and Co. Ltd for extracts from 'Introduction to the Structural Analysis of Narrative' and 'The Death of the Author' in R. Barthes, *Image, Music, Text* (tr. S. Heath) (1977); University of California Press for extract from W. Wright, *Sixguns and Society: a Structural Study of the Western* (1975); the author and BFI for extracts from S. Neale, *Genre* (1980); Macdonald and Co. for extracts from U. Eco, *The Bond Affair* (tr. Downie) (1966); Verso for extract from L. Althusser, *Lenin and Philosophy* (tr. B. Brewster) (1971); Centre for Contemporary Cultural Studies, University of Birmingham, for extracts from S. Hall, D. Hobson, A. Lowe and P. Willis (eds) *Culture, Media, Language* (1980) and A. McRobbie, '*Jackie*: an Ideology of Adolescent Femininity', Stencilled Occasional Paper, Women Series, no. 53 (1978); the author and *Red Letters* for extracts from R. Bromley, 'Natural Boundaries: the Social Function of Popular Fiction', in *Red Letters* No. 7, (1978); the author for extracts from P. Macherey, *A Theory of Literary Production* (1978); the author for S. Hall, 'A Critical Survey of the Theoretical and Practical Work of the Past Ten Years', in *Literature, Society and the Sociology of Literature,* University of Essex, (1976); Drake Marketing Services for extracts from B. Dixon, *Catching Them Young 2: Political Ideas in Children's Fiction* (1977); the author and editors for extracts from J. Palmer 'Thrillers: the Deviant behind the Consensus' in I. Taylor and L. Taylor (eds), *Politics and Deviance* (1973); the author and Methuen and Co. for extracts from T. Moylan, *Demand the Impossible: Science Fiction and the Utopian Imagination* (1986); the author for C. Kaplan, 'An Unsuitable Genre for a Feminist?' in *Womens Review*, No. 8, (1986); the author and *Spare Rib* for J. Batsleer, 'Pulp in the Pink' in *Spare Rib*, No. 109 (1981); the author for extracts from A. Light '"Returning to Manderley" Romance Fiction, Female Sexuality and Class' in *Feminist Review*, No. 16 (1984); the author and Methuen and Co. for extracts from C. Belsey, *Critical Practice* (1980); the estate of the author and Cambridge University Press for extracts from Q.D. Leavis, 'The Case of Miss Dorothy Sayers' in *Encounter*, (1937); the author and *Foundation: the Review of Science Fiction* for extracts from E. Kwasniewski, 'Thrilling Structures? Science Fiction from the early "Amazing"and Detective Fiction', in *Foundation*, no. 38, (1986/7); extracts from Vladimir Propp, *Morphology of the Folktale*, second edition (tr. Laurence Scott, revised and edited with a preface by Louis A. Wagner), ©1968, by permission of the University of Texas Press; the editor and Cambridge University Press for extracts from J.A. Miller (ed.), *The Seminar of Jacques Lacan*; extracts reprinted from Otto Rank, *The Double: A Psychoanalytic Study*, (tr. and ed. Harry Tucker Jr.), © 1971 University of North Carolina Press, used by permission of the publisher; extract from Julia Kristeva, *The Powers of Horror*, ©1982 Columbia University Press, reprinted with permission of the publisher; the author and Routledge for extract from pp. 9–12 of J. Grixti, *Terrors of Uncertainty: the Cultural Contexts of Horror Fiction* (1989); the authors and the BFI for extracts from C. Clover, *Men, Women and Chain Saws: Gender in the Modern Horror Film* (1992) and R. Dadoun, 'Fetishism in the Horror Film', in J. Donald (ed.) *Fantasy and the Cinema*; the author and Routledge for extracts from B. Creed, the *Monstrous-Feminine*; excerpts from Roland Barthes, *The Pleasure of the Text* (tr. Richard Miller), translation © 1975 Farrar, Straus and Giroux Inc., reprinted by permission of Hill and Wang, a division of Farrar, Straus and Giroux Inc.; the author and Scarecrow Press for extracts from R. Wood, 'An Introduction to the the American Horror Film'; extract reprinted from N. Carroll, *The Philosophy of Horror*, (1990) by permission of Routledge; extract reprinted by permission of Sage Publications Ltd from E. Frazer, *Teenage Girls Reading 'Jackie'*, (1987); extracts from Sigmund Freud, *Introductory Lectures on Psychoanalysis*, (tr. James Strachey), translation © 1965, 1964, 1963 James Strachey, reprinted by permission of Liveright Publishing Corporation; extracts from S Freud, *Totem and Taboo*, by permission of Routledge; to Sigmund Freud Copyrights, The Institute of Psychoanalysis and The Hogarth Press for permission to quote from *The Standard Edition of the Complete Psychological Works of Sigmund Freud* (tr. and ed. James Strachey).

PART 1

Introduction: the reading of popular texts: some initial problems

1 K. Worpole, *Reading by Numbers: Contemporary Publishing and Popular Fiction* (1984), Chapter 2
2 L.A. Fiedler, 'Towards a Definition of Popular Literature' (1975)
3 R.B. Rollin, 'Against Evaluation: the Role of the Critic of Popular Culture' (1975)
4 P. O'Flinn, 'Production and Reproduction: the Case of *Frankenstein*' (1983)

The study of popular narrative is the serious examination of material widely dismissed as trivial and there is a tendency to assume that such study is in some way 'easy'. At a frivolous level, easy because the narrative is short and undemanding. More seriously, easy because popular texts are 'accessible' and students allegedly respond in terms of their own experience far more readily and vividly than they would respond, say, to a novel of 'substance' by George Eliot or D.H. Lawrence. Valid as this may be of individual responses to particular texts, as a statement about popular forms in general it will not do. It envisages the popular as an undifferentiated, composite construct in which consumers are uniformly immersed. Experience suggests otherwise: that there are real distinctions to be drawn between, for example, popular musical or televisual forms and narrative forms such as detective novels or horror films. There is no necessary correlation between the latter forms and the leisure experience of those who seek to study them and the obstacles are, in fact, numerous, complex and formidable. It is a premise of this collection that life as a student of popular narrative is far from easy. The introduction will explore some of the problems.

The student who confesses an interest in popular fiction may encounter a varied but predictable range of uncomprehending responses, from the genuinely incredulous parent – 'do they really study that kind of thing in the colleges these days?' – to the aggressively utilitarian – 'reading Shakespeare's bad enough, but I think it's a disgrace people are getting state money for reading this trash'. Some students even have to cope with the misgivings of tutors on other, more traditional courses whose vision still identifies courses in popular fiction as 'soft options'. And all this is to assume that the student has no lingering doubts of his own as to the validity of the topic.

Such doubts seldom bother the student of 'traditional' English literature. 'The classics' are, even today, widely respected, seen to be self-evidently important,

1

'good things' to study. And there's not very much doubt *which* texts are to be studied. The literary canon – that is the authors and texts widely deemed important – is remarkably stable. Shakespeare, Chaucer and Milton, Austen, Hardy and Lawrence are among the dozen or so writers who appear time and again in the syllabuses of English courses at all levels. There may be space occasionally (and increasingly) for lesser known authors, but any controversy is usually at the periphery: the centre remains unmoved. For the student there is no problem of definition of field of study: her task is simply to become skilled in writing about well-established texts. The student of popular fiction enjoys few such certainties. Indeed the very problem of defining the field of study is central, fundamental and demands the attention of anyone who thinks seriously about non-canonical texts.

What then is signified by the 'popular' of popular narrative? Most definitions would include 'enjoyed (and probably purchased) by many readers and viewers' and in differentiating popular from 'serious' narrative it is widely assumed that its consumers, as well as being overwhelmingly numerous, possess little capacity for aesthetic discrimination. The sources of this assumption will be returned to. As to the earlier, common-sense formulation, the identification of popular with commercial success and the enjoyment of many would seem straightforward enough and, within fairly obvious limits, it is. The popular–serious distinction, however, is a theoretical mine-field.

In 1961 the best-selling paperback here in the United Kingdom was Lawrence's Lady Chatterley's Lover. Sales totalled three million copies in the first three months after publication. It so happens that this figure is substantially higher than that achieved in any one year by any single one of Fleming's James Bond novels, overwhelmingly the best-selling popular novels of the 1960s.[1] In quantitative terms, then, the popularity of Lady Chatterley's Lover is inescapable. But what of our qualitative nuance? Clearly the suggestion that D.H. Lawrence is a second-rate novelist appealing to readers of depraved taste would be widely rejected. Are we, then, to conclude that the best-selling paperback of 1961 was not in fact popular? The problem is focused the more sharply if we cite the familiar examples of Dickens and Shakespeare (both popular in their day, subsequently designated serious). Clearly the categories are both overlapping and historically variable. Paul O'Flinn's essay (4) on the shifting significance of Frankenstein demonstrates that there can be no transhistorical, immutable popularity. As for Lady Chatterley's Lover, in 1961 and for the years of its notoriety it *was* a popular novel. It did not simultaneously cease to be serious fiction. Texts do not behave as those seeking definitional precision might like: lines distinguishing popular and serious as mutually exclusive entities cannot be drawn.

And yet, in spite of all the problems of definition, there can be little doubt as to significance in our culture of this nuance, in shaping responses to popular forms. Its source is located ultimately in the practice of literary criticism and it is that negative usage which regards popular fiction as second-rate fiction (or worse), a kind of cultural detritus, left over after literature of permanent value has been identified. Thus 'good' literature is identified, 'canonised', and takes its place within high culture as serious art. What is left is part of popular culture and the best that can be said of it is that it provides harmless entertainment (many commentators, of course, have disputed 'harmless'). More likely it will be ignored. And this is the starting point of this collection: what is to be said about the left-overs? For the residuum is overwhelmingly substantial. It constitutes the principal, perhaps only, fictional reading of the majority of the population of *modern industrialised societies; it is widely assumed to influence lives profoundly; and is surely of major significance in the understanding of those lives, particularly the processes by which meanings are constructed and exchanged.*

It would be wrong to overstate the case here. The silence on popular fiction has been broken and the bulk of the material in this collection indicates the progress which has been made, slowly, since the 1960s, both within the practices of literary criticism and, much more significantly, beyond it, via the influence of other academic disciplines. And yet my early premise stands: it is not easy to study popular fiction; much resistance persists, as do the old prejudices of the mass-culture debate. It is important to re-emphasise the intrusiveness of these prejudices. Such is the prestige and influence of the institution of Literature that its evaluations reverberate beyond its own disciplinary confines. This is why the very idea of the intensive study of popular romance or science fiction invariably provokes a response – no matter how non-literary the respondent. And this is why the student's difficulties are compounded.

And so, what is a student, perhaps, though not necessarily, fresh from 'A' level study in English Literature, going to make of the following passage? (The passage is from Mickey Spillane's novel I The Jury *and records the hero Mike Hammer's encounter with a young woman who, he's been warned in advance, may be a nymphomaniac. The reader is urged to pause for a few minutes after reading it and note briefly his responses.)*

Her eyes were blazing into mine. They were violet eyes, a wild blazing violet. Her mouth looked soft and wet and provocative. She was making no attempt to keep the negligee on. One shoulder had slipped down and her brown skin formed an interesting contrast with the pink. I wondered how she got her tan. There were no strap marks anywhere. She uncrossed her legs deliberately and squirmed like an overgrown cat, letting the light play with the ripply muscles in her naked thighs.
I was only human. I bent over her, taking her mouth on mine. She was straining in the divan to reach me, her arms tight around my neck. Her body was a hot flame; the tip of her tongue searched for mine. She quivered under my hands wherever I touched her. Now I knew why she hadn't married. One man could never satisfy her. My hand fastened on the hem of the negligee and with one motion flipped it open, leaving her body lean and bare. She let my eyes search every inch of her brown figure.
I grabbed my hat and jammed it on my head.

I have occasionally confronted new students of popular fiction with this extract in a seminar situation. Invariably it provokes laughter, though the laughter is usually uncomfortable and ambiguous, reflecting the reader's uncertainty as to how, in a serious academic context, to respond to material of this kind. Fundamentally the laughter proclaims the reader's distance: she clearly knows the difference between good writing and this writing. She further proclaims herself immune from its effects: she at least won't be depraved and corrupted by writing of this sort. Of course many readers don't get this far: an initial response of aversion or total indifference ensures silence on Spillane. Such silence, or uncertainty, reflects the responses of literary criticism to popular fiction and point what seems to me the only way forward. What is required is, effectively, a form of de-conditioning, a release from these culturally induced reflex rejections into a capacity to undertake, without embarrassment, the dispassionate analysis of Spillane.

The desired analysis, however, involves the exploration of a pleasure which the analyst may or may not share, and this may raise further problems, especially for the politically sensitive student. The very right to analyse 'other people's pleasure' may be questioned as a kind of cultural trespass in which an élite privileged to partake of true culture enters the territory of the uncultured. The exercise is seen as patronising. The argument has become circular and somewhat vicious: the student freed (perhaps miraculously) from the inhibiting influence of Literature nonetheless doubts his credentials as a privileged outsider to comment on life in the ghetto. At this point the position of students of other academic disciplines may seem enviable: not only does the sociologist have no expectation of pleasure in the study object *per se*; it is also an everyday part of the job to investigate the culture of subordinate social groups. Given that such departures within literary studies are, even today, occasional and peripheral, it should not surprise that they constitute politically sensitive areas.

There would seem to be two possible ways out of the impasse. Solution one would be to rid Literature of its hang-ups: a reconstituted criticism and a deconditioned student. Solution two would be to rid the study of popular narrative of Literature, to entrust the work to the social sciences and to regard, for example, an 'A' level qualification in English Literature as a negative qualification for academic study of popular texts. Solution two has its advocates and it represents arguably the easiest route to a dispassionate criticism of texts as cultural practices and whose focus is meaning as opposed to value. And yet a divorce with Literature entails the loss of so much more. Tony Bennett's article 'Marxism and Popular Fiction' (27) argues the failure of much early work on popular fiction to engage with specific texts. Close textual analysis is not of course the prerogative of those with literary backgrounds, but it is fairly clear that the technique has been nurtured within English Literature in such a way that a literary training significantly encourages the capacity for close, sensitive and sophisticated textual study. The productive study of popular texts does not then require a defection from Literature to Sociology but rather a creative synthesis in which detailed textual reading is reinforced by an objectivity and freedom from value judgements rooted in the social sciences. The object of this book is firstly to indicate some of the issues such a reconstituted criticism will address and secondly to provide examples of such critical practice in action.

A further theoretical problem remains. The very notion of a method for the study of popular fiction may be questioned. There may be anxiety lest one simply constructs an alternative tradition, even an 'alternative canon', separate and distinct from that of main-stream literature. Such a separation would certainly contradict the earlier insistence that the popular and the serious are shifting and overlapping categories. And it may further be argued that to remove work on popular texts to a separate terrain, with its own distinctive methodology, is to endorse its marginalisation, to legitimise Literature in its tendency to ignore. The problem is very real and is similar in essence to the dilemma of other interest groups relegated to the periphery of what 'matters' culturally – feminists, blacks, working-class writers, for example. I must confess to a continuing uncertainty on this issue: it is possible that consolidated space on the margins now will lead to invisibility in the long term. What is certain, however, is that continuing silence will not lead to the doors of Literature being flung open and popular fiction welcomed in. What is also certain is that the terms in which the silence is broken should not imply a theoretical endorsement of the popular–serious division. It is manifestly true that the methods of traditional literary studies offer few useful insights into non-canonical texts. The corollary does not, however, apply. The reconstituted criticism I advocate should not be regarded as appropriate to popular texts exclusively. Structuralist narratology has as much to say about Jane Austen's narratives as those of Barbara Cartland and it would be absurd to argue that Conrad's novels are in some sense 'above' the kind of ideological analysis entirely appropriate to those of Le Carré. The ideal to work towards is one in which analysis is directed at 'fiction' with no need of qualitative adjective. Short of that ideal as we are, the distinction, for all its theoretical absurdity, is empirically present and influential. It seems to me that a full recognition, both of its sources and nature, is a precondition of its being broken down.

Note

1   Sources for sales statistics: *Lady Chatterley's Lover*, supplied by Penguin Books Ltd.; for Fleming, see Bennett and Woollacott (1987), pp. 26–27. These figures do not, of course, reflect literary qualities alone: *Lady Chatterley's Lover* was the subject of an infamous (and unsuccessful) prosecution under the Obscene Publications Act in summer 1960, and from 1962 onwards Fleming's novels were adapted into a series of immensely successful feature films.

📖 READING 1

Reading by numbers: contemporary publishing and popular fiction

Ken Worpole

The key ingredient in the success of popular literature is quantity, both in numbers of titles and numbers of sales. The market must continually be stimulated and satisfied. Economic literature is one of economies of scale, and as such requires writers of enormous output. Frank Richards, children's writer and creator of Billy Bunter, wrote up to 18,000 words a day, and in his lifetime is estimated to have written over 60 million words for publication. Dennis Wheatley wrote more than 60 books; Denise Robins more than 170 romantic novels; Ruby Ayres published 143 novels; Barbara Cartland more than 230, though these pale besides the spectacular output of popular novelist Ursula Bloom, who has had 420 novels published to date and is still writing. Modern writers are less prolific but their sales are more spectacular. Dennis Wheatley's total sales of 37 million copies for 60 titles has, more recently, been eclipsed by Stephen King's 40 million sales with only four titles (and within less than one decade)! Modern popular fiction thus very easily attains sales figures far in excess of earlier record numbers, which suggests that the market is still expanding and that the book has by no means exhausted its possibilities as a cultural form.

. . . .

In the modern literary industry the sums of money changing hands for the basic product are high, and the successes and failures spectacular. One million dollars was paid as an advance by an American publisher for Shirley Conran's soft-porn novel *Lace*. (She hadn't written a novel before, but through her journalism was known to be an up-to-the-minute 'name'.) Spy-novelist Ken Follett, 'Britain's youngest author-millionaire', at the end of the 1970s signed a 'three-book, three-million dollar contract in the U.S., obviously where the market is strongest'.[10] Mick Jagger's autobiography was sold in 1978 to Weidenfeld for £1.5 million. The U.K. rights to Martin Cruz Smith's intriguing thriller *Gorky Park* were sold for £150,000; the film rights were sold in America for 1 million dollars and his publishers have earned over 2.5 million dollars from book sales internationally.[11] Cruz Smith is in fact an interesting example of the modern writer of popular fiction. Between the ages of 24 and 39 he wrote over 60 novels for various paperback publishers in America:

> Editors knew I could turn out a better book in two weeks than many which had taken six months to write. That's not immodest. A helluva lot of bad books were being written in six months.

Before the success of *Gorky Park* Cruz Smith had also made a name as a writer of genre fiction with the novel *Nightwing*, commissioned by his publishers 'when the film and publishing industries were in a state of post-*Jaws* euphoria, eager to lay out money on any property which featured biting animals.'[12]

Of such key sensitivities to popular moods and genres are fortunes made. American eye surgeon Robin Cook decided he wanted to write a best-seller, so he took a crash course in the writing of popular fiction, scrutinising the *New York Times* best-seller lists, and making a painstaking study of those novelists '. . . with sales of a million copies or over.'[13] After reading 150 such novels in order to extricate the conventions, he wrote *Coma*, employing every trick of the suspense-thriller. Before publishing it he secured the sale of the film rights and in one day, 'Cook was able to sell hardback, paperback and movie rights and secure the necessary exposure to make *Coma* a hit. The movie was a big success and the novel was a worldwide best-seller.' Cook has since gone on to write *Brain* and *Fever*.

The publishing industry has become one of the brightest jewels in the otherwise rather tarnished crown of entrepreneurial capitalism. It remains one of the few industries where fortunes can still be made overnight, and consequently the press and other media have become obsessed with the rags-to-riches stories of unknown authors who have become millionaires in a very short space of time. Thus we learn that Stephen King 'has a wife and three children, two houses, two Mercedes';[14] that for Sheila Holland 'success has brought her a 20-room mansion, private schooling for her children, a Daimler – the Rolls is on order – and a passion for suites at the Ritz and jolly jaunts on Concorde';[15] and that Roberta Leigh lives in 'a luxurious London penthouse filled with antique furniture, Henry Moore sculptures, even a Renoir. And she stopped counting her money years ago.' East London working class writer Lena Kennedy, having published three 'sexy, gritty novels', now has 'two homes and is feted around the world in five-star hotels'.[16] Len Deighton is the son of a chauffeur with a cottage in Dundalk and a 'second home in California'; and Ken Follett has an 'Edwardian mansion in Surrey. Second home in New York. Wife, two children, one butler. Chauffeur-driven Mercedes'.[17] On the back cover of *Woman's Weekly* Fiction Omnibus, we learn that author Sarah Parkes 'is interested in local history, particularly that of her own sixteenth-century house'.

It shouldn't be thought that such professional writers earn their money through occasional bouts of work triggered off by moments of sudden dramatic inspiration. Writing for them is a daily stint at the coalface of production. It has to be, if like Roberta Leigh you 'once hammered out 24 books in a year – every one a winner.'[18] Sheila Holland 'can write 10,000 words a day'. When interviewed in *The Guardian* Len Deighton said he had been working for the past five weeks 'on his word processor for up to 14 hours a day'. The production of popular fiction is every bit as labour intensive as it was in the days of Gissing's New Grub Street. Today the rewards are much greater and the writers of mass production fiction no longer live in cheap lodging houses in Somerstown or in semi-detached houses in Islington, but work at home in stock-broker belt Surrey with one or two secretaries to answer the fan mail and deal with the accountant.

No longer does the writer type away at an original idea which becomes a novel submitted to the publisher; rather, the publisher, or agent, goes to the writer with the idea for the novel. In a recent interview, actress Angela Douglas talked of 'meeting with my publisher to discuss ideas for a novel he wants me to write'. It was seen earlier how literary agent Carol Smith actually wrote the plot outlines for an entire series of neo-gothic romances. It was the same person who persuaded 'minor American novelist Peter Straub to write the contemporary gothic horror novel – *Ghost Story* – which turned him into a millionaire bestseller overnight.'[19]

Selling up front

In their study of the contemporary book trade Mike Poole and Richard Rayner have shown how 'economic pressures are forcing publishers to look to cover their costs *before* a novel has even been published . . .'[20] Consequently in many publishing houses the editorial department has shrunk as the rights, sales, publicity and marketing departments have grown. Many of the older publishers have only recently started a paperback imprint. Before that they were – in the case of fiction particularly – largely concerned with publishing original hardbacks and selling the paperback rights to another company. Part of any contract made with a paperback imprint would be a delay of at least one year between the appearance of the hardback and the appearance of the paperback. To the outsider the obvious question to ask is why novels are not printed in paperback straight away, a move which would reap the big financial rewards more immediately. To do so, would be to fly in the face of a very deep-grained conservatism on the part of the publishing world and the book-reviewing world. For as has been noted, in Britain and America most newspapers, literary and other cultural journals, will only review hardback books. And since it is largely the book reviews which initially stimulate public interest in a book, nearly everything has to start out in hardback, even though the paperback rights, and possibly the film rights, have been signed and sealed before the actual text gets published in its hardback version.

Apart from selling the paperback and occasionally the film rights to a book, publishers increasingly have to negotiate with two other key agencies – a book club and the mass distributors such as W.H. Smith and Bookwise. Book clubs are a post-war phenomenon, originating in America, which started up quite usefully to provide book-buying facilities by post to people who had little possibility of getting to any kind of bookshop. The popularity of the early book clubs meant that they quickly developed a large and captive book-buying public. Their large sales meant that they could quite easily start to negotiate large discounts from the publishers and thus pass on some of these to their readers in the form of special offers and occasional free offers. Some went so far in indulging their club members they actually abbreviated the novels to make them faster and easier reading (the origin of *The Reader's Digest* book club). In some countries book clubs don't even offer any choice to their members, but send them so many books a month which they pay for without protest.[21] Publishers have no choice but to try to make deals with book clubs, even though they are often forced into giving massive discounts, thus upsetting bookshop owners whose livelihood is threatened. Authors who were originally keen on any form of distribution which increased their sales have recently begun to have doubts about book clubs. In a recent example, popular fiction writer Jeffrey Archer realised that through a book club deal on his best-selling novel *Cain and Abel* he was only getting 4p a copy royalties, whereas the royalty on a bookshop sale of the hardback amounted to £1.04 a copy – a rather large difference. Yet a book club deal can be responsible for 'more than half a best-seller's readership', so both publishers and authors are caught on the horns of a dilemma.[22] But that is what the free market is all about: economies of scale for some, and the law of diminishing returns for others!

It is also important for publishers to get their books liked, and therefore promoted by, the two largest distributors of paperbacks in Britain: W.H. Smith and Bookwise. Smith's and John Menzies totally dominate book sales in the High Street and at railway stations, and can easily be responsible for well over half the sales of a popular paperback in Britain. Like the book clubs they are also able to negotiate very large discounts with publishers for the privilege of using their extensive chain of outlets. The other distribution network in Britain, which accounts for 'some 25 per cent of the total paperback sales in Britain', is Bookwise. This distribution firm – which *selects* only about a third of the titles published in paperback fiction each month – supplies 'supermarkets, chemist shops, newsagents, department stores and motorway service stations', and of the 100 or so titles selected each month picks just five titles to actively promote. A clear monopoly, Bookwise's monthly selection is crucial to publishers. 'If Bookwise don't like something, we would certainly reduce the print-run and possibly stand by for a loss' is the comment of one sales manager.[23] Fontana's marketing director has stated that: 'We're naturally very aware of the attitudes of our two major customers. It may not be every day, but if we were thinking, say, of bidding £50,000 for a new book, we'd put in a couple of calls – one to Smiths, another to Bookwise – to see whether *they* thought it promotable.'[24] So a large part of paperback fiction doesn't even get to the market place, let alone have a chance of displaying its wares. Distribution is one of the most powerful gate-keepers at the entrance to the town square where the books are bought and sold each week, and if you cannot pass through then you have to return home empty-handed.

Notes

10 *Guardian*, 1 October 1983.
11 *Time Out*, 2 July 1982.
12 Ibid.
13 Ibid.
14 *Guardian*, 14 May 1982.
15 *News of the World*, 2 October 1983.
16 Ibid.
17 *Guardian*, 1 October 1983.
18 *News of the World*, op. cit.

19 *Time Out*, op. cit.
20 Ibid.
21 *Literature in the Market Place*, Per Gedin, 1977.
22 *Sunday Times*, 25 April 1982.
23 *Sunday Times*, 6 March 1983.
24 *Sunday Times*, 22 July 1984.

 READING 2

'Towards a definition of popular literature'

Leslie A. Fiedler

Fiedler's article opens with a discussion of the basis on which 'popular' texts are 'denied the quasi-immortality bestowed by . . . critics on the "Classics"'. The distinctions, he argues, are spurious and he goes on: 'critics have been forced to play ridiculous sorting-out games: distinguishing "serious novelists" from "mere entertainers" and "Best Sellers" from "Art Novels".' What follows is Fiedler's historical explanation of the pressures underlying this impulse towards categorisation.

Why were they, then, so reluctant to give up categories so clearly unviable? And why, even more distressingly, are some of our critical contemporaries, admirable in other respects, unwilling to do so? The answer lies in the closed circle of 'aesthetics', but in a larger historical and social overview, which begins by investigating the moment at which modern criticism came into being. If we look hard at the mid-eighteenth century, when it all properly began, it becomes clear to us that the notion of literary standards, along with the emergence of the critic-pedagogues as their official 'enforcers', is a product of the cultural insecurity of the rich merchants and nascent industrialists, who were just then taking over control of society in the Western World. Wielding first economic and then political power seemed to them not quite enough to satisfy hungers bred during their long cultural exclusion. They wanted also to dominate literary culture, as had the ruling classes whom they superseded. They demanded, first and foremost to be the chief consumers (delegating this function to their wives and daughters) and sustainers (this function they reserved for their male selves) of song and story, which for them had become almost exclusively identified with print and the 'book'. But they desired also to be its judges, the guardians of the 'values' which it embodied and re-enforced.

But this they proved incapable, either in their own right or by delegation to the distaff side, of doing – certainly not with the insouciant self-assurance of the feudal aristocracies who had imposed their taste in this area, at first despite, and later even on and through an established clergy which theoretically despised all 'literature'. Unlike the predecessors, the new ruling classes were born with a sense of insecurity which has since grown indurated rather than being mitigated by time and the habit of command.

They were even, perhaps especially, insecure about the Pop forms which first assumed a central importance with their political rise. The earliest and most

9

notable of these is, of course, the novel itself, which reflected in its archetypal plots the communal dreams of the New Class; and embodied in its very shape and substance, those dreams made paper and ink and boards, a commodity, in short, to be hefted and bought and sold. The incarnate myths of the bourgeoisie are commodities, even as the market-place and technology are its collective unconscious. Yet they did not, could not in the nature of the case, understand on the level of full consciousness the significance of the technology which they controlled, or the new methods of production and distribution which such technology made possible.

. . . .

The bourgeoisie were blinded by obsolescent mythologies of Art, which envisaged 'poetry' as the creation of a lonely genius and his Muse, rather than the product of technological man and his machines. Consequently, they thought of literary 'survival', or as they insisted on calling it still, 'immortality', as the result of critical consensus rather than the workings of the market-place. Believing in the division of labour in all fields, they appointed 'experts' to prepare themselves by the study of the Classics, and to tell them (to 'brief' them, we would say these days) whether novels were O.K. in general; and if so, which were more O.K. than others.

Obviously, they did not always take the good advice they sought. Quite often, in fact, they continued to read what their critical mentors had taught them to regard as 'trash' – defiantly in the case of sentimental-pious 'trash', shamefacedly and secretly in the case of pornographic 'trash'. But they did snatch such work from the hands of their children; especially their daughters, when they caught them reading it. In the light of this, it is clear that the function of modern critics and schoolmasters whose subject is literature was from the start rather like that performed by the writers of Etiquette Books, Dictionaries and Grammars. Like the latter, the former responded to the cultural insecurity of the eighteenth century middle classes by providing 'rules' or 'standards' or guides to 'good behaviour'. The new rich wanted to know which fork to pick up; how to spell things 'right'; when, if at all, it was proper to say 'ain't'; and also what books to buy for display in their libraries or on their coffee tables.

At first, the critics had to compete in establishing 'values' or 'standards' in their field of literature with the clergy, who were also assigned by the uncertain masters the task of guiding them right. It was unclear on both sides, and doubly unclear to those caught in the middle, into whose territory literature properly fell, the schoolmaster's or the parson's. Indeed, as long as the critics themselves continued to maintain – borrowing the notion from their pre-Gutenberg predecessors – that literature must 'instruct' as well as 'delight', it proved impossible to separate the domain of Art, in which critics were the 'experts', from that of Prudence, in which the clergy had the final word. And who, in any case, was to mediate between aesthetics and ethics: the critic or the pulpit-moralist?

Since in the hierarchical value system of the bourgeoisie the ethical ranked higher than the aesthetic, it was more than a century before any critic dared confront the power of the church head-on, by asserting the creed of 'art for art's sake'. More typically, critics and pedagogues alike tried instead to beat the moralists at their own game, by dividing all of art along essentially Christian lines into what was Serious, Elevating, Uplifting and of High Moral Purpose, on the one hand; and what was trivial, debasing, vulgar and of no redeeming value, on the other. But such ethical distinctions turned out, to no one's surprise, merely to reinforce distinctions made on presumably aesthetic and formalist grounds, i.e., in the name of Greece and Rome rather than Jerusalem and Galilee. Finally, however, the literary experience confounds moral distinctions, even as it does those based on formal elegance, beauty of structure, precision of language, control of tone, avoidance of sentimentality and cliché or whatever criteria are currently chic. Think of the writers presumably to be excluded from the canon on ethical grounds who have been smuggled into respectability by bending or adjusting moral 'standards', or simply by lying to oneself or the political guardians of morality, or both. And think especially of how in recent days duplicity has become the rule in courtrooms, where the most eminent literary critics rise to defend banned works ranging from the *Kama Sutra* to *Deep Throat*, by claiming for them underlying moral qualities.

. . . .

I must explore a little a profound difference between our own age and that in which criticism was born; the well-advertised Death of God and the slow erosion of Christian morality, which has debouched in the even better advertised New Sexual Morality of the dying twentieth century. Oddly enough (and this unpredictable event casts real light on the subject) those developments have not served to mitigate the conflict between Art and Prudence, or to undercut the distinction between Belles Lettres and Pop. On the contrary, in their initial stages at least, they tended rather to exacerbate the former and to reinforce the latter, as is exemplified very clearly by the line which runs from Matthew Arnold to Henry James and D.H. Lawrence to F.R. Leavis. They are, despite their disagreements on other fronts, crypto-Puritans all of them: convinced that with the death of traditional religion, Art in general and Literature in particular had to become the Scriptures of a New Faith, the Culture Religion. And to do so, they taught each in his own way, it had to subscribe to 'High Seriousness' and to be measured by rigorous 'Standards'.

Such standards were entrusted to a priestly brotherhood of critics, who feeling themselves the sole legitimate heirs of both the lay and clerical taste-makers of the past, sought to establish a New Canon, which would exclude philistine, vulgar, trivial or otherwise heretical stuff, even when, or rather especially when it was enjoyed by the unwary many.

. . . .

Yet Popular Literature moves us all the same, both those of us who also respond to High Literature and those of us who subsist entirely on it. Indeed it may, by this very token, move us all the more, touching levels of response deeper and more archaic than those which abide distinctions between instruction and delight, much less the division into High and Low. If we are interested in *how* it moves us – and how, presumably, *all* literature moves us beyond or beside or below the level of social utility – it will repay us to look briefly at three forms: genres or sub-genres of Popular Literature, of which élitist critics remain distrustful or downright contemptuous, though they have traditionally been favourites of the mass audience. These are:

1 Sentimental Literature, particularly as it has developed from novels written by the first women imitators of Samuel Richardson, down through such late nineteenth century bestsellers as *The Lamplighter* and *The Wide, Wide World*, to present-day 'soaps', the daytime serials on television;

2 Horror Literature from, say, M.G. Lewis's *The Monk*, down through *Varney, The Vampire, Frankenstein, Dr Jekyll and Mr Hyde* and *Dracula*, to the Horror Comics and *The Rocky Horror Show* of this moment;

3 Classic Pornography from Cleland and the Marquis de Sade, to Frank Harris, *The Story of O* and *Fritz the Cat*.

It is possible, of course, to combine all three, as they are combined in the Kung Fu movies starring Bruce Lee; such a film, for instance, as *Fist of Fury*, in which the single erotic scene is clearly a last-minute addition to make sure that the whole range of popular taste is satisfied. Moreover, there is a real sense in which all three of these forms can be regarded as varieties of pornography or titillation-literature: handkerchiefly or female-oriented porn, and sado-masochistic, or universally appealing porn. The last can also be thought of as juvenile-oriented porn; but this amounts perhaps to saying 'universal', since almost everyone is willing to indulge the child in himself, while many are wary about giving rein to what persists of the other sex in their male or female bodies. Terror, indeed, seems sometimes the only form capable of crossing all conventional role boundaries: not only generational and sexual, but ethnic as well (I have seen black and white kids, along with adults of all hues and genders, responding to Bruce Lee movies), and class lines, too. But some types of erotica seem limited in appeal not just because they represent, say, the fantasies of men rather than women; but because they appeal only to readers of a certain social status and educational level – like limericks, for instance, which are apparently an exclusively bourgeois form.

In any case, the pornographic classification seems appropriate in the light of the fact that all three sub-genres aim at 'watering the emotions', rather than purifying or purging them by way of the famous Aristotelian process of 'catharsis'. Indeed, the whole baffling and unsatisfactory theory of catharsis seems to me at this point a pious fraud perpetrated by the dutiful son of a doctor; drawing on the terminology of his father's socially acceptable craft, in order to justify his own shameful taste for what seemed to more serious thinkers of his time exactly what pop literature seems to their opposite numbers in ours. Greek Tragedy, as a matter of fact, aimed at evoking precisely the responses stirred by Sentimental and Horror Porn in all ages, responses which Aristotle called honorifically 'pity and terror'; though Athens of the Golden Age banned the portrayal of sexually exciting scenes from the stage – presumably because they could not be ethically neutralized, like those which stir shudders or tears, even in a ritual setting.

For the sake of the popular drama which he loved as I love soap-operas, Aristotle found it strategic to pretend that the thrill of tragedy and the release of comedy could be subsumed under the rubric of instruction and delight. In our era, however, it seems advisable to readjust the balance by insisting that the plays of Sophocles and Euripides, quite like the three forms of pornography I am considering, at their most effective, cause the audience to get out of control, 'out of their heads', as the modern phrase has it. If such works teach us anything it is *not* to be wise; and if they provide us with pleasure by making us blubber, shiver or sustain an erection, it is a pleasure on the verge of pain. We need, therefore, another term than catharsis to say how we are moved, a term less anal and more erotic; for whatever Aristotle may have urged in his age of genital repression, metaphors of a child on the potty (or even at the mirror) will not do for us. We need to redefine literature in terms of images based on the aspiration of the soul for the divine and the body for other bodies.

Such images are to be found in the single surviving work of one we call 'Longinus', though that is not his name: in an essay we call 'On the Sublime', though the last word is a misleading translation, which allowed 'Longinus' to be co-opted and compromised by eighteenth century formalists. That perhaps-Christian critic used the word *ekstasis* to describe the effect not of popular or debased art alone; but of all art at its peak moments – from the tag 'Let there be light and there was light' in the Scriptures of the barbarous Hebrews, to the most precious poetry of the enlightened Greeks. And what is incumbent on us now, it seems to me as I reach the end of definition and move on to advocacy, is to take a cue from Longinus by creating an approach to literature which will if not quite abandon, at least drastically downgrade both Ethics and Aesthetics in favour of 'Ecstatics'.

Once we have made *ekstatics* rather than instruction and delight the center of critical analysis and evaluation, we will find ourselves speaking less of theme and purport, structure and texture, ideology and significance, irony and symbolism, and more of myth, fable, archetype, fantasy, magic, and wonder. And certainly, when we have granted that the essential function of story and song is to release us temporarily from the limits of rationality, the boundaries of the ego and the burden of consciousness, by creating a moment of privileged insanity, compatible with waking awareness as the analogous experience of dreaming or 'tripping out' are not, we will be out of the trap; delivered at long last from the indignity of having to condescend publicly to works we privately relish; and relieved of the obligation to define, as I began by doing in this essay, distinctions which were from the start delusive and unreal.

(from C. Bigsby (ed.), *Superculture*, 1975).

 READING 3

'Against evaluation: the role of the critic of popular culture'

Roger B. Rollin

To evaluate is human, to explicate, divine.

The epigraph is *ersatz*, of course, but it will serve to introduce the argument of this essay: that some of Popular Culture's leading authorities, among them John Cawelti, Leslie Fiedler, and David Madden, have inadvertently proposed what is in effect an impossible mission – to devise an aesthetics of Popular Culture which will incorporate a value theory. Furthermore, they have suggested that not to accept this "mission" must result in the impeding of the growth and development of Popular Culture study.

The most recent to go on record with this view has been David Madden. In "The Necessity for an Aesthetics of Popular Culture,"[1] he makes it clear that serious students of the Popular Arts have a duty to engage, not only in formulation, but in evaluation as well. He refers approvingly (p. 9) to the English philosopher Bosanquet, who is concerned with the "beauty" and "excellence" of aesthetic objects. Madden also refers to Professor Cawelti (pp. 6–7), whose "Notes toward an Aesthetic of Popular Culture" asserts the necessity of developing "a basic core of assumptions about the *nature and value* of artistic work."[2] Admittedly, neither Cawelti nor Madden centers his discussion upon the question of evaluation: their primary concerns are the obviously essential ones of categorizing the intrinsic and extrinsic qualities of Popular Art and suggesting how these are to be explicated by the critic. Yet Madden also claims that we "*must* decide whether Popular Culture works can be termed *beautiful*" (p. 7; italics added). And from both his essay and Cawelti's it can be inferred that their shared conception of the duties and functions of the critic of Popular Art is not so very different from that conception of the duties and functions of the critic of Elite Art that has dominated Western aesthetics for over two thousand years. Yvor Winters has characterized this traditional view with admirable bluntness: "The primary function for criticism is evaluation, and . . . unless criticism succeeds in providing a useful system of evaluation it is worth very little."[3] . . . Evaluation is indeed human, as this essay's epigraph has suggested. Indeed, few encounters in this life, whether they be with other persons or with objects, do not involve evaluation in some form. Certainly encounters with aesthetic objects, Elite or Popular, are no exceptions to this rule. It needs no B.F. Skinner to tell us that stimulus evokes response and that aesthetic objects are *created* to be stimuli. Nor is there any novelty in the notion that a necessary component of the aesthetic response is emotional, or that emotion, however vaguely, will be positive, negative, or mixed.

In truth, it is *impossible* to have *no* emotive reaction to an aesthetic stimulus. Directions on an aspirin bottle can perhaps evoke a neutral or emotion-free response, but a mere television commercial about aspirin, complete with doctor-like actor urging that "Bayer is better," cannot leave the viewer unaffected: even indifference is the next thing to a clearly negative response, for it entails a rejection of the work's basic intentions.

The evaluation of aesthetic objects then is inevitable. *And because it is inevitable it is unnecessary* – unnecessary at least for the serious critic of Popular Culture, and unnecessary to the construction of a critical theory for Popular Culture. *I Love Lucy* will enchant one viewer, merely pass the time for another, and cause a third to experience acute discomfort in his alimentary system, and no theory is likely to alter these patterns of effect significantly.

One qualification, however. I made a distinction here between the scholar-critic of Popular Culture and the commissioned reviewer. *The New York Times's* "Cyclops," Pauline Kael, and the local newspaper's critic of popular fiction undoubtedly have an obligation to accede to the public's reasonable demand that they, the fraternity of channel switchers, purchasers of movie tickets, and book-buyers, receive some guidance so as to minimize the wastage of their time, money and energy. But no serious student of Popular Culture can lose time, money, or energy by tuning in on *Rhoda*, paying to see *Jaws*, or skimming through Harold Robbins's latest opus. Because for such students these activities are called "research," and whether they entail pleasure or pain is immaterial. Nor is the *argumentum ad academium* relevant here – the argument that since many of these scholar-critics are teachers or would-be teachers of Popular Culture, they need some standard of Popular Culture values in order to be able to design courses or structure curricula. Questions of aesthetic value are irrelevant to such practical matters. . . .

The only possible functions of the teacher and serious student of Popular Culture are *description* and *interpretation* – "illumination," in short. Description, because the field of Popular Culture is so vast and so varied that even its most assiduous students are bound to have *lacunae*. Interpretation, because explaining the dynamics of a work of Popular Culture and of audience-response to that work can reveal that which is lost upon the casual viewer: what happens at the interface between a work's aesthetic form and the desires and anxieties of its audience, and also what extrapolations can be made from that interaction with regard to the society of which the audience is a part.

In rendering this important service to scholarship, (and possibly to society), the scholar-critic's evaluation of the work has no necessary part. The only evaluation which counts is the strictly quantitative one: how large a proportion of the work's potential audience responded to it positively. Did it receive a respectable Nielsen rating? Did *Variety* rate it a box-office success? Did it appear on the best-seller list?

For the only real authority concerning the "beauty" or "excellence" of a work of Popular Culture is the people. "Taste," formal training, teaching experience, publications – all factors which might be construed as validating the "authority" of a critic of Elite Culture – stand for naught when it comes to his or anyone else's evaluation of the "quality" of a Popular Culture work. For, in Popular Culture, the rule is "one person – one vote." . . . For better or for worse (and I am not all that certain it is for worse), Popular Art represents the triumph of a democratic aesthetic – or what is probably the nearest approximation of a democratic aesthetic that is possible within the present capitalistic system.

. . . .

If Popular Culture must make a case for itself that case has to be made – not on the supposed intrinsic aesthetic merits of its subject matter – but upon that subject matter's demonstrable interest and importance. After all, any aesthetic object of the past or present, "good" or "bad," can become what Frye calls "a source of imaginative illumination" (p. 17).[11] How any one individual *feels* about that object is *another* source of *another* kind of illumination. As Professor Frye puts it,

> the experience of literature is not criticism, just as religious experience is not theology. . . . In the experience of literature a great many things are felt and can be said, which have no functional role to play in criticism. [Thus,] the attempt to make criticism either begin or end in value judgments turns the subject wrong side out. . . . The value sense is, as the phenomenological people say, pre-predictive. (p. 18)

Norman N. Holland seems to have been the first to demonstrate as much. His clinical-type experiments at the Center for the Psychological Study of the Arts (the State University of New York at Buffalo) have confirmed what every student of the arts' experience is likely to suggest – that whether or not an aesthetic object will please cannot be accurately predicted, even though an individual's "tastes" are known, even if (as in the case of Holland's subjects) the individual's psychological "profile" or "identity theme" is known.[12] (I refer here only to an individual's private "sincere" response, which can of course be different from his public response – in class, in print, etc. – for that public response can, as Frye has indicated, be to varying degrees conditioned without the individual being aware of it.)

How do we evaluate aesthetic objects? All of Holland's investigations lead him to this conclusion: *"we will enjoy and value those literary works from which we can achieve an exciting balance of fantasy and management of fantasy"* (p. 298). Thus my own evaluation of *The Sting*, for example, is based, not primarily upon my conscious, rational, objective, trained analysis of such elements as its script, direction, acting, camera work, etc., for I will likely be able to find merits in such elements if I enjoyed the movie, defects in them if I did not. Rather, my evaluation will mainly depend upon: (1) the extent to which *The Sting* offered aesthetic materials out of which my mind was able to "shape" a largely unconscious fantasy, thereby "involving" me in the movie; (2) the extent to which my ego was able to cope with, "manage" that fantasy, preventing me from feeling either so threatened or so uninvolved that I walked out of the theatre.

Holland's theoretical model of the complex psychological process which results in such effects is itself complex, but can be generally described as follows:

> A reader responds to a literary work by assimilating it to his own psychological processes, that is, to his search for successful solutions within his identity theme to the multiple demands, both inner and outer, on his ego. (p. 128)

If I enjoyed *The Sting* and evaluated it as "good" – which is usually, but not always, the same thing, for the ego of the trained critic, especially, can "split" itself – according to Holland at least four processes have been simultaneously involved. 1. I have been able to put the elements of the movie together so that they act out at any given moment my hopes with regard to the work as a whole (p. 114) – for example, my desire to have the heroes get away with their scheme. 2. The movie provides me with materials to create a wish-fulfillment fantasy that is characteristic of my personality (pp. 117–21), for example, my tendency to imagine myself to be a handsome, debonair, rogue-hero. 3. I have been able to synthesize from the movie my characteristic strategies of psychological defense or adaptation (pp. 115–17); for example, the movie afforded me sufficient materials to enable me to "defend against" the anxiety I feel (will Robert Redford escape the assassin?) in the ways that I customarily handle anxiety (ranging from outright repression to my scholar's expectation that *The Sting* is a comic romance). 4. I have been able to "make sense" of the movie, have been able to render the fantasy I have synthesized into some intellectual content that is characteristic of – and pleasing to – me (pp. 121–22), for example, that the very powerful can be brought low by the less powerful.

Thus what my statement that "*The Sting* is a good movie" really means is (to paraphrase Holland, p. 125) this: "My ego was able to use the movie to build from my own unconscious drives through my own patterns of adaptation and defense toward a conscious significance and unity that mattered to me." The fact that this mental process has been replicated by millions of movie goers now improves the odds on predicting whether Jane Doe will evaluate *The Sting* as a "good" movie, but at the time of its release the odds would have been much longer, even were we in possession of Jane's identity theme and had tried to match it up with a psychoanalytical analysis of the depth structure of the Newman-Redford film. Movies *are* in a sense ink blots, but some repressed trauma concerning the era in which *The Sting* is set – or even an over-heated theatre – could alter the response she makes. Thus, even the highly formulaic nature of most Popular Culture works cannot be of much help in predicting how any one individual or even a mass audience will evaluate a movie, television program, or popular novel. What is more important, however, is that by recognizing how aesthetic evaluations arise – out of idiosyncratic unconscious processes at one extreme, out of cultural conditioning at the other extreme – theorists will be given pause when they contemplate attempting to construct standards of aesthetic value for Popular Culture. Not only does the best evidence suggest that such an attempt is philosophically unsound and scientifically ill-founded, but of all people students of Popular Culture should be aware of the ways in which standards of aesthetic value can be transformed into moral imperatives which are then employed to celebrate some human beings and oppress others.

"The attempt of genuine criticism," in Professor Frye's words, "is to bring literature to 'life' by annihilating stock responses, which of course are always value judgments, and which regularly confuse literature with life" (p. 20). Frye's concern here is with Elite Literature but the goal he sets is no less valid for Popular Culture criticism. Serious students of Popular Culture, those who write for other serious students, fulfill their high-minded and useful purpose when they penetrate the stock response to *The Waltons*, for example – as Anne Rolphe has done so well[13] – and describe that series accurately, analyze the psychological, mythic, religious, social, political, economic, and ethical components of its structure and texture, and interpret what the fact that America "likes" *The Waltons* tells us about the character of our society in the 1970s. Such information and insights cannot help but be valuable. Dr. Johnson said that "All truth is valuable . . . ,"[14] but although aestheticians may be loath to admit it, the quantifiable aspect of a truth does count for something. This is so whether it be the number of critics who have pronounced *Lycidas* to be a "great" poem versus the number of those who, like Dr. Johnson, regard Milton's pastoral elegy as a "bad" poem, or whether it is the millions of viewers who turned for solace to that American pastoral, *Bonanza*, every week for fourteen years, versus those comparatively few who watched whatever was being offered on competing networks.

It will be argued, as David Madden implicitly has argued, that social, political, psychological and other aspects of the mass audience's response to works of Popular Culture are not the proper concern of aesthetics, are not to be "considered part of the aesthetic experience".[15] But if the aesthetic experience is not deeply involved with the experiencer's id, ego, superego, and external reality, what is it involved with? As has been said above, the aesthetic experience will entail evaluation, but how is the *ranking* of aesthetic objects to be squared with a thorough understanding of the limitations of criticism as an intellectual activity? As Frye astutely observes, "the more consistently one conceives of criticism as the pursuit of values, the more firmly one becomes attached to that great sect of anti-intellectualism" (p. 20). Or as Professor Lipman has put it, "an eagerness to portray the population of works of art as made up of 'good works of art versus bad works of art' is rather akin to the infantile moralism that reduces the human population to a contrast between 'good guys' and 'bad guys'".[16]

While my personal approval of *Paradise Lost* is not only "sincere" but public evidence of my "good taste", I have no way of knowing whether the students to whom I teach Milton or the Milton scholars for whom I write are equally well endowed. – Or even whether they can somehow acquire the faculty through exposure to my own "superior" taste. And if they do not or cannot, what does it matter? I can no more read *Paradise Lost* for them than I can force them to like it: all I can do is to try to illuminate Milton's poem for them.

Likewise, my positive response, for example, to *Deep Throat* and my negative response to *The Godfather* finally must say more about me than they do about the aesthetic merits of those two cinema landmarks. That, of the two, *Deep Throat* has more historical importance and *The Godfather* is more obscene, can, I think, be reasonably argued, although the place to do so is not here. Such issues an aesthetic of Popular Culture can confront, but such a confrontation will only result in confusion if the question of "intrinsic" aesthetic merit be introduced. For such questions constitute a trap in which the experience of literature becomes largely divorced from the experience of life. While we may grant that the experience of literature is not infrequently superior to that of life, the two are inextricably linked through the central nervous system, a physiological fact that the practice of criticism ignores at its peril.

Let there be no more judges then – at least among the scholar-critics of Popular Culture. To describe, analyze, and interpret a mass audience's judgment of a work can be a way of knowing one's society; to judge a work of Popular Art can only be a way of knowing oneself, which unlike true criticism is a personal rather than a public *desideratum*. As one of the most ancient communicators to a mass audience has put it: "Judge not lest ye be judged".

Notes

1 *Journal of Popular Culture*, 7:1 (Summer 1973), 2.
2 *Journal of Popular Culture*, 5:2 (Fall 1971), 255 (italics added).
3 *The Function of Criticism* (Denver: Alan Swallow, 1957), p. 17.
11 See *Problems of Literary Evaluation*, pp. 14–21.
12 *Five Readers Reading* (New Haven: Yale University Press,1975). This work incorporates (with important modifications) ideas advanced by Professor Holland in his seminal study, *The Dynamics of Literary Response* (New York: Oxford University Press, 1968). See also his *Poems in Persons: An Introduction to the Psychoanalysis of Literature* (New York: W.W. Norton & Co.,1973).
13 'The Waltons', *New York Times Magazine* (Nov. 18, 1973), 40ff.
14 *The Critical Opinions of Samuel Johnson*, ed. Joseph Epes Brown (Princeton: Princeton University Press, 1926), p. 253.
15 'The Necessity for an Aesthetics of Popular Culture', *Journal of Popular Culture*, 7:1 (Summer, 1973), 4.
16 *Contemporary Aesthetics* (Boston: Allyn & Bacon, 1973), p. 429.

(from *Journal of Popular Culture*, Vol. 9, 1975)

 READING 4

'Production and reproduction: the case of *Frankenstein*'

Paul O'Flinn

Mary Shelley's Gothic novel *Frankenstein* was published anonymously in 1818. In the same year, a couple of other novels – Peacock's *Nightmare Abbey* and Jane Austen's *Northanger Abbey* – also appeared and their derisive use of Gothic conventions suggested that the form, fashionable for fifty years, was sliding into decline and disrepute. There seemed good reason to suppose that *Frankenstein*, an adolescent's first effort at fiction, would fade from view before its print run was sold out.

Yet several generations later Mary Shelley's monster, having resisted his creator's attempts to eliminate him in the book, is able to reproduce himself with the variety and fertility that Frankenstein had feared. Apart from steady sales in Penguin, Everyman and OUP editions, there have been over a hundred film adaptations and there have been the Charles Addams cartoons in the *New Yorker*, Frankie Stein blunders about in the pages of *Whoopee* and *Monster Fun* comics, and approximate versions of the monster glare out from chewing gum wrappers and crisp bags. In the USA he forged a chain of restaurants; in South Africa in 1955 the work was banned as indecent and objectionable.[1]

None of these facts is new and some of them are obvious to anyone walking into a newsagent's with one eye open. They are worth setting out briefly here because *Frankenstein* seems to me to be a case where some recent debates in critical theory about cultural production and reproduction might usefully be centred, a work whose history can be used to test the claims that theory makes.[2] That history demonstrates clearly the futility of a search for the 'real', 'true' meaning of a work. There is no such thing as *Frankenstein*, there are only *Frankensteins*, as the text is ceaselessly rewritten, reproduced, refilmed and redesigned. The fact that many people call the monster Frankenstein and thus confuse the pair betrays the extent of that restructuring. What I would like to offer is neither a naive deconstructionist delight at the endless plurality of meanings the text has been able to afford nor a gesture of cultural despair at the failure of the philistines to read the original and get it right. Instead I'd like to argue that at its moment of production *Frankenstein*, in an oblique way, was in touch with central tensions and contradictions in industrial society and only by seeing it in those terms can the prodigious efforts made over the last century and a half to alter and realign the work and its meanings be understood – a work that lacked that touch and that address could safely be left, as Marx said in another context, to the gnawing criticism of the mice.

Frankenstein is a particularly good example of three of the major ways in which alteration and realignment of this sort happens: first, through the operations of criticism; second, as a function of the shift from one medium to another; and third, as a result of the unfolding of history itself. The operations of criticism on this text are at present more vigorous than usual. When I was a student twenty years ago I picked up the *Pelican Guide to English Literature* to find the novel more or less wiped out in a direly condescending half-sentence as 'one of those second-rate works, written under the influence of more distinguished minds, that sometimes display in conveniently simple form the preoccupations of a coterie'.[3] *Frankenstein* may have been on TV but it wasn't on the syllabus. A generation and a lot of feminist criticism later and Mary Shelley is no longer a kind of half-witted secretary to Byron and Shelley but a woman writer whose text articulates and has been convincingly shown to articulate elements of woman's experience of patriarchy, the family and the trauma of giving birth.[4]

The second instance – the way a text's meaning alters as it moves from one medium to another – is something I'd like to look at in more detail later in this essay by examining the two classic screen versions: Universal's movie directed in 1931 by James Whale and starring Boris Karloff, and Terence Fisher's picture for Hammer Films in 1957 with Peter Cushing. Literary criticism only metaphorically rewrites texts: the words on the page remain the same but the meanings they are encouraged to release differ. But a shift of medium means the literal rewriting of a text as novel becomes script becomes film. Scope for the ideological wrenching and reversing of a work and its way of seeing is here therefore even larger. [. . .] The third category is one I suggested earlier – namely the way in which the movement of history itself refocuses a text and reorders its elements. *Frankenstein*, I would like to argue, meant certain things in 1818, but meant and could be made to mean different things in 1931 and 1957, irrespective of authorial 'intention'. [. . .]

Mary Shelley's monster, in short, is ripped apart by one or more of at least three processes in each generation and then put together again as crudely as Victor Frankenstein constructed the original in his apartment. Faced with these processes, traditional literary criticism can either, with a familiar gesture, pretend not to notice and insist instead that *Frankenstein* 'spanned time' with 'timeless and universal themes' that 'live beyond literary fashion'.[5] Or it can pay attention to those changes but slip past the power and the politics that they imply, so that shifts in the work's presentation become a plain mirror of human evolution: 'the Monster . . . is no longer separate, he is quite simply ourselves';[6] it is a magnified image of ourselves.'[7] Capitalism creates and recreates monsters; capitalist ideology then invites us to behold ourselves. I'd like to try to do something else.

First I would like to argue that much of the text's strength that continues to be released derives from certain issues in the decade of its composition, issues that the text addresses itself to in oblique, imaginative terms and that remain central and unresolved in industrial society. In that decade those issues erupted more turbulently than ever before: they were, briefly, the impact of technological developments on people's lives and the possibility of working-class revolution. Those issues fuel the Luddite disturbances of 1811–17 and the Pentridge rising of 1817.

There had been instances of machine-breaking before in British history but never with the same frequency and intensity. The size of the army marshalled to squash the Luddites – six times as big as any used previously for internal conflicts in the estimate of one historian – is a measure of the extent to which the new technologies, in the first generation of the industrial revolution, threatened traditional livelihoods and provoked violent resistance. There is the same sort of new and disruptive energy evident in the Pentridge rising of June 1817, when 300 men marched towards Nottingham on the expectation of similar marches, designed to overthrow the Government, occurring across the country. The group was soon rounded up by Hussars and three of its leaders executed in November. The revolt ended in shambles and failure but its significance for E.P. Thompson is epochal – it was 'one of the first attempts in history to mount a wholly proletarian insurrection, without any middle-class support'.[9]

The composition of *Frankenstein* needs to be seen in the context of these deep changes in the nature of British society. Mary began work on the novel in June 1816 at the Maison Chapuis, Montalègre, near Geneva, where she was living with Shelley. Byron lived nearby at the Villa Diodati (and the book's impetus came from Byron's challenge – 'We will each write a ghost story' – during one of their regular evening visits). The point is that as Mary set about writing her first novel she was working alongside two men who had responded publicly and politically to the Luddite crisis. Byron's magnificent maiden speech in the House of Lords in February 1812 had attacked Tory proposals to extend the death penalty for machine-breaking, denouncing a process whereby men were 'sacrificed to improvements in mechanism'. And then in January 1813, when fourteen men were executed at York for Luddite activities, Harriet Shelley had written to the radical London bookseller Thomas Hookham on Shelley's behalf: 'I see by the Papers that those poor men who were executed at York have left a great many children. Do you think a subscription would be attended to for their relief? If you think it would, pray put down our names and advertise it in the Papers.'[10] Mary and Percy returned to England from Geneva in September 1816 and Luddites were still being hanged in April 1817 as Mary made the last revisions to her manuscript. Before *Frankenstein*'s publication in March 1818, Shelley reacted to the execution of the leaders of the Pentridge rising with *An Address to the People on the Death of Princess Charlotte*, a forceful political pamphlet published in November 1817 and eagerly read by Mary, as she noted in her journal. The pamphlet lamented the 'national calamity' of a country torn between abortive revolt and despotic revenge – the alternatives of anarchy and oppression'.[11]

What was Mary Shelley's own response to these events and reactions? . . . Her letters around the time of *Frankenstein* reveal a woman who shared the radicalism of Byron and Shelley. The result was a politics shaped by a passion for reform, a powerful hatred of Tory despotism with its 'grinding & pounding & hanging and taxing' and a nervousness about the chance of the revolutionary violence such despotism might provoke. Thus, for example, she wrote to Shelley in September 1817 between the completion of *Frankenstein* in May and its publication the following March:

> Have you seen Cobbett's 23 No. to the Borough mongers – Why he appears to be making out a list for proscription – I actually shudder to read it – a revolution in this country would (not?) be *bloodless* if that man has any power in it. . . . He encourages in the multitude the worst possible human passion *revenge* or as he would probably give it that abominable Christian name retribution.[15]

Her politics here in short are those of a radical liberal agonizing in the face of the apparent alternatives of 'anarchy and oppression', to use the phrase which, as we have already seen, Shelley was to deploy six weeks later in his *Princess Charlotte* pamphlet. That politics also addressed itself to contemporary scientific and technological developments and their social implications. Discussion and speculation at the Villa Diodati ranged across galvanism and Darwin's experiments, as Mary carefully notes in her 1831 introduction to the novel. In the autumn of 1816, as she completed her manuscript, she read Davy's *Elements of Chemical Philosophy*.

It is out of these politics and this way of seeing that *Frankenstein* emerges. It is a multi-layered work; it includes odds and ends like her passing interest in recent British and Russian polar exhibitions, and it is padded in parts with wads of her tourist's diary of a trip to Chamonix.[16] What I would like to show by turning to the text itself in the next two sections is that one of these layers, a layer that accounts for a lot of the story's vigorous, protean life, is an imaginative rendering of the two issues – scientific-technological developments and working-class revolt – which, as we have seen, asserted themselves violently in the half-dozen years preceding the text's production. It is a layer whose boundaries are drawn by the author's politics. . . . Mary Shelley's interest in scientific questions has been well documented[17] and this interest is built into the very narrative structure of her novel. Frankenstein's story is itself framed by the story of Walton, the polar explorer whom Frankenstein meets and to whom he tells his tale. Through the twin narratives of Walton and Frankenstein Mary Shelley presents two models of scientific progress. Both men are obsessed by the urge to discover and both pursue that obsession, enticed by the possibility of 'immortality and power' that success would bring. In the end the pursuit kills Frankenstein whereas Walton survives. What is the difference?

The difference is the sailors on Walton's expedition ship. Frankenstein works alone but Walton works with a crew and it is the crew who force Walton to turn back when they realize that the reckless drive through the polar ice will cost everyone's lives. Several things are worth noting at this point. First, Frankenstein makes a forceful speech aimed at changing the sailors' minds by reminding them of the honour that even failure will bring and still holding out the dream of heroic success. Second, Walton turns back not, as has been argued, for altruistic reasons or for the sake of his sister,[18] but simply because he is forced to by the threat of mutiny, to his own fury and frustration:

> The die is cast; I have consented to return, if we are not destroyed. Thus are my hopes blasted by cowardice and indecision; I come back ignorant and disappointed. It requires more philosophy than I possess, to bear this injustice with patience. (p. 215)

And third, Mary Shelley takes care to distance her readers' sympathies from both Frankenstein's pleas and Walton's anger by pushing those sympathies towards the sailors. [. . .] What the text then appears to offer is a straightforward contrast. Scientific development subject to some form of strong democratic control – even in the violent form of mutiny – can avert the dangers its researchers encounter and save human beings from the possibly fatal consequences of those researches. That is Walton's story. But scientific advance pursued for private motives and with no reining and directing social control or sense of social responsibility leads directly to catastrophe. That is Frankenstein's story. . . .

Seen from this angle, the function of certain elements in the text becomes clearer. . . . Walton's project is especially perilous because it 'hurries me out of the common pathways of men, even to the wild sea and unvisited regions I am about to explore' (p. 22) but he has to go with a crew and they save him, as we have seen. From the start he is aware of the need of a colleague 'to approve or amend my plans' (p. 19) and hence his delight on meeting Frankenstein. The latter, by contrast, works deliberately alone. His move to Ingolstadt where he begins his research cuts him off from Geneva where he had 'ever been surrounded by amiable companions' (p. 45) and he stays away from them for two years. He constructs the monster 'in a solitary chamber, or rather cell, at the top of the house . . . separated from all the other apartments' (p. 55), just as later he goes to 'the remotest of the Orkneys' (p. 163) to begin building the monster's mate. . . . The text's thrust on a series of levels is naively clear: for people together, problems can be solved; for the man alone, they can overwhelm.

The monster describes a crucial part of his education as follows:

> Every conversation of the cottagers now opened new wonders to me. When I listened to the instructions which Felix bestowed upon the Arabian, the strange system of human society was explained to me. I heard of the division of property, of immense wealth and squalid poverty; of rank, descent, and noble blood.
>
> The words induced me to turn towards myself. I learned that the possessions most esteemed by your fellow-creatures were high and unsullied descent united with riches. A man might be respected with only one of these advantages; but, without either, he was considered, except in very rare instances, as a vagabond and a slave, doomed to waste his powers for the profits of the chosen few! And what was I? Of my creation and creator I was absolutely ignorant; but I knew that I possessed no money, no friends, no kind of property. (pp. 119–20)

Looking at that passage, it is perhaps worth remembering that the first person to offer the text as a straightforward allegory of the class struggle is not some vulgar Marxist in the twentieth century but one of the book's protagonists. Read as the monster suggests, the novel argues that, just as Frankenstein's creation drives him through exhausting and unstinting conflicts to his death, so too a class called into being by the bourgeoisie and yet rejected and frustrated by it will in the end turn on that class in fury and vengeance and destroy it.

This way of seeing the work, as well as being overtly stated by the work itself, is rendered more likely if we look again for a moment at the text's context. Lee Sterrenburg has documented the extent to which the populace as a monster, bent on the destruction of the ruling class and its property, figures as a standard trope in conservative journalism in the generation after the French Revolution.[20] During the Luddite years, the monster appeared to some to be on the loose. Factories in Yorkshire were fired in January and April 1812 and in March and April in Lancashire; there were murders, attempted assassinations and executions again and again between 1812 and 1917. During the most famous attack, on Rawfolds mill in the Spen Valley in April 1812, two of the Luddites were killed and 'Vengeance for the Blood of the Innocent' appeared chalked on walls and doors in Halifax after one of the funerals.

In the midst of this crisis, Mary Shelley picks up a way of seeing – the populace as a destructive monster – provided by Tory journalism and tries to re-think it in her own radical-liberal terms. And so in the novel the monster remains a monster – alien, frightening, violent – but is drenched with middle-class sympathy and given central space in the text to exercise the primary liberal right of free speech which he uses to appeal for the reader's pity and understanding. The caricatured people-monster that haunts the dominant ideology is reproduced through Mary Shelley's politics and becomes a contradictory figure, still ugly, vengeful and terrifying but now also human and intelligent and abused.

In addition, incidents in the class struggles of the 1810s are projected into the text. The monster too turns on the De Lacey family he has worked for and, in chapter 16, burns their property to the ground. That pattern of murders and reprisals that characterizes the history of the decade also constitutes much of the plot of the novel. The demand for vengeance flared on the walls of Halifax in 1812 and again and again the terms 'vengeance' and 'revenge' erupt in the text to describe the relations of Frankenstein and monster – on, for example, pages 92, 136, 138, 142, 145, 168, 202 and 220. It is of course precisely a violent class politics fuelled principally by 'the worst possible human passion *revenge*' that Mary wrote in fear of to Shelley, as we saw earlier, shortly before the publication of *Frankenstein*.

To see the text in these terms is not, as I have argued already, a daft left-wing distortion but a reading suggested by the text itself and one that is also apparent if we turn to the way the text was taken up in the nineteenth century. In 1848, for example, the year of revolutions and of the *Communist Manifesto*, Elizabeth Gaskell published *Mary Barton*, the first English novel with a Communist as its protagonist. Describing John Barton she writes at one point:

> And so on into the problems and mysteries of life, until, bewildered and lost, unhappy and suffering, the only feeling that remained clear and undisturbed in the tumult of his heart, was hatred to the one class, and keen sympathy with the other.
>
> But what availed his sympathy. No education had given him wisdom; and without wisdom, even love, with all its effects, too often works but harm. He acted to the best of his judgment, but it was a widely-erring judgment.
>
> The actions of the uneducated seem to me typified in those of Frankenstein, that monster of many different human qualities, ungifted with a soul, a knowledge of the difference between good and evil.
>
> The people rise up to life; they irritate us, they terrify us, and we become their enemies. Then, in the sorrowful moment of our triumphant power, their eyes gaze on us with mute reproach. Why have we made them what they are; a powerful monster, yet without the inner means for peace and happiness?[21]

23

What is intriguing about this reference is that Elizabeth Gaskell obviously hasn't read the book – she confuses Frankenstein with the monster and she doesn't know that the monster has a very clear knowledge of the difference between good and evil. What she has absorbed instead and passes on is the dominant political reading of the text, the sense that the middle classes are threatened by a monster of their own making. That monster, as we have seen, was manufactured out of the violence and anxieties of the Luddite decade; a generation later, at the peak of the Chartist decade, Elizabeth Gaskell reaches into cultural mythology to find the imaginative terms for her own predicament and that of her class.

It is significant that this political reproduction of the text persists and tends to surface at times of sharpening conflict. The 1961 Supplement to the *Oxford English Dictionary* notes Sidney Webb's use in *Fabian Essays*, published in 1889 at the height of the socialist revival: 'The landlord and the capitalist are both finding that the steam engine is a Frankenstein which they had better not have raised.' And the 1972 Supplement quotes the *Daily Telegraph*, 3 May 1971: 'There are now growing indications that the Nationalists in South Africa have created a political Frankenstein which is pointing the way to a non-white political revival.' Again, in both cases, monster and Frankenstein are muddled, indicating a level in ideology at which the text itself has ceased to exist but a myth and a metaphor torn and twisted from it is being strenuously put to work.

This separating of myth and metaphor from text and constructing something entirely new in ideology begins very early. In September 1823, Mary Shelley wrote to Leigh Hunt that she found herself famous – not for her novel but for a stage adaptation of it called *Presumption, or the Fate of Frankenstein* by Richard Brinsley Peake that was having a successful run in London. The title betrays the way the work is already being realigned as one idea in the complex structure is pulled out and foregrounded, and this foregrounding is underscored by a statement on the playbills for the opening performance on 28 July at the English Opera House: 'The striking moral exhibited in this story is the fatal consequence of that presumption which attempts to penetrate, beyond prescribed depths, into the mysteries of nature.'[22] Frankenstein certainly concludes from his own experience that the pursuit of knowledge ought to be prohibited, but the text does not endorse that kind of obscurantist morality, particularly by its placing of the contrasting Walton story. But the later, more conservative and religious Mary Shelley slides towards this position, so that we find her insisting in the 1831 introduction: 'supremely frightful would be the effect of any human endeavour to mock the stupendous mechanism of the Creator of the world'. She herself, in fact, is among the first to nudge the text into the space occupied by the dominant ideology, and we can also see that nudging going on in some of the revisions she makes for this third 1831 edition; for example, Elizabeth Lavenza is no longer Frankenstein's cousin, so that the potentially offensive hint of incest is deleted, while the orthodox notion of the family as moral and emotional sanctuary is boosted by the addition of several passages in the early chapters idealizing the domestic harmony of Frankenstein's childhood.[23] If ideology has taken hold of *Frankenstein* and remade it for its own purposes, Mary Shelley led with her own suggestions about how it might be done.

What I would like to do in the rest of this essay is to look at the two most famous reproductions of *Frankenstein* in the twentieth century, namely Universal's *Frankenstein* directed in 1931 by James Whale and starring Boris Karloff as the monster, and Hammer Films' *The Curse of Frankenstein* directed by Terence Fisher with Peter Cushing as Baron Frankenstein. The constructions and the operations of ideology are complex, and within the scope of an essay I cannot hope to do more than gesture at what seem to me to be the implications of the content of those two versions; wider questions about, for example, the precise relationship within the movie industry between honest popular entertainment, calculated profit-seeking, capitalist propaganda and painstaking aesthetic practice must inevitably be left to one side. [. . .]

That said, there seem to me to be at least three different types of shift that need to be borne in mind when looking at the gap between Mary Shelley's book and twentieth-century films; those shifts concern medium, audience and content. In the case of *Frankenstein*, the shift of medium is particularly important because it must inevitably obliterate and replace what is central to the novel's meaning and structure – namely the patterned movement through three narrators as the reader is taken by way of Walton's letters into Frankenstein's tale and on to the monster's autobiography before backing out through Frankenstein's conclusions to be left with Walton's last notes. That process cannot be filmed and so the very medium demands changes even before politics and ideology come into play.

The turning of novel into film also involves a change in the nature of the work's audience. David Punter has convincingly argued that the Gothic novel is pre-eminently a middle-class form in terms of authors and values as well as readership.[24] The films in question are middle-class in none of these senses, produced as they are by large businesses in search of mass audiences. That different site of production and area of distribution will again bear down on the work, pulling, stretching and clipping it to fit new needs and priorities.

Where this pulling, stretching and clipping appears most obviously is in the alterations in the third category mentioned earlier, namely the work's content, and I would like to detail some of those in a moment. What needs emphasizing here is that the radical change in the class nature of producer and audience hacks away at the content of the original, so that the book is reduced to no more than an approximate skeleton, fleshed out in entirely and deliberately new ways.

. . . .

In looking at the content of this movie I'd like to confine my comments to those three areas where the shifts from the novel seem to me most important in terms of the ideological and political re-jigging that they betray; those areas are the Walton story, the nature of the monster and the ending.

The point about the Walton story is a simple one: it has gone. . . . To take away half of Mary Shelley's statement is to change it. It was argued earlier that the function of the Walton story within the text's meaning is to offer a different model of scientific and technological progress, one in which human survival is ensured as long as that progress is under firm and effective popular control. Remove that narrative and the work collapses into Frankenstein's experience alone which can then be presented as a universal model, replete with the sort of reactionary moralizing about the dangers of meddling with the unknown and the delights of tranquillity which are implicit in that tale and made explicit at more than one point. The film can then more easily slide towards a wider statement about the perils of any kind of progress and change, feeding fears of the unknown that change brings and reinforcing those conservative values that stand in its way.

On the question of the nature of the monster, the most important revision here concerns the creature's brain. The film adds a new episode in which an extra character called Fritz, Frankenstein's assistant, is sent to a laboratory to steal a brain for the monster. In that laboratory are two such pickled organs, in large jars boldly labelled NORMAL BRAIN and ABNORMAL BRAIN. Before the theft, the audience hears an anatomy lecture from Professor Waldman in which he draws attention to various features of the normal brain, 'the most perfect specimen', and contrasts them with the abnormal brain whose defects drive its owner to a life of 'brutality, of violence and murder' because of 'degenerative characteristics'. Its original owner was, in fact, 'a criminal'. The lecture over, Fritz creeps in, grabs the normal brain and then lets it slip so that jar and contents are smashed on the floor. He is forced to take the abnormal brain instead.

The implications for the monster and his story are immense. A central part of Mary Shelley's thesis is to insist that the monster's eventual life of violence and revenge is the direct product of his social circumstances. The monster summarizes his own life in terms that the text endorses: 'Everywhere I see bliss, from which I alone am irrevocably excluded. I was benevolent and good; misery made me a fiend. Make me happy, and I shall again be virtuous' (p. 100). The film deletes this reading of the story through its insistence that the monster's behaviour is not a reaction to its experience but biologically determined, a result of nature, not nurture.

Most commentators on the film are bewildered by this change. . . . It has been variously dismissed as an 'absurd and unnecessary sequence . . . a cumbersome attempt at establishing motivation', 'ridiculous' and 'the main weakness.'[27] If seen from Mary Shelley's stance, these comments are true; seen in terms of the film's ideological project, they miss the point. At one level in the text, Mary Shelley was concerned to suggest, in the imaginative terms of fiction, that Luddite violence was not the result of some brute characteristics of the nascent English working class but an understandable response to intolerable treatment. The Universal film, consciously or unconsciously, destroys the grounds for such a way of seeing with its radical political implications and instead sees violence as rooted in personal deficiencies, to be viewed with horror and to be labelled, literally, ABNORMAL and so sub-human. Bashing the monster ceases to be the problem but becomes instead the only way that the problem can be met and solved. So it is that Mary Shelley is stood on her head and *Frankenstein* is forced to produce new meanings for 1931.

This upending of Mary Shelley's book and its meaning explains two other profound changes in the monster's presentation that the film introduces. In the text, the monster spends chapters 11 to 16 describing his life – a huge speech that is placed right in the centre of the novel and fills over 20 per cent of its pages. In the film the monster can't speak. Again, in the novel, the monster saves a child from drowning in chapter 16; in the film, the monster drowns a child. Both reversals are of a piece with the Abnormal Brain scene and flow from it in that both deliberately seek to suppress audience sympathy for the monster. (Hence, when in the 1935 sequel *Bride of Frankenstein* the monster did speak, Boris Karloff protested that it made him seem 'more human', so that in the second sequel, *Son of Frankenstein* in 1939, he is again wordless.) The changes sharpen a re-focusing which is itself part of the shift from novel to film: reading the book, we hear the monster at eloquent length but we don't see him except vaguely, in imagination, and so reader sympathy is easily evoked; watching the film, we hear nothing from him but instead we see a shambling goon with a forehead like a brick wall and a bolt through his neck, and so audience revulsion is promptly generated. Thus the novel makes him human while the film makes him sub-human, so that in the novel his saving of the drowning child is predictable while equally predictable is his drowning of the child in the film.

The way the film ends flows directly from the drowning of the child and so brings me to the third and last piece of ideological restructuring in the Universal movie that I'd like to look at. In the novel, Frankenstein dies in his pursuit of the monster across the icy Arctic while the latter, in the final sentence, is 'borne away by the waves, and lost in darkness and distance'. In the film, the drowning of the child provokes the villagers to pursue the brute and trap it in an old windmill which is then burnt down; a brief, single-shot coda shows a recovered Frankenstein happily reunited with his fiancée Elizabeth. The politics of the mill-burning scene are overt: as the blaze engulfs the blades they form a gigantic fiery cross that deliberately suggests the Ku-Klux Klan, virulently active at the time, and so, as Tropp crudely puts it, 'points up the mob violence that does the monster in' (p. 97). Similarly, another observer sees the film ending 'with what Whale called "the pagan sport of a mountain man-hunt"; at the finale, the film's sympathies are with the monster rather than with the lynch mob'.[28]

These may have been Whale's intentions but there is a wide gap between director's aims and the movie as distributed. In Whale's original version, in the drowning scene, the girl dies because the monster innocently tries to make her float on the water like the flowers they are playing with and then searches frantically for her when she sinks. But these moments were chopped from the print of the film put out for general release: there we simply see the monster reaching out towards the girl and then cut to a grief-stricken father carrying her corpse. Child rape and murder are the obvious assumptions, so that the immediate response of the community in organizing itself to eliminate the savage culprit comes across as a kind of ritual cleansing of that community, the prompt removal of an inhuman threat to civilized life which is comfortably justifiable within routine populist politics and at the same time provides the firm basis for and so receives its sanction from the conventionally romantic final scene of hero and heroine at last happy and free from danger. If Mary Shelley's monster alludes indirectly to working-class insurrection, one answer to that canvassed in the 1930s was counter-revolutionary mob violence.

Political readings of the film tend to see it either in simple reflectionist terms (Tropp, for example, regards the monster as 'a creature of the '30s shaped by shadowy forces beyond its control, wandering the countryside like some disfigured veteran or hideous tramp' (p. 93), while another finds 'a world in which manipulations of the stock-market had recoiled on the manipulators; in which human creatures seemed to be abandoned by those who had called them in being and those who might have been thought responsible for their welfare'[29]) or as escapist – 'Large sections of the public, having difficulty in dealing with the Depression, were glad to spend some time in the company of a monster that could more easily be defeated.'[30] Readings of that sort can only be more or a lot less inspired speculation. I'd prefer to look within the film and see it as a *practice*, as an intervention in its world rather than just a picture of it or a retreat from it, a practice whose extent is marked out by the reconstruction of the text that I have indicated. Certainly it was released in the depths of the Depression, depths which can shock even when seen from Thatcherite Britain. The value of manufactured goods and services produced in the USA in 1929 had stood at 81 billion dollars and output at 119 (1923 = 100); as the film criss-crossed the nation in 1932, the value of goods and services had more than halved to 40 billion dollars and output was down to 64. There were 14 million unemployed. How the film reflects that catastrophe or seeks to escape from it is less important than what it says to it. As we saw earlier, it is historically at precisely such moments of crisis that Frankenstein's monster tends to be summoned by ideology and have its arm brutally twisted till it blurts out the statements that ideology demands. What Universal's *Frankenstein* seeks to say specifically to the mass audience at whom it is aimed concerns above all mass activity in times of crisis: where that activity might be assertive and democratic and beneficial (the Walton story), it is removed and concealed; where it is violent and insurrectionary (the monster's story), it is systematically denigrated; and where it is traditional and reactionary (the mill-burning), it is ambiguously endorsed. The extent to which the film powerfully articulates those familiar stances of the dominant ideology in the 1930s is measured by its box-office success. The fact that Frankenstein's monster is most urgently hailed at times of crisis perhaps accounts for the fact that, with the jokey exception of Universal's *Abbott and Costello Meet Frankenstein* in 1948, the English-speaking movie industry left the brute alone between 1945 (Universal's *House of Dracula*) and 1957 (Hammer's *The Curse of Frankenstein*) as the long post-war boom slowly built up. The Hammer film marked the end of the lengthiest break in Frankenstein pictures in the past fifty years and was the first attempt by a British studio to reproduce the story.

The relationships between, say, *Roderick Random* and early capitalism are complex and highly mediated. The links between Hammer films and late capitalism are less obscure; the executive producer of *The Curse of Frankenstein*, Michael Carreras, whose family founded Hammer Film Productions in 1947 and have run it for three generations, has put it simply enough: 'The best film is the one that makes money. Our job is to entertain and promote something that is really exploitable. Exploitation is the thing.'[31] Hammer's policy proceeded directly from this philosophy and has been well analysed by David Pirie.[32] It specialized in stories that were already 'pre-sold' to the public by tradition or by radio or television so that public recognition of the product was not a problem – hence early films like *PC 49*, *The Man in Black*, *Robin Hood* and so on. At the same time, it sought for itself an area of the market left untouched by the dimpled complacencies of Rank and Ealing Studios. These two strands of policy combined to push it towards horror films, first with *The Quatermass Experiment* in 1955, a spin-off from the 1953 BBC serial *Quatermass*. The success of both serial and film prompted Hammer to explore the genre further, and the filming of *The Curse of Frankenstein* began in November 1956.

The result was a cultural phenomenon whose scale and importance has certainly been noted but whose significance has not really been investigated. *The Curse of Frankenstein* is, it has been claimed, 'the biggest grossing film in the history of the British cinema in relation to cost.'[33] When it opened in the West End in May 1957 it at once started breaking box-office records and it did the same across the USA that summer. . . . In the decade and a half after the success of *The Curse of Frankenstein* Hammer made six sequels, all starring Peter Cushing as the eponymous hero.

In looking at the first of this series, it's Cushing and the part he plays that I would like to focus on, because it is there that the efforts of ideology in putting the myth to work for fresh purposes are most strenuous. At other points – the dropping of the Walton framework, for example – the film simply follows previous practices whose implications have been argued already. It is in the reconstruction of the protagonist that the Hammer film is distinctive, and here the director Terence Fisher was not encumbered by any sense of the original which indeed he had not read. Thus, although Fisher's script (by Jimmy Sangster) was based on the novel, the way was clear for an alignment of the material that was not inhibited by considerations of accuracy, of being 'faithful to the text', but which was free to rework the elements towards those broad Hammer policies of exploitation and money-making.

The singularity of Cushing's role has been spotted by several observers without much attempt being made to see why this should be so.[34] The fact that the film is centred on creator rather than monster in this version is signposted by the way that Boris Karloff, the monster in the Universal movie, at once became a star while Colin Clive, who was Frankenstein, remained obscure; conversely, in the Hammer picture, it was Peter Cushing who featured in the sequels, whereas Christopher Lee never took the part of the monster again.

Central to the specificity of Cushing's part is the way he makes Frankenstein unambiguously the villain of the story and this shift is produced by at least three major changes in his presentation. First and most obviously there are the crimes he commits which have no basis in the text or in previous film versions: to get a brain for his creature he murders a colleague, Professor Bernstein, and later on he sets up the killing of his servant Justine to conceal from his fiancée Elizabeth the fact that he has got her pregnant. Second, there is a marked class mutation that takes a tendency that is apparent in earlier versions several stages further. Mary Shelley's hero is a student, the son of a magistrate; in the Universal movie he becomes the son of a baron; in the Hammer film for the first time he himself is styled Baron Frankenstein and is given decadent aristocratic trappings to go with his title – he becomes, in Pirie's eyes, 'a dandy'. And then thirdly there is the change in age: Mary Shelley's youthful student is turned into Peter Cushing's middle-aged professor. The relevance of that emerges if we remember that 70 per cent of the audience for horror movies in the 1950s were aged twelve to twenty-five, a fact of which the commercially alert Hammer were well aware. A film pitched largely at adolescents could evoke hostility towards the protagonist more easily by transforming him from one of their own kind into a standard adult authority figure.

In short, the ambiguity of earlier readings of the story is removed by these revisions and we are given a Frankenstein to hate. ... Peter Cushing's Baron Frankenstein is a lethal nutter, an archetypal mad scientist.

It is here that the break with the Universal version is sharpest. James Whale had worked specifically to avoid a mad scientist reading of the story and had written to actor Colin Clive insisting that Frankenstein is 'an intensely sane person . . . a sane and lovable person'.[36] And the one moment in Whale's film when this analysis wavers – namely Frankenstein's megalomaniac cry of 'Now I know what it feels like to be God' as his creature moves for the first time – was chopped by pious censors before anybody else got to see it.

What I'd like to argue is that close to the root of this transformation in the reading and reproduction of *Frankenstein* is a shift in the structure of fears within the dominant ideology. The possibility of working-class insurrection that had concerned Mary Shelley and terrified Universal was no longer a prime source of anxiety in 1956. To take one crude statistical indicator of working-class discontent: the number of working days lost, or rather won, in strikes in Britain in the 1940s and 1950s was the lowest in the twentieth century. But on the other hand the development of atomic and hydrogen bombs created a new and dire nightmare of the risk of world destruction flowing from a single, deranged individual –

a cultural neurosis that the James Bond novels and films, for instance, were to run and run again through the 1960s and beyond. . . . Equally importantly, we need to remember events in the very week that filming began. The cameras turned for the first time on 19 November; two days earlier, the first Hungarian refugees had arrived in Britain driven out by the Russian tanks that smashed their revolution; a fortnight earlier, on 5 November, Anglo-French airborne troops had landed at Port Said at the depths of the fiasco of the Suez invasion.

The Curse of Frankenstein was therefore made at a unique and over determined conjuncture in world history when, for the first time, both the technology and the crises existed to threaten the very survival of the planet. Once again Mary Shelley's novel was pulled off the shelf and ransacked for the terms to articulate cultural hysteria. In one sense, of course, the movie represents a flight from the politics of Eden and the Kremlin into a spot of escapist Gothic knockabout; but to see it and then dismiss it as no more is to wipe out a series of factors including Fisher's ideology, Hammer's business sense, American investment and contemporary critical responses,[37] all of which mark out the seriousness of the project at one level. To put it baldly, at a time of genuine and multi-layered public fears, *The Curse of Frankenstein* addresses itself to a predominantly young audience and locates the source of anxiety in a deranged individual, focuses it down to the point where its basis is seen as one man's wider systematic and social readings and other possibilities (the Walton story for one) are repressed, as a structure whose values go unquestioned is presented as threatened by a loony rather than as being itself at the root of instability. Responsibility for imminent catastrophe is limited to a single intellectual standing outside both ordinary lives and the political establishment, so that the film can flow from and then feed back into a populist politics and a scrubby anti-intellectualism frustrated by its own impotence. *The Curse of Frankenstein* is the curse of blocked democracy looking for a scapegoat and being sidetracked from an analysis.

What I have tried to show is that there is no eternal facet of our psyche that horror stories address themselves to. The reworkings of Frankenstein's story in the last century and a half prove that if there are, in Mary Shelley's phrase in the 1831 introduction, 'mysterious fears of our nature' to which her tale seeks to speak, those fears, like our nature itself, are produced and reproduced by the process of history itself.

Notes

1 Details from W.H. Lyles, *Mary Shelley: An Annotated Bibliography* (Garland, New York 1975), and Peter Haining (ed.), *The Frankenstein File* (New English Library, London 1977).

2 See in particular Tony Bennett, *Formalism and Marxism* (Methuen, London 1979), chs 7, 8 and 9; Catherine Belsey, *Critical Practice* (Methuen, London 1980), chs 2 and 6; and Terry Eagleton, *Walter Benjamin: Or, Towards a Revolutionary Criticism* (Verso, London 1981), part II, ch.3.

3 D.W. Harding, 'The character of literature from Blake to Byron', in Boris Ford (ed.), *The Pelican Guide to English Literature. Vol 5: From Blake to Byron* (Penguin, Harmondsworth 1957), p. 45.

4 See, for example, Ellen Moers, *Literary Women* (The Women's Press, London 1977); Kate Ellis, 'Monsters in the garden: Mary Shelley and the bourgeois family', in George Levine and U.C. Knoepflmacher (eds), *The Endurance of Frankenstein: Essays on Mary Shelley's Novel* (University of California Press, Berkeley 1979); and Sandra M. Gilbert

and Susan Gubar, *The Madwoman in the Attic: The Woman Writer and the Nineteenth-Century Literary Imagination* (Yale University Press, New Haven 1979).

5 Jane Dunn, *Moon in Eclipse: A Life of Mary Shelley* (St Martin's Press, New York 1978), pp. 131,134.

6 Christopher Small, *Ariel Like a Harpy: Shelley, Mary and Frankenstein* (Gollancz, London 1972), p. 331.

7 Martin Tropp, *Mary Shelley's Monster* (Houghton Mifflin, Boston 1976), p. 156.

8 Malcolm I. Thomis, *The Luddites: Machine-Breaking in Regency England* (David & Charles, Newton Abbot 1970), p. 144.

9 *The Making of the English Working Class* (Penguin, Harmondsworth 1968), p. 733.

10 Frederick L. Jones (ed.), *The Letters of Percy Bysshe Shelley. Vol 1: Shelley in England* (Oxford University Press, Oxford 1964), p. 351.

11 Roger Ingpen and Walter E. Peck (eds), *The Complete Works of Percy Bysshe Shelley. Vol. VI* (Benn, London 1965), p. 81.

15 *The Letters of Mary Wollstonecraft Shelley. Vol I*, pp. 138, 49.

16 For details, see Appendix C of Mary Wollstonecraft Shelley, *Frankenstein or The Modern Prometheus*, ed. M.K. Joseph (Oxford University Press, London 1969). All subsequent references to the text are to this edition.

17 See Elizabeth Nitchie, *Mary Shelley, Author of Frankenstein* (Greenwood, Connecticut 1953), pp. 26–33.

18 See, for example, Tropp, *Mary Shelley's Monster*, p. 82, and Mary Poovey, 'My hideous progeny: Mary Shelley and the feminization of romanticism', *Proceedings of the Modern Languages Association*, 95 (May 1980).

20 See 'Mary Shelley's Monster: politics and psyche in *Frankenstein*', in Levine and Knoepflmacher, *Endurance of Frankenstein*.

23 *Mary Barton* (Penguin edn., Harmondsworth 1970), pp. 219–20.

22 Quoted in App. IV, 'The stage history of *Frankenstein*', Nitchie, *Mary Shelley*, p. 221.

23 For details, see Poovey, 'My hideous progeny'.

24 See the concluding chapter, 'Towards a theory of the Gothic', in David Punter, *The Literature of Terror, A History of Gothic Fictions from 1765 to the Present Day* (Longman, Harlow 1980).

27 See, respectively, Tropp, *Mary Shelley's Monster*, pp. 87, 90; David Pirie, *A Heritage of Horror: The English Gothic Cinema 1946–1972* (1973) p. 69; and Jensen, *Boris Karloff*, p. 30.

28 Jensen, *Boris Karloff*, p. 41.

29 S.S. Prawer, *Caligari's Children: The Film as Tale of Terror* (Oxford University Press, Oxford 1980), p. 22.

30 Jensen, *Boris Karloff*, p. 44.

31 Quoted in Prawer, *Caligari's Children*, p. 241.

32 See Pirie, *Heritage of Horror*, p. 26.

33 Allan Eyles, Robert Adkinson and Nicholas Fry (eds), *The House of Horror: The Story of Hammer Films* (Barnes, San Diego 1973), p. 16.

34 See, for example, Pirie, *Heritage of Horror*, pp. 69 ff.; Tropp, *Mary Shelley's Monster*, pp. 125 ff.; Donald Glut, 'Peter Cushing: Doctor Frankenstein I presume', in Haining, *Frankenstein File*; and Albert J. La Valley, 'The stage and film children of *Frankenstein*: a survey', in Levine and Knoepflmacher, *Endurance of Frankenstein*.

36 Quoted in Jensen, *Boris Karloff*, p. 35.

37 *Tribune*, for example, found the movie 'depressing' and 'degrading', and for C.A. Lejeune in the *Observer* it was 'among the half-dozen most repulsive films I have encountered'. The inadequacy of a dismissal of horror stories as merely escapist has recently been powerfully argued by Rosemary Jackson, *Fantasy: The Literature of Subversion* (Methuen, London 1981).

(from *Literature and History*, Autumn 1983)

Mass society theory: British 'literary' and continental 'sociological' approaches

Theory and methodology

5 Q.D. Leavis, *Fiction and the Reading Public* (1932), Introduction, Chapters 3, 10
6 R. Williams, *The Long Revolution* (1961), Part I, Chapter 2
7 T.W. Adorno, 'Culture Industry Reconsidered' (1967)
8 S. Hall and P. Whannel, *The Popular Arts* (1964), Chapter 13
9 W. Benjamin, 'The Storyteller'

Applications

10 Q.D. Leavis, 'The Case of Miss Dorothy Sayers' (1937)
11 T.W. Adorno, 'On Popular Music' (1941)

The extracts in this chapter originate from writers of widely diverse cultural experience and political tendency. Together they illustrate many of the central assumptions of what is conventionally referred to as 'mass society theory'.

The Leavis and Williams extracts represent two important early recognitions by literary academics of the significance of popular forms. In the early 1930s Leavis's interest was shared by few of her Cambridge colleagues. Fiction and the Reading Public was thus very genuinely a pioneering study of new territory. Its central thrust is the denunciation of a general decline in the level of 'culture' in industrial societies: popular fiction is implicated as both symptom and cause of that decline. Its appeal is to 'herd prejudice' and its effect is to 'debase the emotional currency by touching basely on fine issues'. Its popularity ensures that not only is quality literature appreciated by increasingly few readers but that the very existence of such literature is threatened. Leavis's cultural pessimism and unrepentant élitism will doubtless be noted by most readers. Responses to the extracts ought, however, to go beyond the unhistorical 'Queenie-bashing' Mrs Leavis so opens herself to. Her avowed commitment to an 'unbiased', 'inquisitive', 'anthropological' analysis of popular texts can hardly be faulted, and though we must observe her failure to live up to these aspirations, and indeed her role in compounding the problems facing the contemporary student of popular forms, we should never lose sight of her text as a 1930s recognition of what needed to be done. In a real sense Q.D. Leavis cleared some of the space for subsequent study.

Raymond Williams probably contributed more than any other British theorist to the filling of that space. Amid the intellectual upheaval and dramatic expansion in higher education in the 1960s there evolved a new academic discipline: cultural studies. It emerged at a point of convergence of radical literary critics, historians and sociologists. The Long Revolution (1961) is partially concerned with exploring the relations between popular fiction and the wider culture, especially during the 1840s in Britain. Williams's approach was to exert a substantial influence on the subsequent development of cultural studies, notably through certain key concepts represented in Extract 6 – 'dominant social character', 'structure of feeling', and, especially, 'magical resolutions'. The latter phrase is rightly celebrated. In The Long Revolution it signals a fictional reconciliation of how people in real life actually think, feel, behave with the ways in which dominant ideology would have them. (This is the accommodation of the dominant social character within the much broader structure of feeling). Real-life contradictions disappear in the constructed world of fiction. The concept has subsequently been extensively borrowed and adapted. The notion that popular fiction offers magical resolutions to problems, conflicts and contradictions which are in real life intractable is a productive idea and remains of great value to the student.

Williams's development as a theorist is widely perceived in terms of his 'dialogue with Marxism'.[1] And yet for all his sensing, in The Long Revolution, of the importance of subordinate culture, taken as a whole Williams's literary criticism invariably addresses canonical texts. One might perhaps expect to find the serious analysis of specific popular texts in writers less ambiguously committed to Marxism. Adorno and Benjamin reflect some of the interest in popular culture expressed among continental Marxists between the wars and immediately post-1945. Any expectation of close textual analysis is not fulfilled.

Adorno was a member, and Benjamin a close associate, of the Frankfurt Institute for Social Research, founded at the University of Frankfurt in 1923 and later forced to emigrate to the USA. Its research is known collectively as 'critical theory' and is committed to a radical critique of the social order. Sociological, psychological and aesthetic insights contribute to an analysis of the role of the 'culture industry' (by which is meant approximately 'mass media', though see Adorno's important note at the beginning of Extract 7) in the subordination of the working classes in Western Europe and the USA. Media products reflect and reproduce the ideology of monopoly capitalism, and the effect is the endorsement and perpetuation of the system. 'All mass culture is identical', and the impact on the individual is destructive: 'consciousness' is 'fettered' and 'The culture industry as a whole has moulded men as a type unfailingly reproduced in every product'.

The quotations are from a seminal Frankfurt School essay, 'The Culture Industry: Englightenment as Mass Deception' published by Adorno in collaboration with Max Horkheimer in 1947. Reading 7 is Adorno's much briefer reconsideration (published in 1967) of the earlier essay. In the intervening years the study of popular forms had, as we have seen, gained some ground. Adorno, however, firmly endorses his earlier judgement and warns against any tendency to conflate social significance with value. In judgements of quality there is a measure of agreement between Adorno and Q.D. Leavis: popular forms offer nothing more valuable than a 'deceptive glitter' and the critic should not feel constrained *from saying so. Adorno's sense of a fading 'grasp on the idea of the good life' fur- ther recalls Leavis's cultural pessimism, and also shared is the equation of declining cultural standards with the rapid expansion of an industrial society in which material values prevail. Distinctive to Adorno is the reading of effects in ideological terms – one notes especially his formulation 'social cement' in 'On Popular Music' (11) – and, in the same essay, his attempt at theorising the listener, though one may well wish to question his construction of the uniformly passive recipient of popular forms.*

It is striking and probably surprising that there should be such common ground between positions as fundamentally opposed as those of the bourgeois British intelligentsia and continental Marxist social theory. On another level the similarities underline the extent to which mass society theory, with its equation popular = mass = debased, has suffused thinking about popular forms not only in the UK but in Europe and the USA too. In Extract 8 Hall and Whannel sum- marise briefly the terms in which the equation is commonly expressed. Though published in 1964, this fairly represents the frame within which so many contem- porary rejections of popular fiction are formulated.

*Frankfurt School theory is not uniformly dismissive of popular forms. The stu- dent who instinctively reacts against the despondency of much analysis and who wishes to translate that aversion into a fully theorised argument will gain consid- erable help from Walter Benjamin. Benjamin shares Leavis's and Adorno's high regard for art and his analysis, like theirs, insists that the position of serious art in the total culture has changed with the growth of the culture industry. He is not, however, despondent about these changes. Their implication is not the destruction but the democratisation of culture and the transformed relationship between artists and their public participates in the wider revolutionary social change Benjamin believed in.[2] Like Adorno, Benjamin does not write principally about written fiction, but his essay The Story Teller, as has been observed elsewhere,[3] offers suggestions which may usefully be applied to contemporary popular fiction. The essay is organised around the distinction between the 'novel' and the 'story'. In contemporary society the novel, whose 'birthplace' is the 'solitary individual', has replaced the story, whose base was the communal exchange of personal expe- riences in pre-industrial cultures. It is valid to explore connections between story-telling as characterised by Benjamin and the contemporary practice of popu- lar fiction, and a starting point should be Benjamin's stress on **repetition** as crucial to the retention and exchange of stories. We are familiar enough with denunciations of the predictability of the commodities of mass culture. What level of repetition and predictability is compatible with the pleasurable experience of texts? The issue is crucial and will become prominent in Chapter 3 in discussions of genre, formula and the analysis of narrative.*

Notes

1 The phrase is Stuart Hall's (see Extract 26)
2 The reader is referred in particular to two of Benjamin's essays, 'The Work of Art in the Age of Mechanical Reproduction' (1936) and 'The Author as Producer' (1934).
3 See Batsleer (1985), Chapter 4.

Theory and methodology

Fiction and the reading public

Q.D. Leavis

The system of working adopted in this study demands some explanation. There are two accepted methods of dealing with the Novel, and neither has scope for a kind of interest in fiction that I feel to be of great urgency. Henry James in *Notes on Novelists*, and to a much lesser degree Mr Lubbock in *The Craft of Fiction*, have made serious attempts to grapple with the criticism of the novel, but both books, the former in part and the latter wholly, are approaches from the academic angle. I mean by this that they imply the same restrictions as the phrase used by Mr Eliot when he refers to 'the few who can talk intelligently of Stendhal, Proust, and Henry James'. Now this method, which is that of literary criticism, can necessarily take no heed of the majority of novels – nearly everything indeed that comes under the head of 'fiction' – which have been very extensively read for the last three centuries. Yet this body of writing has exerted an enormous influence upon the minds and lives of the English people; till recently it has superseded for the majority every other form of art and amusement; and it forms the only printed matter beside newspapers and advertisements which that majority reads; from the cultural point of view its importance cannot be exaggerated. A tangle of pregnant issues is involved, questions of standards and values are raised which bear on the whole history of taste. And for this purpose it is at least as important to take account of the fiction that does not happen to be, or to have become, literature as of the novels which ultimately get into the text-books. But the text-book is the only method that has so far appeared for dealing with fiction as distinct from literature. Even as I write, the bulky and authoritative volumes of what looks like being a final *History of the English Novel* are being ground out of the press. Here are recorded the plots and histories of all the well-known and many of the less well-known English novels; but there is no indication that they ever had readers, much less that they played any part in shaping the human spirit and were shaped by it; and this method precludes any serious discussion of values. ... I soon found myself committed to a method of investigation which I prefer to describe as 'anthropological'. It consisted in examining all the material that seemed to bear on this question in an unbiased but inquisitive frame of mind and concentrating on registering shifts of taste and changes in the cultural background, allowing such conclusions as I arrived at to emerge simply by comparison and contrast and analysis.

. . . .

It would not be true to suggest a stratification of novel writers and novel readers in 1760, for example, when anyone who could read would be equally likely to read any novel, or every novel, published, and the only division of the novelists of that age that can be made is between good and indifferent (effective and ineffective); even a century later the same conditions hold, for though at that time Dickens,

Reade, and Wilkie Collins were the idols of the man in the street and George Eliot and Trollope of the educated, yet each class read or perfectly well might have read the entire output of all the contemporary novelists, who all live in the same world, as it were, understand each other's language, live by the same code, and employ a common technique presenting no peculiar difficulty to the reader.

Comparison of the situations at these dates (chosen at random) with that exhibited in the previous chapters has brought out a significant fact: that it is a peculiarity of this last generation that a consistent selection by the majority of the 'worst' novels ('worst' by consensus of the critical minority) has created a state exactly contrary to what the Martian or the innocent eighteenth-century observer might expect, so that 'bestseller' is an almost entirely derogatory epithet among the cultivated.... To illustrate the curiously inverse relation now existing between esteem and popularity, a state of affairs that has come to be considered normal, the literary column of the *Evening Standard* (19 July 1928) may be cited, where the writer (Mr Arnold Bennett), explaining with some apologies that he has read a novel by Edgar Wallace out of curiosity, urges that –

> Nearly all bookish people are snobs, and especially the more enlightened among them. They are apt to assume that if a writer has immense circulation, if he is enjoyed by plain persons, and if he can fill several theatres at once, he cannot possibly be worth reading and merits only indifference and disdain.

The twentieth-century reader who would let this pass as a common-place could only be brought to realize that it is indeed something new in English history by considering as a norm Dr Johnson rejoicing to concur with the common reader – a position that for the modern critic of equivalent standing would be ridiculous.

It is not perhaps surprising that, in a society of forty-three millions so decisively stratified in taste that each stratum is catered for independently by its own novelists and journalists, the lowbrow public should be ignorant of the work and even of the names of the highbrow writers, while to the highbrow public 'Ethel M. Dell' or 'Tarzan' should be convenient symbols, drawn from hearsay rather than first-hand knowledge. But what close at hand is apparently trivial becomes a serious development when we realize that this means nothing less than that the general public – Dr Johnson's common reader – has now not even a glimpse of the living interests of modern literature, is ignorant of its growth and so prevented from developing with it, and that the critical minority to whose sole charge modern literature has now fallen is isolated, disowned by the general public and threatened with extinction. Poetry and criticism are not read by the common reader: the drama, in so far as it ever overlapped literature, is dead, and the novel is the only branch of letters which is now generally supported.

. . . .

It is wish-fulfilment in various forms that the modern bestseller and magazine story provide, though it is never quite so simple as this suggests. Take the case of the novel which deals in romantic action: the classical instance – *The Three Musketeers* – at once springs to mind. Its modern equivalent, *Beau Geste* and its successors, have sold half a million each since *Beau Geste* appeared in 1924. But whereas Dumas has commonly served as a stage in the normal boy's development, the works of P.C. Wren are now the reading of adults, for whom they are doing something more than kill time or assuage a craving for adventure. They serve to stabilize a certain attitude, confirm certain prejudices, as the following extracts from their author's reply show:

The bulk of my readers are the cleanly-minded virile outdoor sort of people of both sexes, and the books are widely read in the Army, the Navy, the Universities, the Public Schools, and the Clubs.... My favourite reading is the memoirs of people who have done things, and I admit, without shame, that my favourite novelists are Hergesheimer, A.E.W. Mason, Conrad and R.L. Stevenson.... Although I now make a good many thousands per annum, I still am not a 'professional novelist', nor, as I have said, a long-haired literary cove. I prefer the short-haired executive type.

When the round well-varnished tale is finished, I send it to 'Mr John Murray'. The late Sir John Murray, Colonel John Murray, Lord Gorell and the other partners, are sportsmen and gentlemen who have somehow strayed into the muddy paths of commerce, and somehow contrived to remain sportsmen and gentlemen and jolly good businessmen as well.

The novels of Scott and Dumas had a different mentality behind them, that might perhaps not absurdly be described as cultured; at least it could be said of them that their authors did not despise the profession of letters and that what they wrote was not unrelated to literature. The difference between literature and 'clean entertainment' for 'the cleanly-minded virile sort of people' with 'tone definitely good' lies perhaps as much in the difference between the nineteenth-century public and the public of the twentieth century as in the novelists themselves.

. . . .

These novelists are read by the governing classes as well as by the masses, and they impinge directly on the world of the minority, menacing the standards by which they live. And whereas their forerunners were innocent of malice, devoting themselves to assuring their readers of 'the beauty of human affection and the goodness of God', these writers are using the technique of Marie Corelli and Mrs Barclay to work upon and solidify herd prejudice and to debase the emotional currency by touching grossly on fine issues. In this, as we have noticed earlier, they are at one with their background. They also exhibit a persistent hostility to the world of letters which is quite unprecedented.

. . . .

The best that the novel can do, it may be suggested, is not to offer a refuge from actual life but to help the reader to deal less inadequately with it; the novel can deepen, extend, and refine experience by allowing the reader to live at the expense of an unusually intelligent and sensitive mind, by giving him access to a finer code than his own. But this, we have seen, the popular novels of the age do not do. On the contrary, they substitute an emotional code which, as Part II will try to show, is actually inferior to the traditional code of the illiterate and which helps to make a social atmosphere unfavourable to the aspirations of the minority. They actually get in the way of genuine feeling and responsible thinking by creating cheap mechanical responses and by throwing their weight on the side of social, national, and herd prejudices. The most popular contemporary fiction, it has been shown, unfits its readers for any novel that demands readjustment.

. . . .

First, I have here isolated and shown the workings of a number of tendencies which, having assumed the form of commercial and economic machinery, are now so firmly established that they run on their own and whither they choose; they have assumed such a monstrous impersonality that individual effort towards controlling or checking them seems ridiculously futile. This is probably the most terrifying feature of our civilization. If there is to be any hope, it must lie in conscious and directed effort. All that can be done, it must be realized, must take the form of resistance by an armed and conscious minority.

This minority has two main modes of usefulness, between which communication would have to be kept up. The first is in the field of research. It is of the utmost importance that as many as possible should be made aware of what is happening, and a fully documented presentment of the history of the reading public is an essential means to this end. It may be further argued that what we have here is a type case, a particular instance of a general process at work in the modern world. Many other studies of the same kind are needed in order to examine and document the cultural situation in as many relevant fields as possible, with a view to informing and equipping the active minority. . . .

The profit would be not only a matter of books designed to foster general awareness. It would also mean the training of a picked few who would go out into the world equipped for the work of forming and organizing a conscious minority. And this leads us to the second mode of usefulness of the minority, that of educational work in schools and universities... experience shows that when the young are made aware of these forces they readily see the necessity for resisting. They may even be fired with a missionary spirit. In fact, the possibilities of education specifically directed against such appeals as those made by the journalist, the middleman, the bestseller, the cinema, and advertising, and the other more general influences discussed in this study, are inexhaustible; some education of this kind is an essential part of the training of taste. Such a missionary spirit, however amusing to the psychologizing observer, has played a considerable part in history. As a minor instance of what may be done by conscious resistance, the case of British Honduras comes to hand. Here, I am informed, we have a community which in deliberately setting out to resist American influence is actually preserving a traditional way of life.

READING 6

The long revolution

Raymond Williams

Williams is writing about the culture of Britain in the 1840s.

The dominant social character of the period can be briefly outlined. There is the belief in the value of work, and this is seen in relation to individual effort, with a strong attachment to success gained in these terms. A class society is assumed, but social position is increasingly defined by actual status rather than by birth. The poor are seen as the victims of their own failings, and it is strongly held that the best among them will climb out of their class. A punitive Poor Law is necessary in order to stimulate effort; if a man could fall back on relief, without grave hardship in the form of separation from his family, minimum sustenance, and such work as stone-breaking or oakum-picking, he would not make the necessary effort to provide for himself. In this and a wider field, suffering is in one sense ennobling, in that it teaches humility and courage, and leads to the hard dedication to duty. Thrift, sobriety, and piety are the principal virtues, and the family is their central institution. The sanctity of marriage is absolute, and adultery and fornication are unpardonable. Duty includes helping the weak provided that the help is not of such a kind as to confirm the weakness: condoning sexual error, and comforting the poor, are weaknesses by this definition. Training to the prevailing virtues must be necessarily severe, but there is an obligation to see that the institutions for such training are strengthened.

This can be fairly called the dominant social character of the period, if we look at its characteristic legislation, the terms in which this was argued, the majority content of public writing and speaking, and the characters of the men most admired. Yet, of course, as a social character, it varied considerably in success of transmission, and was subject to many personal variations. The more serious difficulty arises as we look more closely at the period and realize that alternative social characters were in fact active, and that these affected, in important ways, the whole life of the time. A social character is the abstract of a dominant group, and there can be no doubt that the character described – a developed form of the morality of the industrial and commercial middle class – was at this time the most powerful. At the same time, there were other social characters with substantial bases in the society. The aristocratic character was visibly weakening, but its variations – that birth mattered more than money; that work was not the sole social value and that civilization involved play; that sobriety and chastity, at least in young men, were not cardinal virtues but might even be a sign of meanness or dullness – are still alive in the period, all in practice, some in theory. In attitudes to the poor, this character is ambiguous: it includes a stress on charity, as part of one's station, very different from punitive rehabilitation, but also a brutality, a willingness to cut down troublemakers, a natural habit of repression, which again differ from the middle-class attitude. The 1840s are very interesting in this respect, for they show the interaction of different social characters: Tory charity against Whig rehabilitation; brutality and repression against positive civilization through institution. Some of the best criticism of the Whig Poor Law came from Tories with a conscious aristocratic ideal, as most notably in Young England. Brutality and repression are ready, in crisis, but as compared with the twenties and thirties, are being steadily abandoned in favour of positive legislation. Play may be frowned on by the social character, but the decade shows a large increase in light entertainment, from cheap novels to the music-halls. Not only is the dominant social character different, in many ways, from the life lived in its shadow, but alternative social characters lead to the real conflicts of the time. This is a central difficulty of the social character concept, for in stressing a dominant abstraction it seriously underestimates the historical process of change and conflict, which are found even when, as in the 1840s, such a social character is very strong. For we must add another alternative, of major importance: the developing social character of the working class, different in important respects from its competitors. As the victims of repression and punitive rehabilitation, of the gospel of success and the pride of birth, of the real nature of work and the exposure to suffering, working-class people were beginning to formulate alternative ideals. They had important allies from the interaction of the other systems, and could be a major force either in the Corn Laws repeal or in the Factory legislation, when these were sponsored by different sections of the ruling class. But the 1840s show an important development of independent aims, though these are to be realized, mainly, through alliance with other groups. Thus Chartism is an ideal beyond the terms of any dominant group in the society, and is more than an expression of democratic aspirations; is also an assertion of an individual dignity, transcending class. The Ten Hours Bill, in working-class minds, was more than a good piece of paternal legislation on work: it was also the claim to leisure, and hence again to a wider life. At the same time, in their own developing organizations, the most radical criticism of all was being made: the refusal of a society based either on birth or on individual success, the conception of a society based on mutual aid and co-operation.

We can then distinguish three social characters operative in the period, and it is with the study of relations between them that we enter the reality of the whole life. All contribute to the growth of the society: the aristocratic ideals tempering the harshness of middle-class ideals at their worst; working-class ideals entering into a fruitful and decisive combination with middle-class ideals at their best. The middle-class social character remains dominant, and both aristocrats and working people, in many respects, come to terms with it. But equally, the middle-class social character as it entered the forties is in many respects modified as the forties end. The values of work and self-help, of social position by status rather than birth, of the sanctity of marriage and the emphasis on thrift, sobriety and charity, are still dominant. But punitive rehabilitation, and the attitudes to weakness and suffering on which it rests, have been, while not rejected, joined by a major ideal of public service, in which the effort towards civilization is actively promoted by a genuine altruism and the making of positive institutions.

This is one level of change, and such analysis is necessary if we are to explore the reality of the social character. In some respects, the structure of feeling corresponds to the dominant social character, but it is also an expression of the interaction described. Again, however, the structure of feeling is not uniform throughout the society; it is primarily evident in the dominant productive group. At this level, however, it is different from any of the distinguishable social characters, for it has to deal not only with the public ideals but with their omissions and consequences, as lived. If we look at the fiction of the forties, we shall see this clearly.

The popular fiction of the periodicals, so carefully studied by Dalziel, is very interesting in this context. At first sight we find what we expect: the unshakeable assumptions of a class society, but with the stress of wealth rather than birth (aristocrats, indeed, being often personally vicious); the conviction that the poor are so by their own faults – their stupidity and depravity stressed, their mutual help ignored; the absolute sanctity of marriage, the manipulation of plot to bring sexual offenders to actual suffering; the fight against weakness, however terrible, as one of the main creators of humble virtue. All this, often consciously didactic, is the direct expression of the dominant social character, and the assumptions tend to be shared by the pious 'improving' fiction (cf. Mrs Tonna's *Helen Fleetwood*) and by the sensational fiction which the improvers condemned. But then we are reminded of the extent to which popular fiction retains older systems of value, often through stereotyped conventions of character. The 'fashionable novel' of high life only became unfashionable late in the decade. The typical hero is sometimes the successful exponent of self-help, but often he is an older type, the cultivated gentleman, the soldier governed by a code of honour, even the man who finds pleasure a blessing and work a curse. To the earlier hero, loss of income and the need to work were misfortunes to be endured; to have a safe fortune was undoubtedly best. The new attitude to work came in only slowly, for understandable reasons. (Ordinary middle-class life was still thought too plain and dull for a really interesting novel.) Further, heroes of either kind are capable

41

of strong overt emotion; they can burst into public tears, or even swoon, as strong men used to do but were soon to do no more. Heroines have more continuity: they are weak, dependent, and shown as glad to be so, and of course they are beautiful and chaste. One interesting factor, obviously related to a continuing general attitude in the period, is that schools, almost without exception, are shown as terrible: not only are they places of temptation and wickedness, mean, cruel and educationally ridiculous, but also they are inferior to the home and family, as a way of bringing up children. This is perhaps the last period in which a majority of English public opinion believed that home education was the ideal. From the sixteenth century, this belief had been gaining ground, and its complete reversal, with the new public school ethos after Arnold, is of considerable general importance. But the new attitude does not appear in fiction until *Tom Brown's Schooldays* in 1857.

In the popular fiction of the forties, then, we find many marks of older ways of feeling, as well as faithful reproduction of certain and standard feelings of the approved social character. We find also, in an interesting way, the interaction between these and actual experience. The crucial point, in this period, is in the field of success and money. The confident assertions of the social character, that success followed effort, and that wealth was the mark of respect, had to contend, if only unconsciously, with a practical world in which things were not so simple. The confidence of this fiction is often only superficial. What comes through with great force is a pervasive atmosphere of instability and debt. A normal element, in these stories, is the loss of fortune, and this is hardly ever presented in terms consistent with the social character: that success or failure correspond to personal quality. Debt and ruin haunt this apparently confident world, and in a majority of cases simply happen to the characters, as a result of a process outside them. At one level, the assumptions of the social character are maintained: if you lose your fortune, you get out of the way – you cannot embarrass yourself or your friends by staying. But this ruthless code is ordinarily confined to subsidiary characters: the parents of hero or heroine. For the people who matter, some other expedient is necessary. It is found, over the whole range of fiction, by two devices: the unexpected legacy, and the Empire. These devices are extremely interesting, both at the level of magic and at the level of developing attitudes necessary to the society.

Magic is indeed necessary, to postpone the conflict between the ethic and the experience. It is widely used in sexual situations, where hero or heroine is tied to an unloved wife or husband, while the true lover waits in the wings. Solutions involving infidelity or breaking the marriage are normally unthinkable, and so a formula is evolved, for standard use: the unsuitable partner is not merely unloved, but alcoholic or insane; at a given point, and after the required amount of resigned suffering, there is a convenient, often spectacular death, in which the unloving partner shows great qualities of care, duty, and piety; and then, of course, the real love can be consummated. In money, the process is similar: legacies, at the crucial moment, turn up from almost anywhere, and fortunes are restored. Nobody has to go against the principle that money is central to success, but equally very few have to be bound by the ethic preached to the poor: that the deserving prosper by effort. This element of cheating marks one crucial point of difference between the social character and the actual structure of feeling.

The use of the Empire is similar but more complex. Of course there were actual legacies, and these eventually changed the self-help ethic, in its simplest form: the magic, at this stage, lay in their timing. But the Empire was a more universally available escape-route: black sheep could be lost in it; ruined or misunderstood heroes could go out and return with fortunes; the weak of every kind could be transferred to it, to make a new life. Often indeed, the Empire is the source of the unexpected legacy, and the two devices are joined. It is clear that the use of the Empire relates to real factors in the society. At a simple level, going out to the new lands could be seen as self-help and enterprise of the purest kinds. Also, in the new lands, there was a great need for labourers, and emigration as a solution to working-class problems was being widely urged, often by the most humane critics of the existing system. In 1840, 90,000 people a year were emigrating, and in 1850 three times as many. In a different way, in terms of capital and trade, the Empire had been one of the levers of industrialization, and was to prove one major way of keeping the capitalist system viable. These factors are reflected in fiction, though not to the same extent as later in the century, when Imperialism had become a conscious policy. Meanwhile, alongside this reflection of real factors, there was the use as magic: characters whose destinies could not be worked out within the system as given were simply put on the boat, a simpler way of resolving the conflict between ethic and experience than any radical questioning of the ethic.

 READING 7

'Culture industry reconsidered'

T.W. Adorno

The term culture industry was perhaps used for the first time in the book *Dialectic of Enlightenment*, which Horkheimer and I published in Amsterdam in 1947. In our drafts we spoke of 'mass culture'. We replaced that expression with 'culture industry' in order to exclude from the outset the interpretation agreeable to its advocates: that it is a matter of something like a culture that arises spontaneously from the masses themselves, the contemporary form of popular art. From the latter the culture industry must be distinguished in the extreme. The culture industry fuses the old and familiar into a new quality. In all its branches, products which are tailored for consumption by masses, and which to a great extent   determine the nature of that consumption, are manufactured more or less according to plan. The individual branches are similar in structure or at least fit into each other, ordering themselves into a system almost without a gap. This is made possible by contemporary technical capabilities as well as by economic and administrative concentration. The culture industry intentionally integrates its consumers from above. To the detriment of both it forces together the spheres of high and low art, separated for thousands of years. The seriousness of high art is destroyed in speculation about its efficacy; the seriousness of the lower perishes with the civilizational constraints imposed on the rebellious resistance inherent within it as long as social control was not yet total. Thus, although the culture industry undeniably speculates on the conscious and unconscious state of the millions towards which it is directed, the masses are not primary, but secondary, they are an object of calculation; an appendage of the machinery. The customer is not king, as the culture industry would like to have us believe, not its subject but its object. The very word mass-media specially honed for the culture industry, already shifts the accent onto harmless terrain. Neither is it a question of primary concern for the masses, nor of the techniques of communication as such, but of the spirit which sufflates them, their master's voice. The culture industry misuses its concern for the masses in order to duplicate, reinforce and strengthen their mentality, which it presumes is given and unchangeable. How this mentality might be changed is excluded throughout. The masses are not the measure but the ideology of the culture industry, even though the culture industry itself could scarcely exist without adapting to the masses.

The cultural commodities of the industry are governed, as Brecht and Suhrkamp expressed it thirty years ago, by the principle of their realization and value, and not by their own specific content and harmonious formation. The entire practice of the culture industry transfers the profit motive naked onto cultural forms. Ever since these cultural forms first began to earn a living for their creators as commodities in the market-place they had already possessed something of this quality. But then they sought after profit only indirectly, over and above their autonomous essence. New on the part of the culture industry is the direct and undisguised primacy of a precisely and thoroughly calculated efficacy in its most typical products. The autonomy of works of art, which of course rarely ever predominated in an entirely pure form, and was always permeated by a constellation of effects, is tendentially eliminated by the culture industry, with or without the conscious will of those in control. The latter include both those who carry out directives as well as those who hold the power. In economic terms they are or were in search of new opportunities for the realization of capital in the most economically developed countries. The old opportunities became increasingly more precarious as a result of the same concentration process which alone makes the culture industry possible as an omnipresent phenomenon. Culture, in the true sense, did not simply accommodate itself to human beings; but it always simultaneously raised a protest against the petrified relations under which they lived, thereby honoring them. Insofar as culture becomes wholly assimilated to and integrated in those petrified relations, human beings are once more debased. Cultural entities typical of the culture industry are no longer *also* commodities, they are commodities through and through. This quantitative shift is so great that it calls forth entirely new phenomena. Ultimately, the culture industry no longer even needs to directly pursue everywhere the profit interests from which it originated. These interests have become objectified in its ideology and have even made themselves independent of the compulsion to sell the cultural commodities which must be swallowed anyway. The culture industry turns into public relations, the manufacturing of 'good will' per se, without regard for particular firms or saleable objects. Brought to bear is a general uncritical consensus, advertisements produced for the world, so that each product of the culture industry becomes its own advertisement.

Nevertheless, those characteristics which originally stamped the transformation of literature into a commodity are maintained in this process. More than anything in the world, the culture industry has its ontology, a scaffolding of rigidly conservative basic categories which can be gleaned, for example, from the commercial English novels of the late 17th and early 18th centuries. What parades as progress in the culture industry, as the incessantly new which it offers up, remains the disguise for an eternal sameness; everywhere the changes mask a skeleton which has changed just as little as the profit motive itself since the time it first gained its predominance over culture.

Thus, the expression 'industry' is not to be taken literally. It refers to the standardization of the thing itself – such as that of the Western, familiar to every movie-goer – and to the rationalization of distribution techniques, but not strictly to the production process. Although in film, the central sector of the culture industry, the production process resembles technical modes of operation in the extensive division of labor, the employment of machines and the separation of the laborers from the means of production – expressed in the perennial conflict between artists active in the culture industry and those who control it – individual forms of production are nevertheless maintained. Each product affects an individual air; individuality itself serves to reinforce ideology, insofar as the illusion is conjured up that the completely reified and mediated is a sanctuary from immediacy and life. Now, as ever, the culture industry exists in the 'service' of third persons, maintaining its affinity to the declining circulation process of capital, to the commerce from which it came into being. Its ideology above all makes use of the star system, borrowed from individualistic art and its commercial exploitation. The more dehumanized its methods of operation and content, the more diligently and successfully the culture industry propagates supposedly great personalities and operates with heart throbs. It is industrial more in a sociological sense, in the incorporation of industrial forms of organization even where nothing is manufactured – as in the rationalization of office work – rather than in the sense of anything really and actually produced by technological rationality. Accordingly, the misinvestments of the culture industry are considerable, throwing those branches rendered obsolete by new techniques into crises, which seldom lead to changes for the better.

The concept of technique in the culture industry is only in name identical with technique in works of art. In the latter, technique is concerned with the internal organization of the object itself, with its inner logic. In contrast, the technique of the culture industry is, from the beginning, one of distribution and mechanical reproduction, and therefore always remains external to its object. The culture industry finds ideological support precisely insofar as it carefully shields itself from the full potential of the techniques contained in its products. It lives parasitically from the extra-artistic technique of the material production of goods, without regard for the obligation to the internal artistic whole implied by its functionality (*Sachlichkeit*), but also without concern for the laws of form demanded by aesthetic autonomy. The result for the physiognomy of the culture industry is essentially a mixture of stream-lining, photographic hardness and precision on the one hand, and individualistic residues, sentimentality and an already rationally disposed and adapted romanticism on the other. Adopting Benjamin's designation of the traditional work of art by the concept of aura, the presence of that which is not present, the culture industry is defined by the fact that it does not strictly counterpose another principle to that of aura, but rather by the fact that it conserves the decaying aura as a foggy mist. By this means the culture industry betrays its own ideological abuses.

It has recently become customary among cultural officials as well as sociologists to warn against underestimating the culture industry while pointing to its great importance for the development of the consciousness of its consumers. It is to be taken seriously, without cultured snobbism. In actuality the culture industry is important as a moment of the spirit which dominates today. Whoever ignores its influence out of skepticism for what it stuffs into people would be naive. Yet there is a deceptive glitter about the admonition to take it seriously. Because of its social role, disturbing questions about its quality, about truth or untruth, and about the aesthetic niveau of the culture industry's emissions are repressed, or at least excluded from the so-called sociology of communications. The critic is accused of taking refuge in arrogant esoterica. It would be advisable first to indicate the double meaning of importance that slowly worms its way in unnoticed. Even if it touches the lives of innumerable people, the function of something is no guarantee of its particular quality. The blending of aesthetics with its residual communicative aspects leads art, as a social phenomenon, not to its rightful position in opposition to alleged artistic snobbism, but rather in a variety of ways to the defense of its baneful social consequences. The importance of the culture industry in the spiritual constitution of the masses is no dispensation for reflection on its objective legitimation, its essential being, least of all by a science which thinks itself pragmatic. On the contrary: such reflection becomes necessary precisely for this reason. To take the culture industry as seriously as its unquestioned role demands, means to take it seriously critically, and not to cower in the face of its monopolistic character.

Among those intellectuals anxious to reconcile themselves with the phenomenon and eager to find a common formula to express both their reservations against it and their respect for its power, a tone of ironic toleration prevails unless they have already created a new mythos of the 20th century from the imposed regression. After all, those intellectuals maintain, everyone knows what pocket novels, films off the rack, family television shows rolled out into serials and hit parades, advice to the lovelorn and horoscope columns are all about. All of this, however, is harmless and, according to them, even democratic since it responds to a demand, albeit a stimulated one. It also bestows all kinds of blessings, they point out, for example, through the dissemination of information, advice and stress reducing patterns of behavior. Of course, as every sociological study measuring something as elementary as how politically informed the public has proven, the information is meager or indifferent. Moreover, the advice to be gained from manifestations of the culture industry is vacuous, banal or worse, and the behavior patterns are shamelessly conformist.

The two-faced irony in the relationship of servile intellectuals to the culture industry is not restricted to them alone. It may also be supposed that the consciousness of the consumers themselves is split between the prescribed fun which is supplied to them by the culture industry and a not particularly well-hidden doubt about its blessings. The phrase, the world wants to be deceived, has become truer than had ever been intended. People are not only, as the saying goes, falling for the swindle; if it guarantees them even the most fleeting gratification they desire a deception which is nonetheless transparent to them. They force their eyes shut and voice approval, in a kind of self-loathing, for what is meted out to them, knowing fully the purpose for which it is manufactured. Without admitting it they sense that their lives would be completely intolerable as soon as they no longer clung to satisfactions which are none at all.

The most ambitious defense of the culture industry today celebrates its spirit, which might safely be called ideology, as an ordering factor. In a supposedly chaotic world it provides human beings with something like standards for orientation, and that alone seems worthy of approval. However, what its defenders imagine is preserved by the culture industry is in fact all the more thoroughly destroyed by it. The color film demolishes the genial old tavern to a greater extent than bombs ever could: the film exterminates its *imago*. No homeland can survive being processed by the films which celebrate it, and which thereby turn the unique character on which it thrives into an interchangeable sameness.

That which legitimately could be called culture attempted, as an expression of suffering and contradiction, to maintain a grasp on the idea of the good life. Culture cannot represent either that which merely exists or the conventional and no longer binding categories of order which the culture industry drapes over the idea of the good life as if existing reality were the good life, and as if those categories were its true measure. If the response of the culture industry's representatives is that it does not deliver art at all, this is itself the ideology with which they evade responsibility for that from which the business lives. No misdeed is ever righted by explaining it as such.

The appeal to order alone, without concrete specificity, is futile; the appeal to the dissemination of norms, without these ever proving themselves in reality or before consciousness, is equally futile. The idea of an objectively binding order, huckstered to people because it is so lacking for them, has no claims if it does not prove itself internally and in confrontation with human beings. But this is precisely what no product of the culture industry would engage in. The concepts of order which it hammers into human beings are always those of the status quo. They remain unquestioned, unanalyzed and undialectically presupposed, even if they no longer have any substance for those who accept them. In contrast to the Kantian, the categorical imperative of the culture industry no longer has anything in common with freedom. It proclaims: you shall conform, without instruction as to what; conform to that which exists anyway, and to that which everyone thinks anyway as a reflex of its power and omnipresence. The power of the culture industry's ideology is such that conformity has replaced consciousness. The order that springs from it is never confronted with what it claims to be of; with the real interests of human beings. Order, however, is not good in itself. It would be so only as a good order. The fact that the culture industry is oblivious to this and extols order *in abstracto*, bears witness to the impotence and untruth of the messages it conveys. While it claims to lead the perplexed, it deludes them with false conflicts which they are to exchange for their own. It solves conflicts for them only in appearance, in a way that they can hardly be solved in their real lives. In the products of the culture industry human beings get into trouble only so that they can be rescued unharmed, usually by representatives of a benevolent collective; and then in empty harmony, they are reconciled with the general, whose demands they had experienced at the outset as irreconcilable with their interests. For this purpose the culture industry has developed formulas which even reach into such non-conceptual areas as light musical entertainment. Here too one gets into a 'jam,' into rhythmic problems, which can be instantly disentangled by the triumph of the basic beat.

Even its defenders, however, would hardly contradict Plato openly who maintained that what is objectively and intrinsically untrue cannot also be subjectively good and true for human beings. The concoctions of the culture industry are neither guides for a blissful life, nor a new art of moral responsibility, but rather exhortations to toe the line, behind which stand the most powerful interests. The consensus which it propagates strengthens blind, opaque authority. If the culture industry is measured not by its own substance and logic, but by its efficacy, by its position in reality and its explicit pretentions; if the focus of serious concern is with the efficacy to which it always appeals, the potential of its effect becomes twice as weighty. This potential, however, lies in the promotion and exploitation of the ego-weakness to which the powerless members of the contemporary society, with its concentration of power, are condemned. Their consciousness is further developed retrogressively. It is no coincidence that cynical American film producers are heard to say that their pictures must take into consideration the level of eleven year olds. In doing so they would very much like to make adults into eleven year olds.

It is true that thorough research has not, for the time being, produced an airtight case proving the regressive effects of particular products of the culture industry. No doubt an imaginatively designed experiment could achieve this more successfully than the powerful financial interests concerned would find comfortable. In any case, it can be assumed without hesitation that steady drops hollow the stone, especially since the system of the culture industry that surrounds the masses tolerates hardly any deviation and incessantly drills the same formulas of behavior. Only their deep unconscious mistrust, the last residue of the difference between art and empirical reality in the spiritual makeup of the masses explains why they have not, to a person, long since perceived and accepted the world as it is constructed for them by the culture industry. Even if its messages were as harmless as they are made out to be – on countless occasions they are obviously not harmless, like the movies which chime in with currently popular hate campaigns against intellectuals by portraying them with the usual stereotypes – the attitudes which the culture industry calls forth are anything but harmless. If an astrologer urges his readers to drive carefully on a particular day, that certainly hurts no one; they will, however, be harmed indeed by the stupefication which lies in the claim that advice which is valid every day and which is therefore idiotic, needs the approval of the stars.

Human dependence and servitude, the vanishing point of the culture industry, could scarcely be more faithfully described than by the American interviewee who was of the opinion that the dilemmas of the contemporary epoch would end if people would simply follow the lead of prominent personalities. Insofar as the culture industry arouses a feeling of well-being that the world is precisely in that order suggested by the culture industry, the substitute gratification which it prepares for human beings cheats them out of the same happiness which it deceitfully projects. The total effect of the culture industry is one of anti-enlightenment, in which, as Horkheimer and I have noted, enlightenment, that is the progressive technical domination of nature, becomes mass deception and is turned into a means for fettering consciousness. It impedes the development of autonomous, independent individuals who judge and decide consciously for themselves. These, however, would be the pre-condition for a democratic society which needs adults who have come of age in order to sustain itself and develop. If the masses have been unjustly reviled from above as masses, the culture industry is not among the least responsible for making them into masses and then despising them, while obstructing the emancipation for which human beings are as ripe as the productive forces of the epoch permit.

Translated by Anson G. Rabinbach   (from *New German Critique*, Vol. 6, 1975)

The popular arts

Stuart Hall and Paddy Whannel

. . . it will be useful to catalogue the general indictment of the mass society. . . . It is doubtful if any one person would adhere to all of them. . . . The following could rather be regarded as the doctrines of an imaginary composite critic of mass culture.

1. Power

Power is concentrated in a few hands, and methods of maintaining it have been refined by the techniques of manipulation. Armies of people are employed to test and analyse, to seek out needs and hidden desires and to create needs where they do not already exist:

> Before high-pressure salesmanship, emphasis was upon the salesman's knowledge of the product, a sales knowledge grounded in apprenticeship; after it, the focus is upon hyponotizing the prospect, an art provided by psychology. (C. Wright Mills, *White Collar*)

But the ethics of salesmanship have infected every area of life. Politics has become a branch of public relations. Persuasion has been substituted for debate and the search for the right image has replaced the search for the right policy.

2. Mass production

Cultural products are mass produced to a formula that allows no place for creativity. Experiment and growth have been replaced by gimmicks and fashion. Mass production demands an audience so large that it can only be held together by appeals to people's most unthinking responses:

> When we are dealing with figures like this, we are no longer considering a mass audience at all: it has ceased to be an audience, in the sense that one can ever hope to communicate with a majority of it in any but the most superficial way. (Henry Fairlie, *Encounter*, March 1962)

3. Consumers

People are not seen as participants in the society but as consumers of what others produce. Their needs and attitudes as consumers are assessed and analysed but their judgement as men and women is not called upon. They are asked to distinguish between washing powders but not whether they would prefer schools to strip clubs. Their role is passive and they play no part in the world of decision-making. The language of persuasion can be soft and subtle but when the persuaders speak to each other it becomes harsh and aggressive. The people are 'masses' awaiting exploitation:

To other people, we also are masses. Masses are other people. There are in fact no masses; there are only ways of seeing people as masses. . . . The fact is, surely, that a way of seeing other people which has become characteristic of our kind of society, has been capitalized for the purposes of political or cultural exploitation. (Raymond Williams, *Culture and Society*)

4. The pseudo-world

Increasingly the media define our sense of reality and organize our experience into stereotypes. We cease to believe in events until the media sanction them. We come to believe more in the pictures of life than in life itself and in the end may accept the distorting mirror of the media as a portrait of our true selves:

The studio audience, I should say, provides the perfect image of mid-20th century democracy. At the time of Suez, I saw a photograph of troops by the Canal, all looking very glum, except for one small party, which was being televised: thumbs up and smiling, as required. (Malcolm Muggeridge, *New Statesman*, 14 February 1959)

5. The unambiguous world

Mass culture makes us more alike. It does this not merely by manufacturing standardized products but by trivializing the important things until they are reduced to the level of the commonplace. Magazine pages and television programmes flicker past us – religion and quiz games, criticism and gossip columns, art lovers and animal lovers, all cemented by colourful advertising. Communication and salesmanship become inextricably intertwined, so that there is a continuous blurring of distinctions:

Not all celebrities have equal value and the same symbolic status. This simple fact is the basis for one of Mr Murrow's most fascinating wiles: *Person to Person* consists of two 'visits' on the same night, and he strives for incongruity rather than harmony. An early programme epitomized this strategy – Krishna Menon and one of the Gabor sisters within the same half hour. Such a juxtaposition, while it tickles our fancy, also manages to blur the distinction between the meaning of a Krishna Menon and a Gabor; by giving both equal value it trivializes the significance of one... if you throw a Krishna Menon in with a Gabor, bill the entire 'package' as entertainment, and sell it by way of television, you have gone a long way towards creating an image of an unambiguous world. (Murray Hausknecht, 'The Mike in the Bosom', *Mass Culture*)

6. The break with the past

Mass culture destroys folk art, dehydrates popular art and threatens fine art. It has little sense of tradition, of values being modified by change. Instead there is an obsession with fashion and novelty; to be the latest thing is thought in itself a sufficient recommendation.

Most people are subjected to a sustained and ever-increasing bombardment of invitations to assume that whatever is, is right so long as it is widely accepted and can be classed as entertaining. This and the older sense that it is important to 'enjoy y'self while y'can' are connected. To these a third element attaches itself, that of 'progressivism'. Progressivism assists living for the present by disowning the past; but the present is enjoyed only because, and so long as, it is the present, the latest and not the out-of-date past; so, as each new 'present' comes along, the others are discarded. (Richard Hoggart, *The Uses of Literacy*)

7. Corruption of the feelings

The media exploit rather than satisfy our needs and desires. Not only are appeals made to our worst instincts, such as greed and snobbery, but our best instincts are distorted and our finest feelings squandered on objects unworthy of them:

> The history of popular taste is largely bound up with the discovery by the writing profession of the technique for exploiting emotional responses. (Q.D. Leavis, *Fiction and the Reading Public*)

8. The flattery of mediocrity

This is the age of the Common Man, the Ordinary Person, the Man in the Street. He is interviewed, researched and polled, and no issue is thought too complicated to be judged by a counting of heads so that in the end the controllers and manipulators go in fear of the Mass Man, the monster creation of their own fantasies:

> The characteristic of the hour is that the commonplace mind, knowing itself to be commonplace, has the assurance to proclaim the rights of the commonplace and to impose them wherever it will. (Ortega y Gasset, *The Revolt of the Masses*)

9. The cult of personality

In an age of conformity, in which the mass replaces a community of publics, a substitute for true individuality is found in the glorification of personality. This emphasizes not what a man is or what he has done but his image, his public face. The stars of the world of show business have taken over, and in politics grooming the personality becomes as important as brushing up the facts:

> I wish men who call themselves public relations counsellors and have three coronets on their notepaper would stop ringing me up and saying in carried-away voices: 'Decca have just signed Fannie Bloggs. She's receiving the Press at the Savoy, 5.30.' I wish that after I have told the men with the three coronets to drop dead, I could come back from lunch and not find a note from my secretary saying Decca have just signed Fannie Bloggs . . .
>
> By the time I get to the Savoy, I find that Fannie Bloggs, whom nobody ever heard of before that morning, is already famous, anyway. Or as good as.
>
> Next morning some hay-haired girl, grasping a guitar by the throat leers up at you from the breakfast table.
>
> Unconsciously you start to believe in her, reasoning innocently that since her picture is in the paper she's sufficiently important to have her picture in the paper.
>
> That's all Fannie needs. With this aberration of logic, which works time after time in our purblind community, the men with the three coronets have you nailed. (Leslie Mallory, quoted in the *News Chronicle*)

10. Escape from reality

The audience receives the products of the mass media, and is encouraged to receive them, in a state of dream-like passivity:

> Why encourage the art that is destined to replace literature? But still, there is a kind of soggy attraction about it. To sit on the padded seat in the warm smoke-scented darkness, letting the flickering drivel on the screen gradually overwhelm you – feeling the waves of its silliness lap you round till you seem to drown, intoxicated, in a viscous sea – after all, it's the kind of drug we need. The right drug for friendless people.
>
> (George Orwell, *Keep the Aspidistra Flying*)

The media provide us with an endless series of dreams through which we can escape from the reality of the world and ourselves. We are invited to identify ourselves with fictitious characters whose conflicts are resolved by magical solutions, and to indulge in corroding fantasies:

> This car is very personal property: once you get the feel of it, you won't want to hold back. Behind the wheel a man feels power – and a woman feels freedom. Turn the key and feel the Capri spring to life, gliding like a panther, hugging the road, clinging to the curves, responding instantly . . . a sleek and elegant extension of your own personality. (advertisement)

These ten points make up an unambiguous indictment. Before we proceed to set other points of view against this, the words of the late C. Wright Mills might be quoted as a general summary:

> The media tell the man in the mass who he is – they give him identity.
> They tell him what he wants to be – they give him aspirations.
> They tell him how to get that way – they give him technique.
> They tell him how to feel that he is that way even when he is not – they give him escape. (*The Power Élite*)

 READING 9

'The storyteller'

Walter Benjamin

I

Familiar though his name may be to us, the storyteller in his living immediacy is by no means a present force. He has already become something remote from us that is getting even more distant. . . . Less and less frequently do we encounter people with the ability to tell a tale properly. More and more often there is embarrassment all around when the wish to hear a story is expressed. It is as if something that seemed inalienable to us, the securest among our possessions, were taken from us: the ability to exchange experiences.

One reason for this phenomenon is obvious: experience has fallen in value. And it looks as if it is continuing to fall into bottomlessness. Every glance at a newspaper demonstrates that it has reached a new low, that our picture, not only of the external world but of the moral world as well, overnight has undergone changes which were never thought possible With the [First] World War a process began to become apparent which has not halted since then. Was it not noticeable at the end of the war that men returned from the battlefield grown silent – not richer, but poorer in communicable experience? What ten years later was poured out in the flood of war books was anything but experience that goes from mouth to mouth. And there was nothing remarkable about that. For never has experience been contradicted more thoroughly than strategic experience by tactical warfare, economic experience by inflation, bodily exercise by mechanical warfare, moral experience by those in power. A generation that had gone to school on a horse-drawn streetcar now stood under the open sky in a countryside in which nothing remained unchanged but the clouds, and beneath these clouds, in a field of force of destructive torrents and explosions, was the tiny, fragile human body.

II

Experience which is passed on from mouth to mouth is the source from which all storytellers have drawn. And among those who have written down the tales, it is the great ones whose written version differs at least from the speech of the many nameless storytellers. Incidentally, among the last named there are two groups which, to be sure, overlap in many ways. And the figure of the storyteller gets its full corporeality only for the one who can picture them both. 'When someone goes on a trip, he has something to tell about', goes the German saying, and people imagine the storyteller as someone who has come from afar. But they enjoy no less listening to the man who has stayed at home, making an honest living, and who knows the local tales and traditions. If one wants to picture these two groups through their archaic representatives, one is embodied in the resident tiller of the soil, and the other in the trading seaman. Indeed, each sphere of life has, as it were, produced its own tribe of storytellers.

. . . .

IV

An orientation toward practical interests is characteristic of many born storytellers . . . this points to the nature of every real story. It contains, openly or covertly, something useful. The usefulness may, in one case, consist in a moral; in another, in some practical advice; in a third, in a proverb or maxim. In every case the storyteller is a man who has counsel for his readers. But if today 'having counsel' is beginning to have an old-fashioned ring, this is because the communicability of experience is decreasing. In consequence we have no counsel either for ourselves or for others. After all, counsel is less an answer to a question than a proposal concerning the continuation of a story which is just unfolding. To seek this counsel one would first have to be able to tell the story. (Quite apart from the fact that a man is receptive to counsel only to the extent that he allows his situation to speak.) Counsel woven into the fabric of real life is wisdom. The art of storytelling is reaching its end because the epic side of truth, wisdom, is dying out. This, however, is a process that has been going on for a long time. And nothing would be more fatuous than to want to see in it merely a 'symptom of decay', let alone a 'modern' symptom. It is, rather, only a concomitant symptom of the secular productive forces of history, a concomitant that has quite gradually removed narrative from the realm of living speech and at the same time making it possible to see a new beauty in what is vanishing.

V

The earliest symptom of a process whose end is the decline of storytelling is the rise of the novel at the beginning of modern times. What distinguishes the novel from the story (and from the epic in the narrower sense) is its essential dependence on the book. The dissemination of the novel became possible only with the invention of printing. What can be handed on orally, the wealth of the epic, is of a different kind from what constitutes the stock in trade of the novel. What differentiates the novel from all other forms of prose literature – the fairy tale, the legend, even the novella – is that it neither comes from oral tradition nor goes into it. This distinguishes it from storytelling in particular. The storyteller takes what he tells from experience – his own or that reported by others. And he in turn makes it the experience of those who are listening to his tale. The novelist has isolated himself. The birthplace of the novel is the solitary individual, who is no longer able to express himself by giving examples of his most important concerns, is himself uncounselled, and cannot counsel others.

. . . .

VIII

There is nothing that commends a story to memory more effectively than that chaste compactness which precludes psychological analysis. And the more natural the process by which the storyteller forgoes psychological shading, the greater becomes the story's claim to a place in the memory of the listener, the more completely is it integrated into his own experience, the greater will be his inclination to repeat it to someone else some day, sooner or later. . . . . For storytelling is always the art of repeating stories, and this art is lost when the stories are no longer retained. It is lost because there is no more weaving and spinning to go on while they are being listened to. The more self-forgetful the listener is, the more deeply is what he listens to impressed upon his memory. When the rhythm of work has seized him, he listens to the tales in such a way that the gift of retelling them comes to him all by itself. This, then, is the nature of the web in which the gift of storytelling is cradled. This is how today it is becoming unraveled at all its ends after being woven thousands of years ago in the ambience of the oldest forms of craftsmanship.

. . . .

XVI

A great storyteller will always be rooted in the people, primarily in a milieu of craftsmen. But just as this includes the rural, the maritime, and the urban elements in the many stages of their economic and technical development, there are many gradations in the concepts in which their store of experience comes down to us. (To say nothing of the by no means insignificant share which traders had in the art of story telling; their task was less to increase its didactic content than to refine the tricks with which the attention of the listener was captured. They have left deep traces in the narrative cycle of *The Arabian Nights*.) In short, despite the primary role which storytelling plays in the household of humanity, the concepts through which the yield of the stories may be garnered are manifold. What may most readily be put in religious terms in Leskov seems almost automatically to fall into place in the pedagogical perspectives of the Enlightenment in Hebel, appears as hermetic tradition in Poe, finds a last refuge in Kipling in the life of British seamen and colonial soldiers. All great storytellers have in common the freedom with which they move up and down the rungs of the experience as on a ladder. A ladder extending downward to the interior of the earth and disappearing into the clouds is the image for a collective experience to which even the deepest shock of every individual experience, death, constitutes no impediment or barrier.

'And they lived happily ever after', says the fairy tale. The fairy tale, which to this day is the first tutor of children because it was once the first tutor of mankind, secretly lives on in the story. The first true storyteller is, and will continue to be, the teller of fairy tales. Whenever good counsel was at a premium, the fairy tale had it, and where the need was greatest, its aid was nearest. This need was the need created by the myth. The fairy tale tells us of the earliest arrangements that mankind made to shake off the nightmare which the myth had placed upon its chest. In the figure of the fool it shows us how mankind 'acts dumb' toward the myth; in the figure of the youngest brother it shows us how one's chances increase as the mythical primitive times are left behind; in the figure of the man who sets out to learn what fear is it shows us that the things we are afraid of can be seen through; in the figure of the wiseacre it shows us that the questions posed by the myth are simple-minded, like the riddle of the Sphinx; in the shape of the animals which come to the aid of the child in the fairy tale it shows that nature not only is subservient to the myth, but much prefers to be aligned with man. The wisest thing – so the fairy tale taught mankind in olden times, and teaches children to this day – is to meet the forces of the mythical world with cunning and with high spirits. . . . The liberating magic which the fairy tale has at its disposal does not bring nature into play in a mythical way, but points to its complicity with liberated man. A mature man feels this complicity only occasionally, that is, when he is happy; but the child first meets it in fairy tales, and it makes him happy.

. . . .

XIX

. . . the storyteller joins the ranks of the teachers and sages. He has counsel – not for a few situations, as the proverb does, but for many, like the sage. For it is granted to him to reach back to a whole lifetime (a life, incidentally, that comprises not only his own experience but no little of the experience of others; what the storyteller knows from hearsay is added to his own). His gift is the ability to relate his life; his distinction, to be able to tell his entire life. The storyteller: he is the man who could let the wick of his life be consumed completely by the gentle flame of his story. This is the basis of the incomparable aura about the storyteller, in Leskov as in Hauff, in Poe as in Stevenson. The storyteller is the figure in which the righteous man encounters himself.

(from W. Benjamin, *Illuminations*, 1968)

Applications

 READING 10

'The case of Miss Dorothy Sayers'

Q.D. Leavis

Gaudy Night (Gollancz)
Busman's Honeymoon (Gollancz)

With the above two novels Miss Sayers stepped out of the ranks of detective writers into that of the best-seller novelists, and into some esteem as a literary figure among the educated reading public. . . . Miss Sayers belongs with Naomi Mitchison and Rosamond Lehmann . . . and some others who are representative of the new kind of best-seller, the educated popular novelist. Like the Ouidas and Marie Corellis and Baron Corvos of the past they are really subjects for other kinds of specialist than the literary critic, but unlike those writers these are to some extent undoubtedly conscious of what they are doing (and so are able to practise more adroitly on their readers). Thus, for instance, the heroine of *Gaudy Night* is a Harriet Vane who writes detective stories, merely for a living and in all modesty, for was she not an Oxford Scholar and a first-class in English? But returning to her Shrewsbury College after many years for an Old Students' celebration, she finds, with what grateful surprise, that not only her coevals but all the best dons clear up to the Warden (Philosophy) are 'fervent admirers' and 'devotees' (in their own words) of her writings. Miss Sayers can hardly be as artless as all that, and it is not surprising that the world has taken her tip and proceeded to talk obediently about her 'artistry' and 'scholarly English'. The hero is of course Harriet's suitor and ultimate husband, and here again I think Miss Sayers has overstepped the limits of what even a best-seller's public can be expected to swallow without suspicion. Lord Peter is not only of ducal stock and all that an Ouida hero was plus modern sophistication and modern accomplishments – such as being adored by his men during the Great War and able to talk like a P.G. Wodehouse moron – he is also a distinguished scholar in history, a celebrated cricketer, an authority on antiques, a musician, a brilliant wit, a diplomat on whom the F.O. leans during international crises, a wide and deep reader and no doubt some other things I've overlooked. Whatever he does he does better than anyone else and he is one of those universal geniuses like Leonardo. Women naturally find him irresistible. Miss Sayers only omits to add like Ouida that 'he has the seat of the English Guards'. He does say, however, to his bride, 'In the course of a mis-spent life I have learnt that it is a gentleman's first duty to remember in the morning who it was he took to bed with him' and Miss Sayers does actually write of him (thus going one better than Ouida, who was a lady), 'He remembered that it had once been said of "ce blond cadet de famille ducale anglaise" – said, too, by a lady who had every opportunity of judging – that "il tenait son lit en Grand Monarque et s'y démenait en Grand Turc".'

I will not comment further on the large part played in these novels by passages such as I have quoted, Miss Sayers being (unlike Mr James Joyce and the late

D.H. Lawrence, of whom reviewers could say what they liked with impunity) in such good standing with the respectable. But there is no harm in saying, since it is demonstrably true, that these two passages are fair samples of what Miss Sayers thinks on the one hand witty and on the other daringly outspoken; and we are accordingly in a position to draw some conclusion about the taste of the public which likes such stuff and recommends it with conviction not merely as entertainment but as Good Stuff. For it's not as you might have thought, as a successor to Marie Corelli and Ouida that Miss Sayers is valued.

This odd conviction that she is in a different class from Edgar Wallace or Ethel M. Dell apparently depends on four factors in these novels. They have an appearance of literariness; they profess to treat profound emotions and to be concerned with values; they generally or incidentally affect to deal in large issues and general problems (e.g. *Gaudy Night*, in so far as it is anything but a bundle of best-selling old clothes, is supposed to answer the question whether academic life produces abnormality in women); and they appear to give an inside view of some modes of life that share the appeal of the unknown for many readers, particularly the life of the older universities.

Literature gets heavily drawn upon in Miss Sayers's writings, and her attitude to it is revealing. She displays knowingness about literature without any sensitiveness to it or any feeling for quality. . . . Impressive literary excerpts, generally 17th century . . . head each chapter. She – I should say Harriet Vane – proudly admits to having 'the novelist's habit of thinking of everything in terms of literary allusion'. What a give away! It is a habit that gets people like Harriet Vane firsts in 'English' examinations, no doubt, but no novelist with such a parasitic, stale, adulterated way of feeling and living could ever amount to anything. And Miss Sayers's fiction, when it isn't mere detective story of an unimpressive kind, is exactly that: stale, second-hand, hollow. Her wit consists in literary references. Her deliberate indecency is not shocking or amusing, it is odious merely as so much Restoration Comedy is, because the breath of life was never in it and it is only the emanation of a 'social' mind wanting to raise a snigger. . . .

The patter about value and the business of delving into emotional deeps seems to me more nauseating than anything else in the productions of this kind of novelist, not because anything much is said but because such clumsy fumblings stir up mud in the channels of life that, heaven knows, we all know, it is hard enough to keep clear anyway. And in the matter of ideas, subject, theme, problems raised, she similarly performs the best-seller's function of giving the impression of intellectual activity to readers who would very much dislike that kind of exercise if it were actually presented to them; but of course it is all shadow-boxing. With what an air of unconventionality and play of analysis Miss Sayers handles her topics, but what relief her readers must feel – it is part, no doubt, of her success – that they are let off with a reassurance that everything is really all right and appearances are what really matter. You may be as immoral and disillusioned as Lord Peter, and in fact immorality, etc., are rather fetching qualities and humorous too, but you MUST go to Church and be married in it, and whether you are intellectual, nudist or hard up your frock MUST be well cut – this seems to be the moral burden of these books. It would be unkind to boil Miss Sayers's wisdom down to this and label it What Oxford Has Meant to Me, but evidently Miss Sayers's spiritual nature, like Harriet Vane's, depends for its repose, refreshment and sustenance on the academic world, the ideal conception, that is, of our older universities – or let us say a rationalized nostalgia for her student days.

I think indeed that the real draw of *Gaudy Night* was its offering the general public a peepshow of the senior university world, especially of the women's college, which has been less worked at by novelists than undergraduate life and has the appeal of novelty. (*Dusty Answer* made a similar hit.) It is a vicious presentation because it is popular and romantic while pretending to realism. Miss Sayers produces for our admiration an academic world which is the antithesis of the great world of bustle and Big Business that her readers know. Whereas in their world, she says, everything is 'unsound, unscholarly, insincere' – the implication being that the academic world is sound and sincere because it is scholarly – you have here invulnerable standards of taste charging the charmed atmosphere ('Thank Heaven, it's extremely difficult to be cheap in Oxford,' says Lord Peter). If such a world ever existed, and I should be surprised to hear as much, it does no longer, and to give substance to a lie or to perpetuate a dead myth is to do no one any service really. . . . it would surely be healthier from every point of view if the critical winds of the outside world could be let blow through these grimy edifices, and perhaps they would if the facts ever leaked out and left a loophole for criticism to get in by. But popular novelists like Miss Sayers are busy shoring up these hallowed fragments against their ruin; if Miss Sayers were more intelligent you could call it the latest case of *trahison des clercs*, but you suspect her of being a victim of propaganda herself.

But Miss Sayers is after all a product of Shrewsbury College as well as its producer. Who is responsible for this combination of literary glibness and spiritual illiteracy? Are her vices unique and personal? We all know they are not, experience confirms what her style of writing suggests, that she is representative. That inane wit, that unflagging sense of humour, those epigrams, that affectation of unconventionality, that determined sociality, what a familiar chord they strike! 'Are the women at S____ College really like that?' someone says she enquired, after reading *Gaudy Night*, of someone on the spot. 'My dear, they are *much worse*!' At any rate Miss Sayers's fictions are clearly the product of a sympathetic *milieu* somewhere and one that pretty evidently had a university education. . . .

What does seem indisputable is that Miss Sayers as a writer has been a vast success in the senior academic world everywhere. The young report that their elders recommend *Gaudy Night* to them, Miss Sayers has the *entrée* to literary societies which would never have opened their doors to Edgar Wallace, she is canonized as a stylist by English lecturers already, and so on; after all, her reputation as a literary figure must have been made in such quarters. Speculation naturally turns on how anyone can devote himself to the study and teaching of the humanities (we will let off the scientists in spite of their living in a place that alters all one's values) and yet not be able to place a Dorothy Sayers novel on inspection if it comes his way. Well it does seem queer, but such a lapse is not without precedent. Run your eyes over enough academic bookshelves – not those housing shop but those where they keep what they really choose to read – and you get accustomed to a certain association of authors representing an average taste which is at best negative: Edward Lear and Ernest Bramah's *Kai Lung* (delicious humour), Charles Morgan and C.E. Montague (stylists), Rupert Brooke (or Humbert Wolfe Wolfe or some equivalent) . . . we can all supplement. Dorothy Sayers can take her place alongside without raising any blushes; these or their kind are the writers she admires herself. But doesn't it raise some awkward questions? What is the value of this scholarly life Miss Sayers hymns if it doesn't refine the perceptions of those leading it? If your work was of any value to you would you want, would you be able to relax on Edgar Wallace (much less on Dorothy Sayers)? Miss Sayers innocently presents her typical admirable scholar and 'English' don engaged on her life's work of what but a History of English Prosody (an all too plausible undertaking)! Apart from the fact that the lady was engaged in perpetrating a sort of public nuisance, think of the effect on the teaching of English in her college of that attitude to the study of poetry. No education could take place there; studying English Prosody will not show anyone why Miss Sayers isn't a good novelist. That kind of scholarship never gears in with life. But is there any other kind? Miss Sayers, however, finds it wholly admirable. By this code, she says, the only unpardonable thing is to be unscholarly; evil consists in producing a popular life of Carlyle without any research. But which is really worse, to be unscholarly or to pass writers like Miss Sayers? Mistakes about Carlyle are not a menace to civilization.

I once conversed on these or similar lines with a Professor of Classics, a man of genuine but diffident literary tastes. He remarked that it seemed unaccountable to him that the writings of a fellow Classic were so highly esteemed by his colleagues. He himself, he said modestly, had an unconquerable aversion to them, they seemed to him empty, the man's 'style' cheap and his wit puerile, but none of his friends agreed with him, it was so discouraging and he felt he must be in the wrong. I said, Not at all, his colleagues' insensitiveness to their native literature seemed to me an illustration of the evident fact that you could spend a lifetime in the study of any language ancient or modern, or any branch of the humanities, without acquiring the rudiments of literary taste or any apparatus for forming a just estimate of a piece of writing. And I added, no doubt brutally, 'What's the good of Classics, what justification for a Classical training can there be if it doesn't form a decent taste?' My friend was taken aback. But he was a conscientious professor and he tried to find an answer. After a bit he brought out hopefully, 'Well, some people are interested in philology.'

I have always tried to bear that maxim in mind. After all, philology is as legitimate a study as mathematics, and every branch of the humanities has its philological aspect, so to speak. I recommend anyone at a loss before the spectacle of the scholar's bedside reading to adopt the above explanation. Miss Sayers, who might evidently have been an academic herself, is probably quite sound on the philological side.

(from *Scrutiny*, 1937)

📖 READING 11

'On popular music'

T.W. Adorno

A clear judgement concerning the relation of serious music to popular music can be arrived at only by strict attention to the fundamental characteristic of popular music: standardization.[1] The whole structure of popular music is standardized, even where the attempt is made to circumvent standardization. Standardization extends from the most general features to the most specific ones. Best known is the rule that the chorus consists of thirty-two bars and that the range is limited to one octave and one note. The general types of hits are also standardized: not only the dance types, the rigidity of whose pattern is understood, but also the 'characters' such as mother songs, home songs, nonsense or 'novelty' songs, pseudo-nursery rhymes, laments for a lost girl. Most important of all, the harmonic cornerstones of each hit – the beginning and the end of each part – must beat out the standard scheme. This scheme emphasizes the most primitive harmonic facts no matter what has harmonically intervened. Complications have no consequences. This inexorable device guarantees that regardless of what aberrations occur, the hit will lead back to the same familiar experience, and nothing fundamentally novel will be introduced.

The details themselves are standardized no less than the form, and a whole terminology exists for them such as break, blue chords, dirty notes. Their standardization, however, is somewhat different from that of the framework. It is not overt like the latter but hidden behind a veneer of individual 'effects' whose prescriptions are handled as the experts' secret, however open this secret may be to musicians generally. This contrasting character of the standardization of the whole and part provides a rough, preliminary setting for the effect upon the listener.

The primary effect of this relation between the framework and the detail is that the listener becomes prone to evince stronger reactions to the part than to the whole. His grasp of the whole does not lie in the living experience of this one concrete piece of music he has followed. The whole is pre-given and pre-accepted, even before the actual experience of the music starts; therefore, it is not likely to influence, to any great extent, the reaction to the details, except to give them varying degrees of emphasis. Details which occupy musically strategic positions in the framework – the beginning of the chorus or its re-entrance after the bridge – have a better chance for recognition and favorable reception than details not so situated, for instance, middle bars of the bridge. But this situational nexus never interferes with the scheme itself. To this limited situational extent the detail depends upon the whole. But no stress is ever placed upon the whole as a musical event, nor does the structure of the whole ever depend upon the details.

Serious music, for comparative purposes, may be thus characterized.

Every detail derives its musical sense from the concrete totality of the piece which, in turn, consists of the life relationship of the details and never of a mere enforcement of a musical scheme. For example, in the introduction of the first movement of Beethoven's Seventh Symphony the second theme (in C-major) gets its true meaning only from the context. Only through the whole does it acquire its particular lyrical and expressive quality, – that is, a whole built up of its very contrast with the *cantus firmus*-like character of the first theme. Taken in isolation the second theme would be disrobed to insignificance. . . .

Nothing corresponding to this can happen in popular music. It would not affect the musical sense if any detail were taken out of the context; the listener can supply the 'framework' automatically, since it is a mere musical automatism itself. The beginning of the chorus is replaceable by the beginning of innumerable other choruses. The interrelationship among the elements or the relationship of the elements to the whole would be unaffected. In Beethoven, position is important only in a living relation between a concrete totality and its concrete parts. In popular music, position is absolute. Every detail is substitutable; it serves its function only as a cog in a machine.

. . . .

To sum up the difference: in Beethoven and in good serious music in general – we are not concerned here with bad serious music which may be as rigid and mechanical as popular music – the detail virtually contains the whole and leads to the exposition of the whole, while, at the same time, it is produced out of the conception of the whole. In popular music the relationship is fortuitous. The detail has no bearing on a whole, which appears as an extraneous framework. Thus, the whole is never altered by the individual event and therefore remains, as it were, aloof, imperturbable, and unnoticed throughout the piece. At the same time, the detail is mutilated by a device which it can never influence and alter, so that the detail remains inconsequential. A musical detail which is not permitted to develop becomes a caricature of its own potentialities.

Standardization
The previous discussion shows that the difference between popular and serious music can be grasped in more precise terms than those referring to musical levels such as 'lowbrow and highbrow' 'simple and complex', 'naive and sophisticated'. For example, the difference between the spheres cannot be adequately expressed in terms of complexity and simplicity. All works of the earlier Viennese classicism are, without exception, rhythmically simpler than stock arrangements of jazz. Melodically, the wide intervals of a good many hits such as 'Deep Purple' or 'Sunrise Serenade' are more difficult to follow per se than most melodies of, for example, Haydn. . . . . Standardization and non-standardization are the key contrasting terms for the difference.

Structural standardization aims at standard reactions. Listening to popular music is manipulated not only by its promoters, but as it were, by the inherent nature of this music itself, into a system of response mechanisms wholly antagonistic to the ideal of individuality in a free, liberal society. This has nothing to do with simplicity and complexity. In serious music, each musical element, even the simplest one, is 'itself', and the more highly organized the work is, the less possibility there is of substitution among the details. In hit music, however, the structure underlying the piece is abstract, existing independent of the specific course of the music. This is basic to the illusion that certain complex harmonies are more easily understandable in popular music than the same harmonies in serious music. For the complicated in popular music never functions as 'itself' but only as a disguise or embellishment behind which the scheme can always be perceived. In jazz the amateur listener is capable of replacing complicated rhythmical or harmonic formulas by the schematic ones which they represent and which they still suggest, however adventurous they appear. The ear deals with the difficulties of hit music by achieving slight substitutions derived from the knowledge of the patterns. The listener, when faced with the complicated, actually hears only the simple which it represents and perceives the complicated only as a parodistic distortion of the simple.

No such mechanical substitution by stereotyped patterns is possible in serious music. Here even the simplest event necessitates an effort to grasp it immediately instead of summarizing it vaguely according to institutional prescriptions capable of producing only institutionalized effects. Otherwise the music is not 'understood'. Popular music, however, is composed in such a way that the process of translation of the unique into the norm is already planned and, to a certain extent, achieved within the composition itself.

The composition hears for the listener. This is how popular music divests the listener of his spontaneity and promotes conditioned reflexes. Not only does it not require his effort to follow its concrete stream; it actually gives him models under which anything concrete still remaining may be subsumed. The schematic build-up dictates the way in which he must listen while, at the same time, it makes any effort in listening unnecessary. Popular music is 'pre-digested' in a way strongly resembling the fad of 'digests' of printed material. It is this structure of contemporary popular music which, in the last analysis, accounts for those changes of listening habits which we shall later discuss.

So far standardization of popular music has been considered in structural terms – that is, as an inherent quality without explicit reference to the process of production or to the underlying causes for standardization. . . .

Imitation offers a lead for coming to grips with the basic reasons for it. The musical standards of popular music were originally developed by a competitive process. As one particular song scored a great success, hundreds of others sprang up imitating the successful one. The most successful hits, types, and 'ratios' between elements were imitated, and the process culminated in the crystallization of standards. Under centralized conditions such as exist today these standards have become 'frozen'. . . .

This 'freezing' of standards is socially enforced upon the agencies themselves. Popular music must simultaneously meet two demands. One is for stimuli that provoke the listener's attention. The other is for the material to fall within the category of what the musically untrained listener would call 'natural' music: that is, the sum total of all the conventions and material formulas in music to which he is accustomed and which he regards as the inherent, simple language of music itself, no matter how late the development might be which produced this natural language. . . .

In terms of consumer-demand, the standardization of popular music is only the expression of this dual desideratum imposed upon it by the musical frame of mind of the public, – that it be 'stimulatory' by deviating in some way from the established 'natural', and that it maintain the supremacy of the natural against such deviations. The attitude of the audience toward the natural language is reinforced by standardized production, which institutionalizes desiderata which originally might have come from the public.

Pseudo-individualization

The paradox in the desiderata – stimulatory and natural – accounts for the dual character of standardization itself. Stylization of the ever identical framework is only one aspect of standardization. Concentration and control in our culture hide themselves in their very manifestation. Unhidden they would provoke resistance. Therefore the illusion and, to a certain extent, even the reality of individual achievement must be maintained. The maintenance of it is grounded in material reality itself, for while administrative control over life processes is concentrated, ownership is still diffuse.

In the sphere of luxury production, to which popular music belongs and in which no necessities of life are immediately involved, while, at the same time, the residues of individualism are most alive there in the form of ideological categories such as taste and free choice, it is imperative to hide standardization. The 'backwardness' of musical mass production, the fact that it is still on a hand-icraft level and not literally an industrial one, conforms perfectly to that necessity which is essential from the viewpoint of cultural big business. If the individual handicraft elements of popular music were abolished altogether, a synthetic means of hiding standardization would have to be evolved. Its elements are even now in existence.

The necessary correlate of musical standardization is *pseudo-individualization*. By pseudo-individualization we mean endowing cultural mass production with the halo of free choice or open market on the basis of standardization itself. Standardization of song hits keeps the customers in line by doing their listening for them, as it were. Pseudo-individualization, for its part, keeps them in line by making them forget that what they listen to is already listened to for them, or 'pre-digested'.

The most drastic example of standardization of presumably individualized fea-tures is to be found in so-called improvisations. Even though jazz musicians still improvise in practice, their improvisations have become so 'normalized' as to enable a whole terminology to be developed to express the standard devices of individualization: a terminology which in turn is ballyhooed by jazz publicity agents to foster the myth of pioneer artisanship and at the same time flatter the fans by apparently allowing them to peep behind the curtain and get the inside story. This pseudo-individualization is prescribed by the standardization of the framework. The latter is so rigid that the freedom it allows for any sort of impro-visation is severely delimited. . . .

This subservience of improvisation to standardization explains two main socio-psychological qualities of popular music. One is the fact that the details remain openly connected with the underlying scheme so that the listener always feels on safe ground. The choice in individual alterations is so small that the perpetual recurrence of the same variations is a reassuring signpost of the identical behind them. The other is the function of 'substitution' – the improvisatory features forbid their being grasped as musical events in themselves. They can be received only as embellishments. It is a well-known fact that in daring jazz arrangements worried notes, dirty tones, in other words, false notes, play a conspicuous role. They are apperceived as exciting stimuli only because they are corrected by the ear to the right note. This, however, is only an extreme instance of what happens less conspicuously in all individualization in popular music. Any harmonic bold-ness, any chord which does not fall strictly within the simplest harmonic scheme demands being apperceived as 'false', that is, as a stimulus which carries with it the unambiguous prescription to substitute for it the right detail, or rather the naked scheme. Understanding popular music means obeying such commands for listening. Popular music commands its own listening-habits.

III Theory about the listener

Popular music and 'leisure time'
In order to understand why this whole *type* of music maintains its hold on the masses, some considerations of a more general kind may be appropriate.

The frame of mind to which popular music originally appealed, on which it feeds, and which it perpetually reinforces, is simultaneously one of distraction and inattention. Listeners are distracted from the demands of reality by entertainment which does not demand attention either.

The notion of distraction can be properly understood only within its social setting and not in self-subsistent terms of individual psychology. Distraction is bound to the present mode of production, to the rationalized and mechanized process of labor to which, directly or indirectly, masses are subject. This mode of production, which engenders fears and anxiety about unemployment, loss of income, war, has its 'non-productive' correlate in entertainment: that is, relaxation which does not involve the effort of concentration at all. People want to have fun. A fully concentrated and conscious experience of art is possible only to those whose lives do not put such a strain on them that in their spare time they want relief from both boredom and effort simultaneously. The whole sphere of cheap commercial entertainment reflects this dual desire. It induces relaxation because it is patterned and pre-digested. Its being patterned and pre-digested serves within the psychological household of the masses to spare them the effort of that participation (even in listening or observation) without which there can be no receptivity to art. On the other hand, the stimuli they provide permit an escape from the boredom of mechanized labor.

The promoters of commercialized entertainment exonerate themselves by referring to the fact that they are giving the masses what they want. This is an ideology appropriate to commercial purposes, the less the mass discriminates, the greater the possibility of selling cultural commodities indiscriminately. Yet this ideology of vested interest cannot be dismissed so easily. It is not possible completely to deny that mass-consciousness can be molded by the operative agencies only because the masses 'want this stuff'.

But why do they want this stuff? In our present society the masses themselves are kneaded by the same mode of production as the arti-craft material foisted upon them. The customers of musical entertainment are themselves objects or, indeed, products of the same mechanisms which determine the production of popular music. Their spare time serves only to reproduce their working capacity. It is a means instead of an end. The power of the process of production extends over the time intervals which on the surface appear to be 'free'. They want standardized goods and pseudo-individualization, because their leisure is an escape from work and at the same time is molded after those psychological attitudes to which their workaday world exclusively habituates them. Popular music is for the masses a perpetual busman's holiday. Thus, there is justification for speaking of a pre-established harmony today between production and consumption of popular music. The people clamor for what they are going to get anyway.

To escape boredom and avoid effort are incompatible – hence the reproduction of the very attitude from which escape is sought. To be sure, the way in which they must work on the assembly line, in the factory, or at office machines denies people any novelty. They seek novelty, but the strain and boredom associated with actual work leads to avoidance of effort in that leisure-time which offers the only chance for really new experience. As a substitute, they crave a stimulant. Popular music comes to offer it. Its stimulations are met with the inability to vest effort in the ever-identical. This means boredom again. It is a circle which makes escape impossible. The impossibility of escape causes the wide-spread attitude of inattention toward popular music.

. . . .

The social cement

. . . .

Music today is largely a social cement. And the meaning listeners attribute to a material, the inherent logic of which is inaccessible to them, is above all a means by which they achieve some psychical adjustment to the mechanisms of present-day life. This 'adjustment' materializes in two different ways, corresponding to two major socio-psychological types of mass behavior toward music in general and popular music in particular, the 'rhythmically obedient' type and the 'emotional' type. . . .

This obedient type is the rhythmical type, the word rhythmical being used in its everyday sense. Any musical experience of this type is based upon the underlying, unabating time unit of the music, – its 'beat'. To play rhythmically means, to these people, to play in such a way that even if psuedo-individualizations – counter-accents and other 'differentiations' – occur, the relation to the ground metre is preserved. To be musical means to them to be capable of following given rhythmical patterns without being disturbed by 'individualizing' aberrations, and to fit even the syncopations into the basic time units. This is the way in which their response to music immediately expresses their desire to obey. However, as the standardized metre of dance music and of marching suggests the coordinated battalions of a mechanical collectivity, obedience to this rhythm by overcoming the responding individuals leads them to conceive of themselves as agglutinized with the untold millions of the meek who must be similarly overcome. Thus do the obedient inherit the earth.

. . . .

As to the other, the 'emotional' type, there is some justification for linking it with a type of movie spectator. The kinship is with the poor shop girl who derives gratification by identification with Ginger Rogers, who, with her beautiful legs and unsullied character, marries the boss. Wish-fulfillment is considered the guiding principle in the social psychology of moving pictures and similarly in the pleasure obtained from emotional, erotic music. This explanation, however, is only superficially appropriate.

Hollywood and Tin Pan Alley may be dream factories. But they do not merely supply categorical wish-fulfillment for the girl behind the counter. She does not immediately identify herself with Ginger Rogers marrying. What does occur may be expressed as follows: when the audience at a sentimental film or sentimental music become aware of the overwhelming possibility of happiness, they dare to confess to themselves what the whole order of contemporary life ordinarily forbids them to admit, namely, that they actually have no part in happiness. What is supposed to be wish-fulfillment is only the scant liberation that occurs with the realization that at last one need not deny oneself the happiness of knowing that one is unhappy and that one could be happy. The experience of the shop girl is related to that of the old woman who weeps at the wedding services of others, blissfully aware of the wretchedness of her own life. Not even the most gullible individuals believe that eventually everyone will win the sweepstakes. The actual function of sentimental music lies rather in the temporary release given to the awareness that one has missed fulfillment. . . . Emotional music has become the image of the mother who says, 'Come and weep, my child'. It is katharsis for the masses, but katharsis which keeps them all the more firmly in line. One who weeps does not resist any more than one who marches. Music that permits its listeners the confession of their unhappiness reconciles them, by means of this 'release', to their social dependence.

Note

1   The basic importance of standardization has not altogether escaped the attention of current literature on popular music. 'The chief difference between a popular song and a standard, or serious, song like Mandalay, Silvia, or Trees, is that the melody and the lyric of a popular number are constructed within a definite pattern or structural form, whereas the poem, or lyric, of a standard music number has no structural confinements, and the music is free to interpret the meaning and feeling of the words without following a set pattern or form. Putting it another way, the popular song is '"custom built", while the standard song allows the composer freer play of imagination and interpretation'. (Abner Silver and Robert Bruce, *How to Write and Sell a Song Hit*, New York, 1939, p. 2) The authors fail, however, to realize the externally super-imposed, commercial character of those patterns which aims at canalized reactions or, in the language of the regular announcement of one particular radio program, at 'easy listening'. They confuse the mechanical patterns with highly organized, strict art forms: 'Certainly there are few more stringent verse forms in poetry than the sonnet, and yet the greatest poets of all time have woven undying beauty within its small and limited frame. A composer has just as much opportunity for exhibiting his talent and genius in popular songs as in more serious music' (pp. 2–3). Thus the standard pattern of popular music appears to them virtually on the same level as the law of a fugue. It is this contamination which makes the insight into the basic standardization of popular music sterile. It ought to be added that what Silver and Bruce call a 'standard song' is just the opposite of what we mean by a standardized popular song.

(from *Studies in Philosophy and Social Science*, Vol. 9, 1941)

PART 3

Formula, genre and the structuralist analysis of narrative

Theory and methodology

12 J.G. Cawelti, 'The Concept of Formula in the Study of Popular Literature' (1969)
13 V. Propp, *Morphology of the Folk Tale* (1928), Chapters 2,3
14 R. Barthes, 'Introduction to the Structural Analysis of Narratives' (1966)
15 W. Wright, *Sixguns and Society: A Structural Study of the Western* (1975)
16 S. Neale, *Genre* (1980), Chapter 2

Applications

17 J.G. Cawelti, *The Six-Gun Mystique* (n.d.)
18 E. Kwasniewski, 'Thrilling Structures? Science Fiction from the Early *Amazing* and Detective Fiction' (1987)
19 U. Eco, 'The Narrative Structure in Fleming' (1966)

The argument of the general introduction was for a reconstituted criticism and we may look to structuralism for a major contribution. A systematic exposition is not appropriate here. What should be emphasised is the collision between structuralism and many of the assumptions of 'traditional' literary criticism(s) – in particular the emphasis conventionally placed on evaluation. As a critical strategy which presents a way of by-passing the block of evaluation, structuralism has much to offer.

Meaning

Structuralists are not generally interested in value – certainly not in the aesthetic merits of particular texts. The central issue rather is meaning and the project is the systematic analysis of the production and consumption of the meanings of narratives – not as much 'what do they mean?' as 'how do they mean?' In Reading 12 value and meaning are in tension. Cawelti's principal concern is clearly 'a new understanding of the phenomenon of popular literature and new insights into the patterns of culture'. R.B. Rollin, however, has taken Cawelti to task for a continuing interest in the question of evaluation (see Extract 3), and although the indictment is not addressed specifically at the essay reprinted here, it is obvious that Cawelti does not discount the possible relevance of aesthetic value judgement to popular forms. His distinction between 'formula' and 'genre' is value-based and its implicit assumption of the inadmissibility of the concept of 'popular genre' is certainly problematic.

Cawelti's essay was published in 1969, before the methods of structuralism had been applied at all widely to fiction in the USA or in Europe. The beginnings of his essay are tentative; he regards his approach as no more than 'promising' and he confesses to a self-conscious concern to reconcile approaches from 'the traditional arsenal of humanistic disciplines' with the analysis of popular culture whose demands are, he recognises, 'somewhat different' from those of 'the fine arts'. Among more confident structuralist practitioners such tensions are less in evidence and the issue of meaning is addressed with considerable analytic rigour.

System

The nature of the address is best understood in the light of some at least of the 'basic principles' of structuralism. These are conventionally traced back to work on language, in particular the scientific *study of language ('Linguistics'), beginning with Ferdinand de Saussure's* Course in General Linguistics *(1916). The concern of structural linguistics is to identify the rules which govern language usage and which enable meanings to be exchanged. An example of a familiar kind will illustrate the approach. If my father refers to a child as 'a little monkey' most experienced users of the language will know that he is referring to mischievous behaviour rather than physical deformity. A non-native speaker of English on the other hand may well have serious difficulties with the meaning. Effective communication requires that both speaker and listener be fully acquainted with the conventions within which a word may acquire meanings – especially where the range of conventional meanings includes apparently bizarre possibilities. The sum of these conventions contribute to the* **system** *of language in terms of which individual utterances become meaningful and it is the system, rather than the individual utterances, which provides the key to an understanding of the production of meaning. The system does not of course operate exclusively at the level of the meanings of individual words but also in the relationships between words in phrases or more extended utterances. Thus 'that lad's a little monkey' observes conventions governing the arrangement of words in a way that 'lad's a monkey little that' doesn't. The kind of word puzzle which involves the unscrambling of such 'nonsensical' sentences is implicitly an invitation to reassert the system within which the words become meaningful. We can now usefully turn to the structuralist analysis of fiction whose concern, in common with structuralism in general, is the dispassionate, objective,* **scientific** *study of its object. In the same way that systems of language confer meaning on individual utterances so the meanings of texts are to be located in the conventions governing narrative: the systems of fiction within which particular examples operate.*

Formula and genre

The primary interest of structuralists, then, is not as much the individual text in and for itself but rather its relation to a whole range of other texts, and the exploration of those relations identifies the systems of fiction within which texts offer meanings to readers. This is why so many of the extracts which follow discuss the related concepts of formula *and* genre. *The following is the opening sentence of a novel: 'All I saw was the dame standing there in the glare of the headlights waving her arms like a huge puppet and the curse I spat out filled the car and my own ears.' It would arouse in most readers certain expectations as to what is to follow, and they would be very different from the following:*

The Rolls-Royce had its bonnet open and its engine running. The chauffeur, as he cleaned it, was whistling the latest tune, with which, only a few weeks old, London was already satiated. Children were playing in the early morning sunshine on the cobble-stones of the mews. Fiona stirred in her narrow bed, and finally awoke.

The reader who registers this difference is sufficiently experienced in systems of fiction to distinguish codes characteristic of hard-boiled American thrillers from those of popular romance written by Barbara Cartland.[1] As early as the first sentences of these novels certain kinds of meaning are more probable than others. The structuralist analysis of narrative seeks to identify the 'units' which combine to produce meaningful narrative and to explore the principles governing their relations within the individual text and the wider fictional system.

Extract 13 is from one early such attempt, Propp's Morphology of the Folk Tale *(1928). That folk tales do constitute a specific fictional genre is assumed a priori, and the task of analysis is seen as 'a description of the tale according to its component parts and the relationship of these components to each other and to the whole'. To Propp the laws of narrative are as accessible as those governing any other phenomena: 'just as cloth can be measured with a yardstick to determine its length, tales may be measured by the scheme and thereby defined'. It is significant that Propp's appendices 'summarise' his analyses of tales in a series of diagrammatic charts and mathematical formulas and the tone of his conclusions is strongly suggestive of 'Q.E.D.'. Propp's scientific conclusions do not, of course, constitute the final word on narrative in general and we may readily cite examples which refuse to conform to Propp's mould – those which do not end 'happily' are the most obvious example. Propp is also silent on the reading of narrative and on the cultural context in which this takes place. And yet as with Leavis we should refrain from scoring too easily off this early text. The emphasis on the mechanics of narrative as something constructed (as opposed to inexplicably and magnificently there) is crucially important and most commentators would still regard a reading of Propp as an important contribution to an understanding of structuralist approaches to narrative. We are immediately aware of the influence of Propp on Eco's analysis of Ian Fleming's novels (see Reading 19).*

It was during the 1960s, especially in France, that the methods of structuralism were first applied extensively to the analysis of fiction and a prominent practitioner was Roland Barthes. In Reading 14 Barthes is very clearly working by analogy with language in seeking a 'grammar' of narrative to correspond to that which regulates the selection and combination of words in sentences. Barthes refers to narrative as 'a second order' language combining sentences into larger units with distinct functions. Four functions are identified which together account for every unit within the narrative: all units are functional and narrative is never made up of anything but functions. The student who takes time to analyse, say, the opening few pages of a novel in terms of Barthes's functions will immediately sense the way in which the narrative constructs, unit by unit, a framework of meaning in the mind of its reader. She will also perhaps point to some of the dimensions missing from this work which Barthes himself regarded as 'provisional'. It should be recognised that there are senses in which the Barthes of this essay is already looking towards his own later development: many 'omissions' are made good in his 'post-structuralist' work (see Readings 24 and 25).

Pleasure

In Readings 15 and 16 there is a stronger awareness of the responses of readers to narrative. Both Wright and Neale argue that part at least of the pleasure of fiction is to be located at the strictly formal level of analysis: narrative is in itself pleasurable. This, for Wright, explains why it is that 'stories appear in every human society'. He argues that the construction of narratives is essentially the organisation of events in such a way that interrelations become clear: narrative 'makes sense of experience'. In the same way human consciousness makes sense of experience by seeing it in narrative terms. Fiction is thus doubly beneficial: its pleasure is immediately accessible and the experience of narrative constitutes a useful training ground on which readers sharpen the skills necessary for making sense of life. Neale locates pleasure in contrasting tendencies inherent in narrative. The reader who moves through a text experiences conflicting 'pleasures' – on the one hand 'process' on the other 'position'. The former implies the condition of movement, the latter that of being stationary and the pleasures are mutually dependent; movement guarantees against the boredom of endless stasis (in which nothing happens); stasis against the potentially demoralising experience of perpetual motion (in which too much happens). Neale's work focuses a further problem which arises from structuralist analysis of narrative. At one level, Neale points out, narrative structure is monumentally predictable. An initial order is enigmatically or threateningly disturbed; the narrative traces the progression towards final 'closure' or 'resolution' in which the initial order is restored or a new equilibrium negotiated. If it is indeed the case that all narratives participate in this system (albeit in the generically distinctive ways Neale demonstrates) the problem should be obvious. The pleasure of narrative, it is commonly assumed, involves suspense, exploits the reader's uncertainty as to what will happen next and how things will end. How is suspense to be reconciled with the high level of predictability which characterises popular narratives? It is not incidental that the problem is focused at least implicitly by all the readings in this section: it is at the very interface of structuralist analysis and attempts to account for the pleasures of fiction.

The gulf in sophistication between Propp and Neale is substantial. The eight extracts which follow are various and do not collectively encourage the notion of a single, uniform, 'classic structuralism'. Indeed the reader may soon begin to question the validity of grouping them all under the single heading. The common ground should be repeated: in their concern to locate systems of fictional meaning, their focus is primarily – often exclusively – formal, and the object of their analysis is the process of narrative. In Part 4 we shall see a shift in emphasis: from formal narrative on to the analysis of narrative in a wider cultural context. The perspective will by then no longer be 'structuralist', but something else.

Note

1   The first example is Spillane again – *Kiss me Deadly*; the second is from Barbara Cartland, *Dance on My Heart*.

Theory and Methodology

 READING 12

'The concept of formula in the study of popular literature'

John G. Cawelti

Let me begin with a kind of axiom or assumption which I hope I can persuade you to accept without elaborate argumentation: all cultural products contain a mixture of two kinds of elements: conventions and inventions. Conventions are elements which are known to both the creator and his audience beforehand – they consist of things like favorite plots, stereotyped characters, accepted ideas, commonly known metaphors and other linguistic devices, etc. Inventions, on the other hand, are elements which are uniquely imagined by the creator such as new kinds of characters, ideas, or linguistic forms. Of course it is difficult to distinguish in every case between conventions and inventions because many elements lie somewhere along a continuum between the two poles. Nonetheless, familiarity with a group of literary works will usually soon reveal what the major conventions are and therefore, what in the case of an individual work is unique to that creator.

Convention and invention have quite different cultural functions. Conventions represent familiar shared images and meanings and they assert an ongoing continuity of values; inventions confront us with a new perception or meaning which we have not realized before. Both these functions are important to culture. Conventions help maintain a culture's stability while inventions help it respond to changing circumstances and provide new information about the world. The same thing is true on the individual level. If the individual does not encounter a large number of conventionalized experiences and situations, the strain on his sense of continuity and identity will lead to great tensions and even to neurotic breakdowns. On the other hand, without new information about his world, the individual will be increasingly unable to cope with it and will withdraw behind a barrier of conventions as some people withdraw from life to compulsive reading of detective stories.

Most works of art contain a mixture of convention and invention. Both Homer and Shakespeare show a large proportion of conventional elements mixed with inventions of great genius. Hamlet, for example, depends on a long tradition of stories of revenge, but only Shakespeare could have invented a character who embodies so many complex perceptions of life that every generation is able to find new ways of viewing him. So long as cultures were relatively stable over long periods of time and homogeneous in their structure, the relation between convention and invention in works of literature posed relatively few problems. Since the Renaissance, however, modern cultures have become increasingly heterogeneous and pluralistic in their structure and discontinuous in time. In consequence, while public communications have become increasingly conventional in order to be understood by an extremely broad and diverse audience, the intellectual élites

71

have placed ever higher valuation on invention out of a sense that rapid cultural changes require continually new perceptions of the world. Thus we have arrived at a situation in which the model great work of literature is Joyce's *Finnegan's Wake*, a creation which is almost as far as possible along the continuum toward total invention as it is possible to go without leaving the possibility of shared meanings behind. At the same time, there has developed a vast amount of literature characterized by the highest degree of conventionalization.

This brings us to an initial definition of formula. A formula is a conventional system for structuring cultural products. It can be distinguished from form which is an invented system of organization. Like the distinction between convention and invention, the distinction between formula and form can be best envisaged as a continuum between two poles; one pole is that of a completely conventional structure of conventions – an episode of the Lone Ranger or one of the Tarzan books comes close to this pole; the other end of the continuum is a completely original structure which orders inventions – *Finnegan's Wake* is perhaps the best example of this, though one might also cite such examples as Resnais' film *Last Year at Marienbad*, T.S. Eliot's poem 'The Waste Land', or Becket's play *Waiting for Godot*. All of these works not only manifest a high degree of invention in their elements but unique organizing principles. 'The Waste Land' makes the distinction even sharper for that poem contains a substantial number of conventional elements – even to the point of using quotations from past literary works – but these elements are structured in such a fashion that a new perception of familiar elements is forced upon the reader.

I would like to emphasize that the distinction between form and formula as I am using it here is a descriptive rather than a qualitative one. Though it is likely for a number of reasons that a work possessing more form than formula will be a greater work we should avoid this easy judgement in our study of popular culture. In distinguishing form from formula we are trying to deal with the relationship between the work and its culture, and not with its artistic quality. Whether or not a different set of aesthetic criteria are necessary in the judgement of formal as opposed to formulaic works is an important and interesting question, but necessarily the subject of another series of reflections.

We can further differentiate the conception of formula by comparing it to genre and myth. Genre, in the sense of tragedy, comedy, romance, etc., seems to be based on a difference between basic attitudes or feelings about life. I find Northrop Frye's suggestion that the genres embody fundamental archetypal patterns reflecting stages of the human life cycle, a very fruitful idea here. In Frye's sense of the term genre and myth are universal patterns of action which manifest themselves in all human cultures. Following Frye, let me briefly suggest a formulation of this kind – genre can be defined as a structural pattern which embodies a universal life pattern or myth in the materials of language; formula, on the other hand is cultural; it represents the way in which a culture has embodied mythical archetypes and its own preoccupations in narrative form.

An example will help clarify this distinction. The Western and the spy story can both be seen as embodiments of the archetypal pattern of the hero's quest which Frye discusses under the general heading of the mythos of romance. Or if we prefer psychoanalytical archetypes these formulas embody the oedipal myth in fairly explicit fashion, since they deal with the hero's conquest of a dangerous and powerful figure. However, though we can doubtless characterize both Western and spy stories in terms of these universal archetypes they do not account for the basic and important differences in setting, characters, and action between the Western and the spy story. These differences are clearly cultural and they reflect the particular preoccupations and needs of the time in which they were created and the group which created them: the Western shows its nineteenth century American origin while the spy story reflects the fact that it is largely a twentieth century British creation. Of course, a formula articulated by one culture can be taken over by another. However, we will often find important differences in the formula as it moves from one culture or from one period to another. For example, the gunfighter Western of the 1950's is importantly different from the cowboy romances of Owen Wister and Zane Grey, just as the American spy stories of Donald Hamilton differ from the British secret agent adventures of Eric Ambler and Graham Greene.

The cultural nature of formulas suggests two further points about them. First, while myths, because of their basic and universal nature turn up in many different manifestations, formulas, because of their close connection to a particular culture and period of time, tend to have a much more limited repertory of plots, characters, and settings. For example, the pattern of action known generally as the Oedipus myth can be discerned in an enormous range of stories from Oedipus Rex to the latest Western. Indeed, the very difficulty with this myth as an analytical tool is that it is so universal that it hardly serves to differentiate one story from another. Formulas, however, are much more specific: Westerns must have a certain kind of setting, a particular cast of characters, and follow a limited number of lines of action. A Western that does not take place in the West, near the frontiers, at a point in history when social order and anarchy are in tension, and that does not involve some form of pursuit, is simply not a Western. A detective story that does not involve the situation of a mysterious crime is not a detective story. This greater specificity of plot, character, and setting reflects a more limited framework of interest values, and tensions that relate to culture rather than to the generic nature of man.

The second point is a hypothesis about why formulas come into existence and enjoy such wide popular use. Why of all the infinite possible subjects for fictions do a few like the adventures of the detective, the secret agent, and the cowboy so dominate the field.

I suggest that formulas are important because they represent syntheses of several important cultural functions which, in modern cultures have been taken over by the popular arts. Let me suggest just one or two examples of what I mean. In earlier more homogeneous cultures religious ritual performed the important function of articulating and reaffirming the primary cultural values. Today, with cultures composed of a multiplicity of differing religious groups, the synthesis of values and their reaffirmation has become an increasingly important function of the mass media and the popular arts. Thus, one important dimension of formula is social or cultural ritual. Homogeneous cultures also possessed a large repertory of games and songs which all members of the culture understood and could participate in both for a sense of group solidarity and for personal enjoyment and recreation. Today, the great spectator sports provide one way in which a mass audience can participate in games together. Artistic formulas also fulfill this function in that they constitute entertainments with rules known to everyone. Thus, a very wide audience can follow a Western, appreciate its fine points and vicariously participate in its pattern of suspense and resolution. Indeed one of the more interesting ways of defining a Western is as a game: a Western is a three-sided game played on a field where the middle line is the frontier and the two main areas of play are the settled town and the savage wilderness. The three sides are the good group of townspeople who stand for law and order, but are handicapped by lack of force: the villains who reject law and order and have force; and the hero who has ties with both sides. The object of the game is to get the hero to lend his force to the good group and to destroy the villain. Various rules determine how this can be done: for example, the hero cannot use force against the villain unless strongly provoked. Also like games, the formula always gets to its goal. Someone must win, and the story must be resolved.

This game dimension of formulas has two aspects. First, there is the patterned experience of excitement, suspense, and release which we associate with the functions of entertainment and recreation. Second, there is the aspect of play as ego-enhancement through the temporary resolution of inescapable frustrations and tensions through fantasy. As Piaget sums up this aspect of play:

> Conflicts are foreign to play, or, if they do occur, it is so that the ego may be freed from them by compensation or liquidation, whereas serious activity has to grapple with conflicts which are inescapable. The conflict between obedience and individual liberty is, for example, the affliction of childhood [and we might note a key theme of the Western] and in real life the only solutions to this conflict are submission, revolt, or cooperation which involves some measure of compromise. In play, however, the conflicts are transposed in such a way that the ego is revenged, either by suppression of the problem or by giving it an acceptable solution. . . . it is because the ego dominates the whole universe in play that it is freed from conflict.

Thus, the game dimension of formula is a culture's way of simultaneously entertaining itself and of creating an acceptable pattern of temporary escape from the serious restrictions and limitations of human life. In formula stories, the detective always solves the crime, the hero always determines and carries out true justice, and the agent accomplishes his mission or at least preserves himself from the omnipresent threats of the enemy.

Finally, formula stories seem to be one way in which the individuals in a culture act out certain unconscious or repressed needs, or express in an overt and symbolic fashion certain latent motives which they must give expression to, but cannot face openly. This is the most difficult aspect of formula to pin down. Many would argue that one cannot meaningfully discuss latent contents of unconscious motives beyond the individual level or outside of the clinical context. Certainly it is easy to generate a great deal of pseudo-psychoanalytic theories about literary formula and to make deep symbolic interpretations which it is clearly impossible to substantiate convincingly. However, though it may be difficult to develop a reliable method of analysis of this aspect of formulas, I am convinced that the Freudian insight that recurrent myths and stories embody a kind of collective dreaming process is essentially correct and has an important application on the cultural as well as the universal level, that is, that the idea of a collective dream applies to formula as well as to myth. But there is no doubt that we need to put much more thought into our approach to these additional dimensions of formula and about their relation to the basic dimension of a narrative construction.

My argument, then, is that formula stories like the detective story, the Western, the seduction novel, the biblical epic, and many others are structures of narrative conventions which carry out a variety of cultural functions in a unified way. We can best define these formulas as principles for the selection of certain plots, characters, and settings, which possess in addition to their basic narrative structure the dimensions of collective ritual, game and dream. To analyze these formulas we must first define them as narrative structures of a certain kind and then investigate how the additional dimensions of ritual, game and dream have been synthesized into the particular patterns of plot, character and setting which have become associated with the formula. Once we have understood the way in which particular formulas are structured, we will be able to compare them, and also to relate them to the cultures which use them. By these methods I feel that we will arrive at a new understanding of the phenomena of popular literature and new insights into the patterns of culture.

(from *Journal of Popular Culture*, Vol.3, 1969)

 READING 13

Morphology of the folk tale

Vladimir Propp

. . . this work is dedicated to the study of *fairy* tales. The existence of fairy tales as a special class is assumed as an essential working hypothesis. . . . We are undertaking a comparison of the themes of these tales. For the sake of comparison we shall separate the component parts of fairy tales by special methods: and then, we shall make a comparison of tales according to their components. The result will be a morphology (i.e., a description of the tale according to its component parts and the relationship of these components to each other and to the whole).

What methods can achieve an accurate description of the tale? Let us compare the following events:

1 A tsar gives an eagle to a hero. The eagle carries the hero away to another kingdom.

2 An old man gives Súčenko a horse. The horse carries Súčenko away to another kingdom.

3 A sorcerer gives Iván a little boat. The boat takes Iván to another kingdom.

4 A princess gives Iván a ring. Young men appearing from out of the ring carry Iván away into another kingdom, and so forth.

Both constants and variables are present in the preceding instances. The names of the dramatis personae change (as well as the attributes of each), but neither their actions nor functions change. From this we can draw the inference that a tale often attributes identical actions to various personages. This makes possible the study of the tale *according to the functions of its dramatis personae.*

We shall have to determine to what extent these functions actually represent recurrent constants of the tale. The formulation of all other questions will depend upon the solution of this primary question: how many functions are known to the tale?

Investigation will reveal that the recurrence of functions is astounding. Thus Bába Jagá, Morózko, the bear, the forest spirit, and the mare's head test and reward the stepdaughter. Going further, it is possible to establish that characters of a tale, however varied they may be, often perform the same actions. The actual means of the realization of functions can vary, and as such it is a variable. Morózka behaves differently than Bába Jagá. But the function, as such, is a constant. The question of *what* a tale's dramatis personae do is an important one for the study of the tale, but the questions of *who* does it and *how* it is done already fall within the province of accessory study. . . . one may say that the number of functions is extremely small, whereas the number of personages is extremely large. This explains the two-fold quality of a tale: its amazing multiformity, picturesqueness, and color, and on the other hand, its no less striking uniformity, its repetition.

Thus the functions of the dramatis personae are basic components of the tale, and we must first of all extract them. In order to extract the functions we must define them. Definition must proceed from two points of view. First of all, definition should in no case depend on the personage who carries out the function. Definition of a function will most often be given in the form of a noun expressing an action (interdiction, interrogation, flight, etc.). Secondly, an action cannot be defined apart from its place in the course of narration. The meaning which a given function has in the course of action must be considered. For example, if Iván marries a tsar's daughter, this is something entirely different than the marriage of a father to a widow with two daughters. A second example: if, in one instance, a hero receives money from his father in the form of 100 rubles and subsequently buys a wise cat with this money, whereas in a second case, the hero is rewarded with a sum of money for an accomplished act of bravery (at which point the tale ends), we have before us two morphologically different elements – in spite of the identical action (the transference of money) in both cases. Thus, identical acts can have different meanings, and vice versa. *Function is understood as an act of a character, defined from the point of view of its significance for the course of the action.*

The observations cited may be briefly formulated in the following manner:

1 Functions of characters serve as stable, constant elements in a tale, independent of how and by whom they are fulfilled. They constitute the fundamental components of a tale.

2 The number of functions known to the fairy tale is limited.

If functions are delineated, a second question arises: in what classification and in what sequence are these functions encountered? . . . The consequence of elements, as we shall see later on, is strictly *uniform*. Freedom within this sequence is restricted by very narrow limits which can be exactly formulated. We thus obtain the third basic thesis of this work, subject to further development and verification:

3 The sequence of functions is always identical.

As for groupings, it is necessary to say first of all that by no means do all tales give evidence of all functions. But this in no way changes the law of sequence. The absence of certain functions does not change the order of the rest. We shall dwell on this phenomenon later. For the present we shall deal with groupings in the proper sense of the word. The presentation of the question itself evokes the following assumption: if functions are singled out, then it will be possible to trace those tales which present identical functions. Tales with identical functions can be considered as belonging to one type. On this foundation, an index of types can then be created, based not upon theme features, which are somewhat vague and diffuse, but upon exact structural features.

. . . .

. . . we arrive at the fourth basic thesis of our work:

4 All fairy tales are of one type in regard to their structure.

We shall now set about the task of proving, developing, and elaborating these theses in detail. Here it should be recalled that the study of the tale must be carried on strictly deductively, i.e., proceeding from the material at hand to the consequences.

The main body of Propp's book consists of a structural analysis of 100 tales in the collection of Afanas'ev. What follows is a much abbreviated version of Chapter 3 in which the thirty-one functions are listed.

A tale begins typically with an 'initial situation', which, though not a function, is an important morphological element.

I	One member of family absents himself from home (Absentation)
II	An interdiction is addressed to the Hero (Interdiction) – a command, a request, a suggestion, etc.
III	The interdiction is violated (Violation). At this point a new personage, the Villain, enters.
IV	The Villain makes an attempt at reconnaissance.
V	The Villain receives information about his Victim (Delivery).
VI	The Villain attempts to deceive his Victim in order to take possession of him or his possessions (Trickery).
VII	The Victim submits to deception and thereby unwittingly helps his enemy (Complicity).
VIII	The Villain causes harm or injury to a member of a family (Villainy). This function is exceptionally important, since by means of it the actual movement of the tale is created.
VIIIa	Some tales may initiate complication through lack or insufficiency (Lack).
IX	Misfortune or Lack is made known; the Hero is approached with a request or command; he is allowed to go or he is dispatched (Mediation, the connective incident). This function brings the Hero into the tale. The Hero can be seeker Hero or victimised Hero.
X	The Hero leaves home (Departure).

At this point a new personage enters the tale, the Donor or Provider, from whom the Hero will receive a (magical) agent which will permit eventual liquidation of misfortune.

XII	The Hero is tested, interrogated, attacked, etc., which prepares the way for his receiving either a magical agent or helper (the first function of the Donor).
XIII	The Hero reacts to the actions of the future Donor (the Hero's reaction).

XIV   The Hero acquires use of the magical agent (provision for receipt of the magical agent).

XV   The Hero is transferred, delivered or led to the whereabouts of an object of search (Guidance).

XVI   The Hero and the Villain join in direct combat (Struggle).

XVII   The Hero is branded (Branding, Marking).

XVIII The Villain is defeated (Victory).

XIX   The initial Misfortune or Lack is liquidated. The narrative reaches a peak in this function.

XX   The Hero returns (Return).

XXI   The Hero is pursued (Pursuit, Chase).

XXII   The Rescue of the Hero from Pursuit (Rescue).

A great many tales end at Rescue but the tale may have another Misfortune in store. An initial Villainy is repeated, everything begins anew, and functions VIII–XV may be repeated. From this point onwards the development of the narrative proceeds differently and the tale gives new functions.

XXIII The Hero, unrecognised, arrives home, or in another country (Unrecognised Arrival).

XXIV   A False Hero presents unfounded claims (Unfounded Claims).

XXV   A difficult task is proposed to the Hero (Difficult Task).

XXVI   The Task is resolved (Solution).

XXVII The Hero is recognised (Recognition).

XXVIII The False Hero or Villain is exposed (Exposure).

XXIX   The Hero is given a new appearance (Transfiguration).

XXX   The Villain is punished (Punishment).

XXXI   The Hero is married and ascends the throne (Wedding).

On the basis of this analysis Propp reasserts his four basic theses. He further concludes:

Now we shall give several individual, though highly important, deductions. We observe that a large number of functions are arranged in pairs (prohibition-violation, reconnaissance-delivery, struggle-victory, pursuit-deliverance, etc.). Other functions may be arranged according to groups. Thus villainy, dispatch, decision for counteraction, and departure from home . . . constitute the complication. Functions XII, XIII, XIV also form something of a whole. Alongside these combinations there are individual functions (absentations, punishment, marriage, etc.). We are merely noting these particular deductions at this point. The observation that functions are arranged in pairs will prove useful later, as well as the general deductions drawn here.

At this point we have to examine individual texts of the tales at close range. The question of how the given scheme applies to the texts, and what the individual tales constitute in relation to this scheme, can be resolved only by an analysis of the texts. But the reverse question, 'What does the given scheme represent *in relation to the tales?*' can be answered here and now. The scheme is a *measuring unit* for individual tales. Just as cloth can be measured with a yardstick to determine its length, tales may be measured by the scheme and thereby defined.

READING 14

'Introduction to the structural analysis of narratives'

Roland Barthes

The narratives of the world are numberless. Narrative is first and foremost a prodigious variety of genres, themselves distributed amongst different substances – as though any material were fit to receive man's stories. Able to be carried by articulated language, spoken or written, fixed or moving images, gestures, and the ordered mixture of all these substances; narrative is present in myth, legend, fable, tale, novella, epic, history, tragedy, drama, comedy, mime, painting (think of Carpaccio's *Saint Ursula*), stained glass windows, cinema, comics, news item, conversation. Moreover, under this almost infinite diversity of forms, narrative is present in every age, in every place, in every society; it begins with the very history of mankind and there nowhere is nor has been a people without narrative. All classes, all human groups, have their narratives, enjoyment of which is very often shared by men with different, even opposing, cultural backgrounds. Caring nothing for the division between good and bad literature, narrative is international, transhistorical, transcultural: it is simply there, like life itself.

Must we conclude from this universality that narrative is insignificant? Is it so general that we can have nothing to say about it except for the modest description of a few highly individualized varieties, something literary history occasionally undertakes? But then how are we to master even these varieties, how are we to justify our right to differentiate and identify them? How is novel to be set against novella, tale against myth, drama against tragedy (as has been done a thousand times) without reference to a common model? Such a model is implied by every proposition relating to the most individual, the most historical, of narrative forms. It is thus legitimate that, far from the abandoning of any idea of dealing with narrative on the grounds of its universality, there should have been (from Aristotle on) a periodic interest in narrative form and it is normal that the newly developing structuralism should make this form one of its first concerns – is not structuralism's constant aim to master the infinity of utterances [*paroles*] by describing the 'language' [*langue*] of which they are the products and from which they can be generated. Faced with the infinity of narratives, the multiplicity of standpoints – historical, psychological, sociological, ethnological, aesthetic, etc. – from which they can be studied, the analyst finds himself in more or less the same situation as Saussure confronted by the heterogeneity of language [*langage*] and seeking to extract a principle of classification and a central focus for description from the apparent confusion of the individual messages. Keeping simply to modern times, the Russian Formalists, Propp and Lévi-Strauss have taught us to recognize the following dilemma: either a narrative is merely a rambling collection of events, in which case nothing can be said about it other than by referring back to the storyteller's (the author's) art, talent or genius – all mythical forms of chance[2] – or else it shares with other narratives a common structure which is open to analysis, no matter how much patience its formulation requires. There is a world of difference between the most complex randomness and the most elementary combinatory scheme, and it is impossible to combine (to produce) a narrative without reference to an implicit system of units and rules.

Where then are we to look for the structures of narrative? Doubtless, in narratives themselves. *Each and every* narrative? Many commentators who accept the idea of narrative structure are nevertheless unable to resign themselves to dissociating literary analysis from the example of the experimental sciences; nothing daunted, they ask that a purely inductive method be applied to narrative and that one start by studying all the narratives within a genre, a period, or a society. This commonsense view is utopian. Linguistics itself, with only some three thousand languages to embrace, cannot manage such a programme and has wisely turned deductive, a step which in fact marked its veritable constitution as a science and the beginning of its spectacular progress, it even succeeding in anticipating facts prior to their discovery. So what of narrative analysis, faced as it is with millions of narratives? Of necessity, it is condemned to a deductive procedure, obliged first to devise a hypothetical model of description (what American linguists call a 'theory') and then gradually to work down from this model towards the different narrative species which at once conform to and depart from the model. It is only at the level of these conformities and departures that analysis will be able to come back to, but now equipped with a single descriptive tool, the plurality of narratives, to their historical, geographical and cultural diversity.

Thus, in order to describe and classify the infinite number of narratives, a 'theory' (in this pragmatic sense) is needed and the immediate task is that of finding it, of starting to define it. Its development can be greatly facilitated if one begins from a model able to provide it with its initial terms and principles. In the current state of research, it seems reasonable that the structural analysis of narrative be given linguistics itself as a founding model.

I. The language of narrative

1. Beyond the sentence

As we know, linguistics stops at the sentence, the last unit which it considers to fall within its scope. If the sentence, being an order and not a series, cannot be reduced to the sum of the words which compose it and constitutes thereby a specific unit, a piece of discourse, on the contrary, is no more than the succession of the sentences composing it. From the point of view of linguistics, there is nothing in discourse that is not to be found in the sentence: 'The sentence,' writes Martinet, 'is the smallest segment that is perfectly and wholly representative of discourse.' Hence there can be no question of linguistics setting itself an object superior to the sentence, since beyond the sentence are only more sentences – having described the flower, the botanist is not to get involved in describing the bouquet.

And yet it is evident that discourse itself (as a set of sentences) is organized and that, through this organization, it can be seen as the message of another language, one operating at a higher level than the language of the linguists.[4] Discourse has its units, its rules, its 'grammar': beyond the sentence, and though consisting solely of sentences, it must naturally form the object of a second linguistics.

. . . .

2. Levels of meaning

From the outset, linguistics furnishes the structural analysis of narrative with a concept which is decisive in that, making explicit immediately what is essential in every system of meaning, namely its organization, it allows us both to show how a narrative is not a simple sum of propositions and to classify the enormous mass of elements which go to make up a narrative. This concept is that of *level of description*.

A sentence can be described, linguistically, on several levels (phonetic, phonological, grammatical, contextual) and these levels are in a hierarchical relationship with one another, for, while all have their own units and correlations (whence the necessity for a separate description of each of them), no level on its own can produce meaning. A unit belonging to a particular level only takes on meaning if it can be integrated in a higher level; a phoneme, though perfectly describable, means nothing in itself: it participates in meaning only when integrated in a word, and the word itself must in turn be integrated in a sentence. The theory of levels (as set out by Benveniste) gives two types of relations: distributional (if the relations are situated on the same level) and integrational (if they are grasped from one level to the next); consequently, distributional relations alone are not sufficient to account for meaning. In order to conduct a structural analysis, it is thus first of all necessary to distinguish several levels or instances of description and to place these instances within a hierarchical (integrationary) perspective.

The levels are operations. It is therefore normal that, as it progresses, linguistics should tend to multiply them. Discourse analysis, however, is as yet only able to work on rudimentary levels . . . . Today, in his analysis of the structure of myth, Lévi-Strauss has already indicated that the constituent units of mythical discourse (mythemes) acquire meaning only because they are grouped in bundles and because these bundles themselves combine together. As too, Tzvetan Todorov, reviving the distinction made by the Russian Formalists, proposes working on two major levels, themselves subdivided: *story* (the argument), comprising a logic of actions and a 'syntax' of characters, and *discourse*, comprising the tenses, aspects and modes of the narrative. But however many levels are proposed and whatever definition they are given, there can be no doubt that narrative is a hierarchy of instances. To understand a narrative is not merely to follow the unfolding of the story, it is also to recognise its construction in 'storeys', to project the horizontal concatenations of the narrative 'thread' on to an implicitly vertical axis; to read (to listen to) a narrative is not merely to move from one word to the next, it is also to move from one level to the next. Perhaps I may be allowed to offer a kind of apologue in this connection. In *The Purloined Letter*, Poe gives an acute analysis of the failure of the chief commissioner of the Paris police, powerless to find the letter. His investigations, says Poe, were perfect *'within the sphere of his speciality'*; he searched everywhere, saturated entirely the level of the 'police search', but in order to find the letter, protected by its conspicuousness, it was necessary to shift to another level, to substitute the concealer's principle of relevance for that of the policeman. Similarly, the 'search' carried out over a horizontal set of narrative relations may well be as thorough as possible but must still, to be effective, also operate 'vertically': meaning is not 'at the end' of the narrative, it runs across it; just as conspicuous as the purloined letter, meaning eludes all unilateral investigation.

. . . .

II. Functions

1. The determination of the units

Any system being the combination of units of known classes, the first task is to divide up narrative and determine the segments of narrative discourse that can be distributed into a limited number of classes. In a word, we have to define the smallest narrative units.

Given the integrational perspective described above, the analysis cannot rest satisfied with a purely distributional definition of the units. From the start, meaning must be the criterion of the unit: it is the functional nature of certain segments of the story that makes them units – hence the name 'functions' immediately attributed to these first units. Since the Russian Formalists, a unit has been taken as any segment of the story which can be seen as the term of a correlation. The essence of a function is, so to speak, the seed that it sows in the narrative, planting an element that will come to fruition later – either on the same level or elsewhere, on another level. If in *Un Cœur simple* Flaubert at one point tells the reader, seemingly without emphasis, that the daughters of the Sous-Préfet of Pont-l'Evéque owned a parrot, it is because this parrot is subsequently to have a great importance in Félicité's life; the statement of this detail (whatever its linguistic form) thus constitutes a function, or narrative unit.

Is everything in a narrative functional? Does everything, down to the slightest detail, have a meaning? Can narrative be divided up entirely into functional units? We shall see in a moment that there are several kinds of functions, there being several kinds of correlations, but this does not alter the fact that a narrative is never made up of anything other than functions: in differing degrees, everything in it signifies. This is not a matter of art (on the part of the narrator), but of structure; in the realm of discourse, what is noted is by definition notable. Even were a detail to appear irretrievably insignificant, resistant to all functionality, it would nonetheless end up with precisely the meaning of absurdity or uselessness: everything has a meaning, or nothing has. . . .

From the linguistic point of view, the function is clearly a unit of content: it is 'what it says' that makes of a statement a functional unit, not the manner in which it is said. This constitutive signified may have a number of different signifiers, often very intricate. If I am told (in *Goldfinger*) that *Bond saw a man of about fifty*, the piece of information holds simultaneously two functions of unequal pressure: on the one hand, the character's age fits into a certain description of the man (the 'usefulness' of which for the rest of the story is not nil, but diffuse, delayed); while on the other, the immediate signified of the statement is that Bond is unacquainted with his future interlocutor, the unit thus implying a very strong correlation (initiation of a threat and the need to establish the man's identity). In order to determine the initial narrative units, it is therefore vital never to lose sight of the functional nature of the segments under consideration and to recognize in advance that they will not necessarily coincide with the forms into which we traditionally cast the various parts of narrative discourse (actions, scenes, paragraphs, dialogues, interior monologues, etc.) still less with 'psychological' divisions (modes of behaviour, feelings, intentions, motivations, rationalizations of characters).

In the same way, since the 'language' [*langue*] of narrative is not the language [*langue*] of articulated language [*langage articulé*] – though very often vehicled by it – narrative units will be substantially independent of linguistic units; they may indeed coincide with the latter, but occasionally, not systematically. Functions will be represented sometimes by units higher than the sentence (groups of sentences of varying lengths, up to the work in its entirety) and sometimes by lower ones (syntagm, word and even, within the word, certain literary elements only). When we are told that – the telephone ringing during night duty at Secret Service head-quarters – *Bond picked up one of the four receivers*, the moneme *four* in itself constitutes a functional unit, referring as it does to a concept necessary to the story (that of a highly developed bureaucratic technology). In fact, the narrative unit in this case is not the linguistic unit (the word) but only its connoted value (linguistically, the word four never means 'four'); which explains how certain functional units can be shorter than the sentence without ceasing to belong to the order of discourse: such units then extend not beyond the sentence, than which they remain materially shorter, but beyond the level of denotation, which, like the sentence, is the province of linguistics properly speaking.

2. Classes of units

The functional units must be distributed into a small number of classes. If these classes are to be determined without recourse to the substance of content (psycho-logical substance for example), it is again necessary to consider the different levels of meaning: some units have as correlates units on the same level, while the sat-uration of others requires a change of levels; hence, straightaway, two major classes of functions, distributional and integrational. The former correspond to what Propp and subsequently Bremond (in particular) take as functions but they will be treated here in a much more detailed way than is the case in their work. The term '*functions*' will be reserved for these units (though the other units are also functional), the model of description for which has become classic since Tomachevski's analysis: the purchase of a revolver has for correlate the moment when it will be used (and if not used, the notation is reversed into a sign of indeci-sion, etc.); picking up the telephone has for correlate the moment when it will be put down; the intrusion of the parrot into Félicité's home for correlate the episode of the stuffing, the worshipping of the parrot, etc. As for the latter, the integra-tional units, these comprise all the '*indices*' (in the very broad sense of the word), the unit now referring not to a complementary and consequential act but to a more or less diffuse concept which is nevertheless necessary to the meaning of the story: psychological indices concerning the characters, data regarding their iden-tity, notations of 'atmosphere', and so on. The relation between the unit and its correlate is now no longer distributional (often several indices refer to the same signified and the order of their occurence in the discourse is not necessarily perti-nent) but integrational. In order to understand what an indicial notation 'is for', one must move to a higher level (characters' actions or narration), for only there is the indice clarified: the power of the administrative machine behind Bond, indexed by the number of telephones, has no bearing on the sequence of actions in which Bond is involved by answering the call; it finds its meaning only on the level of a general typology of the actants (Bond is on the side of order). Indices, because of the, in some sort, vertical nature of their relations, are truly semantic units: unlike 'functions' (in the strict sense), they refer to a signified, not to an 'operation'. . . .

These two main classes of units, functions and indices, should already allow a certain classification of narratives. Some narratives are heavily functional (such as folktales), while others on the contrary are heavily indicial (such as 'psychologi-cal' novels); between these two poles lies a whole series of intermediary forms, dependent on history, society, genre. But we can go further. Within each of the two main classes it is immediately possible to determine two sub-classes of narrative units. Returning to the class of functions, its units are not all of the same 'importance': some constitute real hinge-points of the narrative (or of a fragment of the narrative); others merely 'fill in' the narrative space separating the hinge functions. Let us call the former *cardinal functions* (or *nuclei*) and the latter, having regard to their complementary nature, *catalysers*. For a function to be cardinal, it is enough that the action to which it refers open (or continue, or close) an alternative that is of direct consequence for the subsequent development of the story, in short that it inaugurate or conclude an uncertainty. If, in a fragment of narrative, *the telephone rang*, it is equally possible to answer or not answer, two acts which will unfailingly carry the narrative along different paths. Between two cardinal functions however, it is always possible to set out subsidiary notations which cluster around one or other nucleus without modifying its alternative nature: the space separating *the telephone rang* from *Bond answered* can be saturated with a host of trivial incidents or descriptions – *Bond moved towards the desk, picked up one of the receivers, put down his cigarette*, etc. These catalysers are still functional, insofar as they enter into correlation with a nucleus, but their functionality is attenuated, unilateral, parasitic; it is a question of a purely chronological functionality (what is described is what separates two moments of the story), whereas the tie between two cardinal functions is invested with a double functionality, at once chronological and logical. Catalysers are only consecutive units, cardinal functions are both consecutive and consequential. Everything suggests, indeed, that the mainspring of narrative is precisely the confusion of consecution and consequence, what comes *after* being read in narrative as what is *caused by*; in which case narrative would be a systematic application of the logical fallacy denounced by Scholasticism in the formula *post hoc, ergo propter hoc*[5] – a good motto for Destiny, of which narrative all things considered is no more than the 'language'.

It is the structural framework of cardinal functions which accomplishes this 'telescoping' of logic and temporality. At first sight, such functions may appear extremely insignificant; what defines them is not their spectacularity (importance, volume, unusualness or force of the narrated action), but, so to speak, the risk they entail: cardinal functions are the risky moments of a narrative. Between these points of alternative, these 'dispatchers', the catalysers lay out areas of safety, rests, luxuries. Luxuries which are not, however, useless: it must be stressed again that from the point of view of the story a catalyser's functionality may be weak but not nil. Were a catalyser purely redundant (in relation to its nucleus), it would nonetheless participate in the economy of the message; in fact, an apparently merely expletive notation always has a discursive function: it accelerates, delays, gives fresh impetus to the discourse, it summarizes, anticipates and sometimes even leads astray.[6] Since what is noted always appears as being notable, the catalyser ceaselessly revives the semantic tension of the discourse, says ceaselessly that there has been, that there is going to be, meaning. Thus, in the final analysis, the catalyser has a constant function which is, to use Jakobson's term, a phatic one: it maintains the contact between narrator and addressee. A nucleus cannot be deleted without altering the story, but neither can a catalyst without altering the discourse.

As for the other main class of units, . . . [a] distinction can be made . . . between *indices* proper, referring to the character of a narrative agent, a feeling, an atmosphere (for example suspicion) or a philosophy, and *informants*, serving to identify, to locate in time and space. To say that through the window of the office where Bond is on duty the moon can be seen half-hidden by thick billowing clouds, is to index a stormy summer night, this deduction in turn forming an index of atmosphere with reference to the heavy, anguish-laden climate of an action as yet unknown to the reader. Indices always have implicit signifieds. Informants, however, do not, at least on the level of the story: they are pure data with immediate signification. Indices involve an activity of deciphering, the reader is to learn to know a character or an atmosphere; informants bring ready-made knowledge, their functionality, like that of catalysers, is thus weak without being nil. Whatever its 'flatness' in relation to the rest of the story, the informant (for example, the exact age of a character) always serves to authenticate the reality of the referent, to embed fiction in the real world. Informants are realist operators and as such possess an undeniable functionality not on the level of the story but on that of the discourse.

Nuclei and catalysers, indices and informants (again, the names are of little importance), these, it seems, are the initial classes into which the functional level units can be divided. This classification must be completed by two remarks. Firstly, a unit can at the same time belong to two different classes: to drink a whisky (in an airport lounge) is an action which can act as a catalyser to the (cardinal) notation of *waiting*, but it is also, and simultaneously, the indice of a certain atmosphere (modernity, relaxation, reminiscence, etc.). In other words, certain units can be mixed, giving a play of possibilities in the narrative economy. In the novel *Goldfinger*, Bond, having to search his adversary's bedroom, is given a master-key by his associate: the notation is a pure (cardinal) function. In the film, this detail is altered and Bond laughingly takes a set of keys from a willing chamber-maid: the notation is no longer simply functional but also indicial, referring to Bond's character (his easy charm and success with women). Secondly, it should be noted . . . that the four classes just described can be distributed in a different way which is moreover closer to the linguistic model. Catalysers, indices and informants have a common characteristic: in relation to nuclei, they are *expansions*. Nuclei . . . form finite sets grouping a small number of terms, are governed by a logic, are at once necessary and sufficient. Once the framework they provide is given, the other units fill it out according to a mode of proliferation in principle infinite.

Notes

2 There does, of course, exist an 'art' of the storyteller, which is the ability to generate narratives (messages) from the structure (the code). This art corresponds to the notion of *performance* in Chomsky and is far removed from the 'genius' of the author, romantically conceived as some barely explicable personal secret.

4 It goes without saying, as Jakobson has noted, that between the sentence and what lies beyond the sentence there are transitions; co-ordination, for instance, can work over the limit of the sentence.

5 'After this, therefore because of this.'

6 The detective novel makes abundant use of such 'confusing' units.

(from R. Barthes, *Image–Music–Text*, 1978)

Sixguns and society: a structural study of the Western

Will Wright

Stories appear in every human society: this is a universal social fact that is well known yet does not arouse the speculative interest and respect accorded such solid and dignified universals as the incest taboo and kinship structures. Stories are entertaining, and this generally suffices as an explanation of the form. The particular content of a story may be sociologically significant, but the form itself is rarely, if ever, considered problematic. Stories (myths) relieve boredom, permit escape, relate custom and history, enrich experience, reinforce values, relieve psychological conflict, produce social cohesion, create social conflicts (Leach), strengthen status demands, teach children violence; but all these alleged functions of stories are performed by their content. What is it about the form itself that gives stories this remarkable ability to accomplish such varied tasks? What is the relation between narrative and consciousness?

I cannot answer this question, but I can suggest a direction in which an answer might lie. Narratives explain change; they have a beginning, middle, and end. A narrative is a temporal account of a sequence of events related by similarity of topic and by a relationship of explanation, or causality. . . . There is also another very important aspect of narrative which we have not sufficiently considered. In a story, everything is important, all the actions and events are meaningful with respect to the unifying topic. To one degree or another all stories reconstruct events based upon the actual, possible, or desirable experiences of life. Yet all stories share a basic difference from life: every event experienced in a narrative is relevant to the success or failure of its actors, whereas many, if not most, of the events experienced by an individual in life are not at all relevant to his success or failure. If a man accidentally cuts his finger in a story, it will sooner or later save his life as well as the allied invasion of Europe (*36 Hours*); if he cuts his finger in life, it simply hurts. . . . Events in life must be *interpreted* as significant, events in narratives are *inherently* significant. In a story, if someone is late for an appointment, either something *has* happened or *will* happen as a result, or it gives an insight into the character important for an understanding of the conclusion – that is, either the event has been caused by something, will cause something, or provides the basis for another event to cause something. *Every* event is a beginning, middle, or end of a narrative sequence that explains a significant change.

It may be objected that many writers and directors have recently attempted to include just such unimportant details in their novels and films in order to change and revolutionize their respective media in exactly this way. But the point is that all such details and irrelevant events become important and relevant simply by being included in a story. They may not be central to the action of the narrative, but they are central to our understanding of the action and its context. The narrative form itself makes them significant; they have been selected for inclusion because they provide the necessary context for understanding. If as the audience or readers of a story we can find no way to relate the details to the action, then we reject the story as unsuccessful. The ability to make the connections may depend on education, intelligence, or experience, but the story is either dismissed as a failure or seen as simply a list of events, not a story at all.

Thus, the narrative form is maximumly meaningful. It provides a far greater context of understanding than is possible in life itself. Yet it reproduces the order and experiences of life, at least in terms of motivations and communication. As humans – the users of symbols – we seek to find meaning in our ordinary experience. We must constantly choose, consciously or unconsciously, which of our experiences to consider significant and which insignificant, which to invest with emotional force and which to ignore. One way, perhaps the only way, to make this choice is to determine whether or not the experience can be connected with another significant experience as either its beginning, its cause, or its result. By locating an experience in a narrative sequence with other experiences, experiences are given meaning. The form stories take can be seen as a paradigm for making sense of life. Not only do stories demonstrate that experience *can* make sense, they also demonstrate *how* it makes sense, by showing that one important event causes another and by ignoring the unimportant events. Narrative *form* – the thing that makes a story a story and not a list of events – is also the form which human consciousness imposes on real experience to give it meaning. If I lose my job, it is because of the boss's perfidy, not my incompetence. Thus, the narrative sequence – I have a job, the boss is unfair, I lose the job – gives meaning to the experience and allows me to incorporate it into a larger sequence – I am happily married, I lose my job, my wife leaves me – and so on. Thus, narratives resonate, with human consciousness: one naturally by selecting events to fit the form, and one less naturally by forcing the form to fit all experience.

In life meaning is problematic, in narrative it is not. Narrative form – the fact that in a story all events have meaning and all events are explained – interacts with the content of a narrative – its characters and events – to create a structure that communicates conceptual meaning to the individuals who hear the story. The structure of narrative communicates ideas about social action; the form of narrative establishes the possibility of meaning – it is a primer for making sense of experience. This is probably why stories, even bad ones, are usually entertaining: the meaningful organization of events is in itself psychologically satisfying as well as instructive. This is probably also why all societies tell stories: they not only aid in the understanding of social action but reflect and reinforce the formal process of consciousness itself.

 READING 16

Genre

Stephen Neale

Genre and narrative

Narrative is always a process of transformation of the balance of elements that constitute its pretext: the interruption of an initial equilibrium and the tracing of the dispersal and refiguration of its components. The system of narration characteristic of mainstream cinema is one which orders that dispersal and refiguration in a particular way, so that dispersal, disequilibrium is both maintained and contained in figures of symmetry, of balance, its elements finally re-placed in a new equilibrium whose achievement is the condition of narrative closure.

. . . .

Genres are modes of this narrative system, regulated orders of its potentiality. Hence it may be possible to begin here to indicate some of the elements of their specificity, some of the ways in which particular genres function simultaneously to exploit and contain the diversity of mainstream narrative. Firstly, it is necessary to consider the modes in which equilibrium and disruption are articulated, and the ways in which they are specified, represented differently and differentially, from genre to genre. In each case, the marks of generic specificity as such are produced by an articulation that is always constructed in terms of particular *combinations* of particular types or categories of discourse. The organisation of a given 'order' and of its disruption should be seen always in terms of conjunctions of and disjunctions between multiple sets of discursive categories and operations. For example, in the western, the gangster film and the detective film, disruption is always figured literally – as physical violence. Disequilibrium is inaugurated by violence which marks the process of the elements disrupted and which constitutes the means by which order is finally (re)established. In each case, equilibrium and disequilibrium are signified specifically in terms of Law, in terms of the presence/absence, effectiveness/ineffectiveness of legal institutions and their agents. In each case too, therefore, the discourses mobilised in these genres are discourses about crime, legality, justice, social order, civilisation, private property, civic responsibility and so on. Where they differ from one another is in the precise weight given to the discourses they share in common, in the inscription of these discourses across more specific generic elements, and in their imbrication across the codes specific to cinema. Of course, there are other genres which deploy figurations of violence. But the difference resides in the nature of the discourses and discursive categories employed in the specification of the order disrupted and the disorder instituted by that disruption.

For instance, violence also marks the horror film, most evidently in films where a monster – werewolf, vampire, psychopath or whatever – initiates a series of acts of murder and destruction which can only end when it itself is either destroyed or becomes normalised, i.e. becomes 'the norm', as in some of Polanski's films (*Rosemary's Baby*, *Dance of the Vampires*) or in Herzog's *Nosferatu*. But what defines the specificity of this particular genre is not the violence as such, but its conjunction with images and definitions of the monstrous. What defines its specificity with respect to the instances of order and disorder is their articulation across terms provided by categories and definitions of 'the human' and 'the natural'. The instances where the 'monster' is not destroyed but ends instead by pervading the social fabric in relation to which it functioned as 'monster', thus becoming integrated into it, becoming normalised, constitute a special option for the horror genre, testifying to the relative weight of discourses carrying the human/nature opposition in its discursive regime, relativising or even displacing entirely the Law/disorder dichotomy in terms of which violence operates in the Western, the detective and gangster films.

. . . .

In the musical and the melodrama, violence may figure in an important way, as it does for instance in *West Side Story* or *Written on the Wind*, but it is not a defining characteristic as such, either in terms of the register of disruption or in terms of its diegetic specification. In both genres the narrative process is inaugurated by the eruption of (hetero)sexual desire into an already firmly established social order. That is to say, the discourse of the law and 'criminality' is marginalised although by no means eliminated, while the metaphysical discourse of the horror genre is either refused entirely or explicitly designated as phantasy. The role of the policeman in *West Side Story* and that of the court in *Written on the Wind*, when compared to the roles these agencies of the legal apparatus play in *Anatomy of a Murder* (each in its own way a family romance), illustrate the difference in status of the legal discourse in the different genres. In the melodrama and the musical, the eruption of sexuality is not inscribed primarily across the codes of legality, as it can be in the thriller or the detective genre, and even, occasionally, in the western (e.g. *Stagecoach*). On the contrary, the disequilibrium inaugurating the narrative movement is specified as the process of desire itself and of the various blockages to its fulfilment within an apparently 'common sense', established social order. In other words, the process of desire in melodrama interrupts or problematises precisely the order the discourse and actions of the law have established in the face of 'lawlessness' and social disorder. Melodrama thus puts into crisis the discourses within the domain circumscribed by and defined as the legally established social order, the kind of order instituted at the end of westerns and detective films. Melodrama does not suggest a crisis of that order, but a crisis within it, an 'in house' rearrangement.

In short, it should be clearly understood that in each example mentioned here, I am not referring to elements which, in and of themselves, are absolutely exclusive to particular genres. Generic specificity is a question not of particular and exclusive elements, however defined, but of exclusive and particular combinations and articulations of elements, of the exclusive and particular weight given in any one genre to elements which in fact it shares with other genres. Heterosexual desire, the element mentioned here, is of course by no means exclusive to the musical or to the melodrama. But the role it plays in these genres is specific and distinctive . . . its presence is a necessity, not a variable option.

. . . .

Genre, narrative and subject

. . . Mainstream narrative is a mode of signification which works constantly to produce coherence in the subject through and across the heterogeneity of the effects that it mobilises and structures. Specifying its effects as narrative functions, pulling those functions into figures of symmetry and balance, mainstream narrative binds together, implicating the subject as the point where its binding mechanisms cohere, the point from where the deployment and configuration of discourses makes 'sense'. . . .

Coherence, therefore, is not simply a fact of closure, of the achievement of the stability of an equilibrium, of the production of a final unified position. It is also and equally a fact of the process which leads to that closure, of the balance of the movement of positioning that disequilibrium itself involves. Its operation is complex and multiple rather than simple and single. Narrative disruption, for example, does not involve the disturbance of one subject position as such, but rather the disturbance of a set of positions, the production of a disphasure in the relations between a plurality of positions inscribed in a plurality of discourses.[4]

The coherence of mainstream narrative derives largely from the way in which that disphasure is contained as a series of oscillations that never exceed the limits of 'dramatic conflict' (that never, therefore, exceed the limits of the possibility of resolution), and from the way in which such conflict is always, ultimately, articulated from a single, privileged point of view.

Fundamental, then, to the economy of the subject in mainstream narrative, to the economy of its mode of address, is the achievement of the maintenance of a coherent balance between process (enunciation) on the one hand, and position (enounced) on the other. But this economy can be structured in a variety of ways. Genres represent systematisations of that variety. Each genre has, to some extent at least, its own system of narrative address, its own version of the articulation of the balance. Each genre also, therefore, engages and structures differently the two basic subjective mechanisms which any form of the balance involves: the want for the pleasure of process, and the want for the pleasure of its closure.

For example, consider the detective film and the characteristic mode of its narrative address, suspense. Suspense is not, of course, exclusive to the detective genre, but it is nonetheless essential to it, tying in as it does with a narrative structured around the investigation of the principle of narrative disorder itself in the sense that the enigma is a mystery, an 'incoherence' functioning as the trigger for a story, which, as it unfolds, eliminates the enigma and comes to an end when its disorder has been abolished. The narrative of the detective genre thus directly dramatises the tension inherent in the signifying process through the mobilisation of a series of discourses concerned specifically with the Law, with the symbolic and with knowledge. What the enigma-investigation structure serves to effect is an amplification of the tension inherent in all 'classic' narratives: the tension between process (with its threat of incoherence, of the loss of mastery) and position (with its threat of stasis, fixity or of compulsive repetition, which is the same thing in another form). This tension, which informs all semiotic systems in so far as they are grounded in desire, realises itself in two distinct forms of pleasure: firstly, the potential 'boredom' of stasis; and, secondly, pleasure in position in the face of the anxieties potentially attendant on unlimited process. The amplification of this tension is largely due to the fact that the detective film dramatises the signification process itself as its fundamental problem: the Law is at issue directly in the investigation, that is to say, in the play between two fluctuatingly related sets of knowledge, that of the detective and that of the audience. In the detective film, the detective and the audience have to make sense of a set of disparate events, signs and clues. The 'risk' for the detective being represented in the narrative is a risk of violence and death. The risk for the audience is a loss of sense and meaning, the loss of a position of mastery. On the other hand, though, for the audience the process of the narrative is the primary source of its pleasure. The viewing subject is thus suspended in a structure which stretches the tensions of classic narrative to breaking point though never, axiomatically, beyond it.

. . . .

. . . the function of the enigma is to structure the generation of suspense, but it achieves this not simply by articulating the narrative as a puzzle, but also by specifying the puzzle in particular temporal terms. The enigma focuses two initially separate times, the past time of the story behind the crime and the present time of its reconstruction.[6] Indeed the enigma in many ways is that separation of times.

Eventually, the two times are brought together coherently and the enigma is resolved. A coherent memory is thus constructed across the separate instances of the story of the crime, the story of its investigation, and the process of the text itself: the memory constructed within the film duplicates the memory constructed by the film. This temporal duplication, the creation of a double temporal tension, is precisely that which marks and generates the tension referred to earlier. It is therefore also that which marks and generates its suspense, the temporal dimension of which has been outlined by Barthes as follows:

> On meeting in 'life', it is most unlikely that the invitation to take a seat would not immediately be followed by the act of sitting down; in narrative these two units, continuous from a mimetic point of view, may also be separated by a long series of insertions belonging to quite different functional spheres. Thus is established a kind of logical time which has very little connection with real time, the apparent pulverization of units always being firmly held in place by the logic that binds together the nuclei of the sequence. Suspense is clearly only a privileged – or exacerbated – form of distortion: on the one hand, by keeping a sequence open (through emphatic procedures of delay and renewal), it reinforces the contact with the reader (the listener), has a manifestly phatic function; while on the other, it offers the threat of an uncomplicated sequence, of an open paradigm (if, as we believe, every sequence has two poles), that is to say, of a logical disturbance, it being this disturbance which is consumed with anxiety and pleasure (all the more so because it is always made right in the end).[7]

This point, apparently so banal, is in fact fundamental not only for understanding the economy of pleasure in the mainstream text, but also for understanding the function of genres themselves: genres institutionalize, guarantee coherence by institutionalizing conventions, i.e. sets of expectations with respect to narrative process and narrative closure which may be subject to variation, but which are never exceeded or broken. The existence of genres means that the spectator, precisely, will always know that everything will be 'made right in the end', that everything will cohere, that any threat or any danger in the narrative process itself will always be contained.

Notes

4   P. Willemen, 'Notes on Subjectivity' in *Screen*, Vol 19, no. 1, Spring 1978, pp. 58–59; 'Each text is in fact a network of intersecting and overlapping statements: quotations, references, derivations, inversions, etc. A text, any text, consists of a bundle of discourses, each discourse installing its subject of enunciation. This also means that it is misleading to describe a text as a signifying chain, i.e. *one* discursive operation corresponding to one subject-production. As texts are imbrications of discourses, they must necessarily produce series of subject positions. But these subjects can be (and are) mapped on to each other, pulled into place.'

6   T. Todorov, 'Detective Fiction' in *The Poetics of Prose*, Cornell University Press, 1977, pp. 44–47: 'At the base of the whodunit we find a duality, and it is this duality which will guide our description. This novel contains not one but two stories: the story of the crime and the story of the investigation. We might further characterise these two stories by saying that the first – the story of the crime – tells us "what really happened", whereas the second – the story of the investigation – explains "how the reader (or the narrator) has come to know about it". The fundamental point is that this duality is articulated as a duality of times, of temporal orders.'

7   R. Barthes, 'Structural Analysis of Narratives' in *Image–Music–Text*, S. Heath (ed.), London 1978, p. 119.

Applications

The six-gun mystique

John G. Cawelti

However, though the intrinsic dramatic vigor and unity of the Western formula plays the major role in its success, this is not the whole story of the Western's popularity. For we must still ask why a particular artistic form or structure of conventions possesses dramatic power for the audiences who enjoy it, and what sort of dramatic power this is. There seem to be two levels on which this question can be answered. First, we can refer a particular form to some universal conception of types or genres, based presumably on innate qualities or characteristics of the human psyche. According to this approach, which has been followed by various literary theorists from Aristotle to Northrop Frye, a particular work or group of works becomes successful insofar as it effectively carries out an archetypal structure, which is in turn based on either innate human capacities and needs or on fundamental and universal patterns of experience. Using such a universal system as that suggested in Northrop Frye's *Anatomy of Criticism*, it is fairly simple to outline the relationship between the Western and archetypal forms. The Western is a fine example of what Frye calls the *mythos* of romance, a narrative and dramatic structure which he characterizes as one of the four central myths or story forms in literature, the other three being comedy, tragedy, and irony. As Frye defines it, 'the essential element of plot in romance is adventure', and the major adventure which gives form to the romance is the quest. Thus, 'the complete form of the romance is clearly the successful quest, and such a completed form has three main stages: the stage of the perilous journey and the preliminary minor adventures; the crucial struggle, usually some kind of battle in which either the hero or his foe, or both, must die; and the exaltation of the hero'.[25] These characteristics certainly fit the Western. The central action of chase and pursuit dramatizes the quest, the climactic shoot-down embodies the crucial battle, and the movement of the hero from alienation to commitment is an example of the 'recognition of the hero, who has clearly proved himself to be a hero even if he does not survive the conflict'.

Other characteristics of romance, as Frye defines them are also clearly present in the Western. The struggle between hero and villain; the tendency to present both figures as coming not from the town but from the surrounding landscape; the way in which the hero's action is commonly associated with the establishment of law and order. These qualities also relate the Western to romances of many different cultures and periods.

> The central form of romance is dialectical: everything is focussed on a conflict between the hero and his enemy, and all the reader's values are bound up with the hero. Hence the hero of romance is analogous to the mythical Messiah or deliverer who comes from an upper world, and his enemy is analogous to the demonic powers

of a lower world. The conflict however takes place in, or at any rate primarily concerns, our world in the middle.[26]

Even smaller details of the basic pattern of romance discussed by Frye find their echo in the Western. For example, there is the contrast between schoolmarm and dance-hall girl – 'a polarization may thus be set up between the lady of duty and the lady of pleasure' – the central role of the horse – 'the dragon [has] his opposite in the friendly or helping animals that are so conspicuous in romance, among which the horse who gets the hero to his quest has naturally a central place' – and there is the noble Indian, the natural man who lends some of his power to the hero – 'the characters who elude the moral antithesis of heroism and villainy generally are or suggest spirits of nature. They represent partly the moral neutrality of the intermediate world of nature and partly a world of mystery which is glimpsed but never seen, and which retreats when approached. . . . Such characters are, more or less, children of nature who can be brought to serve the hero'.[27]

Many Western writers have been fully aware of the relationship between the cowboy hero and the traditional figures of romance. Owen Wister, who created his influential Virginian at least partly in the model of the chivalric knight of the middle ages, explicitly expressed this relationship in his essay on 'The Evolution of the Cow-Puncher':

> No doubt Sir Launcelot bore himself with a grace and breeding of which our unpolished fellow of the cattle trail has only the latent possibility; but in personal daring and in skill as to the horse, the knight and the cowboy are nothing but the same Saxon of different environments, the polished man in London and the man unpolished in Texas; and no hoof in Sir Thomas Malory shakes the crumbling plains with quadruped sounds more valiant than the galloping that has echoed from the Rio Grande to the Big Horn Mountains.[28]

However, though we are undoubtedly correct in ascribing some of the shape and effectiveness of the Western to the fact that it is a contemporary embodiment of a literary pattern which has demonstrated nearly universal human appeal by its appearance in most cultures, we are still faced with the problem of the particular cultural formula which has evolved as the major specific example of this universal narrative and dramatic pattern. In addition to the formula's built-in artistic unity and its relation to archetypal patterns, we must also examine its primary cultural dimensions of game, ritual and collective dream.

Romance, as Frye's many examples indicate, comes at all levels of complexity and sophistication. There are romances as elaborate and arcane as Spenser's *Fairie Queen* and as simple as the comic strip adventures of Superman and Batman. These differences in complexity and sophistication reflect the cultural area in which the romance functions. The romances of a leisured aristocratic class with elaborately developed manners and a number of conscious cultural ideals are usually more elaborate than the folk-tales which have grown out of homogeneous village cultures with less complex, less self-conscious cultural ideals. The conditions of successful mass romances are somewhat different from both aristocratic and folk romance. In heterogeneous modern societies, widely successful romances must be so constructed as to be accessible to diverse groups with rather divergent interests and values. Consequently they tend to resemble games in the clarity of their rules and patterns of action. As I have indicated earlier this game-like aspect of the formula permits anyone who knows the 'rules' – and in our culture children are instructed in the rules of the Western from a very early age – to enjoy and appreciate the fine points of play, as well as to experience the sense of ego-enhancement that comes when 'our side' wins.

Part of the Western's wide popularity then is due to the fact that it is a brilliantly articulated game whose formula structure has evolved narrative counterparts to the primary characteristics of a game structure: 1) a game must have clearly opposing players – usually in the large spectator sports, two sides. These form basic moral reference points to which the viewer or participant relates with clearly positive or negative feelings. Similarly in most clearly differentiated popular formulas we have sides: a hero or group of good people – the home team – and a villain or band of evil doers – the visitors. The relations between these sides dominate the action. 2) A game has a set of rules indicating which actions are legitimate and which are not: only certain moves can take place and they must happen in a certain order and move toward a particular result. Analogously, a formula story has a particular pattern of expectations. Certain situations occur and others are definitely excluded by the rules. 3) Finally, a game takes place on a certain kind of board or field whose shape and markings indicate the significance of particular actions. The formula story also depends on a particular kind of setting: an abstracted social structure and landscape which give meaning to particular actions. In this way, the Western hero's relation to the town is analogous to the football player's relation to the line of scrimmage.

Let us now see how these three characteristics are built into the Western formula. First, since a game is basically determined by its board or field, so a popular formula tends to be initially characterized by its setting. Thus, the secret-agent story and the Western differ in that one takes place in a setting dominated by the struggle of rival nations and is usually set in a contemporaneous time, while the other unravels the major points of social and geographical topography with an advancing civilization on one side and a savage wilderness on the other. Against this background, a three-sided game is played out. There is the group of townspeople who stand for the whole complex of values associated with civilization; there are the villains who are characterized by their rejection or perversion of these values and by their closeness to the savagery and lawlessness of the surrounding wilderness; and finally, there is the hero whose part is basically that of the man in the middle. Unlike the townspeople the hero possesses or comes to possess the savage skills of violence and the lawless individualism of the villain group, but he is needed by and finally acts on the side of the group of townspeople. The pattern of expectations which characterizes the Western is too complex to spell out in any detail here, but some of its main lines can be indicated. There must be a series of acts of violence to set the three-sided game in operation and to provoke and justify final destruction of the villain in such a way as to benefit the good group. Usually these acts are worked out in a sequence of chase and pursuit which can make use of the Western field of action and its particular form of movement, the horse, to the greatest extent. The goal of the game is to resolve the conflict between the hero's alienation and his commitment to the good group of townspeople. Thus, Westerns can end in many different ways. Sometimes the hero gets killed; sometimes he rides off into the desert; sometimes he marries the rancher's daughter and becomes a leading citizen. As I have already noted, important differences in cultural attitude are indicated by changes in the kinds of resolution which are the most common ways of ending the 'game' at different times. It is no doubt significant that the great majority of Westerns in the first 3 decades of the twentieth century follow Wister's *The Virginian* in creating plots of romantic synthesis. The typical Zane Grey story or pulp Western of the 20s and 30s associated the hero's victory over the villain with his assimilation into the developing society. Usually, he married the school teacher or the rancher's daughter. After World War II however, the most significant Westerns have dealt with the gunfighter. In the typical gunfighter story the hero's violence, though necessary to the defeat of evil, nonetheless disqualifies him for the civilized society which he is saving. Similarly, in this more recent type of Western, the group of townspeople is usually presented in a far more ambiguous way, as if there were some question whether they merited the hero's sacrifice.

The social implications of these changing resolutions to the Western 'game' indicate another dimension of the formula. I suggested earlier that popular formulas can be partly understood as social rituals. The structure of the Western bears this out. A ritual is a means of reaffirming certain basic cultural values, resolving tensions and establishing a sense of continuity between present and past. The Western, with its historical setting, its thematic emphasis on the establishment of law and order, and its resolution of the conflict between civilization and savagery on the frontier, is a kind of foundation ritual. It presents for our renewed contemplation that epic moment when the frontier passed from the old way of life into social and cultural forms directly connected with the present. By dramatising this moment, and associating it with the hero's agency, the Western reaffirms the act of foundation. In this sense, the Western is like a Fourth of July ceremony. Moreover, while the Fourth of July ceremony has no room for dramatic conflict and ambiguity of values, the Western is able to explore not only what was gained, but what was lost in the movement of American history. In other words, the Western is effective as a social ritual because within its basic structure of resolution and reaffirmation, it indirectly confronts those uncertainties and conflicts of values which have always existed in American culture, but which have become increasingly strong in the twentieth century.

The dialectical structure of the Western – its opposition of townspeople and savages with the hero in the middle – encourages the expression of value oppositions. The same kind of plot patterns which made it possible for Cooper to explore his ambiguous feelings about civilization and nature, served Owen Wister's sense of a conflict between traditional and modern America. Still more recently, the Western dialectic has focussed on mid-twentieth century conflicts about the relation between law and order and private violence. Since Wister demonstrated so clearly that the nineteenth century Western formula could be resurrected from the dime novel, and made to embody contemporaneous adult attitudes and value conflicts, the Western has been important as a popular mode of exploring and resolving cultural tensions. We can still see this process in operation at the present day as Westerns explore some of the primary concerns of our own time such as racial conflict and collective violence. Generally, the Western's treatment of these issues is ritualistic rather than original. The almost wholly commercial circumstances of its creation, the fact that it is defined as entertainment, and the broad popular audience to which it appeals place a premium on the resolution of conflict and the affirmation of existing cultural values. Consequently, the Western rarely makes a truly profound or transcendent statement about the conflicts it expresses. Also, the highly conventionalized tradition of the Western does not encourage new interpretations of the American past. Nevertheless, within its limits, the Western formula does allow serious attempts on the part of creators and audience to relate contemporaneous conflicts to a vision of the American past. Perhaps for this reason, such traditional American rituals as the Fourth of July ceremony have increasingly declined into carnivals and fireworks displays, while the Western has continued to flourish.

Notes

25 Frye, p. 186.
26 Frye, p. 186.
27 Frye, pp. 196–197.
28 Owen Wister, 'The Evolution of the Cowpuncher', in *Red Men and White*, vol. 6 of *The Writings of Owen Wister* (New York: MacMillan Co., 1928), p. xxvii.

READING 18

'Thrilling structures? science fiction from the early *Amazing* and detective fiction'

Elizabeth Kwasniewski

Fully to understand and interpret the popularity of formulaic stories . . . it must be remembered that they are, first of all, created for the purpose of enjoyment and pleasure. In this regard, it is no accident that their plots are quite predictable, and thus are insignificant for their own sake; for their entertainment value lies precisely in their satisfying a demand of their readers, that of emotional reinforcement.

To illustrate how a formulaic structure performs this psychological function, we might consider as typical examples some of the sf short stories published in *Amazing Stories* between 1926 and 1946.

. . . I would suggest that one necessary condition for the popularity of sf stories has to do with the structural elements in them which generate definite emotions in their readers. And it is here that sf and detective fiction intersect.

The affinities between sf and detective fiction are nowhere more astoundingly evident than in the sf short stories published in the earliest days of magazine sf. These stories follow a certain structural pattern derived from the detective story. The basic structural rule of a very large proportion of magazine sf is in fact very much the same as in the classical detective novel: both rigorously observe a chronological sequence of the narrative elements which may be called linear-retrospective. The content analysis of sf stories of this type indicates that all the episodes and incidents lead, in a direct or indirect way, to the explanation of the phenomena that disturb or threaten the initial status quo, much in the same way that the crime intruding into a fairly conventional and familiar world of a detective story is finally solved and thereby disposed of.

The unprecedented change introduced into the fictive world, such as an invasion of aliens whose motive and purpose are unknown or strange phenomena whose origin remains a mystery, is what Frank Cioffi calls an *anomaly*.[5] This anomaly threatens the safety of an individual or a group of individuals, or even society at large. The chain of events, following one another from the moment the anomaly intrudes itself to that which it is disposed of, is almost unvariably linear. Yet, though the plot develops logically, its logic is mad.

The phenomenon which 'initiates' the action often originates in some unknown, usually dramatic, developments in the past history of an alien civilization whose members have been forced or have decided to invade Earth. In Edmond Hamilton's 'The Comet Doom' (January 1928), for instance, the American scientists have noticed that Earth, whose gravity had been suddenly disturbed, is gradually being pulled into the head of an oncoming comet. The collision with the approaching celestial body would mean the swift asphyxiation of all terrestrial life. As the story develops, it turns out that the unaccountable behavior of Earth is caused by an intervention of the alien creatures, whose civilization is on the edge of extinction because they have exhausted their nuclear resources indispensable to the survival of their form of organic life. The purpose of their mission, therefore, is to draw Earth into the comet's body and to secure, in this way, the source of nuclear minerals for themselves.

D.H. Keller's 'The White City' (May 1935), to give another example, tells the story of a New York whose inhabitants are in danger of being exterminated because all the essential functions of the city are being paralysed by a ceaseless fall of snow that keeps covering an entire area up to the roofs of skyscrapers. A similar meteorological anomaly is observed in all big cities throughout the country. Finally, the U.S. government is informed by the members of an alien civilization, whose spaceships hover above Earth, that the snow is produced artificially, and that they intend the destruction of the major cities as a monitory example of what will happen on a world-wide scale if the Earth's governments do not surrender to their rule.

The two stories, as I have briefly summarized them, exemplify a larger body of structurally similar texts. In them, the narrative not only unfolds the plot in linear fashion but also gives pertinent details of the past history which underlies the ongoing sequence of events. To put it differently, the writer gradually provides information allowing the reader to reconstruct, at least fragmentarily, the past history of an alien civilization and to learn about its final stages of development, the period during which its denizens decide to invade Earth. This basically makes the narration retrospective. Obviously sf stories offer an almost unlimited variety of openings, whereas the detective story usually begins with a murder. Yet, in either case, the principal organizing element of the linear-retrospective structure seems to be the same – i.e. the story devolves from the initial mystery.

Of course, not every conceivable puzzle or mystery is able to shape and decide the structure of the story. The puzzle must comprise something serious and decisive, something that is powerful enough to make the action, which naturally goes forward, stop and go back – a sudden death, for example, or a mysterious, unintelligible, and threatening phenomenon. The object is to draw the reader on, not by immediately affording comprehension of what is happening but by immediately withholding it. Precisely because the reader does not understand, he or she is motivated to learn what or who stands behind the surprising and incomprehensible anomaly (in most cases, a result of a vicious act or inextricable from it). . . .

The mysteriousness of the anomaly is initially a source of only a slight uneasiness – of moderate emotional tension – for the reader, who comes to the story expecting to find a description of 'something unusual' at the very outset. Yet as the reader witnesses in the course of action the succeeding stages of struggle between the two thorough-going opponents who invariably figure in such a story, his or her interest, curiosity, and emotional tension increase. These feelings result from the progressive 'crowding' of events and information, the growth of evidence that, through a prolonged period of intensifying or playing with the reader's curiosity, leads him or her to perceive the terrible mystery. Thereupon the reader can enjoy the catharsis of the moment that is the climax of the story, when the puzzle is solved (usually by liquidating the anomaly and reconstructing a distorted reality).

Hamilton's 'The Comet Doom' may serve to illustrate this process. According to the scientific calculations of the speed and movements of the approaching comet, its collision with Earth and the extinction of the human race are inevitable. The reader is led to believe that nothing can be done in the face of such an omnipotent force of nature. His or her anxiety is increased by the lack of information about this phenomenon (something the reader shares with the characters of the story) and also by the growing imminency of the catastrophe. When the aliens, who had orchestrated that event, land on Earth to begin the final preparations for accomplishing their mission, the reader, who is by now in possession of some clues as to their ultimate intentions, 'joins' the attempts of three young men who have decided to baffle the aliens' efforts. Yet the more information the reader obtains about the intent of the comet-creatures – about the technological advances of their civilization over Earth's and the helplessness of homo sapiens in the face of their power – the more his or her curiosity increases, along with emotional uneasiness (and also uncertainty) as to the chances of defeating the aliens. The intensity of the psychological involvement of the reader in the story reaches its peak during the decisive struggle between the two opponents. In formulaic, not necessarily rational terms, the outcome of that struggle is predictable: the individuals with whom the readers empathize must succeed, contrary perhaps to any logical conclusions to which the elements of the narrative might have led. To a fastidious reader, the efforts undertaken by three young men to defeat the all-powerful comet-creatures must seem doomed to failure from the very start. Surprisingly, the protagonists win the battle – which only exemplifies the general rule that the implausible and the improbable are built into the structure of such sf stories, as is also the case with the formulaic structure of a murder mystery; logic is not what the readers are looking for in these texts.

Aydelotte's observations on the reception of the detective fiction formula can likewise be applied to the reception of the early sf stories: '(we) read (detective stories) not to have a new experience, but to repeat in a slightly different form an experience we have had already. Thus, for example, the "surprise" ending is not really a surprise. It is the ending we expect and demand, and we would feel outraged if any other kind of ending were offered to us'.[7] Hence the predictable result of the struggle between the two opponents in 'The Comet Doom', for instance, does not seem to diminish the authenticity of the feelings the reader experiences 'participating' in all the preceding, dramatic developments of the narrative.

. . . .

Even from a quick glance at sf magazine narratives, it is clear that if a story is to be enjoyed by the readers it must, first of all, generate a sensation of fear. In order to perceive fear as a pleasurable experience, however, two conditions must be fulfilled: a dosage of fear cannot be insupportable and it should be immediately followed by the retreat to safety. In his analysis of detective fiction, Porter observes that, the idea of a given level of tolerance to fear suggests that the reason why fans of detective fiction return again and again to a favorite author is that they are certain to find in his works the dosage of fear they know they can enjoy. The movement from exposure to fear and a return from it is characteristic of most popular literature from fairy stories and tales of adventure to gothic novel, mystery story, melodrama, and spy thriller.[8]

In sf stories the protagonist frequently comes under the influence of strange, inexplicable powers, signs, and phenomena which incite a sense of insecurity, then danger, and eventually the feeling of an approaching catastrophe or death. The danger, felt intuitively, 'hangs above' the hero and can hardly be interpreted in any rational terms. It may be manifested in the most innocent gesture, object, or person. This situation frequently makes the protagonist distrust his reasoning, the state of his mental powers (by invariable convention, the protagonist is always male). The hero has a strange urge to submit to danger which counterbalances his urge to resist it – an ambivalence which the reader, too, must feel to be prompted to read on; so that in identifying with the hero the reader likewise becomes a subject within grasp of the hidden powers.

The hero tries to impose a certain order on the unaccountable events and the surrounding hideous chaos. He analyzes the situation in search of the elements which might convince him about some hidden regularity which governs the seemingly unrelated incidents. This period of a deliberately prolonged tension is always followed by 'the return from fear' as the hero manages to suppress the causes responsible for disturbing the status quo of the fictional reality.

Complementing the vast range of emotional feelings stimulated by the structural elements of the sf story are others resulting from the mechanism of projection and identification, by which the reader becomes absorbed with the fictional characters.[9] It may be assumed that readers derive a peculiar kind of psychological satisfaction from the hero's activity: his success creates an illusion of protection and certainty in the fictive world extendable to empirical reality. The protagonists, though obviously stock characters, are presented as shrewd, intelligent men, analytical thinkers whose power of reasoning – of penetrating reality – is overwhelming. . . .

The attractiveness of the sf story's hero seems to be the principal component in the process of identification. The character who lacks vices and is endowed with a strong individuality and 'super human' intelligence stimulates the average imagination by offering a model that invites and inspires emulation. At the same time, the attractive personality remains hollow enough for the reader to fill it with his or her own views, thoughts, and feelings. In other words, it must allow for the reader's construction of an idealized self-image.

A division of characters and moral attitudes into 'black' and 'white' is evident. This clear demarcation line between good and evil becomes blurred in a good many sf novels, making the process of identification more complex if not impossible; but in the magazine sf of the 1930s and '40s there seems to be no place for such moral ambiguities. The evil characters are usually represented by the aliens (e.g. in 'Peril from the Outlands', June 1945), mad scientists (e.g. in 'The Raid from Mars', March 1939), or ordinary criminals (e.g. in 'Suicide Durkee's Last Ride', September 1932).

Several attempts have been made to analyze the relationship between this type of character and the reader.[11] It may be assumed that apart from a reader with a disturbed personality, the process of identification with fictional characters who embody the values hardly acceptable in the reader's empirical world does not take place. Instead one can speak about the process of projecting the inward, subjective feelings of the reader onto outer reality, of endowing the 'bad guys' with those features and emotions the reader does not accept in her or his own personality. This enables the consumers of these stories to justify or act out their aggressive fantasies vicariously, get free from them, and experience a peculiar state of release from the tensions of their own lives.

Unfortunately, the psychological theories which would oppose this last statement are almost equal in number to those which would support it; so that the problem (of identification/projection) remains open from the scientific point of view. It may be suggested, however, that the source of the peculiar pleasure and frequently intense emotions incited by fictional violence and aggressiveness is an awareness of the clash between the personal safety of the reader and the danger to which the fictional characters are exposed. Such fictions, in other words, perhaps offer the possibility 'to explore in fantasy the boundary between the permitted and the forbidden and to experience in a carefully controlled way the possibility of stepping across this boundary'.[12] In his *Poetics*, Aristotle coined a term for this kind of psychological impact a work of art is capable of exerting on its readers: catharsis, understood as a purification of the emotions which are projected onto the fictional object – a process which brings about spiritual renewal or release from these emotional anxieties. Nevertheless, the advocates of a functional approach to the study of literature still await the scientific verification of this concept.

Undertaking to locate the source of the entertainment value of stories, I have been pointing to particular psychological responses which certain structural elements of sf narratives are capable of generating in their readers, as well as to a similarity between sf and detective stories in this respect. These responses resulting from the reader's imaginative ability to enter into the spirit of fictional reality may explain the enduring and widespread popularity of formulaic genres among the mass reading public.

Notes

5 F. Cioffi, *Formula Fiction? An Anatomy of American Science Fiction, 1930–1959,* (Westport, Conn.: Greenwood Press,1982), p. 11.

7 W.O. Aydelotte, 'The Detective Story as a Historical Source', in *Dimensions of Detective Fiction*, eds. Larry N. Landrum, Pat Browne and Ray B. Browne (Popular Press,1976), p. 69.

8 D. Porter, *The Pursuit of Crime: Art and Ideology in Detective Fiction* (Yale University Press,1981), p. 102.

9 E. Morin in his analysis of mass culture regards these mechanisms as inevitable in the reception of all the contents of mass literature. See E. Morin, *Duch Czasu* (Krakow, 1965), p. 11.

11 A detailed analysis of the cathartic theory of represented violence can be found in L. Berkowitz, *Aggression: A Social Psychological Analysis* (New York: McGraw-Hill, 1962).

12 Cawelti, *Adventure*, p. 35.

(From *Foundation*, No. 38, 1986/87)

'The narrative structure in Fleming'

Umberto Eco

It is our plan to devise a descriptive table of the narrative structure in Ian Fleming while seeking to evaluate for each structural element the probable incidence upon the reader's sensitivity. We shall try, therefore, to distinguish such a narrative at five levels:

(1) The juxtaposition of the characters and of values.
(2) Play situations and the plot as a 'game'.
(3) A Manichean ideology.
(4) Literary techniques.
(5) Literature as montage.

Our enquiry covers the range of the following novels listed in order of publication (the date of composition was presumably a year earlier in each case):

Casino Royale, 1953
Live and Let Die, 1954
Moonraker, 1955
Diamonds are Forever, 1956
From Russia with Love, 1957
Dr. No, 1958
Goldfinger, 1959
Thunderball, 1961
On Her Majesty's Secret Service, 1963
You Only Live Twice, 1964

We shall refer also to the stories in *For Your Eyes Only* (1960), and to *The Man with the Golden Gun* published in 1965. But we shall not take into consideration *The Spy who Loved Me* (1962), which seems quite untypical.

1. The juxtaposition of the characters and of values

The novels of Fleming seem to be built on a series of 'oppositions' which allow a limited number of permutations and reactions. These dichotomies constitute a constant feature around which minor couples rotate and they form, from novel to novel, variations on them. We have here singled out fourteen couples, four of which are contrasted to four actual characters, while the others form a conflict of values, variously personified by the four basic characters. The fourteen couples are:

(a) Bond – M
(b) Bond – Villain
(c) Villain – Woman
(d) Woman – Bond
(e) Free World – Soviet Union
(f) Great Britain – Countries not Anglo-Saxon
(g) Duty – Sacrifice
(h) Cupidity – Ideals

(i)   Love – Death
(j)   Chance – Planning
(k)   Luxury – Discomfort
(l)   Excess – Moderation
(m)   Perversion – Innocence
(n)   Loyalty – Disloyalty

These pairs do not represent 'vague' elements but 'simple' ones that are immediate and universal, and if we consider the range of each pair we see that the variants allowed cover a vast field and in fact include all the narrative ideas of Fleming.

. . . .

Started by M on the road of Duty (at all costs), Bond enters into conflict with the Villain. The opposition brings into play diverse virtues, some of which are only variants of the basic couples previously paired and listed. Bond indubitably represents Beauty and Virility as opposed to the Villain, who appears often monstrous and sexually impotent. The monstrosity of the Villain is a constant point, but to emphasize it we must here introduce an idea of the method which will also apply in examining the other couples. Among the variants we must consider also the existence of secondary characters whose functions are understood only if they are seen as 'variants' of one of the principal personages, some of whose characteristics they 'wear'. The vicarious roles function usually for the Woman and for the Villain; also for M – certain collaborators with Bond represent the M figures; for example Mathis in *Casino Royale*, who preaches Duty in the appropriate M manner (albeit with a cynical and Gallic air). As to the characteristics of the Villain, let us consider them in order. In *Casino Royale* Le Chiffre is pallid and smooth, with a crop of red hair, an almost feminine mouth, false teeth of expensive quality, small ears with large lobes and hairy hands. He did not smile. In *Live and Let Die*, Mr. Big, a Haiti Negro, had a head that resembles a football, twice the normal size, and almost spherical; 'the skin was grey-black, taut and shining like the face of a week-old corpse in the river. It was hairless, except for some grey-brown fluff above the ears. There were no eyebrows and no eyelashes and the eyes were extraordinarily far apart so that one could not focus on them both, but only on one at a time. . . . They were animal eyes, not human, and they seemed to blaze'. The gums were pale pink.

. . . .

In *From Russia with Love* the villain appears in the shape of three vicarious figures: Red Grant, the professional murderer in the pay of Smersh, with short, sandy-coloured eyelashes, colourless and opaque blue eyes, a small, cruel mouth, innumerable freckles on his milk-white skin, and deep, wide pores; Colonel Grubozaboyschikov, head of Smersh, has a narrow and sharp face, round eyes like two polished marbles, weighed down by two flabby pouches, a broad and grim mouth and a shaven skull; finally Rosa Klebb, with the humid pallid lip stained with nicotine, the raucous voice, flat and devoid of emotion, is five feet four, no curves, dumpy arms, short neck, too sturdy ankles, grey hairs gathered in a tight 'obscene' bun. She has shiny yellow-brown eyes, thick glasses, a sharp nose white with powder and large nostrils. 'The wet trap of a mouth, that went on opening and shutting as if it was operated by wires under the chin' completes the appearance of a sexually neuter person.

. . . .

The Villain is born in an ethnic area that stretches from central Europe to the Slav countries and to the Mediterranean basin: as a rule he is of mixed blood and his origins are complex and obscure; he is asexual or homosexual, or at any rate is not sexually normal: he has exceptional inventive and organisational qualities which help him acquire immense wealth and by means of which he usually works to help Russia: to this end he conceives a plan of fantastic character and dimensions, worked out to the smallest detail, intended to create serious difficulties either for England or the Free World in general. In the figure of the Villain, in fact, there are gathered the negative values which we have distinguished in some pairs of opposites, the Soviet Union and countries which are not Anglo-Saxon (the racial convention blames particularly the Jews, the Germans, the Slavs and the Italians always depicted as half-breeds), Cupidity elevated to the dignity of paranoia, Planning as technological methodology, satrapic luxury, physical and psychical Excess, physical and moral Perversion, radical Disloyalty.

. . . .

To the typical qualities of the Villain are opposed the Bond characteristics, in particular Loyalty to the Service, Anglo-Saxon Moderation opposed to the excess of the halfbreeds, the selection of Discomfort and the acceptance of Sacrifices as against the ostentatious luxury of the enemy, the stroke of opportunistic genius (Chance) opposed to the cold Planning which it defeats, the sense of an Ideal opposed to Cupidity (Bond in various cases wins from the Villain in gambling, but as a rule returns the enormous sums won to the Service or to the girl of the moment, as occurred with Jill Masterson; thus even when he has money it is no longer a primary object). For the rest some oppositions function not only in the Bond-Villain relationship, but even internally in the behaviour of Bond himself; thus Bond is as a rule loyal but does not disdain to overcome a cheating enemy by a deceitful trick, and to blackmail him (cf. *Moonraker* or *Goldfinger*). Even Excess and Moderation, Chance and Planning are opposed in the acts and decisions of Bond himself. Duty and sacrifice appear as elements of internal debate each time that Bond knows he must prevent the plan of the Villain at the risk of his life, and in those cases, the patriotic ideal (Great Britain and the Free World) takes the upper hand. He calls also on the racialist need to show the superiority of the Briton. In Bond there are also opposed Luxury (the choice of good food, care in dressing, preference for sumptuous hotels, love of the gambling table, invention of cocktails etc.) and Discomfort (Bond is always ready to abandon the easy life, even when it appears in the guise of a Woman who offers herself, to face a new aspect of Discomfort, the acutest point of which is torture).

We have discussed the Bond-Villain dichotomy at length because in fact it embodies all the characteristics of the opposition between Eros and Thanatos, the beginning of pleasure and the beginning of reality, culminating in the moment of torture (in *Casino Royale* explicitly theorised as a sort of erotic relationship between the torturer and the tortured).

This opposition is perfected in the relationship between the Villain and the Woman; Vesper is tyrannised and blackmailed by the Soviet, and therefore by Le Chiffre; Solitaire is the slave of Mr. Big; Tiffany Case is dominated by the Spangs; Tatiana is the slave of Rosa Klebb and of the Soviet Government in general; Jill and Tilly Masterson are dominated, in different degrees, by Goldfinger, and Pussy Galore works to his orders; Domino Vitali is subservient to the wishes of Blofeld through the physical relationship with the vicarious figure of Emilio

Largo; the English girl guests of Piz Gloria are under the hypnotic control of Blofeld and the virginal surveillance of Irma Blunt; while Honeychile has a purely symbolic relationship with the power of Dr. No, wandering pure and untroubled on the shores of his cursed island, except that at the end Dr. No offers her naked body to the crabs (Honeychile has been dominated by the Villain through the vicarious effort of the brutal Mander who had violated her, and had justly punished Mander by causing a scorpion to kill him, anticipating the revenge of No – which had recourse to crabs); and finally Kissy Suzuki lived on her island in the shade of the cursed castle of Blofeld, suffering a domination that was purely allegorical, shared by the whole population of the place. In an intermediate position is Gala Brand, who is an agent of the Service but who became the secretary of Hugo Drax and established a relationship of submission to him. In most of the cases this relationship culminated in the torture which the woman underwent along with Bond. Here the Love-Death pair function, also in the sense of a more intimate erotic union of the two through their common trial.

Dominated by the Villain, however, Fleming's woman has already been previously conditioned to domination, life for her having assumed the role of the villain. The general scheme is (1) the girl is beautiful and good; (2) has been made frigid and unhappy by severe trials suffered in adolescence; (3) this has conditioned her to the service of the Villain; (4) through meeting Bond she appreciates human nature in all its richness; (5) Bond possesses her but in the end loses her.

This curriculum is common to Vesper, Solitaire, Tiffany, Tatiana, Honeychile, Domino; rather hinted at for Gala, equally shared by the three representative women of Goldfinger (Jill, Tilly and Pussy – the first two have had a sad past, but only the third has been violated by her uncle: Bond possessed the first and the third, the second is killed by the Villain, the first tortured with gold paint, the second and third are lesbians and Bond redeems only the third; and so forth); more diffuse and uncertain for the group of girls on Piz Gloria – each had had an unhappy past, but Bond in fact possessed only one of them (similarly he marries Tracy whose past was unhappy because of a series of unions, dominated by her father Draco, and was killed in the end by Blofeld, who realises at this point his domination and ends by Death the relationship of Love which she entertained for Bond. Kissy Susaki has been made unhappy by a Hollywoodian experience which has made her chary of life and of men.

In every case Bond loses each of these women, either by her own will or that of another (in the case of Gala it is the woman who marries somebody else, although unwillingly) – either at the end of the novel or at the beginning of the following one (as happened with Tiffany Case). Thus, in the moment in which the Woman solves the opposition to the Villain by entering with Bond into a purificating-purified, saving-saved relationship, she returns to the domination of the negative. In this there is a lengthy combat between the couple Perversion-Purity (sometimes external, as in the relationship of Rosa Klebb and Tatiana) which makes her similar to the persecuted virgin of Richardsonian memory. The bearer of purity, notwithstanding and in spite of the mire, exemplary subject for an alternation of embrace-torture, she would appear likely to resolve the contrast between the chosen race and the non-Anglo-Saxon halfbreed, since she often belongs to an ethnically inferior breed; but when the erotic relationship always ends with a form of death, real or symbolic, Bond resumes willy-nilly the purity of Anglo-Saxon celibacy. The race remains uncontaminated.

2. Play situations and the plot as a 'game'

The various pairs of opposites (of which we have considered only a few possible variants) seem like the elements of an *ars combinatoria* with fairly elementary rules. It is clear that in the engagement of the two poles of each couple there are, in the course of the novel, alternative solutions; the reader does not know at which point of the story the Villain defeats Bond or Bond defeats the Villain, and so on. But towards the end of the book the algebra has to follow a prearranged pattern: as in the Chinese (sic) game that 007 and Tanaka play at the beginning of *You Only Live Twice*, hand beats fist, fist beats two fingers, two fingers beat hand. M beats Bond. Bond beats the Villain, the Villain beats Woman, even if at first Bond beats Woman; the Free World beats the Soviet Union, England beats the Impure Countries, Death beats Love, Moderation beats Excess, and so forth.

This interpretation of the plot in terms of a game is not accidental. The books of Fleming are dominated by situations that we call 'play situations'. First of all there are several archetypal situations like the Journey and the Meal; the Journey may be by Machine (and here there occurs a rich symbolism of the automobile, typical of our century), by Train (another archetype, this time of obsolescent type), by Aeroplane, or by Ship. But here it is realised that as a rule a meal, a pursuit by machine or a mad race by train, always take the form of a challenge, a game. Bond decides the choice of foods as though they formed the pieces of a puzzle, prepares for the meal with the same scrupulous attention to method as he prepares for a game of Bridge (see the convergence, in a means-end connection, of the two elements in *Moonraker*) and he intends the meal as a factor in the game. Similarly, train and machine are the elements of a wager against an adversary: before the journey is finished one of the two has finished his moves and given checkmate.

At this point it is useless to record the occurrence of the play situations, in the true and proper sense of conventional games of chance, in each book. Bond always gambles and wins, against the Villain or with some vicarious figure. The detail with which these games are described will be the subject of further consideration in the section which we shall dedicate to literary technique; here it must be said that if these games occupy a prominent space it is because they form a reduced and formalised model of the more general play situation that is the novel. The novel, given the rules of combination of opposing couples, is fixed as a sequence of 'moves' inspired by the code, and constituted according to a perfectly prearranged scheme.

The invariable scheme is the following:

A. M moves and gives a task to Bond.
B. The Villain moves and appears to Bond (perhaps in alternative forms).
C. Bond moves and gives a first check to the Villain or the Villain gives first check to Bond.
D. Woman moves and shows herself to Bond.
E. Bond consumes Woman: possesses her or begins her seduction.
F. The Villain captures Bond (with or without Woman, or at different moments).
G. The Villain tortures Bond (with or without Woman).
H. Bond conquers the Villain (kills him, or kills his representative or helps at their killing).
I. Bond convalescing enjoys Woman, whom he then loses.

The scheme is invariable in the sense that all the elements are always present in every novel (so that it might be affirmed that the fundamental rule of the game is 'Bond moves and mates in eight moves' – but due to the ambivalence Love-Death, so to speak, 'The Villain counter-moves and mates in eight moves'). It is not imperative that the moves always be in the same sequence. A minute detailing of the ten novels under consideration would yield several examples of a set scheme which we might call A. B. C. D. E. F. G. H. I. (for example *Dr No*), but often there are inversions and variations. Sometimes Bond meets the Villain at the beginning of the volume and gives him a first check, and only later receives his instructions from M: this is the case with *Goldfinger*, which then presents a different scheme B. C. D. E. A. C. D. F. G. D. H. E. H. I., where it is possible to notice repeated moves. There are two encounters and three games played with the Villain, two seductions and three encounters with women, a first flight of the Villain after his defeat and his ensuing death, etc. In *From Russia* the company of Villains increases, through the presence of the ambiguous Kerim, in conflict with a secondary Villain Krilenku, and the two mortal duels of Bond with Red Grant and with Rosa Klebb, who was arrested only after having grievously wounded Bond, so that the scheme, highly complicated, is B. B. B. B. D. A. (B. B. C.). E. F. G. H. G. H. (I.). There is a long prologue in Russia with the parade of the Villain figures and the first connection between Tatiana and Rosa Klebb, the sending of Bond to Turkey, a long interlude in which Kerim and Krilenku appear and the latter is defeated; the seduction of Tatiana, the flight by train with the torture suffered by the murdered Kerim, the victory over Red Grant, the second round with Rosa Klebb who, while being defeated, inflicts serious injury upon Bond. In the train and during his convalescence, Bond enjoys love interludes with Tatiana before the final separation.

Even the basic concept of torture undergoes variations, and sometimes consists in a direct injustice, sometimes in a kind of succession or course of horrors that Bond must undergo, either by the explicit will of the Villain (*Dr No*) or accidentally to escape from the Villain, but always as a consequence of the moves of the Villain (e.g., a tragic escape in the snow, pursuit, avalanche, hurried flight through the Swiss countryside in *On Her Majesty's Service*).

Beside the sequence of fundamental moves there are numerous side-issues which enrich the narrative by unforeseen events, without, however, altering the basic scheme.

. . . .

. . . the plot of each book by Fleming is, by and large, like this: Bond is sent to a given place to avert a 'science-fiction' plan by a monstrous individual of uncertain origin and definitely not English who, making use of his organisational or productive activity, not only earns more money but helps the cause of the enemies of the West. In facing this monstrous being Bond meets a woman who is dominated by him and frees her from her past, establishing with her an erotic relationship interrupted by capture, on the part of the Villain, and by torture. But Bond defeats the Villain, who dies horribly, and rests from his great efforts in the arms of the woman, though he is destined to lose her. One might wonder how, within such limits, it is possible for the inventive fiction-writer to function, since he must respond to a wealth of sensations and unforeseeable surprises. In fact, it is typical of the detective story, either of investigation or of action; there is no variation of deeds, but rather the repetition of a habitual scheme in which the reader can recognise something he has already seen and of which he has grown fond. Under the guise of a machine that produces information the detective story, on the contrary, produces redundancy; pretending to rouse the reader, in fact it reconfirms him in a sort of imaginative laziness, and creates escape not by narrating the unknown but the already known. In the pre-Fleming detective story the immutable scheme is formed by the personality of the detective and of his colleagues, by his method of work and by his police, and within this scheme events are unravelled that are unexpected (and most unexpected of all will be the figure of the culprit). But in the novels of Fleming the scheme follows the same chain of events and has the same characters, and it is always known from the beginning who is the culprit, also his characteristics and his plans. The reader's pleasure consists of finding himself immersed in a game of which he knows the pieces and the rules – and perhaps the outcome – drawing pleasure simply from following the minimal variations by which the victor realises his objective.

We might compare a novel by Fleming to a game of football, in which we know beforehand the place, the number and the personalities of the players, the rules of the game, the fact that everything will take place within the area of the great pitch; except that in a game of football the final information remains unknown till the very end: who will win? It would be more accurate to compare these books to a game of basketball played by the Harlem Globe Trotters against a small local team. We know with absolute confidence that they will win: the pleasure lies in watching the trained virtuosity with which the Globe Trotters defer the final moment, with what ingenious deviations they reconfirm the foregone conclusion, with what trickeries they make rings round their opponents. The novels of Fleming exploit in exemplarary measure that element of foregone play which is typical of the escape machine geared for the entertainment of the masses. Perfect in their mechanism, such machines represent the narrative structure which works upon obvious material and does not aspire to describe ideological details. It is true that such structures inevitably indicate ideological positions, but these ideological positions do not derive so much from the structural contents as from the method of constructing the contents into a narrative.

3. A Manichean ideology

The novels of Fleming have been variously accused of McCarthyism, of Fascism, of the cult of excess and violence, of racialism, and so on. It is difficult, after the analysis we have carried out, to maintain that Fleming is not inclined to consider the British superior to all Oriental or Mediterranean races, or to maintain that Fleming does not profess a heartfelt anti-Communism. Yet, it is significant that he ceased to identify the wicked with Russia as soon as the international situation rendered Russia less menacing *according to the general opinion*; it is significant that, while he is introducing the coloured gang of Mr. Big, Fleming is profuse in his acknowledgement of the new African races and of their contribution to contemporary civilisation (Negro gangsterism would represent a proof of the cohesion attained in each country by the coloured people); it is significant that the suspect of Jewish blood in comparison with other bad characters should be allowed a note as to his guilt. (Perhaps to prove by absolving the inferior races that Fleming no longer shares the blind chauvinism of the common man.) Thus suspicion arises that our author does not characterise his creations in such and such a manner as a result of an ideological opinion but purely from reaction to popular demand.

Fleming intends, with the cynicism of the disillusioned, to build an effective narrative apparatus. To do so he decides to rely upon the most secure and universal principles, and puts into play archetypal elements which are precisely those that have proved successful in traditional tales. Let us recall for a moment the pairs of characters that we placed in opposition: M is the King and Bond the Cavalier entrusted with a mission; Bond is the Cavalier and the Villain is the Dragon; the Lady and Villain stand for Beauty and the Beast; Bond restores the Lady to the fullness of spirit and to her senses, he is the Prince who rescues Sleeping Beauty; between the Free World and the Soviet Union, England and the non-Anglo-Saxon countries represent the primitive epic relationship between the Chosen Race and the Lower Race, between Black and White, Good and Bad.

Fleming is a racialist in the sense that any artist is one if, to represent the devil, he depicts him with oblique eyes; in the sense that a nurse is one who, wishing to frighten children with the bogey-man, suggests that he is black.

It is singular that Fleming should be anti-Communist with the same lack of discrimination as he is anti-Nazi and anti-German. It isn't that in one case he is reactionary and in the other democratic. He is simply Manichean for operative reasons: he sees the world as made up of good and evil forces in conflict.

Fleming seeks elementary oppositions: to personify primitive and universal forces he has recourse to popular opinion. In a time of international tensions there are popular notions like that of 'wicked Communism' just as there are of the unpunished Nazi criminal. Fleming uses them both in a sweeping, uncritical manner.

At the most, he tempers his choice with irony, but the irony is completely masked, and reveals itself only by being incredibly exaggerated. In *From Russia* his Soviet men are so monstrous, so improbably evil that it seems impossible to take them seriously. And yet in his brief preface Fleming insists that all the atrocities that he narrates are absolutely true. He has chosen the path of fable, and fable must be taken as truthful if it is not to become a satirical fairy-tale. The author seems almost to write his books for a two-fold reading public, aimed at those who will take them as gospel truth or at those who see their humour. But their tone is authentic, credible, ingenious, plainly aggressive. A man who chooses to write in this way is neither Fascist nor racialist; he is only a cynic, a deviser of tales for general consumption.

If Fleming is a reactionary at all, it is not because he identifies the figure of 'evil' with a Russian or a Jew. He is reactionary because he makes use of stock figures. The user of such figures which personify the Manichean dichotomy sees things in black and white, is always dogmatic and intolerant – in short, reactionary; while he who avoids set figures and recognises nuances, and distinctions, and admits contradictions, is democratic. Fleming is conservative as, basically, the fable, any fable, is conservative: it is the static inherent dogmatic conservatism of fairy-tales and myths, which transmit an elementary wisdom, constructed and communicated by a simple play of light and shade, and they transmit it by indestructable images which do not permit critical distinction. If Fleming is a 'Fascist' it is because the ability to pass from mythology to argument, the tendency to govern by making use of myths and fetishes, are typical of Fascism.

In the mythological background the very names of the protagonists participate, by suggesting in an image or in a pun the fixed character of the person from the start, without any possibility of conversion or change. (Impossible to be called *Snow White* and not to be as white as snow, in face and spirit.) The wicked man lives by gambling? He will be called *Red* and *Grant* if he works for money, duly granted. A Korean professional killer by unusual means will be *Oddjob*, one obsessed with gold *Auric Goldfinger*, without insisting on the symbolism of a wicked man who is called *No*, perhaps the half-lacerated face of *Hugo Drax* would be conjured up by the incisive onomatopoeia of his name. . . . And if the name Bond has been chosen, as Fleming affirms, almost by chance, to give the character an absolutely common appearance, then it would be by chance, but also by guidance, that this model of style and of success evokes the luxuries of Bond Street or Treasury Bonds.

By now it is clear how the novels of Fleming have attained such a wide success; they build up a network of elementary associations, achieving a dynamism that is original and profound. And he pleases the sophisticated readers who here distinguish, with a feeling of aesthetic pleasure, the purity of the primitive epic impudently and maliciously translated into current terms; and applaud in Fleming the cultured man, whom they recognise as one of themselves, naturally the most clever and broadminded.

(from *The Bond Affair*, 1966)

PART 4

Ideology, readers, pleasure: post-structuralism, deconstruction, psychoanalysis

Theory and methodology

20 L. Althusser, 'Ideology and Ideological State Apparatuses' (1971)
21 English Studies Group, CCS University of Birmingham, 'Recent Developments in English Studies at the Centre' (1980)
22 R. Bromley, 'Natural Boundaries: The Social Function of Popular Fiction' (1978)
23 P. Macherey, *A Theory of Literary Production* (1978), (Chapters 14 and 15)
24 R. Barthes, 'The Death of the Author' (1968)
25 R. Barthes, *The Pleasure of the Text* (1973)
26 S. Hall, 'A Critical Survey of the Theoretical and Practical Work of the Past Ten Years' (1976)
27 T. Bennett, 'Marxism and Popular Fiction' (1981)
28 S. Freud, 'Anxiety' (1926), 'The Uncanny' (1919), 'Totem and Taboo' (1912–13), 'Fetishism' (1927), 'Medusa's Head' (1922)
29 J. Lacan, 'The Dream of Irma's Injection' (1954–5)
30 O. Rank, *The Double: A Psychoanalytic Study* (1914)
31 J. Kristeva, *The Powers of Horror* (1980)

Applications

32 B. Dixon, *Catching them Young 2 – Political Ideas in Children's Fiction* (1977)
33 J. Palmer, 'Thrillers: the Deviant Behind the Consensus' (1973)
34 T. Moylan, *Demand the Impossible: Science Fiction and the Utopian Imagination* (1986)
35 J. Grixti, *Terrors of Uncertainty: The Cultural Contexts of Horror Fiction* (1989)
36 N. Carroll, *The Philosophy of Horror* (1990)
37 R. Wood, 'An Introduction to the Modern American Horror Film' (1984)
38 C. Clover, *Men, Women and Chain Saws: Gender in the Modern Horror Film* (1992)
39 M. Dolar, '"I shall be with you on your Wedding Night": Lacan and the Uncanny' (1991)
40 R. Dadoun, 'Fetishism in the Horror Film' (1989)

41 B. Creed, *The Monstrous-Feminine: Film, Feminism and Psychoanalysis* (1993)
42 K. Silverman, *The Acoustic Mirror* (1988)
43 C. Kaplan, 'An unsuitable genre for a feminist?' (1986)
44 A. McRobbie, '*Jackie*: An Ideology of Adolescent Femininity' (1978)
45 J. Batsleer, 'Pulp in the Pink' (1981)
46 A. Light, 'Returning to Manderley: Romance Fiction, Female Sexuality and Class' (1984)
47 E. Frazer, 'Teenage Girls Reading *Jackie*' (1987)
48 C. Belsey, *Critical Practice* (1980)

Problems with structuralism

Many readers have emerged from a first encounter with structuralism in a confused frame of mind. Much of the analysis seems helpful – 'correct' even – and yet there remains a problem: somehow the experience of reading doesn't feel like this. The misgivings commonly focus two problems: firstly, structuralism is felt to conceptualise the reader as an overly passive recipient of narrative meanings; secondly, in its emphasis on the formal qualities of narrative, structuralism ignores the cultural context within which reading takes place. Post-structuralism deals far more adequately with the process of reading. The label is at once ominously imprecise (to define anything as 'that which follows an earlier something else' is hardly exact), and yet ultimately realistic in its vagueness, for the variety of the concerns, methods and styles of post-structuralism are not amenable to the constraints of tight definition. The general tendency of post-structuralism is to concern itself with ambiguity, contradiction and incoherence both in language and fiction. It is indeed a reaction against the aspirations of structuralists to scientifically precise analysis which characterises the emergence of post-structuralism in France towards the end of the 1960s. My remarks will concentrate on the extended sense of readers and reading which is the principal contribution of post-structuralist analysis to the study of popular fiction.

The cultural context of reading: ideology

Neither texts nor readers exist in a vacuum. Both are shaped by and participate in a social, political and material context – the 'total culture' – and it is within the systems of this wider culture, as well as in the formal systems of fiction, that post-structuralists locate their analysis. Prominent in this wider context is ideology and the reader is strongly advised to follow up some of the suggestions for further reading: to be 'comfortable' with ideology is to have a head start in reading post-structuralist texts. I shall offer here the briefest of essential introductory remarks, identifying two common but narrow usages, and following with a much broader sense of ideology which is close to that employed in much contemporary debate on popular culture. A first narrow usage equates ideology with specific political principles or propaganda, as in, for example, 'communist ideology' or 'conservative ideology'. A second is specifically Marxist and equates ideology with 'false consciousness' – the acceptance by subordinate classes of an account of their conditions of existence formulated by and in the interests of the ruling class. An example would be the belief that human nature is constant and that its essential depravity can never be 'corrected'. The perpetuation of such a belief and its wider implication of the consequent futility of seeking radical change of any kind is clearly conducive to the ruling class's continuing dominance. This is broader than the first usage but limited in its restricting of ideology to ideas or at least to 'what goes on inside the head'. More recent Marxist theory, notably in the work of the French philosopher Louis Althusser, has substantially expanded the concept. Althusser argues for 'lived ideology' in the sense that it is embedded in all levels of social existence, penetrating even the most commonplace institutions, occurrences and social interactions. In this sense ideology is everywhere and everything is ideological, working insidiously towards the continuance of ruling-class dominance. Althusser seeks to identify those institutions – he refers to them as 'ideological apparatuses' – which disseminate the dominant account of how things are. The notion of fiction as one such apparatus is not made explicit by Althusser but his concept of 'interpellation' (outlined in Reading 20) has been widely applied to the study of popular fiction. Ideologically charged texts so address individual readers as to invite their complicity in particular ways of viewing the world. The reader who responds to the 'hailing' accepts the text's version of reality, and is temporarily the 'subject' of the text whose ideological work is thus effectively discharged. It is of course possible that the reader, who is already sited in ideology, will reject the hailing. It is, however, presumably a condition of the 'popular' text that a large proportion of those hailed will respond positively.

Hegemony

*Antonio Gramsci was an Italian Marxist who died in 1937. Like Althusser he wrote relatively little on fiction specifically, but he too has been drawn on extensively in post-structuralist analysis of popular fiction. Gramsci's account of class relations in capitalist societies, and especially his concept of hegemony, suggests a distinctive role for fiction in the maintenance of bourgeois dominance and also, potentially, its subversion. According to Gramsci the dominance of the ruling classes is secured not through coercion or direct control but rather through the consent of subordinate groups, and his concern is to analyse the processes which secure this consent. Through the operation of 'hegemonic apparatuses' dominant ideology is broadly accepted as 'valid' and 'natural'. It is therefore not recognised as ideology, but becomes a part of what Gramsci calls the 'common sense' of a culture. It is clearly appropriate to explore the possible function of fiction as a hegemonic apparatus, and much post-structuralist work on popular texts draws very directly on Gramsci. Reading 21 brings out the usefulness of the concept 'common sense' in assessing the participation of fiction in the construction of hegemony. Any such analysis must bear in mind the essentially **unstable** nature of hegemony. No single class interest can secure the lasting and unchanging consent of all other groups; hegemony is thus constantly renegotiated and constitutes, Gramsci insists, 'a moving equilibrium'. If we are to read fiction as a hegemonic apparatus then its role is in the continuous reshaping of consent rather than the crude imposition of fixed ruling-class ideology.*

In Reading 32 Bob Dixon effectively exposes the myth of the 'innocence' of the vastly popular children's fiction of Enid Blyton. His analysis locates the texts firmly within the framework of dominant ideology – especially in respect of attitudes to race and class, and also to gender. For Dixon, Blyton's work is 'anti-social, if not anti-human and is more likely to stunt and warp young people than help them grow'. Angela McRobbie (44) offers a more subtle analysis of the teenage girls' magazine Jackie. Her emphasis is on the 'highly privileged site' in which Jackie does its ideological work. Addressing its readers in their leisure time during their single years (between childhood and motherhood), Jackie is well placed (in contrast to the directly coercive school or parents) to win their consent to the dominant image of femininity it embodies. In McRobbie's work we are particularly aware of the fusing of Gramscian and Althusserian perspectives. Adolescent girls are invited to recognise and adopt the subject position inscribed within the interpellating text. A similar fusion may be observed in Roger Bromley's early but still important enquiry into the relations between ideology and popular fiction. Bromley (22) gives useful explication of the application to popular fiction of such Gramscian concepts as 'common sense', 'naturalisation' and 'hegemony' and of Althusser's 'ideological state apparatus'. Bromley's attribution of 'possessive individualism and property' as both the keystones of bourgeois ideology and the 'real foundations of popular fiction' anticipates the ideological analysis of thrillers offered in Jerry Palmer's essay (33).

Two problems of ideological analysis

Ideological analysis does not provide magical access to all that's worth saying about popular texts. Indeed its application may be counter-productive – where, for example, analysis is reduced to a kind of 'spot the ideology' exercise, in which the exposition of the 'imperialist' or 'bourgeois individualist' tendency of the text is offered as the first and last word on its meaning. The inadequacies of such an approach are obvious enough: this view is in its way as reductive of the text as those approaches which see form and form alone. It is doubtless convenient for analysis to discuss ideology and form separately but ultimately their interpenetration must be stressed. Ideology is not an optional, super-imposed 'extra' but in every sense as integral to the life of the text as it is to the culture in which the text operates. Thus, as Palmer demonstrates, thrillers typically depend on their author's skill in generating suspense. And yet this ostensibly literary quality is itself dependent on the positioning of the reader within the ideological framework of the narrative ('identifying' with the hero, caring that he succeeds). Our 'classic' narrative structure of order–enigma–resolution is itself ideological. Inscribed in the pressure towards an ending in which all is clarified and order restored is the 'conservatism' inherent in mainstream narrative.

A second problem concerns effects and acknowledges a feeling current in some contemporary social theory that analysis post-Althusser has greatly exaggerated the role of ideology in determining social behaviour. Any analysis which simply conflates a text's ideological tendency with its readers' real-life behaviour is clearly reductive of the complex of relations in which the encounter between reader and text occurs. Men clearly do not behave in a sexist or jingoistic way simply because they read certain kinds of fiction when they were boys. Experience of family and education will surely have contributed more than the reading of Enid Blyton. It is further crucial that economic determinants be considered. Where readers are in poverty it would clearly be absurd to argue that they steal simply because they read books in which thieves are celebrated as heroes.

Text as a field of force

To focus these problems is not of course to argue that ideological approaches to popular fiction are inappropriate. It is rather to insist that such analysis recognise the reading of fiction as a multi-dimensional process involving ever-shifting complexes of interrelated factors. Some of these are specified by Bernard Bergonzi.[1] Again he is moving away from 'traditional' visions of what texts are like. Drawing on Barthes he proposes a model of the literary text:

> I propose instead a more kinetic model, which makes the text less tangible though no less specific; that is to say the text as a field of force or configuration of energy, or a vortex, to return to one of the dominant images of high modernist poetics, as described by Hugh Kenner in *The Pound Era*. I am influenced in this suggestion by Roland Barthes's model of the text, in *S/Z*, as a system of interlocking codes, of almost indefinite possible extension, though I do not want to take over Barthes's scholastic terminology, nor his attempted fusion of classical rhetoric and psychoanalysis. But Barthes does help one to a more open model of the text. If the text is a field of force then its whirling constituents come from many possible sources as well as the author's creative brain and imagination.

> The Anglo-American critical tradition assumes that a literary text is solely dependent upon its author; it exists, simply, because a particular person has written it. Recent Continental critics, by contrast, give the individual author a very modest place among all the other determinants of the text: the state of the language, the genre, the contemporary literary situation, the ideology of the author's social group or class, the nature of productive relations in society at large, the desires and expectations of the audience. In our tradition, most of these elements would be relegated to the background, to be looked into or ignored, according to the reader's inclinations. But, in the model I propose, all these elements – personal, intellectual, literary, linguistic, social – would be there in the text, as constituent elements, or part of the network of codes that make up the totality.

The image of the 'field of force' seems to me distinctly useful in resisting not simply a disproportionate stress on the influence of ideology but also an oversimplified vision of its operation. We are reminded, for example, that in attempting an account of Ian Fleming's novels we should consider not only 'culture and ideology of the 1960s' but also such literary forerunners as John Buchan's adventure tales from early in the twentieth century. Bergonzi's model also recognises implicitly that some readers will not have been recruited by Enid Blyton's racist ideology and further that some texts might do their ideological work outside the dominant definition we may be in danger of taking for granted.

Oppositional popular fiction

It is widely assumed that popular texts operate 'conservatively' in the maintenance of the status quo. In recent years the possibility of reversing this tendency has been explored, especially in connection with crime novels and thrillers.[2] Cora Kaplan (43) observes the persistence of the connections between crime fiction and dominant ideologies of the social order and gender. In questioning the prospects for writing a 'feminist' crime novel, she raises important questions as to the capacity of popular genres to accommodate radical reshaping. If Kaplan is correct in identifying particular resistance within crime fiction, we are led to ask whether the conservative pressures working on other genres are (a) as strong and (b) of the same kind.

Tom Moylan (34) argues that utopian science fiction 'contributes to the open space of opposition'. His emphasis is not on the articulation of opposition at the level of content – 'the form is itself more significant than any of its content'. Moylan reads utopian narrative as a process which opens up the imagination to the existence of the space which may subsequently be occupied by oppositional social critiques. Its insistent subject is the as yet unformulated 'other of what is'.

Deconstruction

Deconstructionist criticism shares the post-structuralist and post-modernist perception of meaning as slippery, capricious and elusive but embodies an even more radical critique of bourgeois criticism's perception of literary meaning, notably its emphasis on 'unity'. Most students of 'A' level English will have been trained to value (and expect) unity as a quality of a literary text. Crudely this implies the integration of the various discrete 'elements' of the text – its themes, imagery, symbolism, character, etc. – into a coherent whole whose significance is greater than the sum of its parts. (Such assumptions underpin Adorno's distinction between popular and serious music (11).) It is further assumed that the meaning of this unified text is itself unitary, placed there by its author, to be teased out and triumphantly re-expressed by the student. In as far as the student's 'version' is deemed to correspond pretty well to the author's then she is awarded high marks. Such comfortable assumptions as to the coherence, harmony and unity of textual meaning is radically challenged by deconstruction, which places emphasis not on the unity of a text but on the dislocation and contradictions, not on what it confidently articulates but on its incoherencies, silences and absences.

Pierre Macherey has greatly influenced recent work on popular fiction, especially in his application to literature of post-structuralist work on ideology. In A Theory of Literary Production (23) Macherey suggests that literary language embodies contradictory tendencies. On the one hand it seeks to 'explicate', to clarify, to give a rational account of its world; at the same time language is based in ideology and therefore necessarily contained by the perspectives which shape it. It is the tension between the text's aspiration to completeness and the actual incompleteness which it cannot avoid which provides the focus of Macherey's interest: this is the contradiction which proclaims the position of the text within ideology. Macherey draws attention to the silences of texts, insists that what they do not say – what they cannot say – is as important as what they do say. This recognition is central to deconstructionist analysis, and is very directly influential (as the author acknowledges) on Catherine Belsey's reading of Doyle's Sherlock Holmes stories. Belsey (48) points to the silences and the contradictions, especially those surrounding the 'shadowy, mysterious and often silent women'. What they focus is the tension between what the text claims to be about – the resolution of enigma through rational means – and the significant absences, the expansive landscapes of experience which the ideologically rooted text cannot even begin to address.

The pleasure of readers

The total context in which meanings are produced cannot, of course, exclude the reader – a truth recognised by Barthes in 1968 in an essay (24) which clearly indicates its author's own shift from a structuralist to post-structuralist perspective. Starting from the realisation that 'classic criticism has never paid any attention to *the reader; for it the writer is the only person in literature', Barthes argues that it is at the point of consumption that meaning is formulated: 'the birth of the reader must be at the cost of the death of the Author'. In Reading 25 Barthes advocates the reinstatement of another factor traditionally ignored by criticism: pleasure. The Pleasure of the Text is clearly post-structuralist in mood: it is elusive, difficult, brilliant. In as far as it has a central thrust it is to compare the pleasurable reception of narrative with that of a formidable range of other cultural phenomena. Barthes was not, of course, the first theorist of readers and pleasure. His work in the late 1960s, however, contributed substantially to the considerable subsequent interest in these areas among writers on popular fiction.*

Two feminist responses take as their starting point the inadequacy of conventional denunciations of romance 'pulp' as characteristic expressions of oppressive sexist ideology. For both Batsleer and Light (45 and 46) there remains, after the moralising, the inescapable fact of the pleasures of readers (themselves included) and it is this pleasure which their essays address. For Janet Batsleer romance does draw attention to 'the conflicts which have produced feminism' but also, and more interestingly, provides a means of surviving them. She identifies in the novels of Barbara Cartland 'celebrations of women's world' which participate in the feminist foregrounding of experience marginalised in the wider culture. Alison Light goes beyond this in proposing a psychoanalytic framework for analysing this survival mechanism. The pleasure of romance lies in the 'postponement of fulfilment'. On one level readers know the distance between the romance heroine's ultimate fulfilment and the 'deep dissatisfactions' which in the real world flow from the 'limiting regulation of female sexuality'. Set against this knowledge, however, is the continuing insistent desire for something better (both in sexual and wider cultural terms). Thus romance is not only expressive of this desire but also indicative of the extent to which it is conventionally frustrated. Whilst acknowledging this latter function, Light declines to privilege it: romances remain 'in our society, a forbidden pleasure – like cream cakes'.

Elisabeth Frazer's approach (47) is distinctive. Rejecting ideological analysis as either vague or excessively deterministic, she advocates instead an empirical approach, seeking to record and interpret readers' own accounts of what actually happens *when they read the teenage girls' magazine* Jackie. *Doubts as to the reliability of the data must, as the author acknowledges, persist, but her conclusion that individual readers have available a whole repertoire of ways of discussing popular texts ('discourse registers') implies at least the availability of a range of ways of reading. This is surely a more convincing account of reader response than any which implies the reader as* **passive subject** *of text, whether the subjectivity be constructed in ideological or narrative terms or both.*

Post-structuralism does not provide an instant solution to all the problems facing the student of popular fiction. Some of the work available is frankly esoterically inaccessible to even experienced readers. Paul O'Flinn, however, is anxious to dissociate himself from 'a naive deconstructionalist delight at the endless plurality of meanings' (4) and the precision of his historical approach is matched by the clarity of most of the 'Applications' in this section. In developing and refining our own critical approaches to popular fiction it is inevitable that we shall draw heavily on post-structuralism.

Some of the problems touched on here are taken up in Reading 27 where Tony Bennett also provides a clear statement of his own reconstructed critical strategy, appropriate to the study of popular texts.

Psychoanalysis and the horror genre

Since the early 1970s the position of horror among popular genres has shifted from the focus of a somewhat specialist, 'exclusive' interest in, for example 'sci-fi horror' of the 1950s and 1960s to the massively popular success of Stephen King's novels and film adaptations and the high level of visibility of the genre in both book and video shops. A connected tendency in academic work on popular narrative has been the recent consolidation of psychoanalytic approaches as probably the most interesting source of new work in the field in the first half of the 1990s. Much of this work has extended the exploration of the issue of pleasure in the context of horror, and it is appropriate that this section should include a generous representative selection from that work and the 'classic' theory which informs it.

Critical discussion of the horror genre might be said to partake a little of the uncanny! From whatever perspective it engages with the monstrous invasion of the world as we know it – by vampires, werewolves, mysterious seed pods, the undead, creatures that never were in nature – we are returned unerringly to a problem from within. What may at first manifest itself as an eruption of strange, unrecognizable, motiveless malignance about which we know nothing into the world of the social, may eventually be revealed surprisingly to have this world as its origin, its 'home'. Is what comes from the outside also always within? Psychoanalysis is supremely placed to afford an insight into this phenomenon. Freud's great discovery at the end of the nineteenth century was that of the unconscious. By definition, we know nothing of it, but Freud's work with hysterical patients, his observation of phenomena of everyday life such as slips of the tongue and his attempts at dream analysis led him towards a complex body of theoretical work on the unconscious and its relationship to the structure of human mental life as a whole. In 1895, Freud dreamt the 'dream of Irma's injection', an event so momentous for him that he felt that the house where he dreamt it should be commemorated. It confirmed the existence of the unconscious, the process of the dream work and the dawning recognition that a part of the psyche unavailable to conscious control might contain some shocking, even monstrous, wishes and desires (see Totem and Taboo *[28.2]). Lacan was later to readdress this dream and Freud's analysis of it (29). For Lacan, Freud experiences here the 'anxiety provoking', 'primitive object par excellence', the 'abyss of the feminine organ from which all life emerges'; in Lacan's terminology, the 'Real'. This cannot be contemplated and Freud retreats rapidly back into the space of the Symbolic: professional diagnosis and the chemical formula writ large.*

This should remind us of Freud's lifetime concern with sexuality. In particular his theory of the castration complex: the threat to the boy and the girl to give something up in order to line up on the side of the man or the woman. That this is not an easy or schematic passage, particularly for the girl, is evidenced by Freud's many attempts to confront the nature of female sexuality. In the essay 'Fetishism' (28.5), Freud considers the psychic predicament of the fetishist who attempts to disavow castration. The fetishist cannot admit the lack of the phallus in the mother. He constructs a fetish to stand in for this lack of which the sight of the female genitals would forcibly remind him (anxiety-provoking for any man, Freud suggests). The female genitals are the ultimate site/sight in the essay 'The Uncanny' (28.3): the place where what is strange, horrific, is also, at the same time, 'home'. The horror of Medusa's head (28.4) derives from this source.

Dadoun (40) offers us a reading of the recurring figure of Dracula in the horror genre based on the fetishist structure. Creed (41) develops an account of the pre-occupations of the contemporary horror film based on readings of Freud and Kristeva's theory of the abject (where the generative power of the archaic mother is fearful, an aspect of the abject, to be expelled to secure the stability of the ego). Silverman (42) locates the structure of the fetishist in Peeping Tom. *Her emphasis is on the relay of looks, the structure of perverse looking and the cinematic apparatus as a function of the diegesis of the text and of the position of the spectator who may, with this film, find that what is on the 'outside' is brought 'home' to them in a particularly disquieting way.*

In **Totem and Taboo** *(28.2), Freud is emphatic on the violent and sexual nature of desires that may be repressed in the unconscious. In the moment of the son's destruction of the father of the primal horde in this myth of origins, Society and the Law come into being. Far from authorizing their own enjoyment, the sons prohibit it. They may not be in the place of the father (although, through the act of oral incorporation they all retain an element of his 'enjoyment'). The dead father now becomes more powerful than the live one. He stands outside the set. His exclusion guarantees the symbolic order, though he always threatens to return, like the vampire of the horror film perhaps, or like the undead. Or perhaps, as Dolar suggests (39), as Frankenstein's monster; the creature without a double, with no name, who cannot therefore come into signification; the point of too much meaning, where any content projected onto it does not exhaust it. As Dolar says:*

> Psychoanalysis doesn't provide a new and better interpretation of the uncanny; it maintains it as a *limit to interpretation*. Its interpretation tries to circumscribe the point where interpretation fails, where no 'more faithful' translation can be made. It tries to pinpoint the dimension of the object in that tiny crack before different meanings get hold of it and saturate it with sense, the point that can never be successfully recuperated by the signifying chain. In other words, psychoanalysis differs from other interpretations by its insistence on the formal level of the uncannny rather than its content.

Notes

1   B. Bergonzi, *Reading the Thirties*, Macmillan (1978), p. 5.
2   In 1984 Pluto Press offered a prize of £2,000 plus publication for the best new crime novel providing a perspective 'on contemporary social reality'. This coincided with their launching a series of detective novels and thrillers addressing such conventionally improbable themes as socialist feminism (Gillian Slovo's *Morbid Symptoms*) and the internal affairs of the Chinese Communist party (Nancy Milton's *The China Option*).

Theory and methodology

 READING 20

'Ideology and ideological state apparatuses'

Louis Althusser

I shall then suggest that ideology 'acts' or 'functions' in such a way that it 'recruits' subjects among the individuals (it recruits them all), or 'transforms' the individuals into subjects (it transforms them all) by that very precise operation which I have called *interpellation* or hailing, and which can be imagined along the lines of the most commonplace everyday police (or other) hailing: 'Hey, you there!'[18]

Assuming that the theoretical scene I have imagined takes place in the street, the hailed individual will turn round. By this mere one hundred-and-eighty-degree physical conversion, he becomes a *subject*. Why? Because he has recognized that the hail was 'really' addressed to him, and that 'it was *really him* who was hailed' (and not someone else). Experience shows that the practical telecommunication of hailings is such that they hardly ever miss their man: verbal call or whistle, the one hailed always recognizes that it is really him who is being hailed. And yet it is a strange phenomenon, and one which cannot be explained solely by 'guilt feelings', despite the large numbers who 'have something on their consciences'.

Naturally for the convenience and clarity of my little theoretical theatre I have had to present things in the form of a sequence, with a before and an after, and thus in the form of a temporal succession. There are individuals walking along. Somewhere (usually behind them) the hail rings out: 'Hey, you there!' One individual (nine times out of ten it is the right one) turns round, believing/suspecting/knowing that it is for him, i.e. recognizing that 'it really is he' who is meant by the hailing. But in reality these things happen without any succession. The existence of ideology and the hailing or interpellation of individuals as subjects are one and the same thing.

I might add: what thus seems to take place outside ideology (to be precise, in the street), in reality takes place in ideology. What really takes place in ideology seems therefore to take place outside it. That is why those who are in ideology believe themselves by definition outside ideology: one of the effects of ideology is the practical *denegation* of the ideological character of ideology by ideology: ideology never says, 'I am ideological'. It is necessary to be outside ideology, i.e. in scientific knowledge, to be able to say: I am in ideology (a quite exceptional case) or (the general case): I was in ideology. As is well known, the accusation of being in ideology only applies to others, never to oneself.

Note

18 Hailing as an everyday practice subject to a precise ritual takes a quite 'special' form in the policeman's practice of 'hailing' which concerns the hailing of 'suspects'.

(from *Lenin and Philosophy*, 1971)

'Recent developments in English Studies at the Centre'

English Studies Group, CCCS,
University of Birmingham

In Britain the use of Gramscian concepts for the analysis of literature has been developed by Raymond Williams in a theory of 'cultural materialism',[93] by Colin Mercer[94] and, most specifically, by Roger Bromley in two essays on the analysis of popular fiction.[95] Although we have disagreements with Bromley's use of Gramscian concepts, it was his work which in many ways set us in a new direction. He draws analogies between the forms of narrative and characterization in the popular fiction of the 1930s and the crisis of hegemony and the reformation of the class alliance in the ruling bloc which was occurring at the same time the texts were written. It seems to us, however, that to see characters in texts standing in for social classes is too fast and easy a leap from text to society, as well as creating a curious blindness to non-class representations in a text. For example, Bromley sees woman characters as representatives of the petty bourgeoisie, not particularly as caught in patriarchal relations. However, the basic thesis that popular fiction has a particular work to do in the maintenance and struggle for hegemony is important. Gramsci insists that hegemony is struggled for in every sphere of society, even in those areas which seem most private and removed from the incursions of politics or the state.

One of the ways in which Gramsci analyses the presence of domination and subordination in unlooked-for areas of social life is his discussion of what he calls 'spontaneous philosophy', and particularly his delineation of common sense. 'Spontaneous philosophy' is a term rather similar to Williams's 'structure of feeling': it does *not* mean that ideas come from nowhere, spontaneously, into the minds of the subordinate classes. It holds in tension the idea of 'philosophy', a developed body of ideas (rather like an earlier meaning of the term *ideology*), and the recognition that our ideas do seem to be our own, that we speak as much as we are spoken by language and that the words we *do* address the real situation in which they are spoken.

Gramsci calls common sense the philosophy of the non-philosophers. It is not a single, unique conception, identical in time and space. It is the folklore of philosophy and, like folklore, it takes countless different forms. The personality formed within common sense is

> strangely composite: it contains stone age elements and principles of a more advanced science, prejudices from all past phases of history at a local level and intuitions of a future philosophy which will be that of a human race united the world over.[96]

This fragmentary, proverbial view of the world is the inheritance of the subordinate classes; it has been formed in a long history of struggle for domination and can be seen as the negotiated terms of consent which we give to our continuing subordination. It is partly because common sense has been formed over a very long period that it presents itself as timeless knowledge. Ideologies of previous historical moments, at one time generated and enshrined in institutions, have become embedded in a set of assumptions about 'the way things are'. The explanations of subordination may be contradictory, containing both pragmatism and fatalism: 'God helps those who help themselves'. Gramsci suggests that at moments of heightened struggle common sense crystallizes into a more critical, coherent and oppositional 'good sense'.

It was initially certain striking similarities between the romances and thrillers we were reading and Gramsci's characterization of common sense which suggested that the two might fruitfully be thought together. First, popular female romances are characteristically formed from an amalgam of modern and pre-capitalist elements. The simplified characterization, the withdrawal from society on the part of reader and romance heroine, the happy ending, the strongly enforced code of conduct are all continuing formal elements of romance as a genre which predate capitalist society. Second, Gramsci points to an analysis of language as part of an analysis of 'spontaneous philosophy', language determined by, and carrying the signs of, culture and 'not just words grammatically devoid of content'. The simple, didactic, clichéd language of Cartland's novels does share the proverbial 'written on stone' quality of common sense. Third, the persistent moralizing of popular fiction suggests a relation to the *content* of common sense – for example, true love never runs smoothly, money can't buy you happiness (but it helps). Last, and most tentatively, there may be a similarity between Gramsci's definition of popular religion as a more systematic fragment of common sense providing 'a unity of faith between a conception of the world and corresponding norm of conduct' and the work of narrative form in popular fiction. The narrative organizes a plot, produces coherence, leads the reader from confusion and disarray to a happy ending and links the happy ending with the triumphs of one common-sense conception over others. It is the tendency of popular fiction to be linked with the production of moral norms which suggests the analogy with popular religion. The similarity may also point to the Utopian elements in popular fiction, in so far as it promises, in the end, a world without contradictions.

We are *not* saying that popular fiction is the same as common sense. But whereas previously we defined popular fiction solely by its relation to the institutions which structure the field of literary production and consumption, 'the literary field', we would now see popular fiction as also placed between highly developed ideologies/philosophies, the language of common sense and the experience of subordinate groups and classes. When a fiction addresses each of these we call it *popular*.

Notes

93 Raymond Williams, *Marxism and Literature*.
94 Colin Mercer, 'Culture and ideology in Gramsci', in *Red Letters*, no.8 (1978).
95 Roger Bromley, 'Natural boundaries: the social function of popular fiction', in *Red Letters*, no. 7 (1978); 'Culture and Hegemony in the 1930s', BSA Conference Paper (1978).
96 Gramsci, *Prison Notebooks*, p. 324.

(from S. Hall *et al.* (eds), *Culture, Media, Language*, 1980)

'Natural boundaries: the social function of popular fiction'

Roger Bromley

Starting from the assumption that popular fiction is one mode of social communication whose re-presentations mark one way in which ideology becomes a material force in society, use has been made of Gramsci's concept of 'common sense'[8] (the 'substrata of ideologies'?). The purpose of this is to discover theoretical bearings for the ways in which moral values and customs, and modes of perception, of the ruling bloc become the 'mass-popular' ways of seeing of those subordinated in the processes of production. If this process of transformation is not static, or once and for all, but ongoing and alterable, then how does popular mediation (fictions in particular, for our purpose) intervene in the process? In other words, how are images/ideas/styles appropriated, in the first instance, in the ruling bloc, and then, mediated to, transformed and received by, the dominated class?

For Gramsci, common sense is seen as aggregated and internally contradictory forms of thought: the incoherent (not systematic) set of generally held assumptions and beliefs common to any given society, the product of concrete social activity by the ruling bloc seen from a historical perspective. Common sense is not ideology, but has been generated by its processes and social transformations. It has the force of obviousness. 'Mass-popular' ways of seeing are not critical and coherent, but disjointed and episodic; a series of fragmentations of what were originally produced, in ideology, as unitary and coherent. Though a popular fictional text offers itself as a resolved and coherent unity, it contains within it many 'references' from the disjointed and episodic features of common sense. The popular text is, like personality in Gramsci's analysis

> strangely composite: it contains Stone Age elements and principles of a more advanced science, prejudices from all past phases of history at the local level . . .[9]

Later, in the same analysis, he refers to the ways in which philosophy has left stratified deposits in popular philosophy, and it is this phrase, together with 'an infinity of traces' (which has not left an inventory), which help to identify quite precisely certain features of popular fictional forms in relation to ideology (stratified deposits, ideological and stylistic, and an infinity of 'natural' traces from conceptual, psychological, social and literary sources, present but without reference or evidence of an inventory. The inventory can be seen as analogous to the 'consciousness of its historicity').

Many popular fictions present contemporary phenomena . . . with a mode of thought, expression and perception elaborated for a past which is often remote and superseded in terms of real social relations, yet which persist as *real* through ideological processes. The text, therefore, becomes a living anachronism, a structure of fossils. How and why such fossil-texts are produced and read in vast quantities is a problematic issue (25 million new romantic novels are sold in this country each year, and one publisher alone – Mills and Boon – sold 70 million titles through the world last year). The composite nature of popular texts has to be examined with reference to the social history of literary forms as well as to modes of ideological representations in society.

Popular fiction forms, while signalling at the surface level their place in the contemporary, are in fact carriers of the residual, bearers of the historically displaced and imaginary relations of experience: like perhaps the status and function of a dialect in relation to a national (class-specific) language, as structures they inhabit (occupy) regions of the dominant ideology: regions which, for many people, are their reality. This is not to say that people who read popular fiction have a mode of conduct or action derived from those fictions, but that there is a contradiction between action and the recognition of, and identification with, ideological sets and fragments in these fictions. Each fiction contains a sedimentation of the dominant ideology, which in its complex circuit of diffusion has fractured along certain lines and in certain directions. It is relatively easy to demonstrate these things from an analysis of the forms and themes of a sample of popular texts. This is necessary 'empirical' work but the most urgent task is that of trying to locate the precise relations between the structuration of the fragmented and sedimented elements of ideology in the fictional bloc and key mechanisms in the process of ideology.

In dealing with common sense, Gramsci was concerned with ideology at its lower levels (levels which do not simply repeat the dominant, but assimilate, transpose and domesticate it), as the repository of popular beliefs, myth etc. and as a means of dealing with everyday life. It has a confirmatory and consensual effect. This consensualising effect is one of the functions of popular fictions, a mode of inserting the reader, through its various devices, at the level of consent, not just to its 'story' but to its structurings of that story. It offers as obvious and natural and universal what are, in fact, the values and ideas of the ruling bloc, or one of its allied fractions. 'Naturalisation' was seen by Gramsci as a key mechanism of common-sense thought, as it closes knowledge, ends debate, and dissolves contradictions. Similarly, as we read a popular fiction, meanings are composed by blocks or groups of signification, of which we grasp only the smooth surfaces, imperceptibly joined together by the movement of sentences, flowing discourse of narration, the 'naturalness' of ordinary language.[10] The ways in which common sense 'naturalises' the social order is analogous to the ways in which the structures of fictional discourse 'naturalise' the order of signification in the text, so that the reader responds to their formal solidity (however 'neophobe' and conservative) and their imperative character in producing common-sensical norms of conduct.

. . . .

Popular literature is categorical in Gramsci's use of the term (non-historical and non-dialectical), and, in fact, is structured around a series of categories which are adduced as timeless and universal. It is a mode of writing dominated by 'feeling', 'personal experience', and immediate empirical perception. Like common-sense thinking it fails to grasp or to acknowledge, by omission, the *political* as the crucial level of the social formation. The evacuation from the novel *The Spy Who Came in from the Cold* of the political (or, more precisely, what is offered as the political) by a constant personal/political antithesis which is resolved in terms of the 'personal' is a critical instance of this. The suppressions and absences are part of the social function of this kind of text.

Popular literature is one among many of the material forms which ideology takes (or through which it is mediated) under capitalism, and is an instance of its social production through the medium of writing. If we as marxists hope to intervene in the class struggle at the level of cultural production, then we have to concern ourselves with the specific analysis of ideologies and their concrete mediations. We need a theoretical basis for the examination of specific, historical conjunctures, in order to see how, or in what ways, for example, the domination of the ruling bloc is, or can be, exercised over a social formation at the level of consent. Class rule is legitimised and universalised through the giving of the form of 'general interest' (by, that is, naturalising the boundaries in society) to what are the interests of particular class sections. Popular literature is a local instance of the generalisation/naturalisation of class domination – it has a function in the hegemonic process. It is not a primary site of ideology (cf. the educational system, for example) but it is one of the secondary areas where ideological components are represented, and reinforced, as, for the ruling class, the class struggle has to be fought constantly and on as many fronts as possible.

Factors which facilitated the mass production, marketing, and reading of popular novels (cheap print and paper, literacy, Mudie's Select Library, Smith's etc.)[11] were features which coincided roughly with the early Victorian crisis of hegemony which marked the closing stages of the first period of industrial capitalism, and witnessed the reiteration of certain bourgeois imperatives.[12] This crisis produced a shift in the form of hegemony from coercion to consent (through liberalisation, incorporation, use and role of the labour aristocracy etc. – bourgeois domination became increasingly hegemonic. This was a particular conjuncture which led to a consolidation of bourgeois economic power through social, political, cultural and ideological process which altered the prevailing relation of class forces, and subordinated consensually the potentially subversive. The bourgeoisie consolidated their economic industrial power, while the aristocracy retained a significant place in the governing stratum of the State, and maintained privileges in the army, administration, and land. As Gramsci says in 'Notes on Italian History':

> The class relations created by industrial development, with the limits of bourgeois hegemony reached and the position of the progressive classes reversed, have induced the bourgeoisie not to struggle with all its strength against the old regime, but to allow a part of the latter's facade to subsist, behind which it can disguise its own real domination.[13]

It is, arguably, the style of that mode of hegemony which is still being rehearsed and reproduced in masculine and feminine romance. Time and time again in both masculine and feminine romance an aristocratic facade subsists, and acts as both an alibi for and a disguise of the bourgeois forms, values, and perceptions which the text consecrates and naturalises. The *locus classicus* of this fictional representation of the main class alliance in the ruling bloc is chapter four of Buchan's *Thirty-Nine Steps*.[14]

This fusion of old and new in the ruling bloc in the early Victorian period produced the conditions for certain features and attitudes – a renewed, egotistical, individualism, imperialism, and the position of women in Victorian society – the ideological components of which still persist long after the real conditions which produced them have passed. They persist in our common-sense thinking, and in the themes and structures of popular fiction. The *harmonising* effect of popular romance serves to unstratify the stratified, hides the real foundations of capitalistic production (surplus value), and naturalises (without ever referring to) the market and exchange relations between free individuals. Add to this the concepts of possessive individualism and property, and what is produced is a map of the real foundations of popular fiction, i.e. bourgeois ideology.

The marxist analysis of popular culture has a part to play in raising the question of the extremely complex, diffuse, and indirect means by which the whole fabric of capitalist society is drawn into conformity with the long-term needs of capital. How, in other words, is a consensual harmony realised, and why is there a constant emphasis on coherence, in the face of dislocation and contradiction? The ideological closure and the specious mode of causality common to popular fiction contribute to this consensual harmony.

If ideological relations can be conceived of as specific social determinants borne by individuals, and if ideology is a relatively coherent ensemble of representations, values and beliefs *given* to individuals not once, but repeatedly and through diverse structures then analysis has to focus on the forms used to diffuse the ensemble, and on the ways in which specific individuals come to see, perceive, and feel the material forces of ideology.

For Althusser, ideology represents *individual* relationships to reality and exists in material apparatuses (cultural among others) and their system of rituals and practices.[15] The problem is how these rituals and practices are addressed to individuals: popular fiction operates by constructing and implicitly personifying a privileged reader, its very structure serves to individualise its consumer to such an extent that once inside the framework of confidence and privilege, the contradiction that actually exists between the fictional representation of the *really* privileged figures in the dominant social relations and the really subordinated (including the consumer) is dissolved. Popular literature should properly be regarded as a specific ideological practice within an ideological apparatus (publishing, communication, media etc.) and as such participates in the permanent insertion of individuals and their actions in practices governed by ideological apparatuses.

All romance (whether masculine or feminine) is based on an exchange relation. Feminine romance is not about love, but about marriage (in its form appropriated by the bourgeoisie), whereas masculine romance is based on exchange at the level of mental or physical conflict (game etc.) between two males. Both modes of exchange *reduce* social connectedness to the *couple*.

This formulation of the couple (the only grouping usually acknowledged in romance, other than those seen as inimical, e.g. political party, mob etc.) is crucial to an understanding of popular fiction in its romance forms (arguably, to all its forms, but the evidence is not available), because it is an ideological premise in direct contradiction to the social relations of production which are *collective*, and to the whole purpose of capitalist production which is the production of surplus value, the missing or hidden dimension in the relations of exchange seemingly between equals. The 'couple formulation' (actually, two discrete individuals in an act of exchange, or preparing for an act of exchange) is also related to the fundamental contradiction in capitalism between the (private) ownership of the means of production and the (collective) social relations of production. By the rendering of society as a medium for the expression of individuals in relations of exchange, (at the level of symbol, metaphor, and ritual), and by the permanent *absence* of the economic base from the structure of fictional discourse, the popular work effectively removes the real relations in society from immediate experience: it mediates an imaginary relationship to the real relations. The only model of relationship represented in mass formulaic fiction is that of 'ownership'.

A materialist analysis of a popular text will concern itself with the absences (social, collective, profit, production and reproduction) from the text, but a mass-popular reading will/can only respond to the natural/individual/exchange/

creativity structures. A highly developed, popular/collectivist consciousness alone could construct a dialectical model (natural/social; individual/collective; equivalence/profit; creativity/reproduction) from the absences and presences. Only 'people' are presented in popular fiction; what, of course, is invariably absent is the socially determining economic personifications, e.g. capitalists are present but without their specified relation to the workers which signifies them as capitalist; the worker is in a similar position. What happens is that individuals are presented without their economic definitions (therefore, by implication, they do not exist) which, in a materialist analysis, is socially impossible. So a society is produced, minus its economy but not its money (as though money were somehow real, and not a phenomenal form of capital), which is offered as *natural* (i.e. obvious). It is in fact *asocial*, in so far as it treats people as outside the relations of production (i.e. they are *natural*), but in real terms it presents characters and relationships imprinted with the ideological representations of the relations of production, which are themselves socio-historic in their specificity. The ideological representations are offered as *natural/real*.

If the 'couple formulation' and the basic structure of exchange are, in fact, indispensable conditions of popular romance, then a closer scrutiny of the exchange relation under capitalism is necessary.[16] The sphere of individual exchange (what Marx called the 'noisy sphere') is the space inhabited by the subject; it is the area of freedom, equality, and property. Individuals come together in the free exchange of equivalence, and they only dispose of what is their property. The sphere of circulation and exchange in capitalist relations of production hides the generation and expropriation of the surplus in production; it is what Marx called the 'hidden abode'. He referred to exchange etc. as the 'noisy sphere' presumably because it is the area which has to be signalled actively as the real, what society (in its economic activity) is all about. The noise also silences and conceals the real foundations of economic activity.

In a popular fiction the story-plot is the 'noisy sphere', it is what the narrative discourse is all about (so it is claimed, by directing the reader's attention to it by identification, complication etc.). The story-plot has the ideological function (internal ideological function) of concealing its real foundations, its hidden abode. It hides the generation and expropriation of surplus 'meanings' in the text, which are meanings and forms expropriated by the bourgeoisie. I mean by this the class-specific values and perceptions of the bourgeoisie, which are *surplus* (not necessary, and dispensable) to the relations of people in exchange and reproduction, i.e. individualism to the individual, marriage to relationships (the real exchange – love – is absent), masculinity to the male, femininity to the female, property to the self etc. These are all presented as universal, they are superstructural forms re-presented in the deep, hidden, structures of the discourse: the permanent foundations of life, which are unsigned in the text because in society they are unsigned – not seen as structures but are personalised as natural presences. They are in fact the class specific and historic expropriations of the bourgeoisie which are constantly reproduced in order to guarantee the relations of domination-subordination necessary to capitalism.

The popular story tends to be formulaic, although it is 'uniquely' plotted, and moves around individual activity and a specific mode of personal relationships (man/woman). Its real purpose is to 'advertise' the formal structures in which these are situated under capitalism, as these structures are the containers of ideology. The 'hidden real' in the fiction is the representation of the surplus in the relations of production and reproduction: profit and ideology, both dispensable to socialist relations. These are the structures absorbed in the act of reading; they are 'hidden' in the text, and yet they also 'hide' real relations in so far as their presence signifies a lived, therefore real yet imaginary, relationship to social relations. In the course of reading we react to the phenomenal forms (story-plot, cf. exchange) of the real relations of the text which generate and expropriate the 'surpluses' of bourgeois values and forms. Marx's 'noisy sphere' can be related not only to the mechanisms of story and plot, but also to the status details and the locations (historical and territorial) which are so often meticulously researched and the result of months of 'legwork'. This detail is like noise, in so far as it silences the contradictory by filling in the interstices in the text.

The assurance for the reproduction of the relationships of production is a process which occurs in the consciousness, in the attitudes of the individual subjects. Althusser says of ideology, at one point, that it is

> in class society . . . the relay whereby, and the element in which, the relation between men and their existence is settled to the profit of the ruling class.[17]

If a fiction is read purely in the terms and categories with which the reader is presented in surface narrative discourse, then the deep sources of the exploitation in terms of ideology will be rendered invisible. The reader is thus enabled to 'live' (experience) the exploitative relations of capitalist production as if they were 'exchanges between equivalents'. It is this contradiction, basic to capitalism, that is reproduced in terms of structural metaphor in popular fictional forms. The transformation that takes place is from quantity to quality (cf. wealth = power; wealth and property = quality, leadership, breeding etc.). A similar effect is produced by reducing personality to the physical characteristics of the person, beautiful = good, handsome and tall = good etc.).

Popular literature can be seen as a system of representations, imposed as images and structures in the majority of readers, and producing, through the mechanisms of story-plot and style, stability, duration, and security all rooted in the signifying forms sedimented in the discourse. It is silent on questions which go beyond its boundaries, content to reproduce the key ideological themes and discourse of bourgeois society, in the fictional form of common sense. To paraphrase Marx, the story in a popular novel (what, presumably, we read it for) is simply the individualising sphere of the circuit of ideology's path to expanded reproduction: it is, as simple circulation is the surface of bourgeois society, the surface of the narrative which obliterates (again, like circulation) the deeper operations from which it arises.

Notes

8 Gramsci, *Selections from the Prison Notebooks*, ed. Hoare and Nowell-Smith, London 1971, pp. 322–3 and 419–425, and the discussion in *Working Papers in Cultural Studies*, 10, Birmingham 1977, pp. 45–76.

9 Gramsci, op. cit. p. 324.

10 See Barthes, *S/Z*, London, 1975.

11 See Rachel Anderson, *Purple Heart-Throbs*, London, 1974 and V. Neuberg, *Popular Literature*, London, 1977.

12 Two very stimulating analyses of this conjuncture are Robert Q. Gray's *The Labour Aristocracy in Victorian Edinburgh* (Oxford, 1976) and John Foster's *Class Struggle and the Industrial Revolution* (London, 1974). I attempt a 'literary' analysis in

'The Boundaries of Hegemony: Thomas Hardy and the Mayor of Casterbridge', *Proceedings of the University of Essex Conference*, July 1976, pp. 30–40.
13 Gramsci, op. cit. p. 83.
14 See Buchan, *Thirty-Nine Steps* (London, 1915, Pan 1974) pp. 56–7 especially.
15 Althusser, *Lenin and Philosophy and Other Essays*, London, 1971, especially pp. 123–173 for this point and most of the following comments on ideology, and the discussion in *WPCS 10*, pp. 77–105.
16 *WPCS 10*, pp. 61–2.
17 Althusser, *For Marx*, London 1969, p. 236.

(from *Red Letters*, No. 7, 1978)

 READING 23

A *theory of literary production*

Pierre Macherey

Implicit and explicit

> In order to ascertain their real opinions, I ought to take cognisance of what they practised rather than of what they said, not only because, in the corruption of manners, there are few disposed to speak exactly as they believe, but also because very many are not aware of what it is that they really believe, for as the act of mind by which a thing is believed is different from that by which we know we believe it, the one act is often found without the other. (Descartes, *Discourse on Method*, III).

For there to be a critical discourse which is more than a superficial and futile *reprise* of the work, the speech stored in the book must be incomplete; because it has not said everything, there remains the possibility of saying something else, *after another fashion*. The recognition of the area of shadow in or around the work is the initial moment of criticism. But we must examine the nature of this shadow: does it denote a true absence, or is it the extension of a half-presence? This can be reformulated in terms of a previous question: Will it be the pillar of an explanation or the pretext for an interpretation?

Initially, we will be inclined to say that criticism, in relation to its object, is its *explication*. What, then, is involved in making-explicit? Explicit is to implicit as explication is to implication: these oppositions derive from the distinction between the manifest and the latent, the discovered and the concealed. That which is formally accounted for, expressed, and even concluded, is explicit: the 'explicit' at the end of a book echoes the 'incipit' at the beginning, and indicates that 'all is (has been) said'. To explicate comes from *explicate*: to display and unfold. 'Spread eagle', a heraldic term: one with wings outstretched. And thus the critic, opening the book – whether he intends to find buried treasure there, or whether he wants to see it flying with its own wings – means to give it a different status or even a different appearance. It might be said that the aim of criticism is to *speak the truth*, a truth not unrelated to the book, but not as the content of its expression. In the book, then, not everything is said, and for everything to be said we must await the critical 'explicit', which may actually be interminable. Nevertheless, although the critical discourse is not spoken by the book, it is in some way the property of the book, constantly alluded to, though never announced openly. What is this silence – an accidental hesitation, or a statutory necessity? Whence the problem: are there books which say what they mean, without being critical books, that is to say, without *depending directly* on other books?

Here we recognise the classic problem of the interpretation of latent meaning. But, in this new instance, the problem tends to take a new form: in fact, the language of this book claims to be a language complete in itself, the source and measure of all 'diction'. The conclusion is inscribed even in its initial moments. Unwinding *within a closed circle*, this language reveals only . . . itself: it has only its *own* content and its *own* limits, and the 'explicit' is imprinted on each of these terms. Yet it is not perfect: under close scrutiny the speech inscribed by the book appears interminable: but it takes this absence of a conclusion as its ending. In the space in which the work unfolds, everything is to be said, and is therefore never said, but this does not suffer being altered by any other discourse, enclosed as it is within the definitive limits which constitute its imperfection. This seems to be the origin of criticism's inability to add anything to the discourse of the work: at most, it might extend the work – either in a reduction or in a pursuit of its discourse.

Yet it remains obvious that although the work is self-sufficient it does not contain or engender its own theory; it does not *know* itself. When the critic speaks he is not repeating, reproducing or remaking it; neither is he illuminating its dark corners, filling its margins with annotation, specifying that which was never specific. When the critical discourse begins from the hypothesis that the work speaks falteringly, it is not with the aim of *completing* it, reducing its deficiencies, as though the book were too small for the space it occupied. We have seen that a knowledge of the work is not elaborated within the work, but supposes a distance between knowledge and its object; to know what the writer is saying, it is not enough to let *him speak*, for his speech is hollow and can never be completed at its own level. Theoretical inquiry rejects the notion of the *space* or *site* of the work. Critical discourse does not attempt to complete the book, for theory begins from that incompleteness which is so radical that it cannot be located.

Thus, the silence of the book is not a lack to be remedied, an inadequacy to be made up for. It is not a temporary silence that could be finally abolished. We must distinguish the necessity of this silence. For example, it can be shown that it is the juxtaposition and conflict of several meanings which produces the radical otherness which shapes the work: this conflict is not resolved or absorbed, but simply *displayed*.

Thus the work cannot speak of the more or less complex opposition which structures it: though it is its expression and embodiment. In its every particle, the work *manifests*, uncovers, what it cannot say. This silence gives it life.

The spoken and the unspoken

The speech of the book comes from a certain silence, a matter which it endows with form, a ground on which it traces a figure. Thus, the book is not self-sufficient: it is necessarily accompanied by a *certain absence*, without which it would not exist. A knowledge of the book must include a consideration of this absence.

This is why it seems useful and legitimate to ask of every production what it tacitly implies, what it does not say. Either all around or in its wake the explicit requires the implicit: for in order to say anything, there are other things *which must not be said*. Freud relegated this *absence of certain words* to a new place which he was first to explore, and which he paradoxically *named*: the unconscious. To reach utterance, all speech envelops itself in the unspoken. We must ask why it does not speak of this interdict: can it be identified before one might wish to acknowledge it? There is not even the slightest hint of the absence of what it does not, perhaps cannot, say: the disavowal (dénégration) extends even to the act that banished the forbidden term; its absence is unacknowledged.

This moment of absence founds the speech of the work. Silences shape all speech. Banality?

Can we say that this silence is hidden? What is it? A condition of existence – point of departure, methodical beginning – essential foundation – ideal culmination – absolute origin which lends meaning to the endeavour? Means or form of connection.

Can we make this silence speak? What is the unspoken saying? What does it mean? To what extent is dissimulation a way of speaking? Can something that has hidden *itself* be recalled to our presence? Silence as the source of expression. Is what I am really saying what I am not saying? Hence the main risk run by those who would say everything. After all, perhaps the work is not hiding what it does not say: this is simply *missing*.

Yet the unspoken has many other resources: it assigns speech to its exact position, designating its domain. By speech, silence becomes the centre and principle of expression, its vanishing point. Speech eventually has nothing more to tell us: we investigate the silence, for it is the silence that is doing the speaking.

Silence reveals speech – unless it is speech that reveals the silence.

These two methods of explanation by recourse to the latent or concealed are not equivalent: it is the second which allows least value to the latent, since there appears an absence of speech through the absent speech, that is to say, a certain presence which it is enough to extricate. There is agreement to relate speech to its contrary, figure and ground. But there is a reluctance to leave these terms in equilibrium, an urge to resolve them: figure or ground? Here, once again, we encounter all the ambiguities of the notions of origin and creation. The unacknowledged co-existence of the visible and the hidden: the visible is merely the hidden in a different guise. The problem is merely to *pass across* from the one to the other.

The first image is the more profound, in so far as it enables us to recuperate the form of the second without becoming trapped in a mechanical problematic of transition: in being a necessary medium of expression, this ground of silence does not lose its significance. It is not the sole meaning, but that which endows meaning with a meaning: it is this silence which tells us – not just anything, since it exists to say nothing – which informs us of the precise conditions for the appearance of an utterance, and thus its limits, giving its real significance, without, for all that, speaking in its place. The latent is an intermediate means: this does not amount to pushing it into the background: it simply means that the latent is not another meaning which ultimately and miraculously *dispels* the first (manifest) meaning. Thus, we can see that meaning is in the *relation* between the implicit and explicit, not on one or the other side of that fence: for in the latter case, we should be obliged to choose, in other words, as ever, translation or commentary.

What is important in the work is what it does not say. This is not the same as the careless notation 'what it refuses to say', although that would in itself be interesting: a method might be built on it, with the task of *measuring silences*, whether acknowledged or unacknowledged. But rather than this, what the work *cannot* say is important, because there the elaboration of the utterance is acted out, in a sort of journey to silence.

 READING 24

'The death of the author'

Roland Barthes

In his story *Sarrasine*, Balzac, describing a castrato disguised as a woman, writes the following sentence: '*This woman herself, with her sudden fears, her irrational whims, her instinctive worries, her impetuous boldness, her fussings, and her delicious sensibility*'. Who is speaking thus? Is it the hero of the story bent on remaining ignorant of the castrato hidden beneath the woman? Is it Balzac the individual, furnished by his personal experience with a philosophy of Woman? Is it Balzac the author professing 'literary' ideas on femininity? Is it universal wisdom? Romantic psychology? We shall never know, for the good reason that writing is the destruction of every voice, of every point of origin. Writing is that neutral, composite, oblique space where our subject slips away, the negative where all identity is lost, starting with the very identity of the body writing.

No doubt it has always been that way. As soon as a fact is *narrated* no longer with a view to acting directly on reality but intransitively, that is to say, finally outside of any function than that of the very practice of the symbol itself, this disconnection occurs, the voice loses its origin, the author enters into his own death, writing begins. The sense of this phenomenon, however, has varied; in ethnographic societies the responsibility for a narrative is never assumed by a person but by a mediator, shaman or relator whose 'performance' – the mastery of the narrative code – may possibly be admired but never his 'genius'. The author is a modern figure, a product of our society in so far as, emerging from the Middle Ages with English empiricism, French rationalism and the personal faith of the Reformation, it discovered the prestige of the individual, or, as it is more nobly put, the 'human person'. It is thus logical that in literature it should be this positivism, the epitome and culmination of capitalist ideology, which has attached the greatest importance to the 'person' of the author. The *author* still reigns in histories of literature, biographies of writers, interviews, magazines, as in the very consciousness of men of letters anxious to unite their person and their work through diaries and memoirs. The image of literature to be found in ordinary culture is tyrannically centred on the author, his person, his life, his tastes, his passions, while criticism still consists for the most part in saying that Baudelaire's work is the failure of Baudelaire the man, Van Gogh's his madness, Tchaikovsky's his vice. The *explanation* of a work is always sought in the man or woman who produced it as if it were always in the end, through the more or less transparent allegory of the fiction, the voice of a single person, the *author* 'confiding' in us.

Though the sway of the Author remains powerful (the new criticism has often done no more than consolidate it), it goes without saying that certain writers have long since attempted to loosen it.

. . . .

We now know that a text is not a line of words releasing a single 'theological' meaning (the 'message' of the Author-God) but a multi-dimensional space in which a variety of writings, none of them original, blend and clash. The text is a tissue of quotations drawn from the innumerable centres of culture. Similar to Bouvard and Pécuchet, those eternal copyists, at once sublime and comic and whose profound ridiculousness indicates precisely the truth of writing, the writer can only imitate a gesture that is always anterior, never original. His only power is to mix writings, to counter the ones with others, in such a way as never to rest on any one of them. Did he wish to *express himself*, he ought at least to know that the inner 'thing' he thinks to 'translate' is itself only a ready-formed dictionary, its words only explainable through other words, and so on indefinitely; something experienced in exemplary fashion by the young Thomas de Quincey, he who was so good at Greek that in order to translate absolutely modern ideas and images into that dead language, he had, so Baudelaire tells us (in *Paradis Artificiels*), 'created for himself an unfailing dictionary, vastly more extensive and complex than those resulting from the ordinary patience of purely literary themes'.

Succeeding the Author, the scriptor no longer bears within him passions, humours, feelings, impressions, but rather his immense dictionary from which he draws a writing that can know no halt: life never does more than imitate the book, and the book itself is only a tissue of signs, an imitation that is lost, infinitely deferred.

Once the Author is removed, the claim to decipher a text becomes quite futile. To give a text an Author is to impose a limit on that text, to furnish it with a final signified, to close the writing. Such a conception suits criticism very well, the latter then allotting itself the important task of discovering the Author (or its hypostases: society, history, psyche, liberty) beneath the work: when the Author has been found, the text is 'explained' – victory to the critic. Hence there is no surprise in the fact that, historically, the reign of the Author has also been that of the Critic, nor again in the fact that criticism (be it new) is today undermined along with the Author. In the multiplicity of writing, everything is to be *disentangled*, nothing *deciphered*; the structure can be followed, 'run' (like the thread of a stocking) at every point and at every level, but there is nothing beneath; writing ceaselessly posits meaning ceaselessly to evaporate it, carrying out a systematic exemption of meaning. In precisely this way literature (it would be better from now on to say *writing*), by refusing to assign a 'secret', an ultimate meaning, to the text (and to the world as text), liberates what may be called an anti-theological activity, an activity that is truly revolutionary since to refuse to fix meaning is, in the end, to refuse God and his hypostases – reason, science, law.

Let us come back to the Balzac sentence. No one, no 'person', says it: its source, its voice, is not the true place of the writing, which is reading. Another – very precise – example will help to make this clear: recent research. . . has demonstrated the constitutively ambiguous nature of Greek tragedy, its texts being woven from words with double meanings that each character understands unilaterally (this perpetual misunderstanding is exactly the 'tragic'); there is however, someone who understands each word in its duplicity and who, in addition, hears the very deafness

133

of the characters speaking in front of him – this someone being precisely the reader (or here, the listener). Thus is revealed the total existence of writing: a text is made of multiple drawings, drawn from many cultures and entering into mutual relations of dialogue, parody, contestation, but there is one place where this multiplicity is focused and that place is the reader not, as was hitherto said, the author. The reader is the space on which all the quotations that make up a writing are inscribed without any of them being lost; a text's unity lies not in its origin but in its destination. Yet this destination cannot any longer be personal: the reader is without history, biography, psychology; he is simply that *someone* who holds together in a single field all the traces by which the written text is constituted. Which is why it is derisory to condemn the new writing in the name of a humanism hypocritically turned champion of the reader's rights. Classic criticism has never paid any attention to the reader; for it, the writer is the only person in literature. We are now beginning to let ourselves be fooled no longer by the arrogant antiphrastical recriminations of good society in favour of the very thing it sets aside, ignores, smothers, or destroys; we know that to give writing its future, it is necessary to overthrow the myth; the birth of the reader must be at the cost of the Author.

(from *Image–Music–Text*, 1972)

The pleasure of the text

Roland Barthes

Is not the most erotic portion of a body *where the garment gapes?* In perversion (which is the realm of textual pleasure) there are no 'erogenous zones' (a foolish expression, besides); it is intermittence, as psychoanalysis has so rightly stated, which is erotic; the intermittence of skin flashing between two articles of clothing (trousers and sweater), between two edges (the open necked shirt, the glove and the sleeve) it is this flash itself which seduces or rather; the staging of an appearance-as-disappearance.

The pleasure of the text is not the pleasure of the corporeal striptease or of narrative suspense. In these cases, there is no tear, no edges: a gradual unveiling: the entire excitation takes refuge in the *hope* of seeing the sexual organ (schoolboy's dream), or in knowing the end of the story (novelistic satisfaction). Paradoxically (since it is mass-consumed), this is a far more intellectual pleasure than the other: an (Œdipal pleasure (to denude, to know, to learn the origin and the end), if it is true that every narrative (every unveiling of the truth) is a staging of the (absent, hidden, or hypostatized) father – which would explain the solidarity of narrative forms, of family structures, and of prohibitions of nudity, all collected in our culture in the myth of Noah's sons covering his nakedness.

Yet the most classical narrative (a novel by Zola or Balzac or Dickens or Tolstoy) bears within it a sort of diluted tmesis: we do not read everything with the same intensity of reading; a rhythm is established, casual, unconcerned with the *integrity* of the text; our very avidity for knowledge impels us to skim or to skip certain passages (anticipated as 'boring') in order to get more quickly to the warmer parts of the anecdote (which are always its articulations; whatever furthers the solution of the riddle, the revelation of fate): we boldly skip (no-one is watching) descriptions, explanations, analyses, conversations; doing so, we resemble a spectator in a nightclub who climbs onto the stage and speeds up the dancer's striptease, tearing off her clothing, *but in the same order*, that is: on the one hand respecting, and on the other hastening the episodes of the ritual (like a priest *gulping down* his Mass). Tmesis, source or figure of pleasure, here confronts two prosaic edges with one another; it sets what is useful to a knowledge of the secret against what is useless to such knowledge; tmesis is a seam or flaw resulting from a simple principle of functionality; it does not occur at the level of the structure of languages but only at the moment of their consumption: the author cannot predict tmesis: he cannot choose to write *what will not be read*. And yet, it is the very rhythm of what is read and what is not read that creates the pleasure of great narratives: has anyone ever read Proust, Balzac, *War and Peace*, word for word? (Proust's good fortune: from one reading to the next, we never skip the same passages.)

Thus, what I enjoy in a narrative is not directly its content or even its structure, but rather the abrasions I impose upon the fine surface: I read on, I skip, I look up, I dip in again. Which has nothing to do with the deep laceration the text of bliss inflicts upon language itself, and not upon the simple temporality of its reading.

Whence two systems of reading: one goes straight to the articulations of the anecdote, it considers the extent of the text, ignores the play of the language (if I read Jules Vernes, I go fast: I lose discourse, and yet my reading is not hampered by any verbal loss – in the speleological sense of that word) the other reading skips nothing; it weighs, it sticks to the text, it reads so to speak with application and transport, grasps at every point in the text the asyndeton which cuts the various languages – and not the anecdote, it is not (logical) extension that captivates it, the winnowing out of truths, but the layering of significance: as in the children's game of topping hands, the excitement comes not from a processive haste but from a kind of vertical din (the verticality of language and of its destruction); it is at the moment when each (different) hand skips over the next (and not one *after* the other) that the hole, the gap, is created and carries off the subject of the game – the subject of the text. Now paradoxically (so strong is the belief that one need merely *go fast* in order not to be bored), this second, *applied* reading (in the real sense of the word 'application') is the one suited to the modern text, the limit-text. Read slowly, read *all* of a novel by Zola, and the book will drop from your hands; read fast, in snatches, some modern text, and it becomes opaque, inaccessible to your pleasure: you want something to happen and nothing does, for *what happens to the language does not happen to the discourse*: what 'happens', what 'goes away', the seam of the two edges, the interstice of bliss, occurs in the volume of the languages, in the uttering, not in the sequence of utterances: not to devour, to gobble, but to graze, to browse scrupulously, to rediscover – in order to read today's writers – the leisure of bygone readings: to be *aristocratic* readers.

If I agree to judge a text according to pleasure, I cannot go on to say this one is good, that bad. No awards, no 'critique' for this always implies a tactical aim, a social usage, and frequently an extenuating image-reservoir. I cannot apportion, imagine that the text is perfectable, ready to enter into a play of normative predicates: it is too much *this*, not enough *that*; the text (the same is true of the singing voice) can wring from me only this judgement, in no way adjectival: *that's it!* And

135

further still: *that's for me!* This 'for me' is neither subjective nor non-existential, but Nietzschean ('. . . basically, it is always the same question: What is it *for me? . . .*').

The *brio* of the text (without which, after all, there is no text) is its *will to bliss*: just where it exceeds demand, transcends prattle, and whereby it attempts to overflow, to break through the constraint of adjectives – which are those doors of language through which the ideological and the imaginary come flowing in.

Text of pleasure: the text that contents, fills, grants euphoria; the text that comes from culture and does not break with it, is linked to a *comfortable* practice of reading. Text of bliss: the text that imposes a state of loss, the text that discomforts (perhaps to the point of a certain boredom), unsettles the reader's historical, cultural, psychological assumptions, the consistency of his tastes, values, memories, brings to a crisis his relation with language.

Now the subject who keeps the two texts in his field and in his hands the reins of pleasure and bliss is an anachronic subject, for he simultaneously and contradictorily participates in the profound hedonism of all culture (which permeates him quietly under cover of an *art de vivre* shared by the old books) and in the destruction of that culture: he enjoys the consistency of his selfhood (that is his pleasure) and seeks its loss (that is his bliss). He is a subject split twice over, doubly perverse.

. . . .

Here moreover, drawn from psychoanalysis, is an indirect way of establishing the opposition between the text of pleasure and the text of bliss: pleasure can be expressed in words, bliss cannot.

Bliss is unspeakable, inter-dicted, I refer to Lacan ('What one must bear in mind is that bliss is forbidden to the speaker, as such, or else that it cannot be spoken except between the lines . . .') and to Leclaire ('Whoever speaks, by speaking denies bliss, or correlatively, whoever experiences bliss causes the letter – and all possible speech – to collapse in the absolute degree of the annihilation he is celebrating').

The writer of pleasure (and his reader) accepts the letter: renouncing bliss, he has the right and the power to express it: the letter is his pleasure; he is obsessed by it, as are all those who love language (and not speech), logophiles, authors, letter writers, linguists: about texts of pleasure, therefore, it is possible to speak (no argument with the annihilation of bliss): *criticism always deals with the texts of pleasure, never the texts of bliss*: Flaubert, Proust, Stendhal are discussed inexhaustibly; thus criticism speaks the futile bliss of the tutor text, its *past or future* bliss; *you are about to read, I have read*: criticism is always historical or prospective: the constatory present, the *presentation* of bliss, is forbidden it; its preferred material is thus culture, which is everything in us except our present.

With the writer of bliss (and his reader) begins the untenable text, the impossible text. This text is outside pleasure, outside criticism, *unless it is reached through another text of bliss*: you cannot speak 'on' such a text, you can only speak 'in' it, *in its fashion*, enter into a desperate plagiarism, hysterically affirm the void of bliss (and no longer obsessively repeat the letter of pleasure).

'A critical survey of the theoretical and practical achievements of the past ten years'

Stuart Hall

Such a survey must, by nature of its scope, be merely an incomplete guide, a mapping of some of the tendencies which have developed over the last ten years in the area of cultural studies. Every map, of course, contains its own reading of the nature of the terrain and this paper will do no more than construct a certain area of the field and attempt to suggest connections or disconnections, overlaps or disjunctures. The aim is not to be comprehensive but to construct a part of the field and to 'talk to it', both to attempt to understand its genesis and to consider the consequences of what has been happening.

To understand the origins of the present developments, it is necessary to return to what was the dominant literary practice in criticism, that of Leavis's heritage. The central focus of this tradition was the notion of a radically autonomous and unique text, which expressed the specific configuration of the author's beliefs, feelings, ideas and experience. This by now classical position vis-à-vis the text and the author was combined by Leavis with a systematic concern for the literary, social and historical context of the work. Unlike many conventional critics of the day, Leavis understood, albeit in a special and now unfamiliar manner, that there was something important about the connections between the internal constitution of the text and the social context in which it was produced. Leavis argued that only by attending to the internal organisation of the text could one understand its extrinsic relationship to its social context. This in itself was an important development for a sociology of literature.

For those who wanted to go beyond Leavis's insistence on the autonomous text and the isolated author two paths opened up. The first was to scrutinise the historical contextualization of the work and the second to examine the social relations of the text and the author. The development of an empirical sociology of literature from the latter has given rise to some work, not a great deal, making use of sociological concepts in the evaluation of the external relations of the text. This direction is not one we wish to follow, however. This is not necessarily to relegate it to a lesser status, although it has not been the dominant trend in this country, but merely to indicate the direction of our interest.

The other strand of development is that of 'cultural studies', the area which will be elaborated and discussed here. Rather than discuss it in its own terms we will approach it through the theorist who, chronologically, has contributed the most to its development as a semi-independent area of enquiry, Raymond Williams. Not the full bodied person Raymond Williams, but the various theoretical personae under whose different guises he has appeared in the course of his development. Indeed, many of the theorists considered here will appear in like manner. Raymond Williams I then, that is up to *The Long Revolution*, is a mixed case, as Eagleton has pointed out in his article in *New Left Review*[1], and one must recognise the historical conditions which contribute to this.[2]

Characteristic of Williams's early work is a return to the notion of the importance of the *experiential* which, in its emphasis upon the immediate feel of the text, the quality of its communication, can be traced back to the influence of Leavis. Williams attempts to get underneath the formal social relations of the text, the social, historical and class determinations of the work, to that which in literature captures the essence of the experiential quality of life. One of the most important non-conceptual concepts in *The Long Revolution* is that of the 'structure of feeling',[3] which exactly poses the problem of whether a 'feeling' can have a 'structure'. Nevertheless, Williams still insisted upon the privileged position of the literacy documentation of a period, despite his admission that literature could only be understood alongside other, social, economic and political practices. He argued that it was only literature which could faithfully reproduce what it felt like to live in a certain period. He still paid homage to the witness of literature.

In *The Long Revolution* Williams presents a social model of interactionist elements in which no one practice is dominant or determinant. This quasi-marxist 'parallelogram of practices' does not countenance any determination: rather it postulates an organic inter-penetration of development. Williams's work carries on a continuous, covert dialogue with Marxism in the attempt to develop a theory of literature in relation to culture and society. His refusal of Marxism is denoted by the absence of the terms he is in dialogue with, most importantly that of 'ideology'. Unwilling to openly acknowledge his relationship to Marxism, Williams is forced into a major effort to re-constitute the terms of his mode of analysis.

Raymond Williams II represents an important transformation within cultural studies which would have been unthinkable without the mediation of Stanley Mitchell's translation of the major works of Lukács. The latter's work represents the decisive intervention of the continental Marxist tradition into the parochial field of literary studies. Perhaps the best summation of this new persona is to be found in Williams's article on Goldmann, a disciple of Lukács, in *New Left Review*[4] in which he juxtaposes the new found continental Marxist tradition and the English literary tradition. In so doing he attempts some kind of introductory syntheses between his own notion of 'structure of feeling' and Goldmann's concept of 'genetic structures'. It is at this point that Williams concedes an overlapping interest between the English tradition and that of Lukács and Goldmann. He recognizes a convergence of interest centered on the nature of 'mental structures' internal to the literary work and their relationship to the collective mental structure of the group for whom that text, or corpus of texts, is a collective expression. Goldmann's attempt to establish a 'homology of structures' between the works of Racine, the philosophical writings of Pascal and the material and evaluative world-view of a particular group in France, in relation to a power structure and a mode of production, is undoubtedly the most important contribution to this area of theoretical development.[5] He sought to establish a homology between the 'mental structures' of this group's philosophizing, the shape of their mental world and its most coherent and fully achieved literary expression in the works of Racine. This concern to understand the homology of mental and socio-historical structures is the way in which Williams, through his own interpretation of the process, attempted to reconcile the European Marxist and English literary methodologies. He insists however, that the homology is not one of content but of form, and this line of thinking can be seen in his later work, both on literature and the mass media. This move towards an interest in form, albeit not a developed formalism, partially explains why the work of

Goldmann turned out to be more important than that of Lukács in this input of continental Marxism into the English tradition. Lukács had, in fact, been more concerned with a homology of contents, the way in which the historical conditions of a class found direct expression in the literary work in terms of its aspirations, ideas and forms of consciousness. Goldmann made a radical break from this socio-historical emphasis to consider the aesthetic, literary and philosophical structures of a given work.

Raymond Williams III is that of the essay on base and superstructure[6] and of a collection of essays about to be published on the role of language and linguistic forms in literature.[7] This persona can essentially be seen as an attempt to re-synthesise the earlier positions in the light of his continuing semi-silent dialogue with European Marxism. Althusser, Barthes and linguistics in general are probably the main unspoken opponents of this perversely silent theoretical re-alignment.

The origin of external input now shifts to Germany from where the work of Benjamin and Brecht begins to assert an influence in England. Up to this point one had been dealing with either sophisticated theories of reflection or theories of expressive structure, the most sophisticated version of which being Goldmann's notion of the homology of structures. Benjamin and Brecht's impact was to introduce two concepts which had not been employed in the English field previously; those of practice and production. Central to Benjamin's work was the requirement to develop a Marxist theory of artistic production. In this he is drawing not from the early Marx, but from the later scientific-economic works in which the concept of mode of production is dominant. Benjamin's great importance and revolutionising effect was to displace the notion of the radically autonomous text which had held the centre of English literary studies for so long. His originality was to have transferred the notion of production into cultural studies and to attempt to formulate a thorough-going materialist theory of socio-historical contextualization of the production of the text. How successful he was remains open to question; his importance was to have so originally opened up the materialist basis of theoretical development. There is a theoretical complementarity between Benjamin's theory of artistic production and Brecht's concern with artistic reproduction and exchange. Brecht's more substantial contribution was to enter the previously untouched area of the reader, the audience, to develop a theory of artistic practice. In contrast to the work of Lukács, which was concerned to show the internal coherence, the inner unity of great works of art, both Benjamin and Brecht are concerned with the discontinuous, fragmentary, contradictory forms of the work. Whereas Lukács tried to rework the tradition of bourgeois literature and appropriate it for the revolution Benjamin and Brecht saw the necessity for a fundamental and subversive break with tradition, the rupturing of aesthetic forms. They insisted on the subversive nature of the artistic intervention in both production and practice. In opposition to Lukács' attitude to bourgeois realism, Brecht attacked the whole notion of realism and posited the 'alienation' effect in disjuncturing the passive role of the audience, the reader. Brecht's impact was not exclusively within the sphere of the literary artifact but was to open up the media to which his work was addressed. Alongside the notion of rupture, contradiction and broken progress, there was the realisation of the impact of the historical break-up of the material basis of artistic production. The expansion of the mass media, new modes of production and communication and interest in their material basis are evident in the work of Benjamin and Brecht, especially in Benjamin's famous 'The Author as Producer' (1934).[8]

Brecht was taken up above all in film criticism, his critique of realism and attention to cross media communication providing a sharp focus in the debate. Brecht's intervention was to locate realism as a specific historical form, to suggest the nature of its prescription of complicity between the reader and the text, the audience and the performance. Benjamin and Brecht drew attention to the constructed nature of the aspiring naturalism of the sign in realism which presented itself as the real world. They placed at the centre of the debate the whole process of the social manufacture of messages within communication and nowhere was this more evident than in the visual media where the image is much less arbitrary than in literature. The ideological nature of the process in film and television was clearly brought to the fore by their intervention.

The development from Benjamin and Brecht to Althusser is mediated through Levi-Strauss, Barthes and structuralism. The antecedents of this movement can be found in various forms of linguistics: Prague linguistics, Russian linguistics, Saussure, Jakobson, Russian formalism etc., and are well enough documented for us to merely indicate them here. What is important to note is that although the roots of the linguistic paradigm are in a completely different intellectual tradition to that of Benjamin and Brecht there is a common interest in signification. Roland Barthes, for instance, one of the most important theorists working in this area, although not influenced by Benjamin and Brecht, was important precisely in respect of his interest in, and transformation of, the concepts of linguistic practice. Systems of meaning were no longer accepted as normal, natural modes of practice, they were considered in their specific work within language, their construction of messages as social practice. It was the social, ideological nature of language which came under scrutiny, replacing the primacy of the individual utterance with an interest in its location in the inter-textuality of codes. A text was seen to be spoken not by the individual subject, the isolated author, but by the discourses in which it was located. There was a fundamental decentring from the individual to language and signification as a system under the influence of semiotics. The articulation of this position we can ascribe to Barthes I since he has now moved beyond it.

The importance of this transformation of the field, whether one adjudges it to be right or wrong, should not be under-estimated in the line we are tracing. The scientific nature of its investigation was concentrated on the generative aspect of the code, not on the individual utterance. The text was no longer regarded as having a single meaning, but as bringing together many discourses and as being inscribed across several codes. At the level of literary theory *S/Z* is the most complete working out of this intertextuality of codes, and in *Mythologies* Barthes concentrates on the socio-ideological nature of the code.[9] It is in the work of Kristeva that this development finds its classic expression in the working out of the essential de-centring of the text and of the notion of inter-textuality.[10]

There is considerable argument as to whether the field, as influenced by the first wave of semiotic structuralism, stems from the same problematic as before, even though it shares with that earlier problematic a concern with the concepts of practice and production. The question remains as to whether there is, in fact, the development of a single problematic, whether there is an advance into the constitution of literary and cultural theory within some kind of transformation of Marxist theory. Although the field, as constituted within this linguistic paradigm, has its roots in Marxist theory, in Marx's mature conceptual framework, it is not at all clear that it remains within the terrain of that problematic.

Althusser I, constituted by *For Marx* and *Reading Capital*,[11] assimilates this latter problematic even though he is not directly contributing to the area of a theory of culture and literary production. Nevertheless, Althusser establishes the centrality of the notion of practice in the artistic field and especially that of ideological practice. It should be noted though that this notion of ideological practice is oddly placed in relation to a regional theory of literary production since in his early work, *For Marx,* Althusser goes out of his way to say that art is not ideology.[12] The location of ideological practice in the field of Althusserian practices is, therefore, difficult to understand. However, Althusser's insistence on thinking literary production on the model of practice, that of the transformation of raw material, the means of transformation and the end product, and of the establishment of ideological practice as not being the same as economic and political practice, as having its own relative autonomy, its own internal specificity, both reintroduces certain Marxist concepts, like practice and production, and does so in such a way as to allow the greater development of that regional theory of literature. Once the social formation is thought of in terms of the Althusserian model, the specificity of literary practice is reasserted and the possibility and necessity of a Marxist aesthetics is re-introduced. Macherey, working within the Althusserian paradigm and attempting to think a literary mode of production, seems to share the confusion over the location of the relationship between art and ideology as specific practices.[13]

Althusser II is characterised by a self-criticism of the over-theoreticism of *Reading Capital* and by the radical abandonment of the notion of the opposition of ideology and science.[14] The question is, of course, whether that critique of the over-theoreticism of the early period extends to those who, like Macherey and in this country, Eagleton, have been working within the problematic of Althusser I. However, in this later period between 1973–6 it has not been *Reading Capital* which has been the seminal text but the 'Ideological State Apparatuses' essay.[15] In this essay Althusser returns not to the question of modes of production, of a literary mode of production, but to the question of ideology. The return to ideology does not produce a clarification of the status of the cultural object, whether it is an ideological object or not, but it does raise certain questions which found expression in the work of Barthes and semiology, questions of the unmasking of dominant ideologies, dominant myths in literature, film and the mass media, of the exposure of the cultural ideologies of the dominant class.

There are two kinds of interest in ideology in the essay, which are somewhat divergent, or which have produced two different kinds of reading. The first is the notion, influenced by the work of Gramsci, of the way in which the capitalist social formation depends on the ideological apparatuses to reproduce its own social relations of production. It represents an attempt to ground this interest in ideology in particular practices, in particular institutions and this direction out of the 'Ideological State Apparatuses' essay can be seen in the work of Poulantzas.[16] The second line in the essay is concerned with 'ideology in general' the function of which is to mask social, historical formations through the interpolation of the subject, the positioning of the subject within ideology. These two definitions of ideology seem to stem from different problematics and to be in essential contradiction.

Althusser III is concerned with the subject, not the Sartrean subject of free choice or the Cartesian subject of the ego, but the subject of ideology, the category of the subject as a formative category of ideological discourse. This owes a great deal of course to Lacan and the recent work of Kristeva, based on the Lacanian re-reading of Freud.[17] It is a re-transformation of the Althusserian paradigm by psycho-analysis whose major impact at the present time has been in the film theory. One of the central texts of this is undoubtedly Kristeva II and her concern with the revolution of the word, with aesthetic rupture, with the breaking of literary forms and the contravention of the ideological fixity of the symbolic in heterogeneity, flux and desire. This complex area has not yet been fully assimilated or understood in cultural studies. What has emerged from this long development, however has been the affirmation of, at long last, a fully materialist theory of language. This affirmation does not, however, appear to have been substantiated in the theoretical and empirical work of Lacan and others: it is a materialist theory by affirmation only.

This summary and brief exposition of the contemporaneous developments returns us to the central factor of our analysis which is that every one of these developments has, in some way or another, been generated by Marxism. Since leaving the unsullied English reaches of *The Long Revolution* every subsequent transformation within the field has been a product of, or has claimed to be a product of, various versions of the Marxist problematic. Indeed the whole development of the field could be said to be that problem of the nature of the internal theoretical relations of the transformation, the self-transformation, of paradigms which do stem from Marxist theory or assert a relationship to Marxist theory. The present stage of development, occuring mostly in film theory, but now beginning to produce work in literary studies is based in the psychoanalytic paradigm of the Lacanian re-reading of Freud. Whether it subscribes to the Freudian paradigm seems open to question, and its identity with a materialist theory of ideology, is an uncertain one and by affirmation only.

One of the aims of this mapping exercise of some of the main movements within the theoretical and empirical development of the field has been to draw up certain boundary lines which have become so well established that one cannot go beyond them. This schematism has obviously led to an over-condensation but hopefully this enforced brevity will not detract too much from the over-all purpose. Essentially the field is one which is determined by the reception, development and transformation of Marxist theory; having established this is to lay down some basic protocol, but it is also to open up and expose enormous complexity since this is an area where Marxist theory is not well developed. There is no Marxist aesthetics; there is only the germinal seed of a Marxist theory of ideology – indeed there are two such versions in the mature work of Marx which do not receive any articulation in his definitive works. Therefore, when Marxist theory develops by borrowing concepts from other cognate disciplines that is not necessarily a bad thing, and has proved to be a necessary inter-penetrative discourse for the elaboration of this field. Finally one should note that the development of the field over the last ten years has been a bewildering series of theoretical explosions with the appearance, assimilation and familiarization of one continental theoretician after another.

(transcribed in summary form by Richard Osborne from a recording)

Notes

1   Terry Eagleton, 'Criticism and Politics: the work of Raymond Williams' (*NLR 95*, 1976): now part of Chapter One of his *Criticism and Ideology* (London, 1976).

2 See Eagleton's article for the argument concerning the nature of Williams's suppressed dialogue with Marxism due to the effect of the Cold War.

3 Raymond Williams, *The Long Revolution* (London, 1961).

4 Raymond Williams 'Literature and Sociology: in memory of Lucien Goldmann' (*NLR* 67, 1971).

5 Lucien Goldmann, *Le Dieu caché* (Paris, 1955); *The Hidden God*, trans. Philip Thody (London, 1964).

6 Raymond Williams, 'Base and Superstructure in Marxist Cultural Theory' (*NLR* 82, 1973).

7 Now published as *Keywords* (London, 1976).

8 In Walter Benjamin, *Understanding Brecht* (London, 1973).

9 Roland Barthes, *Mythologies* (Paris, 1957), trans. Annette Lavers (London, 1972); *S/Z* (Paris, 1970), trans. Richard Miller (London, 1975).

10 See for example Julia Kristeva, *Semiotike: Recherches pour une semanalyse* (Paris, 1969).

11 Louis Althusser, *Pour Marx* (Paris, 1966): *For Marx*, trans. B. Brewster (London, 1969): *Lire le Capital* (with Etienne Balibar) (Paris, 1968): *Reading Capital*, trans. B. Brewster (London, 1970).

12 In 'The Picolo Theatre: Berrtolazzi and Brecht' in *For Marx*.

13 Pierre Macherey, *Pour une théorie de la production littéraire* (Paris, 1966).

14 See his collection of essays (1964–1971) published as *Lenin and Philosophy*, trans. B. Brewster (London, 1971).

15 Included in *Lenin and Philosophy*.

16 Especially N. Poulantzas, *Classes in Contemporary Capitalism* (London, 1975).

17 Jacques Lacan, *Écrits* (Paris, 1966); Julia Kristeva, 'Le sujet en procés', *Tel Quel*, 52 (1972), 12–30 and 53 (1973) 17–38.

 READING 27

'Marxism and popular fiction'

Tony Bennett

Against literature

I have stated that popular fiction has been a neglected area of study within Marxist criticism; that the bulk of Marxist critical attention has focused on the canonized tradition is incontestable. However, and especially of late, there are Marxists who have concerned themselves with the study of popular texts – Eco and Barthes for example. Even so, it is noticeable that popular texts have figured more prominently within the project of developing a general semiology than within the distinctively literary-critical region of Marxist theory. So far as the historical formation of Marxist criticism is concerned, however, the degree of critical attention devoted to the study of recognizably popular forms within those major schools of Marxist criticism which – at least until recently – have defined the central terms of reference of Marxist critical debate has been, to say the least, cursory. . . . The result has been for a science which claims to be revolutionary, a highly paradoxical history in which Marxist criticism has functioned largely corroboratively in relation to the distinctions forged by bourgeois criticism: approving of the same body of canonized works but for different reasons, and disapproving the rest – lumped together as a residue – but, again, for different reasons. Bourgeois criticism has thus been simultaneously patted on the back for having recognized which works are truly great and taken to task for having misrecognized the reasons for their greatness. The *real* reason for Tolstoy's greatness, it turns out, has nothing to do with the eternal verities of the human condition, but to his having given coherent expression to the world-view of the peasantry (Lukács) or to his supplying us with a vision of the contradictions inscribed in the ideology to which his works allude (Macherey). Mulhern has warned that 'it would be astonishing if the judgements of Marxist criticism turned out to be so many materialist doppelgänger of those made current by the foregoing idealist tradition'[5]. Yes, astonishing indeed; none the less, so far as the question of literary evaluation is concerned, that has been the main heritage of the tradition so far.

. . . .

Marxist criticism: a deformed materialism

The problem of value

The statement that Marxists have been obsessively concerned with the problem of value is, of course, contestable. Terry Eagleton, for one, has argued that Marxism 'has maintained a certain silence about aesthetic value'[8]. While it is true that attempts to pose the problem of value at an explicitly theoretical level have been few and far between, the problem of value has none the less saturated Marxist critical practice in the sense that it has been routinely present in the background, even when other problems have been addressed. It has been massively present in the way the problem of reductionism has been posed within Marxist criticism. For this has been conceived as a problem only in relation to valued texts; outside this restricted sphere of writing, reductionist formulations have been actively embraced. Reductionism, that is to say, has been shunned less for theoretical reasons than for tactical ones, particularly – in the context of an ideological contest with bourgeois criticism – the need to ward off the ever-ready equation between materialism and philistinism.

I will return to this point later. Meanwhile, it should be noted that to maintain that the problem of value is an improper one for Marxism is not thereby to assert the equivalence of parity of all forms of writing – a self-evident absurdity. Statements to the effect that Joyce opened up the possibilities of language in a way that Conan Doyle, say, did not seem to me to be quite unproblematic. However, such purely technical assessments of the formal effects of different practices of writing do not, of themselves offer grounds for valuing the one above the other. That is a further step which requires the intervention of a discourse of value which argues reasons for preferring forms of writing which stretch the possibilities of language over those which do not (for not all discourses of value have produced such criteria for valuation). Still less is it to advocate a neo-Kantian stance which abdicates the realm of value in the name of a pseudo-neutrality. This is not merely a question of arguing that judgements of value can and should be made; it is more one of recognizing that they inevitably *will* be made and that Marxists cannot afford to stand aloof from the ever ongoing process of the social valorization – and counter-valorization – of texts.

Rather, my chief objection is to the form which the debate about value has predominantly taken within Marxist criticism where it has been conceived as *identical with* and *addressed through* the problem of Literature. This has resulted in the conflation of a whole series of analytically separate problems: the problem of explaining the source of a work's value has been run in with that of explaining its 'literariness' – those formal characteristics which uniquely distinguish it from other forms of fiction – and, worse, problems of aesthetic evaluation and political calculation have been implicitly merged, as in Lukács' attempt to construct a realist aesthetic that would recruit all great realists to the banner of progressivism in art. Most disquieting of all, however, has been the tendency – consistent with an acceptance of the valuations of bourgeois criticisms – to view value as essentially *static*, at least over large periods of time; to regard it as a property that is inherently inscribed within conventionally revered texts; and, as a part of an ideological polemic with bourgeois criticism, to contend that such properties can only be explicated by returning to the text, analytically, to the conditions of its production.

This way of posing the problem is mistaken for a number of reasons, all of which cluster around the fact that value is not – nor, logically, can it be – a property ouf the text *alone*. One cannot pose the question of value without introducing into the analysis the problem of the valuing subject. Texts do not *have* value; they can only *be valued* by valuing subjects of particular types and for particular reasons, and these are entirely the product of critical discourses of valuation, varying from criticism to criticism. What has been offered with Marxist criticism, under the guise of *theories of value,* are in fact merely *specific reasons for valuing*, specific discourses of value begetting valuing subjects of particular types, which cannot logically (although they may, of course, politically) be preferred above those produced by competing critical discourses of valuation.

In the case of Lukácsian aesthetics, for example, texts are valued – that is, they are alleged to contain a value which Marxist critical judgement merely accurately reflects – in proportion to the degree to which they approximate the norm of historical self-knowledge which constitutes the Lukácsian model of literariness. In the case of the Althusserians, value is explained in terms of the extent to which texts distance or rupture the ideological discourses to which they allude; if they do this significantly, they're 'in', they count as Literature and are valued; if they do not, they are consigned elsewhere. As specific political reasons for valuing, such arguments are unexceptionable; they can be debated politically at the level of a strategic calculation of their effects – of the practices of writing they support, of the types of valuing subject they produce, of the categories of readers they imply and so on. However, in so far as they are presented as theories of value (and they are so presented) they are singularly impertinent. For such are not at all the grounds upon which the revered texts of the great tradition have, predominantly been valorized. It is only possible to present such *reasons for valuing* as *theories of value* by simply discounting the positions of valuing subjects produced by and within competing critical discourses.

· ·

In place of a theory of value, then, Marxism's concern should be with the analysis of 'the ideological conditions of the social *contestation* of value'. So far as the *making* of evaluations is concerned, this is a matter for strategic calculation – a question of politics and not of aesthetics.

The literary and the ideological

· ·

No matter which school of criticism – Lukácsan, Frankfurt, Althusserian – the position advanced is substantially the same: Literature is not ideology and is relatively autonomous in relation to it, whereas popular fiction is ideology and is reduced to it. Literature, it is usually argued, either rises above ideology because of its social typicality or the depth of its historical penetration (Lukács), or consists of a specific set of formal operations upon it (Althusser); but 'popular' or 'mass' fiction is viewed as simply a reflection or formulaic reproduction of the ideology on which it is dependent and which it simply passes on. 'Popular literature', as Roger Bromley has put it 'is one among many of the material forms which ideology takes (or through which it is mediated) under capitalism, and is an instance of its social production through the medium of writing'.[11]

The difficulties with such formulations are numerous. It is just not possible to contend, to take Althusser's proposition, that it is only in the case of 'truly authentic' art, and not at all in the case of 'average or mediocre' works, that a distance is opened up between the 'literary' and the 'ideological'. For instance, quite an elaborate play with the dominant forms of narrative ideology is to be found in the detective novel,[12] whereas the detective film, as Stephen Neale has put it, 'dramatizes the signification process itself as its fundamental problem'.[13] More generally, the entire field of popular fiction – especially film and television – is replete with parodic forms in which considerable 'distancing', 'alluding', 'foregrounding', and so on takes place. Whilst an exact categorization of programmes such as *Monty Python's Flying Circus*, *Not the 9 O'clock News* and *Ripping Yarns* may be difficult, it is clear, first, that they are *popular*, and that they are *fiction*, and second, that they are not *just* ideology; they disrupt not merely conventional narrative forms, but are often profoundly, if anarchically, subversive of the dominant ideological discourses of class, nation, sexism and so on.

Such empirical difficulties apart, the very attempt to found a distinction between Literature and popular fiction – so that one is differentiated from, and the other flattened against, ideology – results in a crucial theoretical inconsistency according to which the effectivity that is granted to formal and aesthetic strategies in relation to ideological categories in one area of fiction is witheld from often not dissimilar strategies in other areas of fiction. Such a formulation is, at best, illogical; any area of writing in which fictional devices and strategies are in evidence must, in some way or other, effect a specific *production* of the ideological discourses contained within it. It cannot, if the concept of 'fiction' is to retain any usefulness as a differentiating term, simply be equated with such ideological discourses. Nor, if the logic of reflection theory is faulty elsewhere, can it be construed as a mere reflection or formulaic reproduction of them. At worst, however, it is self-fulfilling, the product of a rift within the critical strategy of Marxism which guarantees that popular texts be viewed reductively. If 'literary' texts have been distinguished from ideology whereas popular texts have been collapsed back into it, this is partly attributable to the fact that these different regions of textual production have received different types of critical attention which serve to buttress the supposition that the distinctions between them are, indeed, organized and explicable in these terms. In their treatment of canonized texts, Marxists have focused on the specifically formal means and mechanisms by which such texts either distance themselves from, or lift themselves above, the merely ideological. When dealing with popular texts, however, they have tended to read through such specifically formal operations, to plunder the texts for the evidence of 'falsifications' of reality which they contain, and, in doing so, have joined hands with bourgeois criticism in reproducing, in the very form of their critical practice itself, the Literature/popular fiction distinction in its ideological form.

Such contradictions are attributable, ultimately, to the pressure which 'Literature' has exerted on the way the problem of relative autonomy has been conceived and addressed. Rather than being posed as a problem concerning the complex and diverse articulation of two different regions of the ideological, the literary (or fictional) and the discursive, it has been construed as a problem concerning the relationship between Literature (as a specific and privileged area of fictional practice) and Ideology viewed, variously, as the domain of false-consciousness, as the opposite of Marxism, or as a specific practice producing specific 'imaginary' subject positions which give rise to the effect of 'misrecognition'. Such a project is misconceived because the categories with which it deals – Literature and Ideology – are, in as much as they have their provenance in different bodies of theory (bourgeois criticism and Marxism respectively), mismatched from the outset. Put simply, there is no *necessary* reason why a space should exist within Marxist theory for the concept of Literature, and the attempt to clear such a space has resulted in the problem of the relationship between the literary or the fictional (in their diverse modes) and the ideological being resolved by definitional *fiat*. Ultimately, the proffered equation of popular fiction with ideology with Marxism is a tautology, a *necessary* definition entailed by the way in which the relations between Literature, Science (Marxism) and Ideology have already been constituted. Once Literature has been distinguished from Ideology and from Science (Marxism) in the formulations of classical Marxism's favoured 'holy trinity of the superstructure', then there is, quite simply, *nowhere that popular fiction can be placed*, other than within the ideological, which does not call into question the category of Literature and the terms in which its specificity has been theoretically constructed. The effect of the category of Literature has been to so constrain Marxists theoretically that they have had *no option* but to argue, time and again, that since popular fiction is not Marxism (it does not contain any analysis of social relationships), and since it is not Literature either (it does not have the critical 'edge' of Literature), then it *must* be ideology.

. . . .

But it is, of course, politically that the effects of this approach are most damaging. For its *en bloc* categorization of popular fiction as a sphere of writing which contributes to the reproduction of dominant ideological formations entails that it be abandoned as a field of struggle. The only relation of political calculation it permits is that of struggling *against* popular fiction (by unmasking it, by opposing to it the knowledge of Marxism or the critical insights of Literature), rather than *within* it. It is necessary to insist, in the face of the essentialism that has blighted much Marxist discussion of the internal economy of the superstructure, that conflict and struggle take place *within* and not just *between* the different regions and spheres of the superstructure. Beating popular fiction over the head with the three volumes of *Capital* is, politically, beside the point; what is needed are terms of theorization which will enable writers and critics to intervene, in a strategically calculated way, *within* the processes of popular reading and writing. Hegemony is to be won, not by sailing against the prevailing wind but by plotting a course across it.

. . . .

The calculation of political effects, however, requires not only that the conjuncture or the prevailing system of intertextual relations be taken into account; there is also the question of the reader – of his/her position in the conjuncture, and of how s/he is placed in relation to the systems of intertextuality which regulate the act of reading. While the 'effects' tradition within media sociology is seldom laudable, it has given serious consideration to questions of the audience; and in recent years, the input of semiological perspectives to the process of 'decoding' has yielded a climate of opinion in film and television studies which is more cautious than that discernible in literary-critical circles concerning the extent to which effects can be inferred from form. Put simply, there are as yet, no serious readership studies, a project which the literary left has culpably neglected.

This is not to suggest that readership studies should replace textual analysis; the text clearly constrains the possible ways in which it may be read, albeit these limits can never be specified in advance. Nor is it to suggest that existing models of audience research should simply be borrowed; these clearly place too much reliance on simple-minded questionnaire techniques. It is rather to recognize that the ground on which the text produces its effects consists not of naked subjectivities but of individuals interpellated into particular subject positions within a variety of different – and sometimes contradictory – ideological formations. This further entails recognizing that such positions vary in accordance with consideration of race, class and gender and, concerning their insertion within the system of intertextual relations, on the degree to which, within the educational apparatus, the institution of Literature has borne upon their ideological formation, upon their positioning as readers. . . .

If such considerations are not allowed a determining role in relation to the process of reading, the result is liable to be an approach to the calculation of the text's effects which, implicitly, is orientated to an assumed reader: white, male and bourgeois. Indeed, only too often (think of Adorno) the implied reader has been none other than the critic himself. More than a theoretical point is at issue here; consideration of the reader also requires that the very practice of Marxist criticism itself be rethought. If texts do not have effects but serve as the site on which effects may be produced, then the question of effects is pre-eminently a practical problem; the problem of how best to intervene within the social process of the production of textual effects. 'In analysing literature', Colin MacCabe has argued, 'one is engaged in a battle of readings, not chosen voluntaristically but determined institutionally. The validity of interpretation is determined in the present in the political struggle over literature.'[15] The object of Marxist criticism is not that of producing an aesthetic, of revealing the truth about an already pre-constituted Literature, but that of intervening within the social process of reading and writing. It is no longer enough, if ever it was, to stand in front of the text and deliver it of its truth. Marxist critics must begin to think strategically about which forms of critical practice can best politicize the process of reading. This may mean different forms of criticism, and different forms of writing, for different groups of readers. As Brecht said: 'You cannot "just write the truth"; you have to write it *for* and *to* somebody, somebody who can do something with it'.[16]

. . . .

Popular fiction/Literature: by-passing the categories

My main purpose so far, has been to suggest that the concept of Literature has intruded an inescapably idealist dimension into the structure of Marxist critical debate, frustrating its historical and materialist ambitions at every turn. Such ambitions can be realized, I want now to argue, only if questions concerning the determination and effects of literary forms, and the articulation of the relations between them, are put in a way that sidesteps the conventional ordering of the relations between texts which 'Literature' implies. In doing so, I shall attempt to outline the part that the study of popular fiction might play within the development of a critical strategy which aims at 'by-passing the categories'.

First, however, I must comment on the spirit in which such an enterprise should be conducted for there is a sense in which simply to speak on popular fiction is to sell the pass from the outset. No matter how much one might wish to contest the assumption that the internal economy of the sphere of writing is organized in relation to the concept of Literature, the mere use of a term derived from the inherited vocabulary of criticism keeps that assumption alive by, and through the very process of contesting it. It is to commit oneself in advance to a position within the system of concepts that should itself be the object of problemization. The problem I face here is one which Derrida has made familiar; it is that of 'the status of a discourse which borrows from a heritage the resources necessary for the deconstruction of that heritage itself'.[18] And that problem, as Derrida goes on to note, is one of *economy* and *strategy*. In the absence of a better alternative, then, I use the term 'popular fiction' for reasons of economy, and mean by it that massive, exceedingly heterogeneous, body of texts which is conventionally defined as residue in relation to 'Literature proper' and which is not normally encompassed within the purview of criticism. Strategically, however, the response that the marginalization of this area of texts requires is not simply one of developing it as an area of study, if it then continues to be regarded as a separate (and marginal) enclave of fiction whose determining characteristics are still defined negatively in relation to the focal point of reference supplied by the concept of Literature. Nor is the development of a fully-fledged theory of popular fiction an appropriate response, for this axiomatically concedes the theoretical and political pertinence of conventional constructions of relations of difference and similarity in the sphere of writing. Instead, it is necessary to dispute the cartography of the field, to question where the centre is and what the margins are. This means treating 'popular fiction' as merely a convenient stopgap concept that can fulfil an economical (if misleading) denotative function until more adequate terms are to hand.

. . . .

. . . the conventional priorities need to be concretely challenged via the production of a criticism which focuses on the specifically formal properties of different types of popular fiction, and which does so at the level of specific texts rather than at the level of genre or period studies. Yet there is a danger here: that of merely aestheticizing a selection of popular texts, of producing a 'little tradition' beneath the 'great tradition'. In conditions of near universal literacy, Eagleton has argued: 'Literature presents itself as a threat, mystery, challenge and insult to those who, able to read, can nonetheless not "read". To be able to decipher the signs and yet remain ignorant: it is in this contradiction that the tyranny of literature is revealed'.[26] Any strategy which compounded that tyranny by producing, so to speak, a new category of cultural illiterates would clearly be anything but progressive; it would merely be to do criticism's dirty work for it, in extending the range of its repressive effects. There is also the further danger that such a strategy might result in a theory of popular fiction *ranged alongside* a theory of Literature. Against this, it is necessary to insist that any strategies of textual analysis should aim to 'occupy' the domain of popular fiction merely provisionally; to treat it as a strategic site upon which to deconstruct the entire system of concepts of which popular fiction is at once a part and the excluded term: and thereby to propose new terms for the theorization of the internal economy of the sphere of fiction as a whole.

The resolution of both difficulties requires that the issue of relative autonomy be radically rethought; indeed, the very form of the problem needs to be altered. The phase 'relative autonomy' always presupposes an answer to the question: 'relatively autonomous in relation to what?' Usually, it has been conceived as a matter of levels: of the relative autonomy of literature in relation to ideology, and of both in relation to the economy or politics. And, classically, the problem of levels has been retrieved as one of categories: of the relative autonomy of the category Literature in relation to the category Ideology. The inconsistencies resulting from this – especially as regards the way popular fiction has been viewed – have already been discussed. More fundamentally, however, it is the very attempt to conceive the internal economy of the superstructure as a set of relations between abstract and static categories that needs to be questioned. For, politically speaking, it is not the analytic separation but the diverse and historically specific modes of articulation of the various elements of the superstructure that should be brought into force.

The problem of relative autonomy, then, should not be viewed as one that concerns the relations between two 'abstract' categories, Literature and Ideology, but as one concerning the diverse and specific forms of the play and interaction between two spheres of the ideological: the *discursive* (those discourses which produce imaginary orderings of the relations of men and women to one another, to the conditions of their social existence and to their history), and the *fictional* or *literary* (those discourses which allude to the *discursive* and recombine its elements by means of specific formal devices). To construct a rigid categorial distinction between these two spheres of the ideological is misleading (for the precise mode of their articulation varies historically) and is politically beside the point: the effects of literature are located not in its separateness from the discursive region of ideology but in the way literary practices connect with that region.

A mere formalism on these questions, however, is not enough. It is not enough to show, within the text, how practices of writing can be distinguished from one another in terms of the differing and specific ways in which they recombine elements of the ideological by means of the formal strategies peculiar to them. True, to construct relations of similarity and difference in accordance with principles and procedures of this kind would be a considerable advance on the simple Literature/middle brow/ popular division which constitutes the only available alternative. But it would still stop short before the point at which analysis can engage, concretely, with the political: the point of the connection between the articulation of the ideological elements contained in the text and those obtaining within the social formation at large. It is here, in the interface between the formation of subjects within the text and the (diverse and plural) formation of subjects outside the text, that the (diverse and plural) effects of literary texts are located. In order to engage with such issues the very notion of textual analysis needs to be jettisoned in favour of an approach which will *reinscribe* the text within, and theorize its action in relation to, the modes of articulation which comprise specific and determinate moments or types of hegemony. Posed in this way, the question of relative autonomy no longer concerns the specificity of determinations or the specificity of effects; nor is it a question of defining one category in relation to another. It is rather a question of articulation: it concerns the diverse ways in which different practices of writing are *bound into* the struggle for hegemony; their *imbrication with* and not *separation from* other regions of ideological struggle.

In a recent presentation of Gramsci's writings on literature, Colin Mercer has argued that these constitute 'a semiotic reading of texts' and 'of the ways in which hegemony, far from being reflected in these texts, is actually, although unevenly, distributed and *inscribed* within them': a method concerned not 'with the text as product or as object, but as a *process* . . . [as] articulated elements of hemegony' rather than as evidence of it.[27] It is always tempting these days – and especially at the end of long essays – to wheel on Gramsci as a 'hey-presto' man, as the theorist who holds the key to all our current theoretical difficulties. Whether or not Gramsci's writings will bear the burden Mercer places on them remains to be seen (they are as yet untranslated). None the less, the concept of hegemony (as it has been reworked and handed down to us since Gramsci) affords a means of rethinking the concerns of Marxist criticism so as to yield, not a theory of literature, but a 'political economy' of writing – and one which will open up the sphere of popular reading to a politics which goes beyond merely opposing it in the name of either Literature or Science.

Notes

5   F. Mulhern 'Marxism in literary criticism', *New Left Review*, no. 108 (1978), p. 96.

8   T. Eagleton *Criticism and Ideology* (New Left books, London 1970) p. 187.

11 R. Bromley 'Natural boundaries: the social function of popular fiction', *Red Letters*, no. 7 (1978), p. 40.

12 See the discussion of the Sherlock Holmes stories in C. Belsey, *Critical Practice* (Methuen, London 1980).

13 S. Neale, *Genre* (British Film Institute, London 1980), p. 26.

15 C. MacCabe, *James Joyce and the Revolution of the Word* (MacMillan, London 1978), p. 26.

16 Cited in P. Slater, *Origins and Significance of the Frankfurt School: A Marxist Perspective* (Routledge & Kegan Paul, London 1977), p. 141.

18 J. Derrida, *Writing and Difference* (Routledge & Kegan Paul, London 1978), p. 282.

26 See Eagleton, *Criticism and Ideology* p. 165.

27 C. Mercer, 'After Gramsci', *Screen Education*, no. 36 (1980), pp. 11–12.

(from *Literature and History*, Autumn 1981)

📖 READING 28

Classic psychoanalytic texts

Sigmund Freud

The five extracts which follow offer some of the 'classic' texts which inform psychoanalytic readings of horror narrative.

1. 'Anxiety'

Freud begins this discussion with the claim that anxiety is a sensation, an 'affective state', that all of us have experienced. He classifies as 'realistic' that anxiety which we might experience in the face of perceptible danger, only to demonstrate that such a reaction is far indeed from a rational and expedient calculation of the anticipated injury and consequent action – normally flight, which excessive anxiety may go so far as to inhibit. One may see in this a parallel with the common vocabulary of the horror narrative.

Freud proceeds to consider those phobic anxieties generated by particular objects and situations. His list, once again, reminds us of the conventions of the horror genre. He attributes the affect of anxiety, finally, to the repression of desire (libido) – a repression which has its origins in the infantile state, to which (given the structure of the unconscious) the adult may always regress.

[One] form of anxiety . . . is bound psychically[2] and attached to particular objects or situations. This is the anxiety of the extremely multifarious and often very strange 'phobias'. Stanley Hall (1914), the respected American psychologist, has recently taken the trouble to present us with a whole series of these phobias in all the magnificence of Greek names. This sounds like a list of the ten Plagues of Egypt, though their number goes far beyond ten.[3] Listen to all the things that can become the object or content of a phobia: darkness, open air, open spaces, cats, spiders, caterpillars, snakes, mice, thunderstorms, sharp points, blood, enclosed spaces, crowds, solitude, crossing bridges, sea voyages and railway journeys, etc., etc. A first attempt at finding one's way about in this confusion suggests a division into three groups. Some of the dreaded objects and situations have something uncanny about them for normal people as well, some relation to danger; and such phobias, therefore, do not strike us as unintelligible, though their strength is greatly exaggerated.

. . . .

What is revealed by a careful examination of apprehensiveness in children? At the very beginning, what children are afraid of is strange *people*; situations only become important because they include people, and impersonal things do not come into account at all until later. But a child is not afraid of these strangers because he attributes evil intentions to them and compares his weakness with their strength, and accordingly assesses them as dangers to his existence, safety and freedom from pain. A child who is mistrustful in this way and terrified of the aggressive instinct which dominates the world is a theoretical construction that has quite miscarried. A child is frightened of a strange face because he is adjusted to the sight of a familiar and beloved figure – ultimately of his mother. It is his disappointment and longing that are transformed into anxiety – his libido, in fact, which has become unemployable, which cannot at that time be held in suspense and is discharged as anxiety. And it can scarcely be a matter of chance, either, that in this situation which is the prototype of the anxiety of children there is a repetition of the determinant of the first state of anxiety during the act of birth – namely, separation from the mother.

In children the first phobias relating to situations are those of darkness and solitude. The former of these often persists throughout life; both are involved when a child feels the absence of some loved person who looks after it – its mother, that is to say. While I was in the next room, I heard a child who was afraid of the dark call out: 'Do speak to me, Auntie! I'm frightened!' 'Why, what good would that do? You can't see me'. To this the child replied: 'If someone speaks, it gets lighter'. Thus a *longing* felt in the dark is transformed into a *fear* of the dark. Far from its being the case that neurotic anxiety is only secondary and a special case of realistic anxiety, we see on the contrary that in a small child something that behaves like realistic anxiety shares its essential feature – origin from unemployed libido – with neurotic anxiety.

. . . .

Let me sum up what we have learnt from our observations of the apprehensiveness of children. Infantile anxiety has very little to do with realistic anxiety, but, on the other hand, is closely related to the neurotic anxiety of adults. Like the latter, it is derived from unemployed libido and it replaces the missing love-object by an external object or by a situation.

. . . .

Adults have long since learnt how to hold such libido in suspense or to employ it in some other way. If, however, the libido belongs to a psychical impulse which has been subjected to repression, then circumstances are re-established similar to those in the case of a child in whom there is still no distinction between conscious and unconscious; and by means of regression to the infantile phobia a passage is opened, as it were, through which the transformation of libido into anxiety can be comfortably accomplished.

Notes

2   Instead of being freely floating.
3   Actually, Stanley Hall enumerates 132 of them. See a review of his paper by Ernest Jones (1916). Stanley Hall (1846–1924) was originally a supporter of Freud's and it was he who invited Freud to lecture in America in 1909, though he later became a follower of Adler.

2. 'Totem and taboo'

Suppose . . . that we were to take into account the finding arrived at by psychoanalysis from the dreams of normal people, to the effect that we ourselves are subject, more strongly and more often than we suspect, to a temptation to kill someone and that that temptation produces psychical effects even though it remains out of sight of our consciousness. Suppose, again, that we were to recognize the compulsive observances of certain neurotics as being guarantees against an intensified impulse to murder or as being self-punishments on account of it. In that case we should have to attach still greater importance to our thesis that where there is a prohibition there must be an underlying desire. We should have to suppose that the desire to murder is actually present in the unconscious and that neither taboos nor moral prohibitions are psychologically superfluous but that on the contrary they are explained and justified by the existence of an ambivalent attitude towards the impulse to murder.

. . . .

Let us call up the spectacle of a totem meal of the kind we have been discussing, amplified by a few probable features which we have not yet been able to consider. The clan is celebrating the ceremonial occasion by the cruel slaughter of its totem animal and is devouring it raw – blood, flesh and bones. The clansmen are there, dressed in the likeness of the totem and imitating it in sound and movement, as though they are seeking to stress their identity with it. Each man is conscious that he is performing an act forbidden to the individual and justifiable only through the participation of the whole clan; nor may anyone absent himself from the killing and the meal. When the deed is done, the slaughtered animal is lamented and bewailed. The mourning is obligatory, imposed by dread of a threatened retribution.

. . . .

Psychoanalysis has revealed that the totem animal is in reality a substitute for the father; and this tallies with the contradictory fact that, though the killing of the animal is as a rule forbidden, yet its killing is a festive occasion – with the fact that it is killed and yet mourned. The ambivalent emotional attitude, which to this day characterizes the father-complex in our children and which often persists into adult life, seems to extend to the totem animal in its capacity as substitute for the father.

If, now, we bring together the psycho-analytic translation of the totem with the fact of the totem meal and with Darwin's theories of the earliest state of human society, the possibility of a deeper understanding emerges – a glimpse of a hypothesis which may seem fantastic but which offers the advantage of establishing an unsuspected correlation between groups of phenomena that have hitherto been disconnected.

There is, of course, no place for the beginnings of totemism in Darwin's primal horde. All that we find there is a violent and jealous father who keeps all the females for himself and drives away his sons as they grow up. This earliest state of society has never been an object of observation. The most primitive kind of organization that we actually come across – and one that is in force to this day in certain tribes – consists of bands of males; these bands are composed of members with equal rights and are subject to the restrictions of the totemic system, including inheritance through the mother. Can this form of organization have developed out of the other one? and if so along what lines?

If we call the celebration of the totem meal to our help, we shall be able to find an answer. One day the brothers who had been driven out came together, killed and devoured their father and so made an end of the patriarchal horde. United, they had the courage to do and succeeded in doing what would have been impossible for them individually. (Some cultural advance, perhaps, command over some new weapon, had given them a sense of superior strength.) Cannibal savages as they were, it goes without saying that they devoured their victim as well as killing him. The violent primal father had doubtless been the feared and envied model of each one of the company of brothers: and in the act of devouring him they accomplished their identification with him, and each one of them acquired a portion of his strength. The totem meal, which is perhaps mankind's earliest festival, would thus be a repetition and a commemoration of this memorable and criminal deed, which was the beginning of so many things – of social organization, of moral restrictions and religion.

. . . .

In order that these latter consequences may seem plausible, leaving their premises on one side, we need only suppose that the tumultuous mob of brothers were filled with the same contradictory feelings which we can see at work in the ambivalent father-complexes of our children and of our neurotic patients. They hated their father, who presented such a formidable obstacle to their craving for power and their sexual desires; but they loved and admired him too. After they had got rid of him, had satisfied their hatred and had put into effect their wish to identify themselves with him, the affection which had all this time been pushed under was bound to make itself felt.[1] It did so in the form of remorse. A sense of guilt made its appearance, which in this instance coincided with the remorse felt by the whole group. The dead father became stronger than the living one had been – for events took the course we so often see them follow in human affairs to this day. What had up to then been prevented by his actual existence was thenceforward prohibited by the sons themselves, in accordance with the psychological procedure so familiar to us in psycho-analyses under the name of 'deferred obedience'. They revoked their deed by forbidding the killing of the totem, the substitute for their father; and they renounced its fruits by resigning their claim to the women who had now been set free. They thus created out of their filial sense of guilt the two fundamental taboos of totemism, which for that very reason inevitably corresponded to the two repressed wishes of the Oedipus complex. Whoever contravened those taboos became guilty of the only two crimes with which primitive society concerned itself.[2]

. . . .

At the conclusion, then, of this exceedingly condensed inquiry, I should like to insist that its outcome shows that the beginnings of religion, morals, society and art converge in the Oedipus complex. This is in complete agreement with the psycho-analytic finding that the same complex constitutes the nucleus of all neuroses, so far as our present knowledge goes. It seems to me a most surprising discovery that the problems of social psychology, too, should prove soluble on the basis of one single concrete point – man's relation to his father. It is even possible that yet another psychological problem belongs in this same connection. I have often had occasion to point out that emotional ambivalence in the proper sense of the term – that is, the simultaneous existence of love and hate towards the same object – lies at the root of many important cultural institutions. We know nothing of the origin of this ambivalence. One possible assumption is that it is a fundamental phenomenon of our emotional life. But it seems to me quite worth considering another possibility, namely that originally it formed no part of our emotional life but was acquired by the human race in connection with their father-complex, precisely where the psycho-analytic examination of modern individuals still finds it revealed at its strongest.

Notes

1 This fresh emotional attitude must also have been assisted by the fact that the deed cannot have given complete satisfaction to those who did it. From one point of view it had been done in vain. Not one of the sons had in fact been able to put his original wish – of taking his father's place – into effect. And, as we know, failure is far more propitious for a moral reaction than satisfaction.

2 'Murder and incest, or offences of a like kind against the sacred laws of blood, are in primitive society the only crimes of which the community as such takes cognizance.' (Smith, 1894, 419.)

3. 'The Uncanny'

The 'uncanny'[1] . . . is undoubtedly related to what is frightening – to what arouses dread and horror; equally certainly, too, the word is not always used in a clearly definable sense, so that it tends to coincide with what excites fear in general. Yet we may expect that a special core of feeling is present which justifies the use of a special conceptual term. One is curious to know what this common core is which allows us to distinguish as 'uncanny' certain things which lie within the field of what is frightening.

. . . .

The theme of the 'double' has been very thoroughly treated by Otto Rank (1914) [see extract 30]. He has gone into the connections which the 'double' has with reflections in mirrors, with shadows, with guardian spirits, with the belief in the soul and with the fear of death; but he also lets in a flood of light on the surprising evolution of the idea. For the 'double' was originally an insurance against the destruction of the ego, an 'energetic denial of the power of death', as Rank says; and probably the 'immortal' soul was the first 'double' of the body. This invention of doubling as a preservation against extinction has its counterpart in the language of dreams, which is fond of representing castration by a doubling or multiplication of a genital symbol. The same desire led the Ancient Egyptians to develop the art of making images of the dead in lasting materials. Such ideas, however, have sprung from the soil of unbounded self-love, from the primary narcissism which dominates the mind of the child and of primitive man. But when this stage has been surmounted, the 'double' reverses its aspect. From having been an assurance of immortality, it becomes the uncanny harbinger of death.

The idea of the 'double' does not necessarily disappear with the passing of primary narcissism, for it can receive fresh meaning from the later stages of the ego's development. A special agency is slowly formed there, which is able to stand over against the rest of the ego, which has the function of observing and criticizing the self and of exercising a censorship within the mind, and which we become aware of as our 'conscience'. In the pathological case of delusions of being watched, this mental agency becomes isolated, dissociated from the ego, and discernible to the physician's eye. The fact that an agency of this kind exists, which is able to treat the rest of the ego like an object – the fact, that is, that man is capable of self-observation – renders it possible to invest the old idea of a 'double' with a new meaning and to ascribe a number of things to it – above all, those things which seem to self-criticism to belong to the old surmounted narcissism of earliest times.[2]

But it is not only this latter material, offensive as it is to the criticism of the ego, which may be incorporated in the idea of a double. There are also all the unfulfilled but possible futures to which we still like to cling in phantasy, all the strivings of the ego which adverse external circumstances have crushed, and all our suppressed acts of volition which nourish in us the illusion of Free Will.

But after having thus considered the *manifest* motivation of the figure of a 'double', we have to admit that none of this helps us to understand the extraordinarily strong feeling of something uncanny that pervades the conception; and our knowledge of pathological mental processes enables us to add that nothing in this more superficial material could account for the urge towards defence which has caused the ego to project that material outward as something foreign to itself. When all is said and done, the quality of uneasiness can only come from the fact of the 'double' being a creation dating back to a very early mental stage, long since surmounted – a stage, incidentally, at which it wore a more friendly aspect. The 'double' has become a thing of terror, just as, after the collapse of their religion, the gods turned into demons.

The other forms of ego-disturbance exploited by Hoffmann can easily be estimated along the same lines as the theme of the 'double'. They are a harking-back to particular phases in the evolution of the self-regarding feeling, a regression to a time when the ego had not yet marked itself off sharply from the external world and from other people. I believe that these factors are partly responsible for the impression of uneasiness, although it is not easy to isolate and determine exactly their share of it.

. . . .

It is possible to recognize the dominance in the unconscious mind of a 'compulsion to repeat' proceeding from the instinctual impulses and probably inherent in the very nature of the instincts – a compulsion powerful enough to overrule the pleasure principle, lending to certain aspects of the mind their daemonic character, and still very clearly expressed in the impulses of small children; a compulsion, too, which is responsible for a part of the course taken by the analyses of neurotic patients. All these considerations prepare us for the discovery that whatever reminds us of this inner 'compulsion to repeat' is perceived as uncanny.

. . . .

One of the most uncanny and wide-spread forms of superstition is the dread of the evil eye, which has been exhaustively studied by the Hamburg oculist Seligmann (1910–11). There never seems to have been any doubt about the source of this dread. Whoever possesses something that is at once valuable and fragile is afraid of other people's envy, in so far as he projects on to them the envy he would have felt in their place. A feeling like this betrays itself by a look[3] even though it is not put into words; and when a man is prominent owing to noticeable, and particularly owing to unattractive, attributes, other people are ready to believe that his envy is rising to a more than usual degree of intensity and that this intensity will convert it into effective action. What is feared is thus a secret intention of doing harm, and certain signs are taken to mean that that intention has the necessary power at its command.

. . . .

If psychoanalytic theory is correct in maintaining that every affect belonging to an emotional impulse, whatever its kind, is transformed, if it is repressed, into anxiety, then among instances of frightening things there must be one class in which the frightening element can be shown to be something repressed which *recurs*. This class of frightening things would then constitute the uncanny; and it must be a matter of indifference whether what is uncanny was itself originally frightening or whether it carried some *other* affect. In the second place, if this is indeed the secret nature of the uncanny, we can understand why linguistic usage has extended *das Heimliche* ['homely'] into its opposite, *das Unheimliche*, for this uncanny is in reality nothing new or alien, but something which is familiar and old-established in the mind and which has become alienated from it only through the process of repression. This reference to the factor of repression enables us, furthermore, to understand Schelling's definition of the uncanny as something which ought to have remained hidden but has come to light.

It only remains for us to test our new hypothesis on one or more examples of the uncanny.

Many people experience the feeling in the highest degree in relation to death and dead bodies, to the return of the dead, and to spirits and ghosts. As we have seen some languages in use to-day can only render the German expression 'an *unheimlich* house' by 'a *haunted* house'. We might indeed have begun our investigation with this example, perhaps the most striking of all, of something uncanny, but we refrained from doing so because the uncanny in it is too much intermixed with what is purely gruesome and is in part overlaid by it. There is scarcely any other matter, however, upon which our thoughts and feelings have changed so little since the very earliest times, and in which discarded forms have been so completely preserved under a thin disguise, as our relation to death.

. . . .

Most likely our fear still implies the old belief that the dead man becomes the enemy of his survivor and seeks to carry him off to share his new life with him. Considering our unchanged attitude towards death, we might rather enquire what has become of the repression, which is the necessary condition of a primitive feeling recurring in the shape of something uncanny. But repression is there, too. All supposedly educated people have ceased to believe officially that the dead can become visible as spirits, and have made any such appearances dependent on improbable and remote conditions; their emotional attitude towards their dead, moreover, once a highly ambiguous and ambivalent one, has been toned down in the higher strata of the mind into an unambiguous feeling of piety.

We have now only a few remarks to add – for animism, magic and sorcery, the omnipotence of thoughts, man's attitude to death, involuntary repetition and the castration complex comprise practically all the factors which turn something frightening into something uncanny.

. . . .

Dismembered limbs, a severed head, a hand cut off at the wrist, as in a fairy tale of Hauff's,[4] feet which dance by themselves, as in the book by Schaeffer which I mentioned above – all these have something peculiarly uncanny about them, especially when, as in the last instance, they prove capable of independent activity in addition. As we already know, this kind of uncanniness springs from its proximity to the castration complex. To some people the idea of being buried alive by mistake is the most uncanny thing of all. And yet psycho-analysis has taught us that this terrifying phantasy is only a transformation of another phantasy which had originally nothing terrifying about it at all, but was qualified by a certain lasciviousness – the phantasy, I mean, of intra-uterine existence.[5]

To conclude this collection of examples, which is certainly not complete, I will relate an instance taken from psycho-analytic experience; if it does not rest upon mere coincidence; it furnishes a beautiful confirmation of our theory of the uncanny. It often happens that neurotic men declare that they feel there is something uncanny about the female genital organs. This *unheimlich* place, however, is the entrance to the former *Heim* [home] of all human beings, to the place where each one of us lived once upon a time and in the beginning. There is a joking saying that 'Love is home-sickness'; and whenever a man dreams of a place or a country and says to himself, while he is still dreaming: 'this place is familiar to me, I've been here before', we may interpret the place as being his mother's genitals or her body. In this case too, then, the *unheimlich* is what was once *heimisch*, familiar; the prefix '*un*' ['un-'] is the token of repression.

Notes

1 The German word, translated throughout this paper by the English 'uncanny' is '*unheimlich*', literally 'unhomely'. The English term is not, of course, an exact equivalent of the German one.

2 I believe that when poets complain that two souls dwell in the human breast, and when popular psychologists talk of the splitting of people's egos, what they are thinking of is this division (in the sphere of ego-psychology) between the critical agency and the rest of the ego, and not the antithesis discovered by psycho-analysis between the ego and what is unconscious and repressed. It is true that the distinction between these two antitheses is to some extent effaced by the circumstance that foremost among the things that are rejected by the criticism of the ego are derivatives of the repressed.

3 'The evil eye' in German is '*der böse Blick*', literally 'the evil look'.

4 *Die Geschichte von der abgehauenen Hand* ('The Story of the Severed Hand').

5 See Section V of Freud's analysis of the 'Wolf Man' (1918*b*).

4. 'Medusa's head'

We have not often attempted to interpret individual mythological themes, but an interpretation suggests itself easily in the case of the horrifying decapitated head of Medusa.

To decapitate = to castrate. The terror of Medusa is thus a terror of castration that is linked to the sight of something. Numerous analyses have made us familiar with the occasion for this: it occurs when a boy, who has hitherto been unwilling to believe the threat of castration, catches sight of the female genitals, probably those of an adult, surrounded by hair, and essentially those of his mother.

The hair upon Medusa's head is frequently represented in works of art in the form of snakes, and these once again are derived from the castration complex. It is a remarkable fact that, however frightening they may be in themselves, they nevertheless serve actually as a mitigation of the horror, for they replace the penis, the absence of which is the cause of the horror. This is a confirmation of the technical rule according to which a multiplication of penis symbols signifies castration.[2]

The sight of Medusa's head makes the spectator stiff with terror, turns him to stone. Observe that we have here once again the same origin from the castration complex and the same transformation of affect! For becoming stiff means an erection. Thus in the original situation it offers consolation to the spectator: he is still in possession of a penis, and the stiffening reassures him of the fact.

Notes

2 This is referred to in Freud's paper 'The Uncanny' (1919), middle of Section II.

5. 'Fetishism'

In the last few years I have had an opportunity of studying analytically a number of men whose object-choice was dominated by a fetish. There is no need to expect that these people came to analysis on account of their fetish. For though no doubt a fetish is recognized by its adherents as an abnormality, it is seldom felt by them as the symptom of an ailment accompanied by suffering. Usually they are quite satisfied with it, or even praise the way in which it eases their erotic life. As a rule, therefore, the fetish made its appearance in analysis as a subsidiary finding.

For obvious reasons the details of these cases must be withheld from publication; I cannot, therefore, show in what way accidental circumstances have contributed to the choice of a fetish. The most extraordinary case seemed to me to be one in which a young man had exalted a certain sort of 'shine on the nose' into a fetishistic precondition. The surprising explanation of this was that the patient had been brought up in an English nursery but had later come to Germany, where he forgot his mother-tongue almost completely. The fetish, which originated from his earliest childhood, had to be understood in English, not German. The 'shine on the nose' [in German *'Glanz auf der Nase'*] was in reality a *'glance* at the nose'. The nose was thus the fetish, which, incidentally, he endowed at will with the luminous shine which was not perceptible to others.

In every instance, the meaning and the purpose of the fetish turned out, in analysis, to be the same. It revealed itself so naturally and seemed to me so compelling that I am prepared to expect the same solution in all cases of fetishism. When now I announce that the fetish is a substitute for the penis, I shall certainly create disappointment; so I hasten to add that it is not a substitute for any chance penis, but for a particular and quite special penis that had been extremely important in early childhood but had later been lost. That is to say, it should normally have been given up, but the fetish is precisely designed to preserve it from extinction. To put it more plainly: the fetish is a substitute for the woman's (the mother's) penis that the little boy once believed in and – for reasons familiar to us – does not want to give up.

What happened, therefore, was that the boy refused to take cognizance of the fact of his having perceived that a woman does not possess a penis. No, that could not be true: for if a woman had been castrated, then his own possession of a penis was in danger; and against that there rose in rebellion the portion of his narcissism which Nature has, as a precaution, attached to that particular organ. In later life a grown man may perhaps experience a similar panic when the cry goes up that Throne and Altar are in danger, and similar illogical consequences will ensue.

. . . .

It is not true that, after the child has made his observation of the woman, he has preserved unaltered his belief that women have a phallus. He has retained that belief, but he has also given it up. In the conflict between the weight of the unwelcome perception and the force of his counter-wish, a compromise has been reached, as is only possible under the dominance of the unconscious laws of thought – the primary processes. Yes, in his mind the woman *has* got a penis, in spite of everything; but this penis is no longer the same as it was before. Something else has taken its place, has been appointed its substitute, as it were, and now inherits the interest which was formerly directed to its predecessor. But this interest suffers an extraordinary increase as well, because the horror of castration has set up a memorial to itself in the creation of this substitute. Furthermore, an aversion, which is never absent in any fetishist, to the real female genitals remains a *stigma indelebile* of the repression that has taken place. We can now see what the fetish achieves and what it is that maintains it. It remains a token of triumph over the threat of castration and a protection against it. It also saves the fetishist from becoming a homosexual, by endowing women with the characteristic which makes them tolerable as sexual objects. In later life, the fetishist feels that he enjoys yet another advantage from his substitute for a genital. The meaning of the fetish is not known to other people, so the fetish is not withheld from him: it is easily accessible and he can readily obtain the sexual satisfaction attached to it. What other men have to woo and make exertions for can be had by the fetishist with no trouble at all.

Probably no male human being is spared the fright of castration at the sight of a female genital. Why some people become homosexual as a consequence of that impression, while others fend it off by creating a fetish, and the great majority surmount it, we are frankly not able to explain. It is possible that, among all the factors at work, we do not yet know those which are decisive for the rare pathological results. We must be content if we can explain what has happened, and may for the present leave on one side the task of explaining why something has *not* happened.

One would expect that the organs or objects chosen as substitutes for the absent female phallus would be such as appear as symbols of the penis in other connections as well. This may happen often enough, but is certainly not a deciding factor. It seems rather that when the fetish is instituted some process occurs which reminds one of the stopping of memory in traumatic amnesia. As in this latter case, the subject's interest comes to a halt half-way, as it were; it is as though the last impression before the uncanny and traumatic one is retained as a fetish. Thus the foot or shoe owes its preference as a fetish – or a part of it – to the circumstance that the inquisitive boy peered at the woman's genitals from below, from her legs up; fur and velvet – as has long been suspected – are a fixation of the sight of the pubic hair, which should have been followed by the longed-for sight of the female member; pieces of underclothing, which are so often chosen as a fetish, crystallize the moment of undressing, the last moment in which the woman could still be regarded as phallic.

 READING 29

'The dream of Irma's injection'

J. Lacan

In this extract from his seminar 'The Ego in Freud's Theory' and in The Technique of Psychoanalysis 1954–1955, *Lacan addresses Freud's own dream, the 'dream of Irma's injection'. This was the dream that revealed to Freud the existence of the unconscious. It was of such significance to him that he called it the 'foundation dream of psychoanalysis'.*

Why does Freud give such importance to this dream? At first glance, this may be surprising. What, in fact, does Freud extract from the analysis of this dream? This truth, which he posits as primary, that the dream is always the fulfilment of a desire, of a wish [*souhait*].

I will read you the contents of the dream, hoping that this will be enough to bring to mind the analysis which follows it.

A large hall – many guests, whom we receive. – Among them Irma, whom I immediately take aside, as if to answer her letter, and to reproach her that she doesn't accept the 'solution' yet. I say to her: 'If you still have pains, it is really only your fault.' – She answers: 'If you knew what pains I have now in my throat, stomach and abdomen, it's tightening me up.' – I am startled and look at her. She looks pallid and puffy; I think, after all I am overlooking something organic. I take her to the window and look into her throat. With that she shows some resistance, like women who wear a denture. I think to myself, she doesn't need to do that. – Her mouth then opens properly, and I find on the right a large white spot, and elsewhere I see some remarkable curled structures which evidently are patterned on the nasal turbinal bones, extensive white-grey scabs. – I quickly call Dr M., who repeats and confirms the examination. . . . Dr M. looks entirely different from usual; he is very pallid, limps, is beardless on the chin . . . My friend Otto now also stands next to her, and my friend Leopold percusses her over the bodice and says: 'She has a dullness below on the left,' points also to an infiltrated portion of the skin on the left shoulder (which I, in spite of the dress, just as he, feel) . . . M. says: 'Without a doubt, it's an infection, but it doesn't matter; dysentery will follow and the poison will be eliminated . . .' We also directly know where the infection comes from. Recently my friend Otto, when she was not feeling well, gave her an injection of a preparation of propyl, propylene . . . proprionic acid . . . trimethylamine (whose formula I see in heavy type before me) . . . one doesn't give such injections so lightly. . . . Probably, too, the syringe wasn't clean.

In the dream itself, Freud shows himself as he is, and his ego is completely at home on the level of his vigilant ego. As psychotherapist, he openly discusses Irma's symptoms, which no doubt are a little, but only slightly, modified compared with what they are in reality. Irma herself is hardly distorted. What she has to show, she would show just the same if one were to look at it closely in the waking state. If Freud analysed his behaviour, his responses, his emotions, his transference at every moment in the dialogue with Irma, he would see just as easily that behind Irma is his wife, her intimate friend, and just as easily the seductive young woman who is just a few steps away and who would make a far better patient than Irma.

This is at the first level, where the dialogue remains subjected to the conditions of the real relation, in so far as it is itself totally stuck within the imaginary conditions which limit it, and which for the moment present Freud with difficulties.

That goes very far. Having got the patient to open her mouth – that is precisely what's at stake in reality, that she doesn't open her mouth – what he sees in there, these turbinate bones covered with a whitish membrane, is a horrendous sight. This mouth has all the equivalences in terms of significations, all the condensations you want. Everything blends in and becomes associated in this image, from the mouth to the female sexual organ, by way of the nose – just before or just after this, Freud has his turbinate bones operated on, by Fliess or by someone else. There's a horrendous discovery here, that of the flesh one never sees, the foundation of things, the other side of the head, of the face, the secretory glands *par excellence*, the flesh from which everything exudes, at the very heart of the mystery, the flesh in as much as it is suffering, is formless, in as much as its form in itself is something which provokes anxiety. Spectre of anxiety, identification of anxiety, the final revelation of *you are this. – You are this, which is so far from you, this which is the ultimate formlessness.* Freud comes upon a revelation of the type, *Mene, Tekel, Peres* at the height of his need to see, to know, which was until then expressed in the dialogue of the ego with the object.

Here Erikson makes an observation which I must admit, is excellent – normally a dream which leads to that should cause one to awaken. Why doesn't Freud wake up? Because he's a tough customer.

. . . .

The phenomenology of the dream of Irma's injection led us to distinguish two parts. The first leads to the apparition of the terrifying anxiety-provoking image, to this real Medusa's head, to the revelation of this something which properly speaking is unnameable, the back of this throat, the complex, unlocatable form, which also makes it into the primitive object *par excellence*, the abyss of the feminine organ from which all life emerges, this gulf of the mouth, in which everything is swallowed up, and no less the image of death in which everything comes to its end, since in relation to the illness of his daughter, which could have been fatal, there's the death of the patient whom he had lost at a time adjacent to that of the illness of his daughter, which he considered to be some mysterious sort of divine retribution for his professional negligence – 'this Mathilde for that Mathilde', he writes. Hence there's an anxiety-provoking apparition of an image which summarises what we can call the revelation of that which is least penetrable in the real, of the real lacking any possible mediation, of the ultimate real, of the essential object which isn't an object any longer, but this something faced with which all words cease and all categories fail, the object of anxiety *par excellence*.

 READING 30

The double: a psychoanalytic study

Otto Rank

In an opening chapter of The Double: a Psychoanalytic Study *entitled 'Stating the Problem', Rank offers an extended summary of the plot of Hans Heinz Ewers' film* The Student of Prague *which appears to have been instrumental in prompting his work on 'the double'. Briefly, the plot concerns the profligate student Balduin, who sells his own mirror image which then proceeds to haunt and frustrate Balduin for the rest of his short life. In desperation at the frustration of his romantic feelings for the count's daughter Margit, Balduin shoots his phantom double, only to discover the fatal wound to his own chest.*

Rank uses his text to identify the essential problem of the double motif in film and literature.

The scenario [of the student Balduin and his double in Ewers' film] does not leave us long in doubt about the intention and meaning of these uncanny happenings. The 'basic idea' is supposed to be that a person's past inescapably clings to him and that it becomes his fate as soon as he tries to get rid of it. This past life is meant to be embodied in Balduin's reflection and also in the enigmatic character of Lyduschka, who pursues him from his former life as a student. It may be that this attempt at an explanation – rather than stressing the basic idea inherent in the subject itself – may in certain respects be sufficient; but certainly this allegorical interpretation is unable either to plumb the content of the film or to justify fully the lively impression of its plot. For there remain enough striking features in it which require explanation – above all, the facts that the eerie double must disturb only 'all hours of sweet company' of the couple, and that he becomes visible only to them. Actually, his interventions become more terrifying in proportion as the demonstrations of their love become more fervent. At Balduin's avowal of love on the terrace, his mirror-image appears, so to speak, as a silent figure of warning; at the meeting of the lovers at night in the cemetery, he interrupts their growing intimacy by preventing their first kiss; and finally, in the decisive meeting of reconciliation, which is sealed by an embrace and a kiss, he forcefully separates the lovers forever. So the hero really turns out to be incapable of love, which seems to find its embodiment in the curious figure of Lyduschka, to whom Balduin, characteristically, pays no attention. Balduin is prevented from loving a woman by his own personified self; and, just as his mirror-image follows him to the meetings with his beloved, so does Lyduschka follow the count's daughter like a shadow. Both these doubles intrude between the main characters in order to separate them.

Aside from these features, which the allegorical key does not explain, we are at a loss to understand what might have motivated the author, or his literary predecessors, to have represented the past in just this figure of the independently generated reflection. We also cannot comprehend, by rational thinking alone, the serious psychic results attending the loss of this image – least of all the strange death of the hero. An obscure but unavoidable feeling takes hold of the spectator and seems to betray that deep human problems are being dealt with here. The uniqueness of cinematography in visibly portraying psychological events calls our attention, with exaggerated clarity, to the fact that the interesting and meaningful problems of man's relation to himself – and the fateful disturbance of this relation – finds here an imaginative representation.

We must arrive at the meaning of these fundamental problems, necessary to understanding the film, by tracing the related forms of the motif in literary models and parallels and by comparing these forms with the corresponding folkloric, ethnographic, and mythical traditions. We should then be able to see clearly how all these motifs, originating in primitive man and his concepts, attain to literary form through those writers who are disposed to accept them. We should see also that this form coincides to a high degree with the original, and later obscured, meaning of these motifs. In the last analysis, they can be traced back to the essential problem of the ego – a problem which the modern interpreter, who is supported or compelled by the new technique of representation, has prominently highlighted by using such a vivid language of imagery.

. . . .

We see primitive narcissism as that in which the libidinous interests and those serving self-preservation are concentrated upon the ego with equal intensity, and which in the same way protect against a series of threats by reactions directed against the complete annihilation of the ego, or else toward its damage and impairment. These reactions do not result merely from the real fear which, as Visscher says, can be termed the defensive form of an exceedingly strong instinct for self-preservation. They arise also from the fact that the primitive, along with the neurotic, exhibits this 'normal' fear, increased to a pathological degree, which 'cannot be explained from the actual experiences of terror.' We have derived the libidinous component, which plays a part here, from the equally-intensively felt threat to narcissism, which resists the utter immolation of the ego just as much as it resists its dissolution in sexual love. That it is actually primitive narcissism which resists the threat is shown quite clearly by the reactions in which we see the threatened narcissism assert itself with heightened intensity: whether it be in the form of pathological self-love as in Greek legend or in Oscar Wilde, the representative of the modern esthete; or in the defensive form of the pathological fear of one's self, often leading to paranoid insanity and appearing personified in the pursuing shadow, mirror-image, or double. On the other hand, in the same phenomena of defense the threat also recurs, against which the individual wants to protect and assert himself. So it happens that the double, who personifies narcissistic self-love, becomes an unequivocal rival in sexual love; or else, originally created as a wish-defense against a dreaded eternal destruction, he reappears in superstition as the messenger of death.[38]

Notes

38 This fundamental trait of the double-problem is further clarified in Freud's essay 'Das Unheimliche', 1919; [see *Gesammelte Schriften* (London, 1947), XII, 227–68].

 READING 31

Powers of horror

Julia Kristeva

The corpse (or cadaver: *cadere*, to fall), that which has irremediably come a cropper, is cesspool, and death; it upsets even more violently the one who confronts it as fragile and fallacious chance. A wound with blood and pus, or the sickly, acrid smell of sweat, of decay, does not *signify* death. In the presence of signified death – a flat encephalograph, for instance – I would understand, react, or accept. No, as in true theater, without makeup or masks, refuse and corpses *show me* what I permanently thrust aside in order to live. These body fluids, this defilement, this shit are what life withstands, hardly and with difficulty, on the part of death. There, I am at the border of my condition as a living being. My body extricates itself, as being alive, from that border. Such wastes drop so that I might live, until, from loss to loss, nothing remains in me and my entire body falls beyond the limit – *cadere*, cadaver. If dung signifies the other side of the border, the place where I am not and which permits me to be, the corpse, the most sickening of wastes, is a border that has encroached upon everything. It is no longer I who expel, 'I' is expelled. The border has become an object. How can I be without border? That elsewhere that I imagine beyond the present, or that I hallucinate so that I might, in a present time, speak to you, conceive of you – it is now here, jetted, abjected, into 'my' world. Deprived of world, therefore, I *fall in a faint*. In that compelling, raw, insolent thing in the morgue's full sunlight, in that thing that no longer matches and therefore no longer signifies anything, I behold the breaking down of a world that has erased its borders: fainting away. The corpse, seen without God and outside of science, is the utmost of abjection. It is death infecting life. Abject. It is something rejected from which one does not part, from which one does not protect oneself as from an object. Imaginary uncanniness and real threat, it beckons to us and ends up engulfing us.

It is thus not lack of cleanliness or health that causes abjection but what disturbs identity, system, order. What does not respect borders, positions, rules. The in-between, the ambiguous, the composite. The traitor, the liar, the criminal with a good conscience, the shameless rapist, the killer who claims he is a savior . . . Any crime, because it draws attention to the fragility of the law, is abject, but premeditated crime, cunning murder, hypocritical revenge are even more so because they heighten the display of such fragility. He who denies morality is not abject; there can be grandeur in amorality and even in crime that flaunts its disrespect for the law – rebellious, liberating, and suicidal crime. Abjection, on the other hand, is immoral, sinister, scheming, and shady: a terror that dissembles, a hatred that smiles, a passion that uses the body for barter instead of inflaming it, a debtor who sells you up, a friend who stabs you. . . .

Applications

 READING 32

Catching them young 2: political ideas in children's fiction

Bob Dixon

Part of Dixon's enquiry addresses the fiction of Enid Blyton. The chapter is called 'Enid Blyton and Her Sunny Stories'.

Over recent years, I've become more and more concerned about how writers influence children. Much of the material in children's books is anti-social, if not anti-human and is more likely to stunt and warp young people than help them grow. So what this book does more than anything is start with a few questions: what are the attitudes, values and opinions found in the most popular fiction young people read? How will these contribute to the ideas and beliefs children form during the most impressionable years of their lives? What picture of the world is presented to children through literature?

Blyton is less a writer than a whole industry, a phenomenon in the world of children's literature. Throughout her lengthy writing life, books bearing her name poured out unendingly and even now something approaching two hundred and fifty titles are more or less constantly in print. Altogether, she published around six hundred titles. Sales are large: in 1968, the year of her death, the Noddy books had sold more than eleven million copies and the *Famous Five* totalled a sale of about three million in British editions alone. In the same year she was also most-translated author in the world, with 399 translations, and came ahead of authors such as Dickens, Zola and Hans Anderson. Amongst British authors, only Agatha Christie and Shakespeare had been more frequently translated. In the winter of 1970, the magazine *Books* estimated that her English language sales totalled seventy-five million.

Attempts to evaluate Blyton's work have, so far, and mostly, not gone much beyond the level of criticism of language and structure in the stories. Certainly, a study of these is very revealing, but here I wish to concentrate mainly on attitudes and values in the content of this writer's work.

· ·

What overwhelmingly pervades every aspect of Blyton's work, both fiction and non-fiction, is the insistence on conformity – and conformity to the most narrow, establishment-type beliefs, practices and values. . . .

Naturally, the stress on the middle-class English (perhaps I should even say upper-middle-class English, judging by the number of servants of all kinds, even governesses) implies its opposite, which is that other people will be held in contempt, despised or hated to the degree that they deviate from this assumed norm. Thus the English working classes, when they appear at all, are figures of fun, if submissive to their natural masters, and only disliked and portrayed as rather stupid if they are rebellious. Gypsies and circus people, and even the Welsh, represent greater degrees of deviation, while foreigners are simply criminals. They are all rather less than human. . . . We are not usually told which countries, precisely, the foreigners come from in Blyton's stories. Specific details of all kinds are almost entirely avoided, probably because their inclusion would make writing too much like hard work. However, the names of the foreigners are often German or Russian. These though are white and racially-related to the English. It's in the case of black people that the greatest degree of deviation possible is reached. . . .

The conformity I'm talking about has to do mainly with ideas, of course. However, the visual aspects . . . have symbolic value. The half-conscious belief that the more closely people resemble one another, the more they'll think alike, is partly true, especially when we take dress and appearance, as well as racial features, into account – even though such a belief isn't very useful in a practical, day-to-day sense. However, a similarity of outlook has to be related, in the first place, to economic considerations. Moral attitudes can only be related to basic economic circumstances, though not in the simple and superficial sense we find in Blyton's work, where the implication is that greater wealth and status mean greater 'goodness'. Although there are certain exceptions, it's easy to see that the opposite is probably nearer the truth. The trouble is that children, in their reading, are almost never invited to consider this.

The common factor, underlying all questions of conformity, is a strong sense of hierarchy. With this in mind, we can see that the class allegiance, jingoism and racism noted above are merely stops on the same line. What's fundamental is the sense of hierarchy. Further underlining this strong hierarchical sense is fear, which is the emotional mainspring.

What strikes me, considering this mental outlook, is . . . the desperate lack of imagination – in human terms the sheer lack of that feeling for others on which all really civilised manners and values are founded. This lack is bound up with fear, which is the fundamental factor in the whole ideological complex – a fear of what is different or unusual, a fear of the non-conformist and the unconventional, a fear of anything that's new and threatens change.

The 'badness' of those who deviate and therefore menace the world of Blyton is usually signalled in some obvious way as though we have to be advised that they are evil. Thus, they are often deformed or crippled. . . . In *The Castle of Adventure*, we have 'a very dangerous spy' called Mannheim or Scar-Neck and 'badness' can be signalled by still more superficial nonconformity in appearance. As the illustrations to the stories often show, people of evil intent tend to be bearded or ill-shaven . . . smell . . . also acts as a signal.

Certain of Blyton's stories are even more specifically about conformity. In *First Term at Malory Towers*, Gwendoline, a 'spoilt' new girl at public school, is gradually broken in and made to conform through a series of petty and spiteful episodes. In one of these, hair, as usual in schools, takes on a symbolic role, and Gwendoline is forced to plait hers. *The Naughtiest Girl in the School* has precisely the same theme. In seeing schools as institutions with a principal aim of enforcing conformity, Blyton isn't, perhaps, very far wrong. In seeing mindless conformity as a good in itself, however, and conformity, moreover, to the kind of ideology we now begin to distinguish, we may be unable to agree with her. In Blyton's work, non-conformity in younger children is virtually the same as naughtiness, and the usual remedy is 'spanking', especially in a school setting. The title of a picture book for younger children, *Dame Slap and Her School*, as well as the contents, give a very clear indication of Blyton's attitudes.

. . . .

Throughout Blyton's work, the attitude to the police is interesting, and here again we find some conflict of values. Conformity to law and order, understood in a purely conventional way, is strongly underlined but, cutting across this, is the powerful sense of class allegiance. As the latter is uppermost, it follows that ordinary policemen, who are working class, are neither feared nor respected and are often held in contempt by children who either go to public schools or are even provided with governesses. Normally, these policemen are respectful, addressing the children as 'Missy' or 'Sir', and they appear conveniently at the ends of the stories to carry off the criminals who have been tracked down by the 'Five', 'the Five Find-outers and Dog' or any of the other self-appointed junior vigilante groups which figure in the stories. Sometimes, however, as Mr Goon does in the series of stories featuring the last named group, ordinary policemen fall foul of the children. Here, Goon comes in for some contempt from 'the Five Find-outers and Dog' seemingly because, in solving 'mysteries', they do his job better than he does. It's perhaps understandable that he's not very deferential towards them. In *The Mystery of the Spiteful Letters*, the fourth book of the series in question, we find that it is, however, a very different matter where *Inspector* Jenks is concerned. The children get on very well with him and he rather sides with them against the wretched Goon.

Enough has been said now, I feel, to establish the ideological framework of Blyton's writings.

. . . .

Blyton has done her work well. If a parent knows the name of only one author of children's books, it's hers. If a shop sells books for children at all, it'll probably have ten times as many Blyton titles as those of any other author. There always seems to be a demand for stories written to a formula, stories which are totally undemanding and conventional, but while children undoubtedly feel a need for security and reassurance, there's no need to suppose that it has to be provided in this way.

'Thrillers: the deviant behind the consensus'

Jerry Palmer

When I gave a version of this paper recently to the Deviancy Symposium I was asked whether I considered the reading of thrillers a deviant activity. My reply should have consisted of a quotation from Rex Stout, an American thriller writer: 'My theory is that people who don't like mystery stories are anarchists'. Another way of putting it would be to refer to the back cover of an early English paperback edition of Mickey Spillane: 'The author with 70,000 sales!' In short, no, I don't consider the reading of thrillers a deviant activity, and I don't see any way in which such a majority pastime could meaningfully be called so.

It is perfectly true that the thriller is based upon the description of deviant acts – murder, rape, burglary, espionage, etc. In the rather genteel thriller of the interwar years (Agatha Christie, Ngaio Marsh, etc.) deviant acts were clearly reprehensible and only performed by the villain of the piece, whereas the hero was the model of probity. There seemed to be good reason for Howard Haycraft to say that thrillers flourish when the population is on the side of law and order[1]. But in later writers, the hero's acts are just as 'deviant' as those of the villain; what difference is there, George Orwell asked, between the policemen and the criminals in No Orchids for Miss Blandish? 'It is implied throughout No Orchids for Miss Blandish that being a criminal is only reprehensible in the sense that it does not pay. Being a policeman pays better, but there is no moral difference, since the police use essentially criminal methods'.[2] If the reader is expected to approve of the representation of deviant actions, even to derive pleasure from them, why is the reading of them not deviant? The answer is that in the modern thriller the representation of deviant acts is used to construct a component of the consensus. It is probably for this reason that the descriptions of sadistic brutality that abound in the pages of – for instance – Mickey Spillane are unlikely to be made the subject of prosecution for obscenity, despite the fact that, as a recent article in the Justice of the Peace and Local Government Review argued, 'the community, particularly the impressionable young, are far more likely to be "depraved and corrupted" by scenes and descriptions in "respectable" books, films, television and radio of horrific brutality, lustful sadism and indiscriminate slaughter.'[3] The thrust of the present article is to show that such representations are quite literally eminently respectable, because they are there to lend support to values that are absolutely central to modern Western civilization. Magazines like Oz, on the other hand are prime targets since they use sexually explicit material in an attempt to make a criticism of major institutions, such as the family, work etc.

The manner in which the description of deviant acts contributes to a consensual view of the world can only be understood on the basis of an analysis of the ideology proposed by the thriller: the world is portrayed in a particular light and its problems are solved in a particular way by a particular kind of person. What it is necessary to demonstrate at the outset is that the categories of 'deviancy' and 'consensus' are appropriate for the discussion, for it is certain that the notion of a moral and rational monopoly inherent in the notion of a 'consensus' is largely a myth: and if 'consensus' goes, then 'deviancy' accompanies it, for the latter can only be defined in terms of 'consensus'.

The concepts are inadequate to a discussion of thrillers in this respect: many of the hero's acts are explicitly presented as 'deviant', but simultaneously as justified, since they help to preserve society:

> I lived only to kill the scum and the lice that wanted to kill themselves. I lived to kill so that others could live. I lived to kill because my soul was a hardened thing that revelled in the thought of taking the blood of the bastards who made murder their business. I lived because I could laugh it off and others couldn't. I was the evil that opposed other evil, leaving the good and the meek in the middle to inherit the earth.[4]

Ian Fleming presents a similar assessment of James Bond:

> This underground war I was talking about, this crime battle that's always going on – whether it's being fought between cops and robbers or between spies and counter-spies. This is a private battle between two trained armies, one fighting on the side of law and of what his own country thinks is right, and one belonging to the enemies of these things. . . . But in the higher ranks of these forces, amongst the toughest of the professionals, there's a deadly quality in common – to friends and enemies . . . The top gangsters, the top F.B.I. operatives, the top spies and the top counterspies are cold-hearted, cold-blooded, ruthless, tough, killers . . .[5]

The body of this article is devoted to resolving this paradox: why is it necessary that the hero should perform acts that are explicitly presented as deviant in order to qualify as the hero?

Professionalism

The world of the thriller is inhabited by sets of contrasting pairs of character types: the good girl and the bad girl, the hero and the villain; one of these pairs is the amateur and the organization man.

. . . .

Analytically, the polarization between the amateur and the organization man can be summarised thus: in a world which has, as it were, rules of play, the amateur is chronically out of place; since he knows none of the rules, he improvises, with the inevitable result that he merely makes things more difficult for the hero. The bureaucrat, on the other hand, tries to foresee and forestall all possible contingencies: he has a perfect knowledge of the rules and the gambits because he makes them. As a result, he is often incapable of improvising, and when a contingency that he had failed to foresee arises, he is completely lost. Fleming's Dr No, for instance, puts Bond through a 'programmed' confrontation with death, the final stage of which consists of Bond being catapulted from a great height into an enclosed inlet inhabited by a 50-foot long squid; no one, the doctor is quite certain, could possibly survive, and the course is designed solely to see how long the victim can endure – the doctor is 'interested in pain'. Bond, however, does survive, takes Dr. No by surprise as a result, and kills him without difficulty.

The mid point between these two alternatives, the point occupied by the hero, consists of professionalism . . .

Another instance occurs in Bond's defeat of Red Grant in *From Russia With Love*. Grant describes, with obvious relish, how Bond has fallen completely for the programmed trap designed for him by SMERSH's planner, a chess Grand Master and – anachronistically, one hopes for the sake of the U.S.S.R. – a Pavlovian psychologist; the detail which especially interests Bond is that he is to be killed with a single bullet through the heart at the exact moment that the train they are in enters the Simplon Tunnel. In the interim, therefore, Bond slips his cigarette case between the pages of his book and, at the appropriate moment, places the book over his heart. The ruse works, Grant believes he is dead, and Bond, profiting from his carelessness, manages to kill him after a brief struggle. . . .

His defeat of Grant depends on a combination of planning for just such contingencies, and the ability to improvise. Pure planning would put him in the position of Grant, unable to respond flexibly to unexpected situations because – according to the plan – there are no unexpected situations. Mere improvisation would leave him defenceless, for through lack of experience and training there would be no expected situations. His ability to assess the possibilities of the situation calmly, given the high probability of imminent death, to make a rapid contingency plan and – above all – to fight, hand to hand, is the result of years of practice: but at the same time, the years of practice have not dulled his capacity for fresh thought. Spillane's heroes are similarly professional.

. . . .

The professionalism of the hero betokens a man who is responsive to socialization (as opposed to the total amateur) but who manages to preserve his individuality, incarnated in initiative (as opposed to the bureaucrat). In him the demands of society and individualism are reconciled. His professionalism is also skill, and it is a skill in acts that are presented as deviant, not recommendable for the majority of the population: the reason why his superior skill should be incarnated in deviant acts will become clear later.

Conspiracy

The professionalism of the hero is dedicated to a confrontation with conspiracy of one kind or another. It is probably the sense of moral outrage provoked by this attempted subversion of the 'normal' world that provides one of the fundamental components of the thriller.

Fleming and Spillane form an excellent contrast in this respect. In Fleming's novels the conspiracy is identified with the character of the villain, a person who is certainly non-British, frequently the result of miscegenation (Dr No, Red Grant, Blofeld etc.), and invariably endowed with moral characteristics calculated to alienate the reader's sympathies; . . . In Spillane, on the other hand, the conspiracy is usually anonymous; the villain is either a shadowy figure with a central European name, who appears only through the traces of brutal killings, and – eventually – in a face-to-face confrontation with the hero in a remote and unlikely location, where he is killed; or the villain is someone whom the hero trusts implicitly and knows well, in 50 per cent of the novels, the girl the hero was sleeping with: in Spillane the essence of villainy is treachery.

In any event, the reader must be made to feel that the security of a world-order that he values is threatened by a conspiracy: not the open antagonism of another nation that declares war, but the covert attacks of thieves, murderers, spies: deviants and perverts of every kind. The theory of deviancy in its early manifestations (deviancy equals social pathology) is very similar to the cosmology of the thriller, for both rest upon the identification of a given social order with the *natural order of* things, and disruptions are therefore *unnatural*. . . .

The threat that the conspiracy constitutes must be averted by the superior professionalism of the hero. This superiority consists of more adequate adaptation to the world in which the action is placed, the underworld. The hero thus has to use the means of the underworld – violence, deceit – and is fully justified in suspending the norms of 'justified suspicion' or habeas corpus, since the conspiracy is aimed precisely at establishing some sort of tyranny where these democratic luxuries would all disappear. It is for this reason that the hero is normally someone whose connections with normal law enforcement agencies is tenuous; a P.I., a spy, an undercover agent of some sort.

When the hero uses violence he does so in hot blood (Bond, on various occasions, expresses great aversion to killing in cold blood) and the passion involved in large part exonerates the hero in the eyes of the reader: this personal hatred fuses with the sense of moral outrage provoked by the behaviour of the conspirators and the sense of exclusion from 'our' world that is projected onto the villain makes his death seem more than justified; for its justice is never questioned.

Competition

It is self-evident that the hero must prove himself superior to the forces of evil that threaten the world in order to emerge the hero, not only morally, but also in his practice: he must win. (The exception is John le Carré, where the hero is a tragic figure). What is less obvious is that the hero also has to prove himself superior to the world he is saving. This is manifest in his relationships with his colleagues.

Despite the fact that he is basically a lone wolf, the hero enjoys the support of a 'back-up team'. Bond has the Secret Service and friends such as Leiter, Mathis and Tanaka: Mike Hammer has Velda and Pat Chambers. However, this support is rarely much use to him: in the last resort, the hero is nearly always solely responsible for victory, and if anyone else is present it is usually in a passive, helpless capacity. . . .

It is no exaggeration to say that the role of the support team is to show how superior the hero is, in other words to demonstrate that he is, in the full sense of the word, the hero. . . .

Not only are the support team here to demonstrate, by their own deficiencies the hero's superiority, but also to provide support for the hero's perspective on the action, his sense of right and wrong. . . .

Put simply, the support team basically have the same perspective on events as the hero, but just as they are incapable of solving the mystery without him, so politically or morally, they are never quite certain about how far they ought to support him: his practical capacities, the need they have for him, enables him to command support; but this support has to be constantly renegotiated. This aspect of heroism was long ago the subject of a perceptive comment by Ralph Waldo Emerson:

> Heroism works in contradiction to the voice of mankind and in contradiction, for a time, to the voice of the great and good. Heroism is an obedience to a secret impulse of an individual's character. . . . Therefore, just and wise men take umbrage at his act, until some little time be past; then they see it to be in unison with their acts. . . .
>
> Self trust is the essence of heroism. It is the state of the soul at war, and its ultimate objects are the last defiance of falsehood and wrong, and the power to bear all that can be inflicted by evil agents.[18]

It is clear that the hero must be a competitive person in order to be the hero: he has to demonstrate that he can always go one better than even the people closest to him. It is the contention here that in the thriller competitiveness is always seen as intrinsically bound in with isolation.

Isolation

Nowhere is this isolation seen more clearly than in the hero's sexual relationships. In Fleming, Bond's relationships with women are clearly demarcated, in true public-school fashion, into the twin categories of companionship and sex. The category of companionship applies to the secretaries at Secret Service headquarters ...

The relationships with the heroines, on the other hand, are of course entirely sexual. What is less obvious is that their premises are antagonisms and hostility ... The hostility is, of course, overcome, in nearly every case, but if happiness is the result, it is invariably temporary. Bond may, at the end of *Diamonds are Forever*, be very happy with Tiffany, and he may even marry Tracy in the final chapter of *On Her Majesty's Secret Service*: Tiffany leaves him and Tracy is shot as they drive off on their honeymoon. The conventions of the thriller demand that the hero be sexually alone at the beginning of any novel.

The second part of Fleming's sexuality that is significant is its therapeutic value for the girl. The great majority of the heroines are, in one way or another, below par when Bond meets them, and the relationship with Bond has an improving effect on them: Vesper, Solitaire, Tiffany, Tatiana, Pussy, Domino, persuaded to abandon their allegiance to Communism or gangsterism and to collaborate with the Secret Service; Tiffany, Honeychile, Pussy, Tracy, Kissy, Vivienne all cured of Lesbianism or frigidity. To point out that in the Bond world it is the male who is dominant is to underline the obvious.

Spillane is in some ways a contrast, for although on the surface his heroes totally dominate their women, this domination overlays fear. One passage will illustrate this:

> ... directing every essence of her nudity towards [me] in a tantalizing manner as if an impenetrable wall of glass separated [us] so that she could taunt and torture with immunity, laying a feast of desire before a starving man who could see, and smell and want, but couldn't get through the barrier ...
>
> She came closer to the invisible wall, tempting me with her delights, daring me, and when she couldn't fathom my response became even more abandoned in her offering.
>
> It was she who broke the barrier down. She had laid the feast, but had given way to her own hunger and knew that the prisoner was really herself and threw herself across the space that separated us with a moan torn from her own throat, then she was a warm slithering thing that tried to smother me with a passion she could no longer suppress.[22]

This is a remarkable passage. The man remains aloof, retaining control over his own sexuality until the woman has abandoned herself to what is presented as an animal appetite ('warm, slithering thing'); sexuality is a 'feast' but a feast that arouses a hunger that is incompatible with self-control, a hunger to which one becomes a 'prisoner'. It is because sexuality is seen in these terms that the man is only willing to abandon himself after the woman has done so; and it is because sexual appetite is incarnated in woman that woman constitutes a threat to the male ego: the temptation is to self-control, and it is the role of the ego to impose this control. This is no doubt also one of the reasons why the hero's mistress is so frequently the villain of the piece. Moreover, even when treachery does not occur, each of the two main heroes has the obsessive memory of a woman who betrayed and attempted to kill him years before: this narrative convention is an excellent portrayal of the threat that the hero feels from any woman.

The heroes' permanent companions (Velda, Rondine) constitute a measure of exception, since they are absolutely to be trusted, and the relationship that the hero has with them is sexual: Hammer breathes heavily whenever he sets eyes on Velda, but never sleeps with her as he wants to marry a virgin; Tiger Mann, being a hero of the sixties does sleep with Rondine. However, it is questionable to what extent their roles as companion and as sexual partner fuse together, for whenever they are in the role of sexual partner, their behaviour and the hero's responses are evoked in the same terms as the confrontations between the hero and other girls. In so far as sex exists in Spillane's world, it is an aggressive and fear-based sexuality.

In neither Fleming nor Spillane can there be the kind of reciprocity and solidarity that is the basis of everyday adult sexual relationships in the real world, for the hero has to be constantly on his guard, constantly aware of the antagonisms between himself and the girl; the nature of the fear and the antagonisms are different in the two authors, but the distance and the isolation are constant.

This sexual isolation is only the most striking example of a general isolation that results from the hero's irregular institutional position (P.I., spy, etc.) and from the necessity to prove himself superior to his support team.

It is hardly the case that the sexuality of thriller heroes is, in any very meaningful sense of the word, 'deviant'. But it is certainly presented as unusual: the sexual encounters, which are intended to titillate the reader, gain their dramatic impact from the implicit contrast with the daily experience of their readers – a *Sunday Times* reviewer, quoted on the cover of *On Her Majesty's Secret Service* suggested that Bond was 'what every man would like to be and what every woman would like between her sheets'. As with the hero's professionalism in violence, the fact that he is glamorously unusual is essential.

The contribution of thrillers to ideology

It is possible to argue that the hero's qualities and behaviour are an eminently rational response to the nature of the world in which he finds himself: this is perfectly true. However, thrillers are fiction, and there is no guarantee that the world is really like this at all. It may be that the world is portrayed in thrillers as hostile and conspiracy-ridden solely in order to justify the hero behaving the way he does. Or – to put it more accurately – the hostile world and the aggressive, competitive, isolated hero are a symbolic pair, each of which is only defined in terms of the other; moreover, the world is only the rotten place that it is in the thriller because everyone else behaves in the same way as the hero, or tries to.

Thus, the focal point of the thriller, its central contribution to ideology, is the delineation of a personality that is isolated and competitive and who wins because he is better adapted to the world than everyone else. This superiority is incarnated in acts that are deliberately and explicitly deviant, and yet justified. The individuality, the personal worth of the hero is presented as inseparable from the performances of actions that in any other circumstances would be reprehensible; yet at the same time the 'circumstances' are a fictional construct designed to justify the pleasure that the reader derives from the representation of such acts. Individualism is inherently anarchic, the thriller asserts, but this is palliated by the objective effects of the hero's actions, the saving of the world. It would appear that only in the performance of such acts is the hero able to assert both his individuality (isolated and competitive) and his sociability (to save the world). It is for this reason too, that his professionalism is important: the amateur is chronically ectopic, totally anarchic by default of personal capability, and the bureaucrat is over-socialised; the hero has the best of both worlds.

What the thriller does, essentially, is explore the various ramifications of the proposition, common enough in our society, that the individual must be competitive in order to be an individual . . .

Notes

1　Howard Haycroft *Murder for Pleasure* (Appleton-Century, 1941), p. 316. I have chosen to deal exclusively with the area of the 'tough thriller' in this article on the grounds that it is now this version that is the commoner of the two in popular entertainment – when one of Dorothy Sayers's Lord Peter Wimsey novels was serialized recently on TV, it was the period nostalgia that was the source of entertainment rather than the tension associated with thrillers nowadays. Given that this restriction is imposed, it is reasonable to concentrate on the most successful writers in the genre – Spillane and Fleming – since others tend to imitate these, for good commercial reasons. In practice it is perfectly possible to integrate into the paradigm both the police thriller, deriving from Sherlock Holmes, and the 'tough thriller' of the 1930s – Chandler, Hammett, Macdonald – with only superficial alterations. Lack of space prevents this here, and the reader is referred to my forthcoming book *Ideology of the Thriller*, which deals with everything from Hollmansthal and Poe onwards.

2　George Orwell, 'Raffles and Miss Blandish', *Collected Essays* (Mercury Books, 1961), p. 258.

3　Quoted in *The Times* (9th August 1971).

4　Mickey Spillane, *One Lonely Night* (Corgi, 1961), p. 207. References are not made to the first editions of any of the thrillers quoted, but to a standard English paperback edition. Since the format of paperbacks changes every now and again, page references can be taken to refer to the edition cited.

5　Ian Fleming *The Spy Who Loved Me* (Pan, 1967), pp. 169–70.

18　Ralph Waldo Emerson, *Essays*, First Series, No.8 (MacMillan, 1911), p. 206.

22　Mickey Spillane, *The Death Dealers* (Corgi, 1967), p. 110.

(from I. Taylor and L. Taylor (eds), Politics and Deviance, 1973)

 READING 34

Demand the impossible: science fiction and the Utopian imagination

Tom Moylan

The literary genres of Utopia and science fiction are forms of the romantic mode that appear to concern themselves realistically with the future. Simplistic readings of these genres speak of their *predicting* or *planning* the future as though they were the narrative tools of some futurological technocrat. On the contrary, Utopia and science fiction are most concerned with the current moment of history, but they represent that moment in an estranged manner. They restructure and distance the present not to a misty past nor to an exotic other place but rather to that one place where some hope for a better life for all humanity still lingers; the future. To be sure, history always requires some mediating narrative to articulate its absent and unreachable reality, but in our time, the historical present has become opaqued and packaged by the reifying mechanisms of contemporary capitalism and ponderous bureaucracy, thus rendering the social situation even more resistant to being radically perceived and transformed. This enclosing of the present by transnational capital makes the estranged genres that critically apprehend that present and hold open the possibility of a different future all the more important in the continuing project of opposition and emancipation. In preserving the expression of otherness and radical difference, the critical Utopias of recent years hold open the activity of the Utopian imagination whilst also being fully aware that the figures of any one utopian society are doomed to ideological closure and compromise.

In examining the Utopian text, three operations can be identified: the alternative society, the world, generated in what can be termed the iconic register of the text; the protagonist specific to Utopias – that is, the visitor to the Utopian society – dealt with in what can be termed the discrete register: and the ideological contestations in the text that bring the cultural artifact back to the contradictions of history.[13] The Utopian text can be pictured as a fabric of iconic images of an alternative society through which the thread of the discrete travelogue of the visitor is stitched: within the weave of the fabric and the strands of the thread are the conflicts and antinomies that articulate the deep ideological engagement which relates the entire text to history itself.

Central to Utopian fiction, and to the entire mode of romance, is the alternative world imaged by the author. What in the realist novel would be considered 'mere' background setting becomes in traditional Utopian writing the key element of the text. The society projected in such a complete manner as to include everything from political and economic structures to the practices and rituals of daily life has long been seen as what the Utopian novel is 'about'. . . . The alternative world tends to absorb many of the actions and causations normally reserved for characters in a realist narrative. Kingsley Amis spoke of science fiction as a literature in which the 'idea' was the 'hero'. So too in Utopia, the social structure, and what it represents and encourages, is traditionally seen as the main protagonist . . .

In the iconic register of the text, then, can be found the conflicting dialogue between the world as we know it and the better world that is not yet. This 'outer discourse' of the text, as Samuel Delaney calls it, produces a map of the other society that in its very creation acts as a neutralization of historical society. This manifesto of otherness, with its particular systems that mark the uniqueness of each Utopian text and carry out the ideological contest in diverse forms, is the commonly accepted *raison d'être* of the utopian narrative.

The traditional way in which the author of a Utopia conveys the alternative world to the reader is by the perambulations and confused, cynical, or excited questionings of the main protagonist of this genre, the visitor to Utopia. More of an investigator or explorer than a hero who conquers villains and reaps rewards, the visitor serves to represent in the text the compelling advantages which the alternative society has over the visitor's own, usually coterminous with the one in which author and contemporary readers live. Along with the visitor are the guides for the Utopian society who take the neophyte around town and comment on the workings of the society and how they do better what was poorly or unjustly done, or not done in the visitor's home. Clearly these characters – guides and traveller – are in the traditional Utopia secondary to the society itself. Through the discrete register, then, the fine points of the social alternative are brought out in the dialogue between guides and visitor. This 'inner discourse', which in realist novels would be privileged as the site of plot and major characters, provides the itinerary across the iconic map and generates the fable which led to the discovery of the utopia, its exploration, and the visitor's return to the home world. By means of this trip, the alternative society is presented, and the contrast with the historical world is highlighted in the questions and actions of the visitor.

In the traditional Utopian novel, the tension occurs between the iconic description of the society and the discrete narrative of the visitor's journey. Utopia is imaged in the social structure and in the experience of that image recorded by the visitor. Underlying both registers however, is the set of binary oppositions between what is and what is not, between the 'evil' of the given world and the 'good' of the alternative. In these oppositions which 'ratify the centrality of a dominant term by means of the marginalization of an excluded or inessential one' can be found the ideological contest of antinomies that symbolically resolves the historical contradictions of the time. What can be identified by the analytical reader at this level is the *ideologeme*: the 'historically determinate conceptual or semic complex which can project itself variously in the form of a "value system" or "philosophical concept", or in the form of a protonarrative, a private or collective narrative fantasy'.[15] Teased from the iconic images and discrete adventures, the ideologeme leads back to history. Here we are at the junction of text and larger society, where the text's discourse with the world confronts the process of historical change in the actual formal operation of Utopian discourse itself, for the Utopian form embodies 'an ideological critique of ideology' (Marin) that outlines the empty places which will later be filled by concepts of social theory or by practices of social change. Utopian writing marks a distanced place of neutrality in which historical contradictions are allowed to play against one another rather than be reduced to ideal blueprints. Within this neutral space is opened an area of critique, of polemic, that can operate without premature closure. . . . To write Utopia is to indicate what cannot yet be said within present conceptual language or achieved in current political action. To write Utopia is to perform the most Utopian of actions possible within literary discourse. The form is itself more significant than any of its content.

Having identified the three operations of the Utopian text, we must now move to that connection between the practice of Utopian discourse and the historical context. Here it must again be emphasized that Utopian narrative is first and foremost a process. Utopia cannot be reduced to the society imaged, the 'Utopia' constructed by the author, or to the experience of the visitor in that society, or even to its basic ideological contestation with present society. That is, Utopia cannot be reduced to its *content*. To do so, would be to cut short the process and limit Utopia to a closed set of images, character activities, or ideological expressions. Instead, the Utopian process must be held open as a symbolic resolution of historical contradictions that finds its importance not in the particulars of those resolutions but in the very *act* of imagining them, in the *form* of Utopia itself.

Utopia is not to be regarded as an ideal blueprint or system. Rather this particular type of romantic discourse should be seen as:

> a determinate type of praxis rather than as a specific mode of representation, a praxis which has less to do with the construction and perfection of someone's 'idea' of a 'perfect society' than it does with a concrete set of mental operations to be performed on a determinate type of raw material given in advance which is contemporary society itself, or rather, what amounts to the same thing, to those collective representatives of contemporary society which inform our ideologies just as they order our experience of daily life.[17]

The 'work' of Utopian discourse by means of its social images, its visiting and guiding characters, and its deep ideological assertion is its response to history by way of neutralizing the historical contradictions that generate the text. Utopia is literally out of this world, a negation of reality. The reader's response to it is the negation of the negation or that playful action which dialectically explodes beyond the status quo of the enclosing ideological version of reality. Whereas myth resolves social contradictions, Utopia neutralizes them by forcing open a consideration of what is not yet, and creating a space as yet unoccupied by a transforming theory of material conditions that would lead to fundamental social change. Utopian figuration anticipates the historical moment which its critique of current reality urges. . . .

Before a change in history, before theories and concepts that help motivate such a change, the 'preconceptual thinking in images' that generates the Utopian text stands in opposition to the status quo and to limiting ideology, even that of a fixed Utopian society that would exist by being imposed on real human beings. In the absence of a radical theoretical discourse yet to be developed, this figural anticipation of what could not yet be conceptualized is the driving impulse of the genre itself. The operation of Utopian narrative, dependent as it is on the radical insufficiency of solutions at hand, can offer no systematic solution of its own. It can only offer itself as an activity which opens human imagination beyond the present limits:

> Utopia's deepest subject, and the source of all that is most vibrantly political about it is precisely our inability to conceive it, our incapacity to produce it as a vision, our failure to project the other of what is, a failure that, as with fireworks dissolving back into the night sky, must once again leave us alone with this history.[19]

Notes

13 For the discussion of the iconic and discrete modes that led to my formulation, see J.M. Lotman, 'The Discrete Text and the Iconic Text: Some Remarks on the Structure of the Narrative', *New Literary History*, 6 (Winter, 1975), 333–8. For Delany's usage of outer and inner discourse with the world, see Samuel R. Delany, *The American Shore* (Elizabethtown, NY: Dragon Press, 1978)

15 Jameson, *Political Unconscious*, 115

17 Fredric Jameson, 'Of Islands and Trenches: Neutralization and the Production of Utopian Discourse' (a review of Louis Marin, *Utopiques: Jeux d'Espace*), *Diacritics*, 7, No. 2 (Summer 1976), 6

19 Jameson, 'Of Islands and Trenches', 21

Terrors of uncertainty: the cultural contexts of horror fiction

Joseph Grixti

Grixti is discussing the final part of the Warner Brothers' 1983 fantasy/horror film The Twilight Zone, *dir. Stephen Spielberg and John Landis.*

In an age when air disasters and highjacks are frequently in the news, this film invites us to consider the fear of flying from the perspective of a hyper-anxious air traveller. The situation is basically that of the boy who cried wolf. Having jeopardized his credibility by over-reacting in a storm, the protagonist finds himself in the unenviable position of being the only person on the plane to realize that the flight's safety is threatened by a supernatural (and grotesquely improbable) force. The opening shot is of a plane flying through a thunderstorm at night. 'This could be the end of a particularly frightful experience,' the narrator's voice informs us; 'it is only the beginning.' Inside the plane the stewardesses are concerned about one of the passengers, a Mr Valentine (played by John Lithgow), who has locked himself in the lavatory and is only with difficulty persuaded to return to his seat. Valentine knows all the statistics about flying being the safest means of transport, but these figures clearly give him little reassurance. He is also a scientist, and has written a highly technical book on computing – a copy of which is seen by one of the stewardesses and mistaken for science fiction. Left alone and wishing to distract himself, Valentine looks out of the window. Through the darkness he thinks he sees something unusual moving about on one of the wings. He peers more closely and a flash of lightning illuminates his view. The shots in this sequence have alternated between close-ups of Valentine's face as he squints through the rain-spattered window, and ill-defined shots of his angle of vision as the viewer too is invited to try to make out exactly what is on the wing. We next see Valentine from a grotesque angle (a hand-held camera looks up at his face) as he jumps from his seat and dementedly shouts that there is a man out on the wing. The initial reaction of his fellow-travellers is one of panic and confusion. They then become patronizing and reproachful: 'You used to be a normal person!' a rather unpleasant little girl tells him reprovingly.

Let us pause here and consider what this introduction to the tale is up to. The segment comes at the end of the film, so that we are viewing and responding to it after we have seen three other tales dealing with fantastic situations. We are, therefore, waiting for something unusual to happen. In this type of film, the unexpected is expected, and the thrill we experience when it arrives partly derives from the satisfaction of having our expectations confirmed in a reassuring and entertaining fashion. Since this story is emphatically presented as belonging to a genre and tradition of fantasy horror, the denouement will have to be out of the ordinary, magical. The audience is in a sense expecting to make again the reassuring discovery that everything is still in its culturally accustomed place: magic and the supernatural belong to fantasy fiction and to films and TV programmes like *The Twilight Zone* – and, within the well-ordered world of popular genres, good fences make good neighbours. Audience expectations and genre conventions are therefore determining (and restricting) factors in the story's development.

At the opening of the segment Valentine is presented as a somewhat ludicrous figure – the wide-angle close-ups of his terrified face in the lavatory mirror, the patronizing attitude of the stewardesses, and the disapproving looks of the other passengers, all suggest that here is a man who needs to get a good hold of himself and stop acting in this absurdly irrational fashion. But the film does not allow us to maintain this patronizing attitude for long. Valentine, we soon discover, is a scientist, well versed in statistics and technicalities, and in all probability more knowledgeable than either the stewardesses or his rather bizarre-looking fellow passengers. He also knows that he is making a fool of himself and understands the need to calm down. But he is still terrified. Logic and scientific knowledge are apparently as ineffective against his fearful gut reactions as are the mild sedatives which the senior stewardess encourages him to swallow.

In its relatively light-handed fashion, the segment can be argued to be inviting us to consider a very disturbing epistemological possibility. Underlying our fascinated consideration of the sequence of events narrated in this story is a vaguely formulated dread that our neatly schematized conceptions of reality and normality might be ill-founded, that there might be vision and truth in the most absurd-sounding claims made by people whose behaviour we 'naturally' take to indicate instability and derangement. The narrative method adopted here only gradually courts us into seeing the situation from Valentine's perspective, and hence to the realization that this ostensibly unbalanced and irrationally terrified individual is in fact the one sensible person in the group. Valentine's most absurd-sounding discovery is thus also witnessed by the film's viewers: there is a gremlin tearing apart one of the engines on the wing outside his window. . . . What I wish to stress here is the manner in which this particular commentary on the ambiguities and uncertainties of our ways of seeing and knowing falls short of being really disturbing because of the context in which it is presented. Our sense of a well-ordered cognitive reality is in fact paradoxically confirmed here, and this reassurance is made possible by our continued awareness of the frame within which the tale is functioning. The story explores a potentially very disturbing consideration – i.e. that the world-view of the condescendingly appraised madman, or absurd-looking doomsday prophet, might not be so ridiculous after all, that it is his version of reality which is the most practical, and that our survival might actually depend on our taking his warnings seriously. But all this is undercut by the frame within which this episode and its underlying ideas are set – the expectations and connotations which we (like the film's makers) have brought to it from our previous experiences of other representatives of this genre, of the TV series, and of the package provided by the film as a whole. It is this frame which provides the undercurrent of reassurance to the effect that our set of reality (our cognitive schemes or mental models) is ultimately still well founded and functional.

📖 READING 36

The philosophy of horror

Noel Carroll

I shall take a look at . . . what might be called the 'paradox of horror'. This paradox amounts to the question of how people can be attracted by what is repulsive. That is, the imagery of horror fiction seems to be necessarily repulsive and, yet, the genre has no lack of consumers. Moreover, it does not seem plausible to regard these consumers – given the vast number of them – as abnormal or perverse in any way that does not beg the question. Nevertheless, they appear to seek that which, under certain descriptions, it would seem natural for them to avoid. How is this ostensible conundrum to be resolved?

. . . .

Most psychoanalytic theories of horror will employ some notion of repression in the discussion of horror and related genres of fantasy. The objects of such genres will be taken as figures of repressed material and their appearance in the fiction will be thought to release repression in a way that is pleasurable. Thus, most psychoanalytic approaches will presume, virtually axiomatically, that if a horrific creature can be designated as a figure of repressed psychic material that will, in turn, support an explanation of the way in which the figure yields pleasure through manifesting what is repressed. A further step would be to regard such manifestations of the repressed as transgressive or subversive, concepts that also, in current usage, seem to have a connection with pleasure, i.e., with a sense of liberation.

The psychoanalytic correlation of repression with such things as monsters and ghosts finds influential precedence in Freud's essay 'The Uncanny'. Though I suspect that the objects Freud thinks are captured under the rubric of the uncanny are more numerous and diverse than what I take to be the objects of art-horror, it does seem fair to surmise that Freud thinks that these latter objects will all fall into the class of uncanny things (along with a lot of other stuff).

Concerning the experience of the uncanny, Freud writes that it 'occurs either when repressed infantile complexes have been revived by some impression, or when the primitive beliefs we have surmounted seem once more to be confirmed'.[36] To experience the uncanny, then, is to experience something that is known, but something the knowledge of which has been hidden or repressed. Freud takes this to be a necessary, though not a sufficient condition, of the experience of the uncanny: 'the uncanny is nothing else than a hidden, familiar thing that has undergone repression and then emerged from it, and that everything that is uncanny fulfills this condition'.

Now many contemporary theorists, such as Rosemary Jackson, think of cultural categories as repressive schematizations of what is.[37] And, in this light, the creatures of art-horror are manifestations of what is repressed by the culture's schematizations. She writes:

> fantastic literature points to or suggests the basis upon which the cultural order rests, for it opens up, for a brief moment, on disorder, onto illegality, onto that which is outside dominant value systems. The fantastic traces the unsaid and the unseen of culture: that which has been silenced, made invisible, covered over and made absent.[38]

and

> Themes of the fantastic in literature revolve around this problem of making visible
> the un-seen, articulating the un-said. Fantasy establishes or dis-covers, an absence of
> separating distinction, violating a 'normal', or commonsense perspective which repre-
> sents reality as constituted by discrete but connected units. Fantasy is preoccupied
> with limits, with limiting categories, and with their projected dissolution. It subverts
> dominant philosophical assumptions which uphold as 'reality', a coherent, single-
> viewed entity. . . . [I]t is possible to see its [fantasy's] thematic elements as deriving
> from the same source: a dissolution of separating categories, a foregrounding of those
> spaces which are hidden and cast into/as darkness, by the placing and naming of the
> 'real' through the chronological temporal structures and three dimensional spatial
> organization.[39]

For Jackson, fantasy and, one assumes, horror (as a subcategory of fantasy),
exposes the limits of a culture's definitional scheme of what is; fantasy problema-
tizes categories in a way that shows that which the culture represses. In this
respect, it is possible to see a subversive function to the genre; by reversing or
inverting the culture's conceptual categories, fantastic literature subverts repressive cultural schemes of categorization. One supposedly repressive category, of
central importance, which is subverted in this way is the idea of a person:
'Fantasies of deconstructed, demolished or divided identities and of disintegrated
bodies, oppose traditional categories of unitary selves.'

Though Jackson does not address the problem of the paradox of horror
directly, it is easy to see what her implicit answer to it would be. The objects of
art-horror violate the culture's standing concepts and categories; they present
figures that cannot be (cannot exist) according to the culture's scheme of
things. Insofar as the culture's scheme of things is repressive, the presentation
of things that defy that schematization lifts or releases repression, if only
momentarily. This, one presumes, is pleasurable; moreover Jackson suggests
that this also has some vague political value, i.e., that it is 'subversive' in the
arena of cultural politics.

. . . .

I can concur with Jackson's notion that such objects are the unseen and the
unsaid of culture. However, unlike Jackson, I see no reason to think that these
categorical permutations are necessarily, in all cases, repressed. Insofar as these
categorical permutations are not part of the standing categories of the culture,
they may be unthought (until the fiction maker does so); and since they are outside our standard repertoire of concepts, they represent possibilities that are
generally unnoticed, ignored, unacknowledged, and so forth. But repression
involves more than lack of awareness. It involves the suppression of awareness for
the sake of some specific dimension of psychic functionality.

But a large number of horrific beings are not repressive figures of this sort. We
are not prepared with a ready cultural category for the large insect slaves in the
film *This Island Earth*. They are part insect and part man while, at the same time,
they confound normal expectations about inside and outside since their brains are
clearly exposed. The possibility of such a recombinative being is not something
our cultural categories lead us to expect; many perhaps never dreamed of the possibility of such a creature until they saw *This Island Earth* or a poster thereof. But
this is not because we have been repressing the possibility of these monsters.

I think that the reasons that support this claim are twofold: first, with many of the monsters of horror fiction, we have no antecedent awareness of them which we are repressing – they are merely unthought; second, with examples like this one, which might be thought to be derived from almost formal operations on our cultural categories, it is difficult to specify the psychic value that repressing them would promote. That is, horrific fictional creatures may be concocted by means of routine deformations, recombinations, subtractions, etc., performed on the paradigms of our cultural categories. But there are no grounds for predicting that these formal operations will, in every case, link up with repressed material. In fact, I have proposed cases – such as Wells's cephalopods and the slave creatures in *This Island Earth* – where the notion of repression appears out of place. Thus, if this argument is convincing, the repression hypothesis championed by Jackson and others does not provide a comprehensive account of the horror genre.'[40]

Jackson's statement of the repression hypothesis is sometimes disconcerting. One way of reading her claim is that what she calls the culture's unseen and unsaid – that which the culture's categorization renders invisible, hidden, and so on – involves some denial, perhaps for ideological purposes, of reality. Undoubtedly, a culture's concepts makes thinking about some possibilities less likely than thinking about other possibilities. However, this need not entail any denial of reality. Our culture's categories may make it unlikely (*unlikely* rather than impossible) that we think about jellyfish as big as houses coming from Mars to conquer the world. However, that's no offense against reality; there are no such jellyfish. Nor am I being enthnocentric, anthropocentric, or naughty in any other way when I say so.

Moreover, Jackson's extreme suspicion of a culture's categorical schemes is virtually paranoid; culture is portrayed as something that stands in the way of our interaction with reality. But one should, in contrast, regard culture – especially in terms of the way in which its concepts organize our negotiations with the world – as a means by which we come to know reality.

I should also say that I find Jackson's notion that fantasy is, by nature, inherently subversive politically or culturally to be strained. The idea seems to be that since the genre affirms that to which the culture denies existence it is oppositional and perhaps Utopian – celebrating as possible states of affairs that are off-limits to the culture's imagination.

This line of argument bears a number of formal similarities with the radical arguments that maintain that fiction – because it represents what is not the case – and art in general – because it is autonomous from the realm of the practical and the instrumental – are emancipatory as such. For fiction and art (according to Herbert Marcuse, for example) celebrate the possibilities of either reality being other than the way it is or other than the way the culture says it is, thereby promoting a sense that reality (notably social reality) can be changed. Fantasy, fiction, and art, given their very nature, are, according to such views, said to be automatically emancipatory by virtue of their ontological preconditions. The content of a particular fantasy story, fiction or artwork does not cancel the inherent Utopian dimension of the form in question.

But I think that these arguments are highly suspect. They hypostasize fiction, art, and fantasy in such a way that they are seen as emancipatory as a function of their very essence. Fiction, art, and fantasy are treated as morally good in virtue of their ontological status. Not only does this seem overly sentimental, but I think it flies in the face of the facts. Surely there can be and have been morally and, more to the point, politically obnoxious fictions, artworks, and fantasies.

. . . .

One cultural conception which Jackson thinks comes under especial subversive fire in the fantasy genre is that of the person as a unitary self. The genre, for example, is populated by beings comprised of multiple selves or creatures that are undergoing disintegration. Jackson reads this as an assault on the dominant culture's conception of the self. However, this characterization hardly withstands scrutiny. Many of the divided. disintegrating selves of fantasy fiction – Dr. Jekyll, Dorian Gray, werewolves, and so on – in fact literalize popular religious and philosophical views of the person (as divided between good and evil, between reason and appetite, between human and beast). Thus, these creatures do not subvert the culture's conceptions of personhood, but rather articulate them, or, at least, certain of them. Jackson's mistake, like that of so many other contemporary theoreticians, is to suppose that our culture has only one concept of the person *and* that that is always of a unitary self. Such views are tragic in the sense in which it was said that Herbert Spencer felt that tragedy was a theory killed by a fact.

. . . .

The present horror cycle and postmodernism correlate insofar as both articulate an anxiety about cultural categories; both look to the past, in many cases with pronounced nostalgia; both portray the person in less than sacrosanct terms. Moreover, this cluster of themes becomes intelligible when one realizes that both the horror genre and the flap about postmodernism have emerged on the heels of the evident collapse of *Pax Americana*. That is, the horror genre with its anxiety over the instability of cultural norms and postmodernist relativisms of every shade, along with their mutual penchants for nostalgia, arise at just that point in history when the international order set in place at the end of the second world war seems to have fallen into unnerving disarray.

That disarray includes not only the demotion of the global power of the United States – illustrated by the loss of the Vietnam War, the oil crises, the ascendency of Japanese industry and commerce (not to mention West Germany, Korea, Taiwan, etc.), the inability of the United States to secure its ends abroad at will – but, also internal tensions which, with reference to the U.S. at least, encompass unending spectacles of political scandals, widely publicized business scams, economic altercations of all sorts including the oil crises and recessions, the debt crisis, the claims for enfranchisement of heretofore disempowered groups such as women and minorities. Predictably, as the verities of the American Imperium falter, an overwhelming sense of instability seizes the imagination in such a way that everything appears at risk or up for grabs, even that which on sober reflection is still intact. Relativism, both conceptual and moral, is a probable response at the level of thought to such social instability, while horror fiction, with its structural commitments to the fragility or instability of standing cultural norms, becomes a ready pop-artistic symbol for feelings that 'the center cannot hold'.

The nostalgia that is apparent in the intertextuality of much horror fiction, and which at least appears to underwrite much of what is called postmodern (i.e., 'after-the-modern'), again looks back to a time that seemed, probably mistakenly, more settled in its convictions than is possible in the present. As well, the world view of *Pax Americana*, which made a kind of extravagant individualism its ideological centerpiece, was a fantasy which was easier to sustain in the context of the rising productivity and international hegemony which reassured the well-being of a majority middle class, as well as their faith in the nostrums of personal efficacy and a secular morality of prosperity and conformism. The undermining of that sense of security may well be symbolized in the extreme iconography of personal vulnerability, rooted in bodily degradation, in the horror genre, on the one hand, and the excessive denial (the defensive lowering of expectations?) of the category of person-hood by postmoderns, on the other hand.

As the shocks of the late sixties and seventies battered (and continue to batter) the American order as a whole, the tenuousness of the individualist creed becomes more and more apparent; confidence is replaced by a sense of the vulnerability, impotence, and contingency of individual lives. Nor can the sense that one is part of a larger national project, manifestly destined, be sustained. And it is this sense of loss which I think the demotion of the person in the contemporary horror fiction emblematizes and to which I think postmodernist slogans, stateside, about 'the death of man' refer. What is passing, attended by feelings of anxiety, is the social myth of the 'American'[80] individualist which, in the case of horror, is enacted in spectacles of indignity, directed at the body, and which, in another register, is articulated in manifestos by postmodernist nihilists, most often those of a literary persuasion.

In characterizing the destruction of the body in contemporary horror fiction in this way, I do not mean to deny that it also is often connected with mobilizing many of the medical anxieties and phobias of the day, but projecting those anxieties, as well, dovetails into expressing an overall sense of vulnerability that itself seems to be a function of the collapse of the American Empire and the culture of the indomitable individual that it was supposed to guarantee.

Contemporary horror fiction, then, articulates the anxieties attending the transition from the American Century to the 'we know not what' for mass audiences, in a manner analogous to the way postmodernism articulates intimations of instability for intellectuals. In both cases, the reactions may seem extreme. The deep norms of the culture need not be thought to be at risk, even if American hegemony is. However, over-reaction in times of social stress is surely comprehensible. And I submit that the undeniable popularity of horror fiction and postmodernism is a response to feelings of instability prompted by the recognition that the post-World War II order and its subtending culture is in turmoil.

Of course, even if my extended analogy here with postmodernism is inaccurate, it may still be the case that we are onto something of contemporary relevance with respect to horror fiction. For even if postmodernism is not a kind of nihilistic response to the demise of *Pax Americana*, it may still be the case that contemporary horror fiction embodies such cultural anxieties. Its expatiation on the instability of norms – both classificatory and moral – its nostalgic allusions, the sense of helplessness and paralysis it engenders in its characters, the theme of the person-as-meat, the paranoia of its narrative structures, all seem to address an uncertainty about living in the contemporary world which is made more urgent since within memory – or the illusions of memory – there is the belief that there was a time, not so long ago, when things seemed stable and a sense of certainty prevailed.

Since the horror genre is, in a manner of speaking, founded upon the disturbance of cultural norms, both conceptual and moral, it provides a repertory of symbolism for those times in which the cultural order – albeit at a lower level of generality – has collapsed or is perceived to be in a state of dissolution. Thus, horror, a genre which may typically only command a limited following – due to its basic powers of attraction – can command mass attention when its iconography and structures are deployed in such a way that they articulate the widespread anxiety of times of stress.

As a consequence of the Vietnam War and the parade of disillusionments that followed in its trail, Americans have recently and continuously – often for good reason – been disabused of their Dream. Understandably, commentators have traded on the suggestive verbal substitutability of the *American Dream* with the *American Nightmare*. The sense of paralysis, engendered not only by massive historical shocks, but by an unrelenting inability to come to terms practically with situations, which persistently seem inconceivable and unbelievable, finds a ready, though not a total, analogue in the recurrent psychic demoralization of the fictional victims left dumbfounded by horrific monsters. For better or for worse, Americans have been irreparably shaken by 'incredible' events and changes for nearly two decades.[81] And horror has been their genre.

Notes

36 Freud, 'The Uncanny', p. 55, in *Studies in Parapsychology*, ed. P. Rieff (New York: Collier Books, 1963).

37 See Rosemary Jackson, *Fantasy: the Literature of Subversion* (London: Methuen, 1981).

38 Jackson, *Fantasy*, p. 4. Note that Jackson speaks of fantasy here and not horror. Nevertheless I feel entitled to criticize her formula with respect to horror because I believe that on her view – given her examples – horror is a subcategory of fantasy and, therefore, the formula is supposed to fit it.

39 Jackson, *Fanatasy*, p. 48.

40 There is another variant of the repression hypothesis that is becoming popular. This construes horror fiction as a drama of reenacted repression. Terry Heller writes: 'We can follow the hints offered by Andrew Griffin and Christopher Craft and hypothesize that the horror thriller offers a reenactment of repression. By bringing readers into carefully controlled contact with symbolic representations of the culturally forbidden and affirming that control, the horror thriller becomes one of a culture's instruments of repression. The reader of Lovecraft or Brown becomes better at repressing the forbidden by meeting it again in another identity – the implied reader – and repeating original acts of repression. Henry James, Edgar Allan Poe, and others, including filmmakers such as Val Lewton, have helped to make us aware that horror images are most effective when minimally specified because the reader is then encouraged to read his own personal versions of cultural repressions into the images. . . . Now we may further hypothesize that works that encourage this kind of reading will be more greatly valued because the individual reader will be enabled to reenact his personal repressions. Both Lovecraft and Brown give the reader opportunities to meet the repressed and to reassert the power of identity over it. The power of choosing ourselves as personalities in whole bodies is one of humanity's major accomplishments; it is something that, on the whole, humans do well. The main visible result of this activity is a rich variety of human cultures. It would seem natural then, to take pleasure in "doing it again".'

(From Terry Heller, *The Delights of Terror: an Aesthetics of the Tale of Terror* [Urbana: University of Illinois Press, 1987], pp. 72–3.) See also Christopher Craft, '"Kiss Me with Those Red Lips": Gender and Inversion in Bram Stoker's *Dracula*' in *Representations* 8 (Fall 1984); and Andrew Griffin, 'Sympathy for the Werewolf,' *University Publishing* 6 (1979).

The idea here seems to be that with horror fictions we re-enact repressions that we have already undergone in the process of acculturation. That is, the plot of a horror thriller introduces the monster – a figure of repressed psychic material – only to (in general) obliterate every vestige of the return of the repressed by the end of the fiction. As we participate in the story as readers, we re-enact the suppression of this psychically troubling material. In turn, repression, on this view, seems to be pleasurable, and, therefore, having the opportunity to repress once more what is culturally unacknowledged again gives us pleasure. Thus the paradox of horror is dissolved by showing that the manifestation of the horrific, though horrifying, affords a pretext for indulging pleasurable repression which more than outweighs the reader's discomfort.

This hypothesis posits that repression is pleasurable. I have no idea whether this is correct, though it sounds suspicious. It does not seem to be the standard view of repression. Nevertheless, it may be true; whether it is is beyond the scope of a book like this.

However, it is important to stress that this view apparently contradicts the standard account of how repression figures in promoting pleasure with respect to horror. In the standard account, repression is not pleasurable. What is pleasurable is the lifting of repression. Therefore, it would appear to be ill-advised – without further explanation – to attempt to combine the repression-re-enactment account of horror with the standard repression hypothesis. That is, repression can't be pleasurable and unpleasurable at the same time. Only one – if either – of these hypotheses can be right; which one – if either – is to be preferred is a debate for psychoanalytic critics and theorists. Since I have questioned the standard repression hypothesis above and since I, on admittedly personal and introspective grounds, question the notion that repression is pleasurable, I shall not enter this debate.

80 Citizens other than those of the United States buy into this myth as well.

81 For the record, though it is not of material consequence to my account of the present horror cycle, let me say that I think that, overall, it is a good thing that the myths of the social system of *Pax Americana* have been contested. At the same time, this does not imply a valorization of the contemporary horror cycle. The cycle is a fact, one which I have tried to explain. That it is a fact and that the fact has an explanation does not imply that the cycle is good as such. When it comes to questions of the goodness of contemporary horror, I would think that it is only really plausible to speak of the goodness of individual works rather than of the goodness of the whole cycle as a block.

Concerning my reservations, alluded to above, with regard to the philosophical claims of the postmodernists, see Noel Carroll, 'The Illusions of Postmodernism,' *Raritan* VII (2) (Fall 1987), p. 154.

📖 READING 37

'An introduction to the American horror film'

Robin Wood

Return of the repressed

I want first to offer a series of general propositions about the American horror film.

1. Popularity and disreputability

The horror film has consistently been one of the most popular and, at the same time, the most disreputable of Hollywood genres. The popularity itself has a peculiar characteristic that sets the horror film apart from other genres: it is restricted to *aficionados* and complemented by total rejection, people tending to go to horror films either obsessively or not at all. They are dismissed with contempt by the majority of reviewer-critics, or simply ignored. (The situation has changed somewhat since *Psycho*, which conferred on the horror film something of the dignity that *Stagecoach* conferred on the Western, but the disdain still largely continues. I have read no serious or illuminating accounts of, for example, *Raw Meat*, *It's Alive*, or *The Hills Have Eyes*.) The popularity, however, also continues. Most horror films make money; the ones that don't are those with overt intellectual pretensions, obviously 'difficult' works like *God Told Me To* (*Demon*) and *Exorcist II*. Another psychologically interesting aspect of this popularity is that many people who go regularly to horror films profess to ridicule them and go in order to laugh – which is not true, generally speaking, of the Western or the gangster movie.

2. Dreams and nightmares

The analogy frequently invoked between films and dreams is usually concerned with the experience of the audience. The spectator sits in darkness, and the sort of involvement the entertainment film invites necessitates a certain switching-off of consciousness: a losing of oneself in a fantasy-experience. But the analogy is also useful from the point of view of the filmmakers. Dreams – the embodiment of repressed desires, tensions, fears that our conscious minds reject – become possible when the 'censor' that guards our subconscious relaxes in sleep, though even then the desires can only emerge in disguise, as fantasies that are 'innocent' or apparently meaningless.

One of the functions of the concept of 'entertainment' – by definition, that which we don't take seriously, or think about much ('It's only entertainment') – is to act as a kind of partial sleep of consciousness. For filmmakers as well as for the audience, full awareness stops at the level of plot, action, and character, in which the most dangerous and subversive implications can disguise themselves and escape detection. This is why seemingly innocuous genre movies can be far more radical and fundamentally undermining than works of conscious social criticism, which must always concern themselves with the possibility of reforming aspects of a social system whose basic rightness must not be challenged. The old tendency to dismiss the Hollywood cinema as escapist always defined escape merely negatively, as escape *from*, but escape logically must also be escape *to*. Dreams are also escapes, from the unresolved tensions of our lives into fantasies. Yet the fantasies are not meaningless; they can represent attempts to resolve those tensions in more radical ways than our consciousness can countenance.

Popular films, then, respond to interpretation as at once the personal dreams of their makers and the collective dreams of their audiences – the fusion made possible by the shared structures of a common ideology. It becomes easy, if this is granted, to offer a simple definition of horror films: they are our collective nightmares. The conditions under which a dream becomes a nightmare are: (a) that the repressed wish is, from the point of view of consciousness, so terrible that it must be repudiated as loathsome; and (b) that it is so strong and powerful as to constitute a serious threat. The disreputability noted above – the general agreement that horror films are not to be taken seriously – works clearly *for* the genre viewed from this position. The censor (in both the common and the Freudian sense) is lulled into sleep and relaxes vigilance.

3. The surrealists

It is worth noting here that one group of intellectuals did take American horror movies very seriously indeed: the writers, painters, and filmmakers of the Surrealist movement. Luis Buñuel numbers *The Beast with Five Fingers* among his favorite films and paid homage to it in *The Exterminating Angel*; and Georges Franju, an heir of the Surrealists, numbers *The Fly* among his. The association is highly significant, given the commitment of the Surrealists to Freud, the unconscious, dreams, and the overthrow of repression.

4. Basic formula

At this stage it is necessary to offer a simple and obvious basic formula for the horror film: normality is threatened by the Monster. I use 'normality' here in a strictly non-evaluative sense, to mean simply 'conformity to the dominant social norms'; one must firmly resist the common tendency to treat the word as if it were more or less synonymous with 'health'.

The very simplicity of this formula has a number of advantages:

a) It covers the entire range of horror films, being applicable whether the Monster is a vampire, a giant gorilla, an extraterrestrial invader, an amorphous gooey mass, or a child possessed by the Devil, and this makes it possible to connect the most seemingly heterogeneous movies.

b) It suggests the possibility of extension to other genres: substitute for 'Monster' the term 'Indians', for example, and one has a formula for a large number of classical Westerns.

c) Although so simple, the formula provides three variables: normality, the Monster, and, crucially, the relationship between the two. The definition of normality in horror films is in general boringly constant: the heterosexual monogamous couple, the family, and the social institutions (police, church, armed forces) that support and defend them. The Monster is, of course, much more protean, changing from period to period as society's basic fears clothe themselves in fashionable or immediately accessible garments – rather as dreams use material from recent memory to express conflicts or desires that may go back to early childhood.

It is the third variable, the relationship between normality and the Monster, that constitutes the essential subject of the horror film. It, too, changes and develops, the development taking the form of a long process of clarification or revelation. The relationship has one privileged form: the figure of the *doppelgänger, alter ego,* or double, a figure that has recurred constantly in Western culture, especially during the past hundred years. The *locus classicus* is Stevenson's Dr. Jekyll and Mr. Hyde, where normality and Monster are two aspects of the same person. The figure recurs throughout two major sources of the American horror film, German Expressionist cinema – the two Marias of *Metropolis*, the presentation of protagonist and vampire as mirror reflections in *Nosferatu*, the very title of F.W. Murnau's lost Jekyll-and-Hyde film, *Der Januskopf* – and the tales of Poe. Variants can be traced in such oppositions as Ahab/the white whale in *Moby Dick* and Ethan/Scar in *The Searchers*. The Westerns of Anthony Mann are rich in doubles, often contained within families or family patterns; *Man of the West*, a film that relates very suggestively to the horror genre, represents the fullest elaboration.

I shall limit myself for the moment to one example from the horror film, choosing it partly because it is so central; partly because the motif is there less obvious, partially disguised; and partly because it points forward to Larry Cohen and *It's Alive*: the relationship of Monster to creator in the *Frankenstein* films. Their identity is made explicit in *Son of Frankenstein*, the most intelligent of the Universal series, near the start of which the title figure (Basil Rathbone) complains bitterly that everyone believes '*Frankenstein*' to be the name of the monster. (We subsequently discover that the town has also come to be called Frankenstein, the symbiosis of Monster and creator spreading over the entire environment.) But we should be alerted to the relationship's true significance from the moment in the James Whale original where Frankenstein's decision to create his monster is juxtaposed very precisely with his decision to become engaged. The *doppelgänger* motif reveals the Monster as normality's shadow.

5. Ambivalence

The principle of ambivalence is most eloquently elaborated in A.P. Rossiter's *Angel with Horns*, among the most brilliant of all books on Shakespeare. Rossiter first expounds this principle with reference to *Richard III*. Richard, the 'angel with horns', both horrifies us with his evil and delights us with his intellect, his art, and his audacity; while our moral sense is appalled by his outrages, another part of us gleefully identifies with him. The application of this to the horror film is clear. Few horror films have totally unsympathetic Monsters (*The Thing* is a significant exception); in many (notably the *Frankenstein* films) the Monster is clearly the emotional center, and much more human than the cardboard representatives of normality. The Frankenstein monster suffers, weeps, responds to music, longs to relate to people; Henry and Elizabeth merely declaim histrionically. Even in *Son of Frankenstein* – the film in which the restructured monster is explicitly designated evil and superhuman – the monster's emotional commitment to Ygor and grief over his death carries far greater weight than any of the other relationships in the film.

But the principle goes far beyond the Monster's being sympathetic. Ambivalence extends to our attitude to normality. Central to the effect and fascination of horror films is their fulfillment of our nightmare wish to smash the norms that oppress us and which our moral conditioning teaches us to revere. The overwhelming commercial success of *The Omen* cannot possibly be explained in terms of a simple, unequivocal horror at the devil's progress.

6. Freudian theses

Finally, one can simply state the two elementary (and closely interconnected) Freudian theses that structure this article: that in a society built on monogamy and family there will be an enormous surplus of sexual energy that will have to be repressed; and that what is repressed must always strive to return.

READING 38

Men, women and chain saws: gender in the modern horror film

Carol Clover

If popularity alone measures the fitness of a form for study, and if profits and sequels are the measure of popularity, then the slasher qualifies. *Halloween* cost $320,000 to make and within six years had grossed more than $75,000,000; even a highly produced film like *The Shining* has repaid its costs tenfold. *Alien* (a science-fiction/slasher hybrid) and *The Hills Have Eyes* are at Part Two. *The Texas Chain Saw Massacre* and *Psycho* are currently at Part Three. *A Nightmare on Elm Street* and *Halloween* have reached Part Five, and *Friday the Thirteenth* Part Eight. These are better taken as remakes than sequels; although the later part purports to take up where the earlier part left off, in most cases it simply duplicates with only slight variation the plot and circumstances – the formula – of its predecessor. Nor do different titles indicate different plots; *Friday the Thirteenth* is set at summer camp and *Halloween* in town, but the story is much the same, compulsively repeated in those thirteen films and in dozens like them under different names. The popularity of the slasher began to tail off in the mid-1980s, and by the end of the decade the form was largely drained.

But for some twelve years the slasher was the 'exploitation' form of choice for junior horror fans. Although girls too went to slasher movies, usually in the company of boyfriends but sometimes in same-sex groups (my impression is that the *Nightmare on Elm Street* series in particular attracted girls in groups), the majority audience, perhaps even more than the audience for horror in general, was largely young and largely male – conspicuously groups of boys who cheer the killer on as he assaults his victims, then reverse their sympathies to cheer the survivor on as she assaults the killer. Young males are also, I shall suggest, the slasher film's implied audience, the object of its address. The question, then, has to do with that particular audience's stake in that particular nightmare; with what in the story is crucial enough to warrant the price of admission, and what the implications are for the current discussion of women and film.

The slasher film

The appointed ancestor of the slasher film is Hitchcock's *Psycho* (1960). Its elements are familiar: the killer is the psychotic product of a sick family, but still recognizably human; the victim is a beautiful, sexually active woman; the location is not-home, at a 'Terrible Place'; the weapon is something other than a gun; the attack is registered from the victim's point of view and comes with shocking suddenness.

. . . .

. . . let us, with *Psycho* as the benchmark, survey the genre by component category: killer, locale, weapons, victims, and shock effects.

Killer

The psychiatrist at the end of *Psycho* explains what we already guessed from the action: that Norman Bates had introjected his mother, in life a 'clinging, demanding woman', so completely that she constituted his other, controlling self. Not Norman but 'the mother half of his mind' killed Marion – *had* to kill Marion – when he (the Norman half) found himself aroused by her. The notion of a killer propelled by psychosexual fury, more particularly a male in gender distress, has proved a durable one, and the progeny of Norman Bates stalk the genre up to the present day. Just as Norman wears his mother's clothes during his acts of violence and is thought, by the screen characters and also, for a while, by the film's spectators, to *be* his mother, so the murderer in the *Psycho*-imitation *Dressed to Kill* (Brian De Palma, 1980), a transvestite psychiatrist, seems until his unveiling to be a woman; like Norman, he must kill women who arouse him sexually. Likewise, in muted form, Hitchhiker/Chop Top and Leatherface in the *Chain Saw* films: neither brother shows overt signs of gender confusion, but their cathexis to the sick family – in which the mother is conspicuously absent but the preserved corpse of the grandmother (answering the treated body of Mrs. Bates in *Psycho*) is conspicuously present – has palpably arrested their development. Both are in their twenties (thirties, in Part Two), but Hitchhiker/Chop Top seems a gangly kid and Leatherface jiggles in baby fat behind his butcher's apron. Like Norman Bates, whose bedroom still displays his childhood toys, Hitchhiker/Chop Top and Leatherface are permanently locked in childhood. Only when Leatherface 'discovers' sex in Part Two does he lose his appetite for murder.

. . . .

Terrible place

The Terrible Place, most often a house or tunnel, in which victims sooner or later find themselves in a venerable element of horror. The Bates mansion is just one in a long list of such venues – a list that continues, in the modern slasher, with the decaying mansion of *Texas Chain Saw I*, the abandoned and haunted mansion of *Hell Night*, the house for sale but unsellable in *Halloween* (also a point of departure for such films as *Rosemary's Baby* and *The Amityville Horror*), and so on.

What makes these houses terrible is not just their Victorian decrepitude, but the terrible families – murderous, incestuous, cannibalistic – that occupy them.

. . . .

The house or tunnel may at first seem a safe haven, but the same walls that promise to keep the killer out quickly become, once the killer penetrates them, the walls that hold the victim in. A phenomenally popular moment in post-1974 slashers is the scene in which the victim locks herself in (a house, room, closet, car) and waits with pounding heart as the killer slashes, hacks, or drills his way in. The action is inevitably seen from the victim's point of view; we stare at the door (wall, car roof) and watch the surface open to first the tip and then the shaft of the weapon. In Hitchcock's *The Birds*, it is the birds' beaks we see penetrating the door. The penetration scene is commonly the film's pivotal moment; if the victim has up to now simply fled, she now has no choice but to fight back.

Weapons

In the hands of the killer, at least, guns have no place in slasher films. Victims sometimes avail themselves of firearms, but like telephones, fire alarms, elevators, doorbells, and car engines, guns fail in a pinch. In some basic sense, the emotional terrain of the slasher film is pretechnological. The preferred weapons of the killer are knives, hammers, axes, ice picks, hypodermic needles, red hot pokers, pitchforks, and the like. Such implements serve well a plot predicated on stealth and the unawareness of later victims that the bodies of their friends are accumulating just yards away.

. . . .

Victims

Where once there was one victim, Marion Crane, there are now many: five in *Texas Chain Saw I*, four in *Halloween*, fourteen in *Friday the Thirteenth III*, and so on. (As Schoell puts it, 'other filmmakers figured that the only thing better than one beautiful woman being gruesomely murdered was a whole series of beautiful women being gruesomely murdered'.) Where once the victim was an adult, now she is typically in her teens (hence the term 'teenie-kill pic'). Where once she was female, now she is both girl and boy, though most often and most conspicuously girl. For all this, her essential quality remains the same. Marion is first and foremost a sexual transgressor. The first scenes show her in a hotel room dressing at the end of a lunch hour, asking her lover to marry her. It is, of course, her wish to be made an honest woman of that leads her to abscond with forty thousand dollars, an act that leads her to the Bates motel in Fairvale. In much the way we watched her dress in the opening sequences, we now watch her undress. Moments later, nude in the shower, she dies.

In the slasher film, sexual transgressors of both sexes are scheduled for early destruction.

. . . .

But even in films in which males and females are killed in roughly even numbers, the lingering images are of the latter. The death of a male is nearly always swift; even if the victim grasps what is happening to him, he has no time to react or register terror. He is dispatched and the camera moves on. The death of a male is, moreover, more likely than the death of a female to be viewed from a distance, or viewed only dimly (because of darkness or fog, for example), or indeed to happen offscreen and not be viewed at all. The murders of women, on the other hand, are filmed at closer range, in more graphic detail, and at greater length. The pair of murders at the therapy pool in *Halloween II* illustrates the standard iconography. We see the orderly in two shots: the first at close range in the control room, just before the stabbing, and the second as he is being stabbed, through the vapors in a medium long shot; the orderly never even sees his assailant. The nurse's death, on the other hand, is shot entirely in medium close-up. The camera studies her face as it registers first her unwitting complicity (as the killer strokes her neck and shoulders from behind), then apprehension, and then, as she faces him, terror; we see the knife plunge into her repeatedly, hear her cries, and watch her blood fill the pool. This cinematic standard has a venerable history, and it remains intact in the slasher film.

. . . .

Final girl

The image of the distressed female most likely to linger in memory is the image of the one who did not die: the survivor, or Final Girl. She is the one who encounters the mutilated bodies of her friends and perceives the full extent of the preceding horror and of her own peril; who is chased, cornered, wounded; whom we see scream, stagger, fall, rise, and scream again. She is abject terror personified.

. . . .

The sequence first appears in full-blown form in *Texas Chain Saw I* with Sally's spirited self-defense and eventual rescue. Her brother and companions were dispatched suddenly and uncomprehending, one by one, but Sally survives the ninth round: long enough to see what has become of her fellows and is in store for her, long enough to meet and even dine with the whole slaughterhouse family, long enough to undergo all manner of torture (including the ancient grandfather's feeble efforts to strike a fatal hammer blow on the temple as they bend her over a washtub), and long enough to bolt and rebolt, be caught and recaught, plead and replead for her life, and eventually escape to the highway. For nearly thirty minutes of screen time – a third of the film – we watch her shriek, run, flinch, jump or fall through windows, sustain injury and mutilation. Her will to survive is astonishing; in the end, bloody and staggering, she finds the highway, Leatherface and Hitchhiker in pursuit. Just as they bear down on her, a truck comes by and crushes Hitchhiker. Minutes later a pickup driver plucks Sally up and saves her from Leatherface.

. . . .

In *Texas Chain Saw II*, from 1986, the Final Girl sequence takes mythic measure. Trapped in the underground slaughterhouse, Stretch repeatedly flees, hides, is caught, tortured (at one point forced to don the flayed face of her murdered technician companion), and nearly killed. She escapes with her life chiefly because Leatherface, having developed an affection for her, is reluctant to ply his chain saw as his father commands. Finally Stretch finds her way out, leaving the Texas Ranger to face certain death below, and clambers up a nearby pinnacle,

Chop Top in pursuit. In a crevice near the summit she finds the mummified grandmother, ceremoniously enthroned in an open-air chamber, and on her lap, a functional chain saw. She turns the saw on Chop Top, gashing open his abdomen and tossing him off the precipice. The final scene shows her in extreme long shot, in brilliant sunshine, waving the buzzing chain saw triumphantly overhead. (It is a scene we are invited to compare to the final scene of *Texas Chain Saw I*, in which the wounded Leatherface is shown staggering after the pickup on the highway and waving his chain saw crazily over *his* head.) In Part One the Final Girl, for all her survivor pluck, is, like Red Riding Hood, saved through male agency. In Part Two, however, there is no male agency; the figure so designated, the Texas Ranger, proves so utterly ineffectual that he cannot save himself, much less the girl.

Shock

One reason that the shower sequence in *Psycho* has 'evoked more study, elicited more comment, and generated more shot-for-shot analysis from a technical view-point than any other in the history of cinema' is that it suggests so much but shows so little.[23] Of the forty-odd shots in as many seconds that figure the murder, only a single fleeting one actually shows the body being stabbed. The others present us with a rapid-fire sequence of shots of the knife, of the shower, of Marion's face, arm, and feet, finally the bloody water as it swirls down the drain and dissolves to the image of a large, still eye. The horror resides less in the actual images than in their summary implication.

Although Hitchcock is hardly the first director to prefer the oblique rendition of physical violence, he may, to judge from current examples, be one of the last. For better or worse, the perfection of special effects has made it possible to show maiming and dismemberment in extraordinarily credible detail. The horror genres are the natural repositories of such effects; what can be done is done, and slashers, at the bottom of the category, do it most and worst. Thus we see heads squashed and eyes popped out, faces flayed, limbs dismembered, eyes penetrated by needles in close-up, and so on.

With this new explicitness also comes a new tone. If the horror of *Psycho* was taken seriously, the 'horror' of the slasher films is of a rather more complicated sort. Audiences express uproarious disgust ('Gross!') as often as they express fear, and it is clear that the makers of slasher films pursue the combination. More particularly: spectators tend to be silent during the stalking scenes (although they sometimes call out warnings to the stalked person), scream out at the first slash, and make loud noises of revulsion at the sight of the bloody stump. The rapid alternation between registers – between something like 'real' horror on one hand and a camp, self-parodying horror on the other – is by now one of the most conspicuous characteristics of the tradition.

The body

On the face of it, the relation between the sexes in slasher films could hardly be clearer. The killer is with few exceptions recognizably human and distinctly male;

his fury is unmistakably sexual in both roots and expression; his victims are mostly women, often sexually free and always young and beautiful.

. . . .

But what this line of reasoning does not take into account is the figure of the Final Girl. Because slashers lie for all practical purposes beyond the purview of legitimate criticism, and to the extent that they have been reviewed at all have been reviewed on an individual basis, the phenomenon of the female victim-hero has scarcely been acknowledged.[28]

. . . .

No one who has read 'Red Riding Hood' to a small boy or attended a viewing of, say, *Deliverance* (an all-male story that women find as gripping as men do) – or, more recently, *Alien* and *Aliens*, with whose space-age female Rambo, herself a Final Girl, male viewers seem to engage with ease – can doubt the phenomenon of cross-gender identification.[34] This fluidity of engaged perspective is in keeping with the universal claims of the psychoanalytic model: the threat function and the victim function coexist in the same unconscious, regardless of anatomical sex. But why, if viewers can identify across gender lines and if the root experience of horror is sex blind, are the screen sexes not interchangeable? . . . The fact that the horror film so stubbornly figures the killer as male and the principal as female would seem to suggest that representation itself is at issue – that the sensation of bodily fright derives not exclusively from repressed content, as Freud insisted, but also from the bodily manifestations of that content.

Nor is the gender of the principals as straightforward as it first seems. The killer's phallic purpose, as he thrusts his drill or knife into the trembling bodies of young women, is unmistakable. At the same time, however, his masculinity is severely qualified: he ranges from the virginal or sexually inert to the transvestite or transsexual, and is spiritually divided ('the mother half of his mind') or even equipped with vulva and vagina [see, e.g. *God Told Me To*].

. . . .

The gender of the Final Girl is likewise compromised from the outset by her masculine interests, her inevitable sexual reluctance, her apartness from other girls, sometimes her name. At the level of the cinematic apparatus, her unfemininity is signaled clearly by her exercise of the 'active investigating gaze' normally reserved for males and punished in females when they assume it themselves; tentatively at first and then aggressively, the Final Girl looks *for* the killer, even tracking him to his forest hut or his underground labyrinth, and then *at* him, therewith bringing him, often for the first time, into our vision as well. When, in the final scene, she stops screaming, faces the killer, and reaches for the knife (sledge hammer, scalpel, gun, machete, hanger, knitting needle, chain saw), she addresses the monster on his own terms.

. . . .

If the slasher film is, 'on the face of it', a genre with at least a strong female presence, it is in these figurative readings a thoroughly male exercise, one that finally has very little to do with femaleness and very much to do with phallocentrism. Figuratively seen, the Final Girl is a male surrogate in things oedipal, a homoerotic stand-in, the audience incorporate; to the extent she means 'girl' at all, it is only for purposes of signifying male lack, and even that meaning is nullified in the final scenes. Our initial question – how to square a female victim-hero with a largely male audience – is not so much answered as it is obviated in these readings. The Final Girl is (apparently) female not despite the maleness of the audience, but precisely because of it. The discourse is wholly masculine, and females figure in it only insofar as they 'read' some aspect of male experience. To applaud the Final Girl as a feminist development, as some reviews of *Aliens* have done with Ripley, is, in light of her figurative meaning, a particularly grotesque expression of wishful thinking.[47] She is simply an agreed-upon fiction and the male viewer's use of her as a vehicle for his own sadomasochistic fantasies an act of perhaps timeless dishonesty.

Notes

23 Spoto, *The Dark Side of Genius*, p. 454. See also William Rotherman, *Hitchcock*, pp. 246–341.
28 Cf. Dika's *Games of Terror*, which, although not particularly concerned with the female heroes of slasher films, does recognize their centrality and does suggest a reason for their emergence at this historical moment. The phenomenon has otherwise tended to be slighted or denied in treatments of modern horror (Carroll, *The Philosophy of Horror*; Tudor, *Monsters and Mad Scientists*; Twitchell, *Dreadful Pleasures*). Wood's essay 'Beauty Bests the Beast' acknowledges the phenomenon but confines itself to a few examples.
34 'I really appreciate the way audiences respond', Gail Anne Hurd, producer of *Aliens*, is reported to have said. 'They buy it. We don't get people, even rednecks, leaving the theater saying "That was stupid. No woman would do that". You don't have to be a liberal ERA supporter to root for Ripley'; as reported in the *San Franciso Examiner Datebook*, 10 August 1986, p. 19. *Time* magazine (28 July 1986) suggests that Ripley's maternal impulses (she squares off against the worst aliens of all in her quest to save a little girl) give the audience 'a much stronger rooting interest in Ripley, and that gives the picture resonances unusual in a popcorn epic'.
47 This would seem to be the point of the final sequence of Brian De Palma's *Blow Out*, in which we see the boyfriend of the victim-hero stab the killer to death but later hear the television announce that the woman herself vanquished the killer. The frame plot of the film has to do with the making of a slasher film ('Co-Ed Frenzy'), and it seems clear that De Palma means his ending to stand as a comment on the Final Girl formula of the genre. De Palma's (and indirectly Hitchcock's) insistence that only men can kill men, or protect women from men, deserves a separate essay.

 READING 39

'"I shall be with you on your wedding night": Lacan and the uncanny'

Mladen Dolar

Freud's examples [of the uncanny] are, although he never explicitly mentions it, historically situated. Hoffmann, the sudden emergence of the doubles in the romantic era, the extraordinary obsession with ghosts, vampires, undead dead, monsters, etc., in Gothic fiction and all through the nineteenth century, the realm of the fantastic – they all point to the emergence of the uncanny at a very precise historical moment. It is Frankenstein, however, that is perhaps the best example of this.

[The] quadruple scheme in Hoffmann's tale . . . was then reduced to a dual relationship with the double. Now we can undertake a further simplification or condensation of the problem by reducing it to a single element best presented by the theme of the monster.

It appears at first sight that Frankenstein is the direct opposite of the theme of the double: the creature created by Frankenstein is a monster without a name, and his basic problem in the novel is precisely that he cannot find his double.[26] It is a creature without filiation or a genealogy, without anybody who would recognize or accept him (not even his creator). His narcissism is thus thwarted from the outset, and the main part of the plot actually springs from his demand for a partner, somebody like him, a wife, so that he could start a line, a new filiation. He is One and Unique, and as such he cannot even have a name – *he cannot be represented by a signifier* (which absence is often 'spontaneously' filled in by his 'father's' name), he cannot be a part of the symbolic. The story itself had the strange fate of becoming a 'modern myth', a very rare occurrence indeed. The huge number of different versions in which the original is virtually lost testifies to this fact. All these versions turn around the same fantasmatic [sic] kernel, retranscribing it to infinity. It is a myth in the Levi-Straussian sense of the word: the myth as 'a logical model to resolve a contradiction (an insoluble task if the contradiction is real)'[27] – ultimately the contradiction between nature and culture.

The myth has its starting point in scientific discourse. Shelley's 'Introduction' takes up Erasmus Darwin as the witness, along with the background of research into electromagnetic occurrences, galvanism, etc. The possibility of creating a human being seems to be just a small extension of the seemingly limitless possibilities of the new science. But the connection with the Enlightenment goes much further.

. . . .

Frankenstein's creature demonstrates [the Enlightenment notion of the link between matter and spirit, nature and culture] in a particularly poignant way: it is the realization of the subject of the Enlightenment, the missing link produced by its scientific project. He is created, so to speak, *ex nihilo*, and he has to recreate the whole complexity of the spiritual world *ex nihilo*. And we have, in the most extraordinary central part of the book, a first-hand account of his subjectivation, a first-person narration of the passage from nature into culture. He is the zero point of natural subjectivity, and herein lies his paradox: as the embodiment of the natural zero state, he is counter to nature, a monster excluded from nature and culture alike. Through his tragedy, culture only gets back its own message: his monstrosity is the monstrosity of culture. The noble savage, the self-educated man, turns bad only because the culture turns him down. By not accepting him society shows its corruption, its inability to integrate him, to include its own missing link. Culture judges by nature (that is, by his looks), not by culture (that is, by his good heart and sensitivity). The creature as the Unique only wants a social contract, but being refused one he wants to destroy the contract that excludes him and so to vindicate himself. Since he cannot found a family – a minimal contract with his like – he exterminates the family of his creator, who wouldn't recognize his offspring, his only link with culture. In the end all the figures of the novel are dead (except for Walton who lives to tell the story).

The paradox of the creature lies in the fact that this embodiment of the subject of the Enlightenment directly disrupts its universe and produces its limit. The creature, that small extension of scientific endeavor, would fill the missing link and make it exist; it would bridge the gap. With its addition, 'the great chain of being' would be complete; one could pass without a break from matter to spirit, from nature to culture. There was an empty space between the two that the monster comes to fill, but what we get with this continuous, full universe is the opposite of the traditional *horror vacui*; it is a *horror plenitudinis*, the horror of an unsplit world. Frankenstein brings to humanity, like Prometheus, the spark of life, but also much more: there is a promise to provide it with its origin, to heal the wound of castration, to make it whole again. But filling the lack is catastrophic – the Enlightenment reaches its limit by realizing it, just as the appearance of the double, in another context, produced the lack of lack.

. . . .

The point where the monster emerges is always immediately seized by an overwhelming amount of meaning – and that is valid for the whole subsequent gallery of monsters, vampires, aliens. etc. It has immediate social and ideological connotations. The monster can stand for everything that our culture has to repress – the proletariat, sexuality, other cultures, alternative ways of living, heterogeneity, the Other.[31] There is a certain arbitrariness in the content that can be projected onto this point, and there are many attempts to reduce the uncanny to just this content. The important thing from a Lacanian point of view, however, is that while this content is indeed always present in the uncanny to a greater or a lesser degree, it doesn't constitute it. The uncanny is always at stake in ideology – ideology perhaps basically consists of a social attempt to integrate the uncanny, to make it bearable, to assign it a place, and the criticism of ideology is caught in the same framework if it tries to reduce it to another kind of content or to make the content conscious and explicit. This criticism is always on the brink of a naive effort to fix things with their proper names, to make the unconscious conscious, to restore the sense of what is repressed and thus be rid of the uncanny. The constant resurgence of 'right-wing' ideologies that find support in the uncanny always comes as a surprise – the fascination won't vanish, the historicization fails, the 'hidden contents' do not exhaust it. Thus the criticism of ideology helplessly repeats the modernist gesture – the reduction of the uncanny to its 'secular basis' through the very logic that actually produced the uncanny in the first place as the objectal remainder. Psychoanalysis doesn't provide a new and better interpretation of the uncanny; it maintains it as *a limit to interpretation*. Its interpretation tries to circumscribe the point where interpretation fails, where no 'more faithful' translation can be made. It tries to pinpoint the dimension of the object in that tiny crack before different meanings get hold of it and saturate it with sense, the point that can never be successfully recuperated by the signifying chain. In other words, psychoanalysis differs from other interpretations by its insistence on the formal level of the uncanny rather than on its content.

Lacan's specification that the best presentification [sic] of the object is the gaze doesn't contradict this formal level of analysis. It seems that it names the object and thus assigns it a place, but the gaze in its formal structure is rather a device to open a 'non-place', the pure oscillation between an emptiness and a fullness. Frankenstein's story again reveals this simply and efficiently. The principal source of the uncanniness of the monster, for Frankenstein, is precisely the gaze. It is the being of the gaze. The point that Frankenstein cannot endure, during the creation of the monster, is the moment when the creature opens its eyes, when the Thing renders the gaze – it is this opening that makes it the Thing. When seeing those 'watery eyes, that seemed almost of the same color as the dun-white sockets in which they were set', Frankenstein runs away in horror.[32] But the gaze comes to pursue him in his bedroom; the monster comes to his bedside – 'his eyes, if eyes they may be called, were set on me'.[33] The emergence of this impossible subject is the emergence of the gaze – the opening of a hole in reality which is immediately also that which comes to fill it with an unbearable presence, with a being more being than being, *vacuum* and *plenitudo* all in one, the plenitude as the direct consequence of the emptiness. One could say that the monster's terrible appearance is only a mask, an imaginary cover to provide a frame for his gaze. The same traumatic presence of the gaze can also be pinpointed in the second 'primal scene', the attempted creation of the monster's bride in a Scottish cottage, the scene that is interrupted precisely because of the appearance of the gaze. It finishes with the announcement of the reappearance of the gaze in the third 'primal scene': 'I shall be with you on your wedding-night'.[34] And he will. The bearer of the gaze will turn from a creature – that is, something created, an offspring, a son – into the figure of the father-*jouissance*.

The gaze that occurs with such precision in all the 'primal scenes' of the novel is an impossible gaze. Jean-Jacques Lecercle has already pointed out that it is situated as the presence of the gaze at the subject's own conception.[35] It emerges together with the emergence of the subject, in the moment of its conception, as an *hors-corps* and an *hors-sexe*. It is this object that would make the subject a *causa sui* if it could be integrated – the missing cause of subjectivity, the missing link of its emergence.

Notes

26 I am greatly indebted to two recent analyses: Chris Baldick, *In Frankenstein's Shadow* (Oxford: Oxford University Press, 1987) and Jean-Jacques Lecercle, *Frankenstein: Mythe et Philosophie* (Paris: P.U.F., 1988). But I concentrate on only one line of argument, neglecting other possibilities offered by the material.

27 Claude Lévi-Strauss, *Structural Anthropology*, trans. Monique Layton (Chicago: University of Chicago Press, 1983).

31 Ibid., p. 236.

32 Mary Shelley, *Frankenstein*, in *Three Gothic Novels*, ed. Peter Fairclough (Harmondsworth: Penguin, 1979), p. 318.

33 Ibid., p. 319.

34 Ibid., p. 438.

35 Lecercle, *Frankenstein*, p. 99.

'Fetishism in the horror film'

Roger Dadoun

Freud's outline interpretation of fetishism, broken down into its component parts – the archaic mother and the mother's phallus, the sexualised phallic object, the missing phallus, the anxiety of castration, the specific defence mechanisms, etc. – will allow us to find our way in the gloomy labyrinths of Dracula's world.

The *imago* of the archaic mother permeates the atmosphere of the horror film and underpins its development. We are dealing with a figure more complex and many-sided than might be thought. An essential aspect, as specified in Freud's analysis of fetishism, is the way she appears as a phallic woman, a woman with a penis, a murderous, all-devouring or castrating mother. She evokes the anxiety of castration in its primordial, founding intensity – more so than the father, with whom the son can struggle on equal terms as it were, even benefiting from maternal complicity and ever-increasing strength.

. . . .

What . . . is perceived and named, what is present and actual, the fullest form, or so it would seem, larger than life, better than anything else, more insistent, more intense, always ready to occupy (with a flourish) the empty spaces and blank frames reserved for him (the big posters, the hoardings, the cinema displays are also, of course, all devoted to him), always there making his presence felt is Dracula – so much so that, thanks to the intervention of a demon-god and Freddie Francis, he becomes the target of a monk's courageous resolve; the form occupying a throne, towering above the castle, the village, the land, the whole universe; the fetish form. As a 'substitute for the mother's penis', according to Freud's definition, he is a phallic form. This form is not directed towards creative erotic development or genital fulfilment, but *stands in for something else*. It depends on the mother figure, whose absence it incorporates as an essential characteristic, and it sets up as a memorial the very thing it should defend itself against. Sexual energy has served to transform the mother form (Form 1) into a complicated, stable, reified product. The Dracula fetish may therefore be called a sexualised total object.

And this is exactly how he appears – not to see Dracula as a relatively full erotic form is one of the commonest mistakes. The vampire's phallic exhibitionism confirms his fetishistic nature. (A remark attributed to a fetishist in Freud's article is relevant here. His 'fetish was an athletic support belt which could also be worn as bathing drawers'.[19] It hid the genitals, says Freud, and the difference between them, and made castration a present reality; but it might be added that the belt also enclosed, immobilised and showed off the genitals.) Dracula carries his body like an erect phallus: you only have to think of his usual stiff posture, his long black cape, his sudden appearances like a bolt from the blue. As if to emphasise this phallic value, the camera often marks a pause – while Dracula poses. In a film like *Nosferatu*, a prototype of the horror film, the human vampire, as it appears to us almost constantly, is nothing other than this erection, a walking phallus or 'phallambulist', as one might say in French.[20] His rigidity is, at the same time, obviously, that of the corpse, but the signs of an aggressive sexuality are abundant and spectacular enough for us to be able to say that the phallic dimension predominates. Nosferatu might be called the Pointed One, bearing in mind all the simple and basic symbolism attached to pointedness. His face is pointed, so are his ears, his shoulders, his knees, his back and of course his nails and fangs. According to a primitive mental operation which prefers not to distinguish the structure of the parts from that of the whole, *Nosferatu* is an agglomeration of points.

The vampire as a walking phallus can only parade in front of us – out there on the catwalk. But the fantasy also needs its anchorage points, just as the story needs action. The (phallic) structure of the global form (Dracula) has to find an echo in other forms. It has to be embodied or reproduced in miniature. It requires precise details and markers around which psychic crystallisation can take place. It is here that the main clichéd images of the horror film come in. The internal form of the castle points towards the archaic mother, but its external form (a huge turreted building surrounded by jagged rocks), announces and demands the presence of the vampire's erect body. The famous fangs, the organs which express an aggressive sexuality, are not only the vampire's favourite sexual tool; they are also unique in that they can emerge from a woman's mouth – transforming her, via a striking return of the repressed, into the very thing that gave birth to the vampire form, the phallic woman, the bad mother. Fangs play a spectacular role in modern horror series, notably Terence Fisher's films; tightly clenched, claw-like hands are a feature of Tod Browning's *Dracula* and long pointed nails of Murnau's *Nosferatu*. The metaphor of the 'penetrating look' or 'piercing eyes' is taken literally – an effective way of displacing the phallic sign. Browning's Dracula has a look that radiates outwards, a laser beam, and the victim is mesmerised and overcome; in *Dracula has Risen from the Grave*, Freddie Francis takes the image of 'blood-shot eyes' to the extreme. Dracula's eyes are just this and, since an erection is produced by a rush of blood, the blood rushing into Dracula's eyes is an erection. The whole body and the various organs (eyes, hands, etc.) participate in the crucial act of the kiss-bite when the fangs, as they are sunk into the woman's neck (sometimes passionately) or the man's (aggressively rather), make two little slits, two little holes with the merest trace of blood around them – a remarkably condensed expression of the fetishistic link between sexuality and castration.[21]

The Dracula form, the phallus-fetish, stands out against the background of the archaic mother and is part of that background. But the substitute for the missing penis, the absent phallus, can only be, in the last resort, an illusion, a delusion. According to the pattern of belief outlined earlier, the mother's penis is there – that's what we set out to demonstrate, and that's what the more spectacular aspects of the horror film insistently proclaim – and it isn't there. The originality of the horror film is that it manages to make us aware of the conjunction: it's there – it isn't there. Dracula makes his entry, he is there, he is seen by spectators and characters alike. And yet, as far as the logic of the fantasy is concerned, *he shouldn't be there*. This is where that remarkable device of the mirror comes in: Dracula is present in the room and he isn't present on the other side of the room, in the other half of reality caught in the mirror. This division, this splitting of reality into two sides which 'deny' each other – which finds its perfect model in the absence of the reflection in the mirror – takes various forms. Dracula has no shadow and makes no noise. We think he is dead and buried, but he isn't. He is all-powerful, he has a whole country under his control, he rules over a huge community, he's a kind of Superman, capable of the most staggering physical exploits. At the same time he is surprisingly weak, so much so that he depends on the services of a sick and deformed servant. By night he is everything, by day nothing. Dracula's fangs, a sharp, intense expression of his energy, are counterbalanced by what they produce, the two little holes where this energy, although it passes into a new recruit, is also lost, since the vampire circuit is never-ending. And even this typical action of the fangs is an illusion. You only have to pass a flame over the fresh wounds for healing to take place immediately: the vampire doesn't really bite, nothing has happened. Another split. Externally Dracula is lord and master, a formidable 'master of men' like Zalmoxis. But the religious form has been emptied, and inside there is nothing. Dracula's body does not bleed. And even that prestigious outer envelope, that impressive silhouette draped in black, is misleading. A stake driven into the heart is all it takes for it to crumble into dust and be blown away on the wind (*Horror of Dracula*).[22]

Notes

19 Vol XXI, p. 156.
20 By analogy with 'somnambule' = sleepwalker.
21 Erections of the fangs, the eyes and even the skin, associated with magnetism and snake-taming, come into their own in John Gilling's *The Reptile* (1966). The reptile woman, who bites her victims and infects them with 'the black death', is nothing but a *montage*: the head is made out of huge, bulging eyes, enormous fangs and scaly skin: it is 'mounted' on a female body which doesn't really exist, is only a pretence. This snake is tamed and 'set up' by an exotic character representing a secret and primitive sect, the Sect of the Snake, which wields its power in a strictly magnetic way: infantile omnipotence of thought! The overdetermination of symbols and archaic references is further enriched by a cosmic dimension: the woman-reptile simulacrum can only be kept in a basement which houses a boiling spring, a true image of the beginning of the world, a primal chaos. Gilling's film is further characterised by a remarkable confrontation between spaces invested with a different value (the castle, the cottage, the inn); it would seem that at a certain level of regression, the characters, who probably depend too much on cultural systems of perception, lose their ability to signify and spatial figures, closely linked to elementary tactile and motor values, take over.
22 The American title of the 1958 remake of *Dracula*, directed by Terence Fisher.

 READING 41

The monstrous-feminine: film, feminism and psychoanalysis

Barbara Creed

One of the major concerns of the sci-fi horror film (*Alien, The Thing, Invasion of the Body Snatchers, Altered States*) is the reworking of the primal scene, the scene of birth, in relation to the representation of other forms of copulation and procreation. *Invasion of the Body Snatchers* explores the themes of bodily invasion and paranoia. The invading creature first exists as a giant egg/pod, which has come to Earth from another galaxy. As the pod silently hatches the creature simultaneously creates a replica of the human it wishes to become. In *The Thing* the primal scene is also presented as a series of grotesque bodily invasions; here the creature is able to take over both the human and animal body and clone itself into an exact replica of the invaded being. In both these films conception and birth are presented as a form of cloning; the sexual act becomes an act of vampirism. In *Altered States* a male scientist is able to take himself back to more primitive stages of existence through the agency of hallucinogenic drugs. He takes these while enfolded in a womb-like bath of special fluids. Eventually he gives birth to himself as an ape-creature. Procreation and birth take place without the agency of the opposite sex; and the creature born is primitive rather than civilized suggesting that a thin line separates the human animal from its ancestors. Central to all of these films are scenes which explore different forms of birth.

The primal scene is also crucial to *Alien* as is the figure of the mother, in the guise of the archaic mother. The archaic mother is the parthenogenetic mother, the mother as primordial abyss, the point of origin and of end. Although the archaic mother, the creature who laid the eggs, is never seen in *Alien*, her presence is signalled in a number of ways. She is there in the text's various representations of the primal scene, and in its depiction of birth and death. She is there in the film's images of blood, darkness and death. She is also there in the chameleon figure of the alien, the monster as fetish-object of and for the archaic mother. Signs of the archaic mother are particularly evident in the film's first section, with its emphasis on at least four different representations of the primal scene.

. . . .

What is most interesting about the mythological figure of woman as the source of all life is that, within patriarchal signifying practices, particularly the horror film, she is reconstructed and re-presented as a *negative* figure, one associated with the dread of the generative mother seen only as the abyss, the all incorporating black hole which threatens to reabsorb what it once birthed.

The central characteristic of the archaic mother is her total dedication to the generative, procreative principle. She is the mother who conceives all by herself, the original parent, the godhead of all fertility and the origin of procreation. She is outside morality and the law. Ash, the Science Officer who is also a cyborg, delivers a eulogy to the eponymous alien of the film which could be a description of this mother: 'I admire its purity; a survivor unclouded by conscience, remorse or delusions of morality'. Clearly, it is difficult to separate out completely the figure of the archaic mother, as defined above, from other aspects of the maternal figure – the maternal authority of Kristeva's semiotic, the mother of Lacan's imaginary, the phallic woman, the castrated and castrating woman. While the different figures signify separate aspects of the monstrous-feminine, as constructed in the horror film, each one is also only part of the whole. At times the horrific nature of the monstrous-feminine results from the merging of all aspects of the maternal figure into one – the horrifying image of woman as archaic mother, phallic woman, castrated body and castrating parent represented as a single figure within the horror film. However, the archaic mother is clearly present in two distinct ways in the horror film.

Constructed as a negative force, she is represented in her phantasmagoric aspect in many horror texts, particularly the sci-fi horror film. We see her as the gaping, cannibalistic bird's mouth in *The Giant Claw*; the terrifying spider of *The Incredible Shrinking Man*; the toothed vagina/womb of *Jaws*; and the fleshy, pulsating womb of *The Thing* and *Poltergeist*. What is common to all of these images of horror is the voracious maw, the mysterious black hole that signifies female genitalia which threatens to give birth to equally horrific offspring as well as threatening to incorporate everything in its path. This is the generative archaic mother, constructed within patriarchal ideology, as the primeval 'black hole', the originating womb which gives birth to all life.

In the horror films mentioned above, it is the suggested presence of the gestating, all-devouring womb of the archaic mother which generates the horror. Nor are these images of the womb constructed in relation to the penis of the father. Unlike the female genitalia, the womb cannot be constructed as a 'lack' in relation to the penis. The womb is not the site of castration anxiety. Rather, the womb signifies 'fullness' or 'emptiness' but always it is its *own point of reference*. This is why we need to posit a more archaic dimension to the mother. For the concept of the archaic mother allows for a notion of the feminine which does not depend for its definition on a concept of the masculine. In contrast, the maternal figure, of the pre-Oedipal is almost always represented in relation to the penis – the phallic mother who later becomes the castrated mother. Significantly, there is an attempt in *Alien* to appropriate the procreative function of the archaic mother, to represent a man giving birth, to deny the mother as signifier of sexual difference – but here birth can exist only as the other face of death. When one of the alien creatures orally rapes Kane, one of the male astronauts, it implants its embryo in Kane's stomach. But the primeval mother does not need the male as a 'father', only as a host body, and the alien creature murderously gnaws its way through Kane's belly. Its birth leads to the male mother's death.

The archaic mother is present in all horror films as the blackness of extinction – death. The desires and fears invoked by the image of the archaic mother, as a force that threatens to reincorporate what it once gave birth to, are always there in the horror text – all-pervasive, all-encompassing – because of the constant presence of death. The desire to return to the original oneness of things, to return to the mother/womb, is primarily a desire for non-differentiation. If, as George Bataille argues in *Death and Sensuality*, life signifies discontinuity and separateness, and death signifies continuity and non-differentiation, then the desire for and attraction of death suggests also a desire to return to the state of original oneness with the mother. As this desire to merge occurs after differentiation, that is after the subject has developed as separate, autonomous self, it is experienced as a form of psychic death. In this sense, the confrontation with death as represented in the horror film gives rise to a terror of self-disintegration, of losing one's self or ego – often represented cinematically by a screen which becomes black, signifying the obliteration of self, the self of the protagonist in the film and the spectator in the cinema. This has important consequences for the positioning of the spectator in the cinema.

One of the most interesting structures operating in the screen-spectator relationship relates to the sight/site of the monstrous within the horror text. In contrast with the conventional viewing structures working within other variants of the classic text, the horror film does not work to encourage the spectator to identify continually with the narrative action. Instead, an unusual situation arises whereby the filmic processes designed to encourage spectatorial identification are momentarily undermined as horrific images on the screen challenge the viewer to run the risk of continuing to look. Here I refer to those moments in the horror film when the spectator, unable to stand the images of horror unfolding before his/her eyes, is forced to look away, to not-look, to look anywhere but at the screen particularly when the monster is engaged in the act of killing. Strategies of identification are temporarily broken and pleasure in looking is transformed into pain as the spectator is punished for his/her voyeuristic desires. For instance, the scene in *Alien* where the alien creature gnaws its way out of the stomach of one of the astronauts is designed to command our attention while simultaneously punishing us for looking. We watch in horrified fascination as we see blood spatter up from underneath his shirt as something tries to push its way up from under. When we realize that the movement is actually coming from inside his stomach it is too late to disavow what we know. Even if we do look away – as do many spectators – we still have a fair idea of what is about to happen. Such scenes satisfy a morbid desire to see *as much as possible* of the unimaginable, such as graphic horrifying images of a man giving birth to a monster, of the human body torn apart before our disbelieving eyes, before we are forced to look away. Graphic displays of gore and bodily dismemberment are repeated each time the alien strikes.

The three main 'looks' which have been theorized in relation to the screen–spectator relationship are: the camera's look at the pro-filmic event; the look of the character(s) in the diegesis; and the look of the spectator at the events on the screen. In his discussion of pornography, Paul Willemen (1980) has specified a fourth look, the possibility of the viewer being overlooked while engaged in the act of looking at something he or she is not supposed to look at. The act of 'looking away' when viewing horror films is such a common occurrence that it should be seen as a fifth look that distinguishes the screen–spectator relationship.

Confronted by the sight of the monstrous, the viewing subject is put into crisis – boundaries, designed to keep the abject at bay, threaten to disintegrate, collapse. According to Lacan, the self is constituted in a process which he called the 'mirror-phase' in which the child perceives its own body as a unified whole in an image it receives from outside itself. Identity is an imaginary construct, formed in a state of alienation, grounded in misrecognition. In 'Some reflections on the ego' Lacan argues that the self, because it is constructed on an illusion, is always in danger of regressing. The horror film puts the viewing subject's sense of a unified self into crisis, specifically in those moments when the image on the screen becomes too threatening or too horrific to watch, when the abject threatens to draw the viewing subject to the place 'where meaning collapses', the place of death. By not-looking, the spectator is able momentarily to withdraw identification from the image on the screen in order to reconstruct the boundary between self and screen and reconstitute the 'self' which is threatened with disintegration. This process of reconstitution of the self, via the fifth look, is also reaffirmed by the conventional ending of some horror narratives in which the monster is 'named' and destroyed.

Fear of losing oneself and one's boundaries is made more acute in a society which values boundaries over continuity, and separateness over sameness. Given that death is represented in the horror film as a threat to the self's boundaries, symbolized by the threat of the monster, death images are most likely to cause the spectator to look away, to not-look. Because the archaic mother is closely associated with death in its negative aspects – death seen as a desire for continuity and the loss of boundaries – her presence is marked negatively within the project of the horror film. Both the mother and death signify a monstrous obliteration of the self and both are linked to the demonic, as *Alien* so terrifyingly demonstrates.

 READING 42

The acoustic mirror

Kaja Silverman

The female subject's involuntary incorporation of the various losses which haunt cinema, from the foreclosed real to the invisible agency of enunciation, makes possible the male subject's identification with the symbolic father, and his imaginary alignment with creative vision, speech and hearing. Indeed, not only is woman made to assume male lack as her own, but her obligatory receptivity to the male gaze is what establishes its superiority, just as her obedience to the male voice is what 'proves' its power.

The diegetic drama of castration described by Mulvey is thus a simulation of the crisis which occurs whenever the male viewer is reminded of his visual and verbal subordination to cinema's absent enunciator – a simulation which covers over that other scene of castration with its representations of phallic men and wounded women. Because it restages what happens elsewhere, in both the history of the subject and the production of the cinematic text, Hollywood's diegetic organization can perhaps best be characterized by a phrase from Bazin: it is 'a mirror with a delayed reflection, the tin foil of which retains the image' of earlier losses. It is scarcely necessary to add that woman is the foil.

. . . .

Peeping Tom gives new emphasis to the concept of reflexivity. Not only does it foreground the workings of the apparatus, and the place given there to voyeurism and sadism, but its remarkable structure suggests that dominant cinema is indeed a mirror with a delayed reflection. It deploys the film-within-a-film trope with a new and radical effect, making it into a device for dramatizing the displacement of lack from the male to the female subject.

There are, in fact, two films-within-the-film. The first, which was completed by the now-deceased Dr. Lewis (Michael Powell) some twenty years prior to the diegetic present, offers a 'scientific' record of his son's childhood, with particular emphasis on moments of fear, loss, and sexual crisis. Completely traumatized by his father's experiments, Mark Lewis (Carl Boehm) attempts as an adult to master that trauma by making a film of his own, which constitutes the second film-within-the-film.

Although both films purport to be documentaries, each is shown to be elaborately staged. Not only does Dr. Lewis orchestrate the crises he then photographs, but these crises are all key moments within the Oedipal narrative (the castration threat, the primal scene, the loss of the mother, and access to the paternal legacy, here represented by the gift of a camera). Throughout these various episodes, the emphasis falls on the father's punishing power and on the son's lack (this is true even at the moment of seeming phallic transmission, since the father's camera remains conspicuously trained on the son's). That lack is dramatically figured here by Mark's exclusion from the site of discursive production – by the evident fact that his meaning comes to him from elsewhere. By constantly turning his camera on his son, Dr. Lewis firmly locates him on the side of the spectacle, within the boundaries of the filmic fiction. Although Mark's position is thus analogous to that of any diegetic character within classic cinema, it is clearly shown to be incompatible with the 'phallic function',[56] and to necessitate extreme defensive measures. Here those measures take the form of Mark's own 'documentary', which performs an analogous displacement to that engineered by Hollywood, obliging woman once again to assume a double burden of lack.

This second film is consequently equally constrained by Oedipal imperatives – by the imperatives of male adequacy. It casts an inverted reflection of the first, manifesting the same obsessive interest in trauma, but now situating Mark outside the fiction, on the side of apparent discursive control. This shift is effected by inserting a series of prostitutes and models into the specular position Mark occupies in Dr. Lewis's film, and by subjecting them to a lethal castration.

Mark's relationship with these women is insistently mediated by the camera; from the moment that he first sights one of them as a bridge to phallic identification, he never looks away from the view-finder, thereby indicating the central role played by the cinematic apparatus in the desired psychic transaction. In each case, he films his victim in an attitude of erotic display which facilitates the inscription of lack onto the female body at precisely that point where Freud would have it be found. (Thus, the key moment in the erotic display of the nameless prostitute is when she separates her legs to remove her stockings. In the case of Vera it is the spreading of her trousered legs as she dances. Millie proves even more cooperative by wearing a corset whose v-shaped lower edge sharply demarcates the looked-for site of absence.)

Mark then films his victims as he kills them. The conflation of these two actions is reiterated by the murder weapon, which is itself a part of the apparatus – a knife at the end of one of the tripod legs. Significantly, Mark forces the women to look at their own faces in a mirror as he stabs them in the throat – to see their own fear, pain, and loss, just as his fathers films have obliged him to see his own.[57] The mirror also functions to disavow male lack even further by suggesting that the female subject reflects only herself, and so denying the place of the male subject within the mimetic circuit.

. . . .

Perhaps the most striking demonstration of the reversibility of Mark's projections occurs during the scene in which he gives Helen a lizard brooch, thereby attempting to locate her in the position he occupied as a child when his father dropped a live lizard into his bed. As Helen tries to decide where to pin the brooch, moving it around on her dress, voyeurism gives way to identification, and Mark fascinatedly mimics her gestures. However, it is while screening his 'documentary' footage that he most consistently crosses the barrier he has been at such pains to construct, slipping over to the side of the victim.

Twice while watching that footage, Mark literally crosses the imaginary dividing line separating viewer from spectacle; rising from his chair, he walks over to the image of a woman experiencing the anguish of death, and places his face against the screen. This physical relocation dramatically attests to the collapse of the fetishistic structure of classic cinema. Far from maintaining the requisite distance from the image of woman-as-lack, Mark recognizes himself in that image, and tips over into it. As he does so, a remarkable transformation occurs, which is more than a little reminiscent of the glance/*Glanz* example. Suddenly the beam of the projector lamp no longer irradiates the spectacle for the viewing subject (Mark); it illuminates him, as well. In so doing it functions much like the flashlight his father used to turn on him as a child. When Mark cries out that 'the lights faded too soon', he speaks not only to his failure to produce technically good footage of Vera's murder, but to his failure to sustain that externalizing displacement which converts the paternal flashlight into the son's projector lamp, and the image into the gaze. He speaks, in other words, to his inability to project the projections necessary to disburden himself of lack – to his inability to transfer 'the shine' from himself to woman.

. . . .

In the concluding moments of *Peeping Tom*, Mark acknowledges the splits and losses that have structured his subjectivity and directs against himself and the whole battery of weapons he has until then reserved for his female victims – camera, mirror, sharpened tripod knife. In a stunning reprise of all the many textual references to light, Mark times numerous flashbulbs to shine on him at half-second intervals as he levels the psychic barrier separating himself from the female subject, and embraces his own castration.

I would argue that it is not so much the film's preoccupation with voyeurism and murder as its refusal to be complicit in a general cultural disavowal of male lack which provoked such hostility from the popular press at the time of its original release. The reviews are revealingly saturated with references to excrement ('The only really satisfactory way to dispose of *Peeping Tom* would be to shovel it up and flush it swiftly down the nearest sewer'; '*Peeping Tom* stinks more than anything else in British Films since *The Stranglers of Bombay*'; 'I was shocked to the core to find a director of his standing befouling the screen with such perverted nonsense'),[59] suggesting intense anxiety about the possible leakage back into a 'clean' and 'proper' space of what has been thrown violently outside it.

. . . .

The critical defense most frequently mounted against *Peeping Tom* at the time of its original release was to relegate it and its admirers to the category of psychic abnormality. Movie audiences were warned that it 'displays a nervous fascination with the perversion it illustrates', that it 'wallows in the diseased urges of a homicidal pervert', and that 'sick minds will be highly stimulated'. Only one reviewer, Isobel Quigly, was prepared to acknowledge that the film attempts to engage its viewer on familiar ground, and her response is consequently worth quoting at some length:

> *Peeping Tom* didn't make me want to streak out of the cinema shrieking . . . it gives me the creeps in retrospect, in my heart and mind more than in my eyes. We have had glossy horrors before . . . but never such insinuating, under-the-skin horrors, and never quite such a bland effort to make it look as if this isn't for nuts but for normal homely filmgoers like you and me.[61]

What is immediately surprising about this passage is its preoccupation with spectatorship. Instead of disavowing her own relation to the film, as the other reviewers were so quick to do, Quigly focuses upon the ways in which *Peeping Tom* destabilized her by triggering a responsive tremor within her own subjectivity. She stresses not only its 'under-the skin horror', but its capacity for generating 'creeps in retrospect'. Both of these phrases have a curious resonance, which reverberates once again in her admission that the film takes as its point of address 'normal homely filmgoers like you and me'. If the emphasis upon interiority and delayed effectivity are not enough to alert the reader to the uncanny nature of Quigly's viewing experience, the adjective 'homely' dispels all doubt. The juxtaposition of this adjective with 'creeps in retrospect' and 'under-the-skin horrors' suggests that if *Peeping Tom* traumatizes and unsettles the viewer, that is because it forces a confrontation with 'that class of the frightening which leads back to what is known of old and long familiar'.

Notes

56 Lacan, 'Seminar of 21 January 1975', p. 186.
57 See Linda Williams, 'When the Woman Looks', in *Re-vision: Essays in Feminist Theory*, ed. Patricia Mellencamp, Mary Ann Doane, and Linda Williams (Los Angeles: American Film Institute, 1984), pp. 83–99, for an extremely interesting discussion of the way in which Mark seeks to trap his female victims in attitudes of narcissism and exhibitionism.
59 Ian Christie provides an excellent summary of those reviews in 'The Scandal of *Peeping Tom*', published in *Powell, Pressburger, and Others*, ed. Ian Christie (London: BFI, 1978), pp. 53–59.
61 Ibid.

READING 43

'An unsuitable genre for a feminist?'

Cora Kaplan

Young, nubile women detectives like P.D. James' Cordelia Gray or Antonia Fraser's Jemima Shore are, without doubt, imaginative by-products of the modern women's movement. Liberated, smart and sexual, these female sleuths challenge fictional convention in which freelance investigators are either incarnations of middle aged machismo (Chandler, McDonald, etc.), intuitive post-menopausal spinsters (Christie, Wentworth, Tey), or certified male eccentrics like Wimsey, Poirot or Gervase Fen. But if feminism has made space for a new breed of female protagonist in a traditional field of popular fiction, can it really affect the politics, sexual and otherwise, of the genre itself? Women have been prominent as authors of detective fiction since the twenties and thirties, and especially in Britain these 'queens of crime' from Christie to Ruth Rendell have been as influential as men in shaping the conventions of the form and determining its readership. We are right to reclaim the women writers of crime fiction as important literary figures, for their books are as ever evocative of the culture and period in which they were written as those of serious novelists.

But we may find both when we look back at the work of the older generations of crime writers, Agatha Christie, Ngaio Marsh, Josephine Tey, Dorothy Sayers, Patricia Wentworth, as well as that of women writers who have dominated the last couple of decades (P.D. James, Ruth Rendell) that women crime writers have been at worst explicitly anti-feminist, and at best highly ambivalent about any disruption of traditional gender relations. Within a genre which in general upholds conservative social values our queens of crime have, with few exceptions, been good royalists, often defending a social order in their fiction that is decidedly on the wane if it has not actually disappeared from the real world some decades before.

Thus Agatha Christie, through Miss Marple 'rescues' the village spinster from the general contempt accorded elderly unmarried, childless women, emphasising instead the acute and sympathetic observer in the figure standing 'outside' the sexual, familial and economic entanglements that make up the lives of most members of a community. At one level this seems a radical move to reinstate the unmarried woman as an independent force, even a public benefactor. At another, Miss Marples' genteel distance from passion highlights the disruptive power of female sexuality in the populace at large.

Moreover, the village life itself becomes, in the Miss Marples books a microcosm of all social relations, a cultural book of knowledge from which a thousand parables about human nature and motivation can be drawn. The nostalgia for a rural, stable, class conscious society, where servants, a modern peasantry and the gentry are clearly defined, runs through much of Christie, Marsh, Wentworth, Tey – and constitutes a consistent theme in British crime fiction from the twenties onwards. The crime that threatens this idyll is often a symptom of the social disruption that social change itself brings about, and its bearer in one form or another is frequently the woman who aspires through sexual attachment or professional insinuation to improve her class position. Cold, independent women who use sex to manipulate men and humiliate women are favoured offenders, either murderers themselves or catalysts in the criminal scenario, but equally women who flout sexual convention are a prime source of suspicion. Harriet Vane, the fictional writer of crime fiction who figures in several of Dorothy L. Sayers' novels, initially as the suspected murderer of her lover, then as a not very competent amateur sleuth, and finally as the wife of Sayers' aristocrat detective, Lord Peter Wimsey, is perhaps the most fully developed character of this latter kind. Sayers' crime fiction written between the wars explicitly centres the related ambivalence about female intellectual and sexual independence.

In *Strong Poison* (1930), Harriet is under suspicion because she has broken social and sexual codes; in *Gaudy Night*, set in an Oxford women's college (Sayers went to Somerville), she is at risk because she attempts to find the culprit, who turns out to be a female servant in the college, in the unnatural enclave of women scholars. While *Gaudy Night* is in many ways a loving portrait of Somerville, the novel ends with Harriet giving up her risky independence and accepting Wimsey. All-women's institutions are similarly used as settings for two other post war detective novels, Josephine Tey's *Miss Pym Disposes* and P.D. James' *Shroud for a Nightingale*. In each of these books a world where men are excluded breeds envy, jealousy, competition, and – worst of all – unnatural attachments. In both books murder and lesbianism are strongly collected, and the negative implication of these female ghettos – a physical training college and a nursing school attached to a country hospital – are fully exploited. It matters little that Tey's detective is another aging spinster writer, Miss Pym, and James', the poet detective, Adam Dalgleish. Each book uses the setting to celebrate normative heterosexuality, and implies that even the most humble professional occupations for women involve a period of single sex education which breeds unhealthy and dangerous emotions.

The presence of these sexually and socially conservative themes in so many of the 'great' women crime writers raises the question of why these women were attracted to the genre in the first place. One point so obvious that it is easy to overlook it, is that crime fiction is a popular genre that is read by both sexes, unlike women's fiction in general which has in most cases a primary audience of women. It allows women to invest a masculine persona with impunity – Margery Allingham's Albert Campion, Sayers' Wimsey, Christie's Poirot, James' Dalgleish, Marsh's Roderick Alleyn, Rendell's Wexford, serve as fictional alter egos, distancing the authority of the investigator who finds out that society's secret from the gendered identity of the female writer. Even when the sleuth is female she has only recently – and usually where the author *is* explicitly feminist in her orientation – become an autobiographical extension of the author. For it is precisely the identification of author and protagonist that is used to criticise the narrowest of women's fiction in general. In the traditional crime novel there must be a culprit who is individually responsible, and suspicion needs to fall on more than one character. The best writers of the traditional crime narrative believe, often with a vengeance, in individual responsibility rather than social causes for acts of violence. Christie, in her wonderfully interesting autobiography – 'The best thing she's ever written' as *Woman's Own* said – makes absolutely clear how out of sympathy she was with 'modern' theories of criminology and penal reform. She began to write, she says, in the wake of 'the 1914 war' when 'the doer of evil was not a hero: the *enemy* was wicked, the *hero* was good: it was as crude and simple as that. We had not then begun to wallow in psychology. I was, like everyone else who wrote books or read them, *against* the criminal and *for* the innocent victim.

This representation of the morality of writers and readers in a simpler moral universe is typical of Christie's nostalgia for a social system long gone. Her example of the new perverse morality which sympathises with the criminal chooses 'the fragile old woman in a small cigarette shop' who is 'attacked and battered to death' by a 'young thug'. She believes such 'wolves' should be executed without a second thought; attempts to reform innate evil are, of course useless. Earlier in the autobiography in an extraordinary passage, Christie links the pleasure of her girlhood – the anticipation of a happy marriage that she and all her friends had – with the fate of the murderer. 'We were like obstreperous flowers – often weeds maybe, but nevertheless, all of us growing exuberantly – pressing violently up through cracks in pavements and flagstones, and in the most inauspicious places, determined to have our fill or life . . . bursting out into the sunlight, until someone came and trod on us. Nowadays, alas, life seems to apply weedkiller. . . . There are said to be those who are "unfit for living". This obscure passage with its sexual and revolutionary metaphors for the emergence of adult feminity, followed by the odd non-sequitur attack on progressive criminology suggests the vital connection between Christie's social and sexual perspectives. In the old order where 'nurses, nannies, cooks and housemaids' told you that 'One day Mr. Right will come along', conventional femininity could be expressive, even radical, because it was contained within an ordered society with a known morality. Now rambunctious young women seem to founder, because society has transferred its sympathies to the working class criminal! To some extent many of the older queens of crime, Tey and Sayers certainly, shared this dubious moral and political perspective; these writers' views of gender and sexuality were imbued with a class snobbery and a nostalgia for a social structure that the second world war would radically change.

So what, today, are the prospects for writing a 'feminist' crime novel that does not, in any way, reproduce the anxieties about dangerous femininity so obtrusive in women's initial development of the genre?

Certainly P.D. James does reproduce much of the moral and political perspectives of the group of writers I have been discussing. If Cordelia Gray is young, nubile, orphaned and gutsy, the convent educated daughter of a peripatetic revolutionary, her sleuthing, in *An Unsuitable Job for a Woman* results in her inciting a 'bad' woman to murder her lover. Ruth Rendell who deserves more attention than I have space to give her has tackled the theme of feminism several times – most recently in *An Unkindness of Ravens* which takes on both feminism and the heated question of 'the real event,' in father-daughter incest. A more politically progressive writer than James, she is better at suggesting the ways in which modern feminism has changed the ambitions of her women characters than in her attempts to deal with self-identified feminists. Would a feminist novel use a woman detective to find a patriarchal villain? Depends what kind of feminist you are, I guess: a number of American feminist crime writers – notably Amanda Cross in *Death in a Tenured Position* – have written really gripping novels set in academia which explore whether the male villain represents society or acts as its agent in innovative ways.

Both Antonia Fraser and Sara Caudwell have used their defiantly promiscuous female protagonists to reject the notion that it is women's transgressive sexuality that is 'the problem – the trigger of social disturbance and violence. In addition, Caudwell in *Thus Was Adonis Murdered* has a rather marginal 'detective' figure called Hilary whose sex is never revealed. But both Fraser and Caudwell, unlike Rendell, write about safely bourgeois society and urban professionals – media people, lawyers. American writers on the whole are, of course, not bound by the conventions, ideologies and history established by British crime fiction. Brilliant writers like Diane Johnson (*The Shadow Knows* and *Lying Low*) appropriate some of the narrative structures of crime fiction to write novels which are implicitly feminist and that have one foot in and one out of the genre. Indeed, an awareness of feminism is even productively used by the best and most prolific writers of contemporary blood and guts crime fiction, Elmore Leonard, whose urban settings, north and south, deal with a much wider social cultural range of characters than any contemporary British writer.

Turning a genre politically inside out while still retaining its narrative pleasure – the chase, the investigation, the mystery – is a tough, if not impossible job. Can crime fiction survive as a recognizable popular form if we no longer 'cherchez la femme'?

(from *Women's Review*, No. 8, 1986)

READING 44

'Jackie: an ideology of adolescent femininity'

Angela McRobbie

D.C. Thompson is not, in *Jackie*, merely 'giving the girls what they want'. Each magazine, newspaper or comic has its own conventions and its own style. But within these conventions and through them a concerted effort is nevertheless made to win and shape the consent of the readers to a set of particular values.

The work of this branch of the media involves 'framing' the world for its readers, and through a variety of techniques endowing with importance those topics chosen for inclusion. The reader is invited to share this world with *Jackie*. It is no coincidence that the title is also a girl's name. This is an unambiguous sign that its concern is with 'the category of the subject'[4], in particular the individual girl, and the feminine 'persona'. *Jackie* is both the magazine and the ideal girl. The short, snappy name carries a string of connotations: British, fashionable (particularly in the 1960s); modern; and cute; with the pet-form '-ie' ending, it sums up all those desired qualities which the reader is supposedly seeking.

Second, we must see this ideological work as being grounded upon certain so-called natural, even 'biological' categories. Thus *Jackie* expresses the 'natural' features of adolescence in much the same way as, say, Disney comics are said to capture the natural essence of childhood. Each has, as Dorfman and Mattelart writing on Disney point out, 'a virtually biologically captive, predetermined audience'.[5] *Jackie* introduces the girl into adolescence outlining its landmarks and characteristics in detail and stressing importantly the problematic features as well as the fun. Of course, *Jackie* is not solely responsible for nurturing this ideology of feminity. Nor would such an ideology cease to exist should *Jackie* stop publication.

Unlike other fields of mass culture, the magazines of teenage girls have not as yet been subject to rigorous critical analysis. Yet from the most cursory of readings it is clear that they too, like those more immediately associated with the sociology of the media – press, TV, film, radio, etc. – are powerful ideological forces.

In fact women's and girls' weeklies occupy a privileged position. Addressing themselves solely to a female market, their concern is with promoting a feminine culture for their readers. They define and shape the woman's world, spanning every stage from childhood to old age. From *Mandy*, *Bunty* and *Judy* to *House and Home*, the exact nature of the woman's role is spelt out in detail, according to her age.

She progresses from adolescent romance where there are no explicitly sexual encounters to the more sexual world of *19*, *Honey* or *Over 21*, which in turn give way to marriage, childbirth, home-making, child care and the *Woman's Own*. There are no male equivalents to these products. 'Male' magazines tend to be based on particular leisure pursuits or hobbies, motorcycling, fishing, cars or even pornography. There is no consistent attempt to link 'interests' with age (though readership of many magazines will obviously be higher among younger age groups), nor is there a sense of a natural inevitable progression or evolution attached to their readers' expected 'careers'. There is instead a variety of possibilities with regard to *leisure* . . . many of which involve active participation inside or outside the home.

It will be argued here that the way *Jackie* addresses 'girls' as a monolithic grouping, as do all other women's magazines, serves to obscure differences, of class for example, between women. Instead it asserts a sameness, a kind of *false* sisterhood, which assumes a common definition of womanhood or girlhood. Moreover, by isolating a particular 'phase' or age as the focus of interest, one which coincides roughly with that of its readers, the magazine is in fact creating this 'age-ness' as an ideological construction. 'Adolescence' and here female adolescence, is itself an ideological 'moment' whose *connotations* are immediately identifiable with those 'topics' included in *Jackie*. And so, by at once defining its readership vis-à-vis age, and by describing what is of relevance to this age group, *Jackie* and women's magazines in general create a 'false totality'. Thus we *all* want to know how to catch a man, lose weight, look our best, or cook well! Having mapped out the feminine 'career' in such all-embracing terms, there is little or no space allowed for alternatives. Should the present stage be unsatisfactory the reader is merely encouraged to look forward to the next. Two things are happening here: 1) The girls are being invited to join a close, intimate sorority where secrets can be exchanged and advice given; and 2) they are also being presented with an ideological bloc of mammoth proportions, one which imprisons them in a claustrophobic world of jealousy and competitiveness, the most unsisterly of emotions, to say the least!

. . . .

What I want to suggest is that *Jackie* occupies the sphere of the personal or private, what Gramsci calls 'Civil Society' ('the ensemble of organisms that are commonly called Private').[14] Hegemony is sought uncoercively on this terrain, which is relatively free of direct State interference. Consequently it is seen as an arena of 'freedom', of 'free choice' and of 'free time'. This sphere includes

> not only associations and organisations like political parties and the press, but also the family, which combined ideological and economic functions[15]

and as Hall, Lumley and McLennan observe, this distinctness from the state has

> pertinent effects – for example, in the manner in which different aspects of the class struggle are ideologically inflected.[16]

Jackie exists within a large, powerful, privately-owned publishing apparatus which produces a vast range of newspapers, magazines and comics. It is on this level of the magazine that teenage girls are subjected to an explicit attempt to win consent to the dominant order – in terms of femininity, leisure and consumption, i.e. at the level of culture. It is worth noting at this point that only three girls in a sample of 56 claimed to read any newspapers regularly. They rarely watched the news on television and their only prolonged contact with the written word was at school and through their own and their mothers' magazines. Occasionally, a 'risqué' novel like Richard Allen's 'Skingirl' would be passed round at school, but otherwise the girls did not read any literature apart from 'love' comics.

The 'teen' magazine is, therefore, a highly privileged 'site'. Here the girl's consent is sought uncoercively, and in her leisure time. As Frith observes:

> The ideology of leisure in a capitalist society . . . is that people work in order to be able to enjoy leisure. Leisure is their 'free' time and so the values and choices,

expressed in leisure are independent of work – they are the result of ideological conditions.[1]

While there is a strongly coercive element to those other terrains which teenage girls inhabit, the school and the family; in her leisure time the girl is officially 'free' to do as she pleases. . . . And this 'freedom' is pursued, metaphorically, inside the covers of *Jackie*. With an average readership age of 10 to 14, *Jackie* pre-figures girls' entry into the labour market as 'free labourers' and its pages are crammed full of the 'goodies' which this later freedom promises. *Jackie* girls are never at school, they are enjoying the fruits of their labour on the open market. They live in large cities, frequently in flats shared with other young wage-earners like themselves.

This image of freedom has a particular resonance for girls when it is located within and intersects with the longer and again ideologically constructed 'phase' they inhabit in the present. Leisure has a special importance in this period of 'brief flowering',[19] that is, in those years prior to marriage and settling down, after which they become dual labourers in the home and in production. Leisure in their 'single' years is especially important because it is here that their future is secured. It is in this sphere that they go about finding a husband and thereby sealing their fate.

Notes

4 L. Althusser, 'Ideology and the State', in *Lenin and Philosophy and Other Essays* (1971), p. 163.
5 A. Dorfman and A.M. Mattlart, *How to Read Donald Duck* (1971), p. 30.
14 Antonio Gramsci, *Selections from the Prison Notebooks*, quoted in S. Hall, B. Lumley, G. McLennan, 'Politics and Ideology: Gramsci' in *On Ideology, Cultural Studies 10* (1977), p. 51.
15 ibid., p.51.
16 ibid., p. 67
17 From an unpublished ms. by Simon Frith.
19 Richard Hoggart, *The Uses of Literacy* (1957), p. 51.

(from CCCS Occasional Paper, Women Series, No. 53, 1978)

📖 READING 45

'Pulp in the pink'

Janet Batsleer

Only when she felt she could bear no more of a happiness that was too glorious, too brilliant and too overwhelming did he let her go. And then, as he looked down at her shining eyes, at her flushed cheeks and her lips parted with ecstasy, he gave a little sigh of utter contentment. 'I have found you again my darling,' he said softly. 'I have found what I have been looking for all my life. This, my sweet, is what I have been waiting for although I didn't know it.'

Wings On My Heart, Barbara Cartland

What do these words mean to you? Do you tear out your hair at the sound of a woman falling one more time for the con-trick of the ages: He Tarzan, You Jane, woman the property of man, claimed by him and his throbbing sexuality? Do you flinch at the thought of such an embrace and grit your teeth at the purple prose, the excess of superlatives, one cliché after another? And do you remember the shiver of delight that used to thrill down your spine when you read these love stories? If you remember it, read on . . .

True Romance, *Womans Weekly*, Georgette Heyer, Barbara Cartland. Before I studied English Literature, first at 'A' Level and then at university, where I was trained in 'appreciation' and 'discrimination', I read romantic fiction indiscriminately. I didn't properly appreciate the difference between *Jane Eyre* and *Regency Buck*. For a while at university, I thought that being able to tell the difference meant success in life. Knowing a great work of literature when I saw one, meant I had miraculously shed subordination. Being a woman from a poor family didn't matter very much. I was one of the cream. I didn't read pulp fiction any more.

Now, as a feminist, I believe I was sold a pup when I gave up books and started reading literature. I have returned to the reading of my teens, which is also the bulk of the reading of thousands and thousands of women of all ages, to ask: why is all this so powerful, and why does it matter?

The answers, so far, to these questions have been mainly short and sharp, even from a criticism which aims to be progressive. On the whole, marxist criticism stresses that romantic fiction is *ideology*, a product of monopoly capitalism and its leisure industry. Like the rest of 'mass culture' it disguises and conceals the truth about our situation and encourages us to believe that as things are, they ever shall be. It is rotten with pleasure which lulls us into accepting the status quo. We're to believe the aristocracy is a fine thing: a marvellous British thing. We shall celebrate the Royal Wedding all the better because we have these stories. White British men are born to rule and marry a pure white English rose. All this is what romantic fiction would have us think.

Feminism, too, has produced some sharp attacks on the ideology of romance. Germaine Greer's assault in *The Female Eunuch* will run and run:

> The domestic romance myth remains the centrepiece of feminine culture. Sexual religion is the opiate of the supermenial. Romance sanctions drudgery, physical incompetence and prostitution.[1]

The case against romance is undoubtedly very strong. It is like so much in this society, a carrier of philosophies which perpetuate injustice. Barbara Cartland's work is racialist and nationalist in its almost obsessive stress on 'stock' and 'breed'; it is full of paternalistic Tory nonsense about the proper relationships between the 'nobility' and the 'lower classes'; it proposes heterosexual monogamy as the only possible sexual relationship; above all, it is incredibly sexist. And many of the most notable romance authors have been explicitly concerned to communicate a 'life-philosophy' through their work. In an early work of philosophy *Touch the Stars: A Clue to Happiness*, which sold, I am glad to say, extremely badly, Barbara Cartland sums up her view of the proper relationship between men and women:

> A man fought for his wife, or for the woman he had acquired, because she was his, and his responsibility. He fed her and protected and provided for her and her children; it was then obviously against his interests that she should be taken or seduced away from him. If this happened, there would be fighting; the clan would be divided

against itself, and in consequence vulnerable to an outside enemy. Therefore the laws of citizenship decreed that women were the property of their husbands and must not be stolen.

Yes, romance from many points of view is a very bad thing indeed. But before we begin a burning of the books or a picket at the publishers, here, with some trepidation, is a defence from the point of view of the thousands of women who read the stuff, and an appeal for an analysis of the contradictions involved. Because, despite recognising that the attacks tell part of the story, the tingle in my spine obstinately refuses to go away.

At present, all women in this society suffer, in various and complicated ways to be sure, a series of troubles and oppressions: apparently just because we are women and not men. Some of us respond to this state of affairs by becoming feminists. Many, many more women do not. But all of us in some way must look for ways of coping with our subordination. Romances are stories of desire for a happy ending. If we look for happy endings in fiction it is because at present it is the only place we can hope to find them. Heroines negotiate a path through a world full of difficulty and danger, and emerge triumphant with a man transformed by their love. And we all have to find a way of negotiating the difficulties of our subordination. However, the negotiations do not end in 'love triumphant'; the negotiations are continuous. In romantic fiction, alongside, or even within the ideology, there are processes which offer clues to answers to our oppressions – imaginary answers to oppressions that obstinately remain in the rest of our reality.

Take, for example, Barbara Cartland, the Queen of Romance. Millions of women around the world have read her stories, 262 or more by now. All her stories work to the same formula:

1 Handsome British nobleman meets lower class English Rose in a fix.

2 Nobleman transfixed by shallow society ladies.

3 English Rose at Country House of Nobleman shows how good she is with children.

4 Nobleman rescues English Rose from clutches of Society Lady and/or Lecherous Bounder.

5 Nobleman ditches Society Lady.

6 English Rose is a flower of noble stock.

7 Nobleman kisses English Rose, and says: I love you.

Within this secure formula there are any number of ways in which the finale can be achieved. Knowing that the happy ending is coming, but not knowing exactly how, is a basis of the pleasure we get from the stories. Formula in romantic fiction is well known and taught by countless schools of writing, and literary agents. The success of Mills and Boon publishing house at a time when other British publishers are in recession is due, in part, to their success in stamping their brand name on the formulas of romance.

Formula writing is a very old mode of writing. Modern romances have sometimes been claimed as the successors to mediaeval 'quest' stories. Nowadays, formula stories are not celebrated as the pinnacle of our civilisation. Despite the profits associated with them, they are left to readers on the edges of the Literary

Establishment; fairy stories for children, comic strips for teenagers, war stories and detective stories for men, love stories for women. The common, easily recognized pattern makes it possible for these stories to represent to us a view of our common state as women. Many more highly valued stories represent femininity too: but often through the detailed construction of one woman's life – a detailed *individual* characterisation, a *unique* story. So *To The Lighthouse*, *Madame Bovary*, and *Middlemarch* are valued because they are seen as unrepeatable stories. Romances, by contrast, are stories that are meant to be repeated over and over again. Romances tell us 'what all women know'; they are part of our common experience as women, and the formula story provides a means of making sense of the troubles which all women share.

The romance story isn't the only place this formula is found: read *The Tatler* or Barbara Cartland's own autobiographies. Read especially these days the story of Prince Charles and Lady Di, in which Miss Cartland herself figures bizarrely as a fairy step-grandmother. The stories of Di's ancestry, her birth, their meeting, her quiet work in a nursery, his farewell to the life of a rake: all this is the stuff from which romantic fiction is made. And it isn't a plot, though it may serve to divert our mind from unemployed Britain. It is as though we are in two places at once; often more fascinated by the gossip page than the financial report. And the harder our lives become, the more we are likely to turn to a world unlike our own – a world of glamour, wealth, pageantry, automatic happiness – seeking a distraction from our own ever more depressing world. So what in romance does fascinate? And what troubles, what aspects of our subordination does romance latch on to? Two examples will do.

Trouble number 1: a woman's place is in the home

Despite the fact that a majority of us now work outside the home, we are still, emotionally and psychologically, the guardians of the hearth. Romantic fiction makes the 'private sphere' not only of home and families, but also the emotions, central. In doing this, it turns the common accounts of power and history topsy-turvy:

> 'You are everything that matters,' Rayburn said. 'Everything that a man wants in his home and his personal world, which should always be private and apart from his public one.' (Cartland, *Vote for Love*)

The noblemen of Cartland's stories are always diplomats, foreign secretaries, rulers of one kind or another, but their only sphere of action in these romances is determined by the world of women. This is true of historical romance more generally. Napoleon is not the director of armies and Empire, but the lover of Josephine. Tudor economics disappear in the face of Henry VIII's treatment of his wives. The few exceptional women who burst onto the stage of history are still women like us: Mary Stuart and Elizabeth I are vain and jealous rivals in love, not the monarchs of contending nation states.

The home is still a place of incredible powerlessness, and women as a group are excluded from public power and decision making. But it is also the only place in which women may claim some semblance of power, knowledge and authority; in the daily ordering of family life and in the care of children, husband and relatives. The stories which Cartland tells again and again are celebrations of women's world. This is in part the process of placing women on a pedestal, an idealisation which serves to deny the realities of power. But it is more than that.

Reading about 'power behind the throne' is a means of turning the tables of power on the princes in an imaginary way. Wars and Governments, the institutions of men's power, can be left in the wings for once, while women take centre stage. And strangely, this celebration of private life and the assertion of its importance, is not a million miles from the feminist perception that what happens in the kitchen and the bedroom is as important for our future as what happens in the corridors of power. Both are born from the common condition of femininity.

Trouble number 2: the battle of the sexes

The Earl had only touched her hand and yet she had instinctively longed to snatch it away and at the same time felt herself shrink back in an effort to avoid him.

(*Vote For Love*)

Women live sexually in a world full of fear of men and other women, and fear of sexuality as a violent physical force alienated from loving. Fear of our own sexuality is dramatised by Cartland in the conflicts between the country girl heroine and the Scarlet Society Lady:

She would certainly not be as fiery, impetuous and over-passionate as Eloise was.

(*Vote for Love*)

and so is the problem of finding one Prince among so many Toads:

Why should there be such a difference between the two men? (*Vote for Love*)

The hero is one apart in a world full of men who are rough, sadistic and only out for one thing. And it is the love of a good woman which transforms him. Rayburn, in *Vote for Love* renounces the sexual double standard and the eleventh commandment 'do not get found out', overwhelmed by the Divine message of the first true kiss. Won over by her love, the kiss is not like any other: it stops when it hurts; there is passion without brutality. Sexual love between men and women is imagined as not a trouble any more.

Although all women know that this promise of romance will not be kept (what mother ever taught her daughter it would be?) and that the price it exacts can be very high, many women return to romance for its promises. Promises of love, security and power. The conflicts of Cartland's fiction are the conflicts which have produced feminism: conflicts *between* the private world of marriage, family and home and the world of public decision making and conflicts *within* the private world of marriage and patriarchal sexuality.

Feminism (my feminism), is a means of seeking an end to these conflicts by an abolition of the unjust sexual and social divisions from which they arise. But it is also a desire and a longing for a new world, in which women, men and children can love without subordination. This longing has been expressed by several generations of feminists: earlier this century it was called 'The Great Love'; today it has been expressed in one form in Marge Piercy's utopia, *Woman on the Edge of Time*. These feminist forms are fictions and formulas too: another and better means of surviving present reality. They fulfil some of the same need as romance does. But even within romance, with all its assumptions of racialism, chauvinism, class power and 'natural, normal' heterosexuality, there are signs of trouble and conflict. This is the perception on which Marilyn French's wonderful novel, *The Bleeding Heart*, is based. It takes all the clichés and the formula of romance on board and makes the troubles and conflicts surface into a conscious struggle:

And then they were pitched into the middle of a battle or a battle began inside them . . .
. . . and they kissed and the war escalated, but they were in the war, and they pressed their bodies together until they felt like a single unit.

Was love always like that, do you suppose? Champing down on the beloved and crushing them like the bound feet of a Chinese girl-child? How could you work it out, the togetherness, the distance? The old way had been to turn the woman into the man's creature; one will, one mind, one flesh, his. But there was no new way, was there?

If romance is our old way of making sense and surviving in the battle of the sexes, there is no sense in the simple act of refusal, denial and rejection. We may turn our backs, but it will still be there. It is only by acknowledging its power as a dream and identifying the troubles it claims to resolve that we can look forward and struggle, with more hope, to a new way of loving.

Note

1   Recent Marxist-feminist work on ideology has taken more trouble in its analysis of popular forms, and I've been very influenced by it, although this probably does not show. But the stress on how texts create and position subjects, and shape oppressed femininity seems to lead to the same dead end of rejection as less sophisticated critiques.

The article that is nearest to this piece that I know of is 'On Reading Trash' by Lilian S. Robinson, in her collection of essays, *Sex, Class and Culture*.

(From *Spare Rib*, No. 109,1981)

 READING 46

'"Returning to Manderley": romance fiction, female sexuality and class'

Alison Light

In the aftermath of Charles and Di, a lot of critical attention has been turned towards romance and its fictions, from Mills and Boon to 'bodice rippers' and the latest high-gloss consumerist fantasies (see, for example, Batsleer, 1981; Margolies, 1982; Harper, 1982). At the centre of the discussion has been the question of the possible political effects of reading romances – what, in other words, do they do to you? Romances have on the whole, been condemned by critics on the Left (although Janet Batsleer's piece is a notable exception). They are seen as coercive and stereotyping narratives which invite the reader to identify with a passive heroine who only finds true happiness in submitting to a masterful male. What happens to women readers is then compared to certain Marxist descriptions of the positioning of all human subjects under capitalism.[1] Romance thus emerges as a form of oppressive ideology, which works to keep women in their socially and sexually subordinate place.

I want to begin by registering the political dangers of this approach to romance fiction, and then to suggest that we should come at the question of its effects rather differently. David Margolies, for example (Margolies, 1982, p. 9), talks in highly dubious ways when he refers to women readers being 'encouraged to sink into feeling' and 'to feel without regard for the structure of the situation'. 'Romance', he continues 'is an opportunity for exercising frustrated sensitivity . . . inward-looking and intensely subjective', it is 'retrogressive' as a form of 'habitual reading for entertainment'. Such an analysis slides into a puritanical Left-wing moralism which denigrates readers. It also treats women yet again as the victims of, and irrational slaves to, their sensibilities. Feminists must baulk at any such conclusion which implies that the vast audience of romance readers (with the exception of a few up-front intellectuals) are either masochistic or inherently stupid. Both text and reader are more complicated than that. It is conceivable, say, that reading Barbara Cartland could turn you into a feminist. Reading is never simply a linear con-job, but a process of interaction, and not just between text and reader, but between reader and reader, text and text. It is a process which helps to query as well as endorse social meanings and one which therefore remains dynamic and open to change.

In other words, I think we need critical discussions that are not afraid of the fact that literature is a source of pleasure, passion *and* entertainment. This is not because pleasure can then explain away politics, as if it were a panacea existing outside of social and historical constraints. Rather it is precisely because pleasure is experienced by women and men within and despite those constraints. We need to balance an understanding of fictions as restatements (however mediated) of a social reality, with a closer examination of how literary texts might function in our lives as imaginative construction and interpretations. It is this meshing of the questions of pleasure, fantasy and language which literary culture takes up so profoundly and which makes it so uniquely important to women. Subjectivity – the ways in which we come to express and define our concepts of ourselves – then seems crucial to any analysis of the activity of reading. Far from being 'inward-looking' in the dismissive sense of being somehow separate from the realities of the state or the marketplace, subjectivity can be recognized as the place where the operations of power and possibilities of resistance are also played out.

A re-emphasis on the imaginative dimensions of literary discourse may then suggest ways in which romance, as much because of its contradictory effects as despite them, has something positive to offer its audience, as readers and as *women* readers. It must at the very least prevent our 'cultural politics' becoming a book-burning legislature, a politics which is doomed to fail, since it refuses ultimately to see women of all classes as capable of determining or transforming their own lives.

Romance fiction deals above all with the doubts and delights of heterosexuality: an institution which feminism has seen as problematic from the start. In thinking about this 'problem' I myself have found the psychoanalytic framework most useful since it suggests that the acquisition of gendered subjectivity is a process, a movement towards a social self, fraught with conflicts and never fully achieved. Moreover, psychoanalysis takes the question of pleasure seriously, both in its relation to gender and in its understanding of fictions as fantasies, as the explorations and productions of desires which may be in excess of the socially possible or acceptable. It gives us ways into the discussion of popular culture which can avoid the traps of moralism or dictatorship.

. . . .

How then does *Rebecca* say anything at all about the formulaic fiction in which frail flower meets bronzed god? I would like to see *Rebecca* as the absent subtext of much romance fiction the crime behind the scenes of Mills and Boon. For it seems to me that perhaps what romance tries to offer us is a 'triumph' over the unconscious, over the 'resistance to identity which lies at the very heart of psychic life' (Rose, 1983: 9). *Rebecca* acts out the process of repression which these other texts avoid by assuming a fully-achievable, uncomplicated gendered subject whose sexual desire is not in question, not produced in struggle, but given. Above all, romance fiction makes heterosexuality easy, by suspending history in its formulae (whether costume, hospital or Caribbean drama) and by offering women readers a resolution in which submission and repression are not just managed without pain and humiliation but managed at all.

Thus although women are undoubtedly represented as sexual objects, there might be a sense in which women are also offered unique opportunities for reader-power, for an imaginary control of the uncontrollable in the fiction of romance. Within the scenario of extreme heterosexism can be derived the pleasure of reconstructing any heterosexuality which is not 'difficult'. Romance offers us relations impossibly harmonized; it uses unequal heterosexuality as a dream of equality and gives women uncomplicated access to a subjectivity which is unified and coherent *and* still operating within the field of pleasure.

Perhaps then, the enormous readership of romance fiction, the fact that so many women find it deeply pleasurable, can be registered in terms other than those of moralizing shock. Romance is read by over fifty per cent of all women, but it is no coincidence that the two largest audiences are those of young women in their teens and 'middle aged housewives'. (See Anderson, 1974, for discussion of readership patterns and responses and Euromonitor for more recent data). I would suggest that these are both moments when the *impossibility* of being successfully feminine is felt, whether as a 'failure' ever to be feminine enough – like the girls in *Rebecca* – or whether in terms of the gap between fulfilling social expectations (as wife and mother) and what those roles mean in reality. That women read romance fiction is, I think, as much a measure of their deep dissatisfaction with heterosexual options as of any desire to be fully identified with the submissive versions of femininity the texts endorse. Romance imagines peace, security, and ease precisely because there is dissension, insecurity and difficulty. In the context of women's lives, romance reading might appear less a reactionary reflex or an indication of their victimization by the capitalist market, and more a sign of discontent and a technique for survival. All the more so because inside a boring or alienating marriage, or at the age of fifteen, romance may be the only popular discourse which speaks to the question of women's sexual pleasure. Women's magazines, for example, do at least prioritize women and their lives in a culture where they are usually absent or given second place.

Patterns of romance reading are also revealing. Readers often collect hundreds, which are shared and recycled among friends. Reading romance fiction means participating in a kind of subculture, one which underlines a collective identity as women around the issue of women's pleasure and which can be found outside a political movement. As Janet Batsleer has pointed out, romances are not valued because like 'Great Art' they purport to be unrepeatable stories of unique characters, they are valued precisely as ritual and as repetition. It is difficult then to assume that these narratives are read in terms of a linear identification – it is not real and rounded individuals who are being presented and the endings are known by *readers* to be a foregone conclusion. Romance offers instead of closure a postponement of fulfillment. They are addictive because the control they gesture towards is always illusory, always modified and contained by the heterosexuality which they seek to harmonize. In a sense, the activity of reading repeats the compulsion to the limiting regulation of female sexuality. Romances may pretend that the path to marriage is effortless (obstacles are there to be removed) but they have to cry off when the action really starts – after marriage. The reader is left in a permanent state of foreplay, but I would guess that for many women this is the best heterosexual sex they ever get.

I want to suggest then that we develop ways of analysing romances and their reception as 'symptomatic' rather than simply reflective. Romance reading then becomes less a political sin or moral betrayal, than a kind of 'literary anorexia' which functions as a protest against, as well as a restatement of, oppression. Their compulsive reading makes visible an insistent search on the part of readers for more than what is on offer. This is not, of course, any kind of argument for romance fictions being somehow progressive. Within the realities of women's lives however, they may well be *trans*gressive Consumerist, yes: a hopeless rebellion, yes: but still in our society a forbidden pleasure – like cream cakes. Romance does write heterosexuality in capital letters but in so doing it is an embarrassment to the literary establishment since its writers are always asking to be taken seriously. Their activity highlights of course the heterosexism of much orthodox and important literature. For, leaving aside the representation of femininity, what other models are available *anywhere* for alternative constructs of masculinity? Romance is not being wilfully different in its descriptions of virility as constituted around positions of authority, hierachy and aggression. Male, left-wing critics might do well to address themselves to projects which set out to deconstruct 'normal' male heterosexuality – a phenomenon which does after all exist outside war stories and cowboy books.

To say, as I have, that subjectivity is at stake in the practices of reading and writing is not to retreat into 'subjectivism'. It is to recognize that any feminist literary critical enterprise is asking questions about social and historical formations, not just as they operate 'out there', but as they inform and structure the material 'in there' – the identities through which we live, and which may allow us to become the agents of political change. Fiction is pleasurable at least in part because it plays with, displaces and resites these other fictions, and we need a language as critics of 'popular culture' which can politicize without abandoning the categories of entertainment. To say that everyone's art is somebody's escapism is not to underestimate the effects of a literary discourse, but to try to situate these effects across the vast spectrum of the production of meaning, of which literary texts are part. It would suggest too that it is not so much the abolition of certain literary forms which feminism necessitates as the changing of the conditions which produce them. I for one think that there will still be romance after the revolution.

If I have a soft spot for romance fiction then it is because nothing else speaks to me in the same way. It is up to us as feminists to develop a rigorous and compassionate understanding of how these fictions work in women's lives, keeping open the spaces for cultural and psychic pleasure whilst rechannelling the dissatisfactions upon which they depend.

Note

1   I am referring here very briefly to the enormous body of theoretical arguments which have emerged largely from the work of the French Marxist Louis Althusser. For

extended discussion of this work, and the different directions it has taken since the late 1960's see, for example, Coward and Ellis (1977), Barrett (1980). For an analysis of the historical and political relations between Marxism, feminism and psychoanalysis, see Rose (1983).

Barrett (1982) takes up some of these points but see also Coward (1982) and Rose (1982) for the importance of psychoanalysis as offering ways into the questions of subjectivity, representation and sexual politics.

References

Anderson, Rachel (1974) *The Purple Heart Throbs: The Sub-Literature of Love* (London: Hodder and Stoughton).

Barrett, Michèle (1980) *Women's Oppression Today* (London: Verso and NLB).

Barrett, Michèle (1982) 'Feminism and the Definition of Cultural Politics in Brunt and Rowan (1982).

Batsleer, Janet (1981) 'Pulp in Pink', *Spare Rib*, no. 109.

Brunt, Rosalind and Rowan, Caroline, eds. (1982), *Feminism, Culture and Politics* (London: Lawrence and Wishart).

Coward, Rosalind and Ellis, John (1977) *Language and Materialism* (London: Routledge and Kegan Paul).

Coward, Rosalind (1982) 'Sexual Politics and Psychoanalysis: Some Notes on the Relation' in Brunt and Rowan (1982).

Euromonitor Readership Surveys.

Harper, Sue (1982) 'History with Frills: Costume Fiction in World War II' *Red Letters* no. 14.

Margolies, David 1982) 'Mills and Boon: Guilt Without Sex' *Red Letters* no. 14.

Rose, Jacqueline (1983) 'Femininity and its Discontents' *Feminist Review* 14.

(from *Feminist Review*, no. 16, 1984)

 READING 47

'Teenage girls reading *Jackie*'

Elizabeth Frazer

I wonder who takes all the pictures and who are the people?

In this article I present some empirical data – the transcripts of discussions among seven groups of girls about a photo story from *Jackie* magazine, and about *Jackie*, and other girls' magazines like it generally. The data are used to underpin an argument about the use of the concept of 'ideology' in social theory and research. Critics complain that the theory of ideology is typically ill-specified and vague, and I discuss these criticisms. Where 'ideology' is more tightly specified, on the other hand, it predicts a certain sort of relationship between readers and the texts which are said to be bearers of ideological meaning and is taken as an explanation of people's beliefs or behaviour. A more or less passive reader is depicted: my data shows that, on the contrary, readers take a critical stand vis-à-vis texts. This theoretical discussion also underpins some remarks about social research method.

The research with girls about reading *Jackie* is part of a wider enquiry into the acquisition of a feminine gender and sexual identity, and about the role of ideology in this process. In recent years, social and cultural researchers have taken feminine heterosexuality as peculiarly 'ideological'. Girls seem to suffer from what we might call 'false consciousness' in sexual matters; the social organisation of sexuality benefits men and boys and disbenefits women and girls; sexual meanings and definitions uphold the valorization of masculinity and the oppression of females; behaviour, values and ideals, which to radicals look highly artificial and political are widely perceived as natural, and so on (for example: Barrett, 1980; Griffin, 1985; Hebron, 1983; Lees, 1986; McRobbie, 1978a, 1978b; Sharpe, 1976; Wilson, 1978; Winship, 1978). Sociologists have studied sexist beliefs and attitudes. Cultural analysis has paid attention to texts which are said to be bearers of the ideology of feminine sexuality, pornography, romantic fiction, girls' and women's magazines, sex education materials. One text which has received a considerable amount of this sort of attention is *Jackie* (Griffin, 1982; Hebron, 1983; McRobbie, 1978b). However, I could not discover any research in which readers were asked about the magazine.

In my fieldwork I had prolonged and regular contact with seven groups of teenage girls. One was a racially mixed working-class group who regularly go to a youth project in Inner London. I have used conventional sociologists' occupational status criteria for determining class; typical parental occupations from among this group are kitchen assistant, factory worker, shop assistant, cleaner. On the other hand, for racial identity I have used the girls' own self-ascriptions; this group is mainly black British, but included two white girls and one Turkish. They attend a variety of schools (mixed, or single-sex comprehensive, or single-sex convents) and range in age from thirteen to seventeen. There were also two groups of fourth formers (fourteen-year-olds), and a group of upper sixth formers from an Oxfordshire single-sex comprehensive. The parental occupations of these girls included secretaries, plumber, police officer, nurse, master butcher, cabinet maker, night porter. They were more homogeneous racially – one fourth former was Afro-Caribbean, and one sixth former was a black African. There were also two groups of sixth formers (one upper and one lower), and a group of third formers (thirteen-year-olds) in an Oxfordshire headmistresses' conference public school for girls. The parental occupations of these girls included barrister, managing director, solicitor, stud manager, stockbroker, landowner, army officer. They were all white.

In the *Jackie* session I gave the girls a photocopy of the story to read, and then just asked them to talk about it[1]. They were not surprised to be asked to do this as we had talked a lot about TV, books, advertising and so on before, and they knew what my research was about. Discussion about the story generally lasted about twenty minutes. After this the talk drifted off, different ways, depending on the group. The comprehensive fourth years, and the public school upper sixth began to talk about problem pages, with interesting results, which I discuss later in this article.

To begin with, though, I want to discuss some philosophical and conceptual problems with 'ideology'. These problems are invariably overlooked, or ignored by social theorists, and researchers, but they have serious implications for the use of 'ideology' as the powerful explanation of social phenomena that it is often taken to be.

. . . It is the argument of this paper that the concept of 'ideology' is overly theoretical, in the sense that it is explanatorily unnecessary. The legitimation of social orders, what texts mean – all of these things must be explained by social theorists; I argue that we can explain them with concepts which are more concrete than 'ideology'.

Paradoxically, I shall also go on to argue that the concept is too monolithic, and, as it stands, predicts that people will be more, or differently affected by 'ideology' than evidence actually shows they are. For there is no doubt that the ordinary language notion of ideology carries with it an implication of 'normativity' and of efficacy – ideology makes people do things. Although it is rarely spelt out as such, researchers and theorists work with an implicit model as follows:

Ideology $\left. \begin{array}{l} \text{unitary or} \\ \text{multiple} \end{array} \right) \longrightarrow$ $\left. \begin{array}{l} \text{meanings} \\ \text{'culture'} \\ \text{representation} \end{array} \right) \longrightarrow$ $\left. \begin{array}{l} \text{belief} \\ \text{attitude} \\ \text{opinion} \end{array} \right) \longrightarrow$ behaviour

Texts as bearers of ideology

Much empirical research has been focused on the third element in this chain, i.e. subjects' beliefs and attitudes. This work tends to take 'attitude' or 'opinion' or 'belief' to be measurable, and fixed. I believe that this in itself is an unwarrantable assumption. In this article, though, I want to concentrate on the work which attends to the second element – the meanings and representations of the culture which are encoded in texts of various sorts. Especially significant are semiotic, and other contents analyses of texts, which carry the implication that from the analysis we can infer the content of ideology, and predict or explain the beliefs and behaviour of readers.

Notable examples are the Glasgow Media Group's contents analyses of television news programmes; various reports on the television programmes children watch; Barthes's semiotic analyses of advertisements and so forth; the analyses of school text books by theorists of socialization; and most pertinent for my present purposes, the several analyses of girls' and women's magazines, including *Jackie*.

All too often theorists commit the fallacy of reading 'the' meaning of a text and inferring the ideological effect the text 'must' have on the readers (other than the theorists themselves, of course!). We may oppose this strategy at two points. First, we may dispute that there is one valid and unitary meaning of a text. Second, we may care to check whether, even if we grant that there is a meaning, it does have this, or an ideological effect on the reader (see Richardson and Corner 1986). In this article I am mainly concerned with the second of these two queries.

Some issues of method

When we had the discussions about the story, I knew the girls in the groups fairly well, as I had had at least half a dozen intensive sessions with each, discussing topics loosely connected with 'femininity' and doing group work exercises, playing communication games and so on. They knew I was interested in what they watched, read and listened to, and that if possible I wanted to find out how these things affected them. A crucial part of my fieldwork methodology is feeding the analysis and concepts *I* use back into the groups, so in previous sessions we had discussed concepts like 'stereotypes', 'roles', 'alternative meanings' and so on. They were not, therefore, in the least bit surprised to be asked to read and discuss the photo-story. I gave them enough time to read it once from start to finish, and then said something like: 'OK – what do you think of that story then?'

. . . .

Obviously, all this means I was far from getting a 'naive reading' of the story from the girls. How one would go about eliciting a naive reading escapes me. . . .

The discussion about the story generally lasted about twenty minutes – I worked quite hard to keep them on the subject (it is a very boring story) – and in the end the talk moved off, in the case of the comprehensive sixth formers into a general discussion on sexism, the double standard and gender stereotypes; in the case of the fourth formers into talk on books, magazines, and how what you read changes as you get older; and the public school third years got onto a very long discussion of class . . .

Above all, though, they read the story as a work of fiction:

Claire	it needs to be a bit dramatic though to get there
Liz	and there wasn't much drama in this one apart from would he or would he not turn up in the cafe
Claire	and that only took one picture in the thing, so it wasn't particularly . . .
Lucy	and it was all a bit of an anti-climax in the end you know, it seems quite good at the beginning, but 'It's my nasty mind', I mean that's not much of a story . . .

(It was Claire who introduced this thought about the dramatic structure of the story, not me.)

Katherine	well there isn't a sort of start and middle and end sort of things, there isn't a real story to it, she just thinks that was wrong and found out that it's wrong in the end, but it wasn't really. I don't know, there wasn't much to it . . .
Liz	OK, what do you think of that story then?
Nanette	well I thought it was a bit obvious that Ben lives next door to the cafe

Although there were other reactions which suggested that the reader was evaluating the characters as if they were real people:

Liz	OK, what d'you think of that story then?
Claire	I've read better ones
Lucy	I think she's quite vain, the girl's quite . . .

(Note that Claire is doing literary criticism from the first, while Lucy is not.)

Liz	right, what d'you think of that story then?
Helen	I don't know, she was just an insecure little person who had to keep shouting down these blokes and he found that attractive, there you go, that's it

Shifts from first to second-order discourse occurred throughout the discussions, but on the whole, second-order talk is dominant; and the discussion tended to focus on why the story was or was not realistic when measured against the girls own lives and experience. Much of their analysis considered the story as normative (or ideological), and evalued the message promulgated:

Fiona	well, he might intend it to be sincere, but it's not true that you need the right bloke to make your life work, you need friends more than that . . .
Sharon	yeah, but if you read that now right, years ago and then you get to be fourteen and you haven't got a boyfriend then you're going to feel even worse from reading this

The comprehensive sixth formers didn't bother measuring the story against their own experience, as they assessed it from the beginning in the light of a pre-existing ideology of gender, of which they took the story to be a reflection as well as a reinforcement:

Liz	and why should she feel guilty?
Lucy	oh perhaps it's because she's expected to put up with it, no, because she's expected to put up with it
Sam	it's OK for a man to have other girlfriends but . . .
Sam	oh yes, well, 'cos I'll tell you one thing that really gets me, it's this bit that says 'you're jealous, that means you really care for me . . .'
(several)	oh yeah, oh, terrible . . .'
Sally	you know I think girls' magazines have a lot to answer for in sort of building up self-confidence, because you don't get the same sort of thing with boys, I mean in these sorts of magazines all the emphasis is put on you know, you do something wrong you won't get a boyfriend, you've got to behave in a certain way to . . .'
Sam	you've got to dress in a certain way
Helen	it's sort of like the girl who has to get the boy. It's not the boy who has to make an effort to get the girl sort of thing

The whole issue of why, if the 'ideology' is as powerful as the girls in this group argue, it has been possible for them to transcend or resist it was a live one between me and them, and was never satisfactorily resolved.

On the whole then, it seems that the girls I asked to read the photo story do not coincide with the implied reader constructed by the text, who we can take to be a sympathetic confidante of Julie, the narrator and heroine. The pretence that Julie is a sixteen-year old talking to a friend didn't come off at all with any of the teenage girls I talked to, (including those who were closest to the fictional heroine in socio-economic status and age – the comprehensive school fourth years). This failure occurred first because, as we have seen, the girls were overwhelmingly reading the story as a fiction, with all that entails. Second, none of them identified with Julie's actions, thoughts or attitudes. That is, these real readers were freer of the text than much theory implies.

However, there was one very significant exception – they could understand her being attracted to Ben because:

Lucy	he's sort of strong, silent
Sam	yeah, caring, yeah
(several)	yeah
Helen	big old beefy jumpers
Sam	that's it, it's the jumper more than anything and the little shirt coming out the top
Lorna	hands in pockets

We've already seen the attraction of the jumper to the public school girls! And:

Lucy	well, it's not that he's good looking, he's got you know
Sophie	he's quite a hunk
Claire	well he's not you know . . . wimpish or anything like that . . .
Lucy	he's so gentlemanly
Zara	yes
Claire	he's quite gentle

But one group thought he was a creep:

Jo	you wouldn't feel offended, you would feel that he's creeping a bit an he's it's not, oh it doesn't show that he's creeping all the time but it's related in a way
Liz	mm
Alison	yeah but it's creepy the way he um . . .
Jo	in that picture there he's got his arms around her like y'know that shows

This straightforward attraction to hero, though, was understood as an ingredient of fantasy:

Jo	cos they're a bit like this you know fairy tales aren't they?
Alison	yes it's all like one of those dream things
Nanette	it all goes so well, it's always like he lives next door to the cafe, she goes walking a dog, her dog runs off
(laughter)	
Jo	all of a sudden there's the boy, exciting eh?
Alison	it's just a dream innit?

and the thirteen year old public school girls were just as clear about the role of fiction in constructing a fantasy life:

Liz	what would you get out of reading this kind of story week in, week out?
Claire	boredom
Zara	I'd begin to know that the boy . . .
Claire	I'd know what's going to happen
Zara	you know because we're sort of I don't know, kind of shut up here we'd get to know about I don't know outside life
Liz	sorry?
Zara	that sort of thing, well because we're
(laughter)	
Zara	not that, well I don't know because we're all prisonized here
Liz	yeah, cos you're shut up in school
Zara	you know we're all just shut up well we've got to get, I don't know in the towns and everything
Claire	cos we're not allowed to go to (nearest town) even
Liz	so, no
Lucy	so you can imagine yourself as the girl

(although it seems Zara might believe that 'life in the town' is like Julie's life).

My preliminary analysis of the transcripts of these discussions, then, strongly suggests that a self-conscious and reflexive approach to texts is a natural understanding, not only of the fiction, but of the genre of publication for girls of which *Jackie* is an example. They were even curious about the production of the text which is entirely obscure in the magazine:

Claire	I wonder who takes all these pictures, and who are the people?

So far then, this empirical evidence suggests that the kinds of meanings which are encoded in texts and which we might want to call ideological, fail to get a grip on readers in the way the notion of ideology generally suggests. Ideology is undercut, that is, by these readers' reflexivity and reflectiveness.

However, I now want to move on to some further data which I believe suggest an alternative formulation to the concept of ideology. The sixth form public school girls and the fourth form comprehensive school girls all began to talk about problem pages during this discussion. They read problem pages, in all sorts of magazines; but they also said that they were 'stupid', that the problems weren't real problems, that the answers were pathetic and not helpful at all. When I asked them if they had problems, they replied 'oh yes, but not like those ones'. Their problems, they said, were to do with issues like work, money and relationships with parents. So I asked them to write problems, serious ones, as if addressed to someone they trusted who might be really helpful. The problems they wrote were then passed on to someone else anonymously, to reply to. I have pulled one of these problems and its reply at random from the pile:

> Dear Melanie, At my bus stop I see a lush boy every morning. He knows me through one of my best friends' friends or ex-boyfriend. He smiles at me every time; I smile back but not much else seems to happen. The problem is I am very shy. Help me. Andy Ridgeway Fan.

> Dear Andy Ridgeway Fan, Don't be shy, pluck up courage to say 'hello' to this boy; smile at him or even ask him how he is. Be patient, and remember, shyness doesn't get you anywhere.

This is absolutely typical of the fifteen or so 'problems' they came up with in this exercise. Other topics include wanting an old boyfriend back, fear of pregnancy, parents not letting you stay out late. That is, they varied in 'gravity'; but were all written in this, what can only be called typical problem page style.

Discourse registers

Here, I introduce the ideal of a *discourse register* which I take roughly as an institutionalized, situationally specific, culturally familiar, public way of talking. My data suggests that the notion of a 'discourse register' is invaluable in analysing talk – the talk of all the girls groups I worked with is marked by frequent and sometimes quite dramatic shifts in register.

Other research has interpreted similar data as 'contradiction'. For example, Shirley Prendergast and Alan Prout interviewed fifteen year old girls about the subject of marriage and motherhood (Prendergast and Prout, 1980). They began by talking informally with the girls and elicited from a large proportion of them evidence of a body of 'knowledge' about the tedium, exhaustion, loneliness and depression which afflict mothers of young children. This knowledge was generally first hand – that is, it was gained from sisters with young children, the experience of babysitting, being asked to help with primary childcare, and so forth. When, later in the interview, the girls were asked to agree or disagree with the statement: 'It's a good life for a mother at home with a young child', and give reasons for their opinion, and it was made clear that it was now *mothers in general* who were being discussed, they practically all *agreed*, and gave a variety of reasons which could all be characterized as in accordance with the sentimental notion or meaning of motherhood which Ann Oakley has argued is so powerful in this society (Oakley, 1979).

Prendergast and Prout characterize these two 'distinct bodies of knowledge' as 'illegitimate' and 'legitimate' respectively. The girls were aware of the 'contradiction' here, and uncertainly and tentatively negotiated means of simultaneously holding onto both. For example, some girls located the problem of motherhood in young mothers, and implied that if you wait until you're older everything will be OK; others came to terms with the negative image of motherhood by inserting into their assessments a series of conditional requirements, such as 'if you establish a routine . . .' or 'if you have a good husband . . .'. In Prendergast and Prout's analysis, illegitimate knowledge is not generalizable, while legitimate knowledge is: the sentimental stereotype is so powerful that when one's own experience comes into conflict with it, it is taken that the experience is invalid.

There are various problems with this. For example, the girls were interviewed alone. Prendergast and Prout comment that some of the girls indicated that the 'illegitimate knowledge' was *private* knowledge. For the girls I know who were talking frankly in groups this was not true – such 'knowledge' was shared among them, as it is among sociologists of the family, women in women's studies classes, consciousness-raising groups, and the like. Prendergast and Prout's girls are ready to discount their experience and try to bring it into line with the perceived wider 'reality'. For the girls I talked to this wasn't the case either. Why should this be so?

I think it is that ways of talking, or 'knowledges', or 'discourse registers' will be dropped in contexts where they are not supported. The knowledge that Prendergast and Prout label 'illegitimate', in other words is not illegitimate in all contexts.

Discourse registers both *constrain* what is sayable in any context, and *enable* saying. Prendergast and Prout's data support this proposition: in informal talk they could voice the unpleasantness of motherhood: in formal talk they could not (the girls were asked to agree or disagree with a statement – this is very like the kind of thing people are asked to do in school). What is said, and how it is said, are covariant. My data about *Jackie* problem pages illustrate the power of a discourse register to structure and shape what people can actually say in a particular context. In this session, the girls wanted to discuss *serious* problems; but it seemed that asking them to write the problems had the immediate effect of undercutting their gravity – they couldn't think 'writing problems' outside of the conventions of the problem page. . . .

It does not seem appropriate to characterize the difference between these two contrasting sorts of discussion of 'problems' as *contradiction*. It is more apposite to say that the girls have available more than one way of discussing this topic, as Prendergast and Prout's girls had at their disposal more than one way of discussing the notion of motherhood.

There were some interesting differences between the groups which make clear that a structurally based analysis of what discourse registers are available to people is necessary. 'The girls from the youth club were very used to playing groupwork games, and in the context of their girls' discussion group, self-disclosure, support and confidentiality came very naturally to them. The public school girls found these games the hardest, and in the first few sessions the sort of exercise where everybody completes the sentence: 'My greatest talent is . . .' made them feel embarrassed and mystified. However, it wasn't many sessions before they really came to enjoy such exercises (they organised our last sessions together, and we played some extremely advanced group-work games, and they quickly came to understand the conventions and rules of being in a girls' group very well. The transcripts of the sessions at the public school show very clearly the process of their grasping a new and alternative discourse register *in which different things can be said.*

It's very clear from the transcripts of the groups' discussions that all the girls have a multiplicity of discourse registers available to use. They could all, for example, switch in and out of the register of 'feminism' according to context, topic and mood. We have already seen that what is available to whom is socially variable – the youth club girls had the register of the discussion group; the public school girls had to learn it. This difference can be explained institutionally. Sometimes shifts made startling contrasts. For example:

Jane   I dislike the ways boys treat girls in the sense that they've got the front to call them slags

Stella   when they're sleeping around more than you are

Jane   yeah and they think they're hard if they go out and do something, like . . . but if a girl does it she's stupid and things like that

Janine   if a girl want to do the same job as a boy it's too hard

Compare this 'feminist' register with this:

Janine   that's what gets me, they beat up their kids and get about six months, especially the mothers right, cos you know in the (local newspaper) there was this woman, she picks up her baby and hit his head on the bannister, and it was just born, it was most probably three months, and she was most probably still giving it milk and it was hungry still so she picked it up right, and she goes it was after feeding and she hit it across the bannister and it died. You get soppy ones right, who leave d'you know metal baths, and you know in some parts of London they ain't got a bathroom, she put the metal thing on the gas ring, and put the baby in it and left it in the boiling water, I think that it's bloody true, and d'you know cot deaths, I think that most of them are already . . .

Fetiye   most of them do that you know

Shortly after this I intervened on the subject of cot death, and there was a shift to a quite different style of talk, a much more thoughtful and analytic style, with participants making much *shorter* contributions to the discussion. The discussion about boys was organised or 'led' by me. This discussion about baby battering had been initiated by them, before the session proper started. In the one case, a feminist discussion group register was appropriate and determined the 'tone' of what was said: in the other, the register, and values of the tabloid press was dominant.

Conclusion

The concept of ideology is unsatisfactory in two main ways, as I have argued. On the one hand real people don't seem to be 'in the grip of' ideology, as the theory (and especially much theory which is based on the analysis of texts) implies. On the other hand, 'ideology' is of altogether too ethereal a nature to be properly researched. Its existence is only and always inferred; we can never examine it directly.

However, I suggest that we take seriously the power of concrete conventions and registers of discourse to constrain and determine what is said and how it is said. Registers are material, and directly researchable. We can compare how real people speak with institutional discourse, for example the discourse of cultural artefacts like *Jackie*, the tabloid press, and with institutional practices like that of the 'discussion group'. We can pay attention to the forums in which people learn different registers, for example, girls in girls' groups learning the appropriate register; what registers are acceptable in school; the influence of popular culture. But we should not take it that people are unselfconscious about these registers, as do theories of ideology.

Note

1. The story is entitled 'It's my Nasty Mind'. Julie, the heroine, tells off her boyfriend, Mike, in no uncertain terms when he arrives late to meet her, accusing him of having been with another girl. He tells her that she has a 'nasty and suspicious mind' but that her jealousy proves she really cares. In response to this she says 'Goodbye Mike, if I never see you again it'll be too soon'. This altercation is overheard by Ben, who admires her spirit: 'That was a great performance' and takes her to a nearby café for a Knickerbocker Glory. When he leaves he says 'Next time you're going to give some guy the big heave, let me know, I'd love to see you in action again'. Julie hangs around the café hoping to see Ben; when she does bump into him he repeats his admiration: 'Is some other guy about to get it in the neck?' Rather than admit that she wants to see him, Julie says that she is going to 'have a showdown' on the following evening and invites him to watch. She then has to find a boy to play the opposite part, but fails. When she arrives at the assignation she admits to Ben that she had treated Mike badly, and that she had made up the boyfriend: 'Do you think I'm dreadful? I don't think I'm a very nice kind of person'. To which Ben says, among other things: 'You're insecure, and you've got a strong sense of justice' and 'You're too self critical' and he invites her to go out with him, and to go for another Knickerbocker Glory.

References

Barrett, Michèle (1980) *Women's Oppression Today: Problems in Marxist Feminist Analysis* (London: Verso/NLB).

DES 1983 *Popular TV and School Children* (The report of a group of teachers).

Glasgow University Media Group (1980) *More Bad News*. (London: Routledge and Kegan Paul).

Griffin, Christine (1982) *The Cultures of Femininity: Romance Revisited*. (Birmingham: CCCS Occasional Paper).

Griffin, Christine (1985) *Typical Girls? Young Women from School to the Job Market*. (London: Routledge and Kegan Paul).

Hebron, Sandra (1983) *'Jackie' and 'Woman's Own': Ideological Work and the Social Construction of Gender Identity*. (Sheffield: City Polytechnic).

Lees, Sue (1986) *Losing Out : Sexuality and Adolescent Girls*, (London: Hutchinson).

McLellan, David (1986) *Ideology*. (Milton Keynes: Open University Press).

McRobbie, Angela (1977) 'Working Class Girls and the Culture of Femininity' Unpub. thesis.

McRobbie, Angela (1978a) 'Working Class Girls and the Culture of Femininity', in CCCS Women's studies Group, *Women Take Issue*. (London: Hutchinson).

McRobbie, Angela (1978b) *'Jackie': An Ideology of Adolescent Femininity*. (Birmingham: CCCS Occasional Paper).

McRobbie, Angela (1982) 'The Politics of Feminist Research: Between Talk, Text and Action'. *Feminist Review*, 12.

Oakley, Ann (1979) *Becoming a Mother*. (Oxford: Martin Robertson).

Prendergast, Shirley and Prout, Alan (1980) 'What Will I Do . . . ?' Teenage Girls and the Construction of Motherhood, *Sociological Review*, 28, 3.

Richardson, Kay and Corner, John (1986) 'Reading Reception: Meditation and Transparency in Viewers' Accounts of a TV Programme' *Media Culture and Society*, 8.4.

Sharpe, Sue (1976) *'Just Like A Girl': How Girls Learn To Be Women*, (Harmondsworth: Penguin).

Thompson, John B (1984) *Studies in the Theory of Ideology*. (Cambridge: Polity Press).

Thompson, Kenneth (1986) *Beliefs and Ideology*. (London: Tavistock).

Wilson, Deirdre (1978) 'Sexual Codes and Conduct: A Study of Teenage Girls', in Carol Smart and Barry Smart (eds) *Women, Sexuality and Social Control*. (London: Routledge and Kegan Paul).
Winship, Janice (1978) 'A Woman's World: *Woman* An Ideology of Femininity' in CCCS Women's Studies Group, *Women Take Issue*. (London: Hutchinson).

(from *Media, Culture and Society*, Vol. 9, No. 4, 1987)

 READING 48

Critical practice

Catherine Belsey

The project of Sherlock Holmes stories is to dispel magic and mystery, to make everything explicit, accountable, subject to scientific analysis. The phrase most familiar to all readers – 'Elementary my dear Watson' – is in fact a misquotation, but its familiarity is no accident since it precisely captures the central concern of the stories. Holmes and Watson are both men of science. Holmes, the 'genius' is a scientific conjuror who insists on disclosing how the trick is done. The stories begin in enigma, mystery, the impossible, and conclude with an explanation which makes it clear that logical deduction and scientific method render all mysteries accountable to reason:

> I am afraid that my explanation may disillusionize you, but it has always been my habit to hide none of my methods, either from my friend Watson or from anyone who might take an intelligent interest in them. ('The Reigate Squires', *The Memoirs of Sherlock Holmes*)

The stories are a plea for science not only in the spheres conventionally associated with detection (footprints, traces of hair or cloth, cigarette ends), where they have been deservedly influential on forensic practice, but in all areas. They reflect the widespread optimism characteristic of their period concerning the comprehensive power of positivist science. Holmes's ability to deduce Watson's train of thought, for instance, is repeatedly displayed, and it owes nothing to the supernatural. Once explained, the reasoning process always appears 'absurdly simple', open to the commonest of common sense.

The project of the stories themselves, enigma followed by disclosure, echoes precisely the structure of the classic realist text. The narrator himself draws attention to the parallel between them:

> 'Excellent' I cried.
> 'Elementary, said he 'It is one of those instances where the reasoner can produce an effect which seems remarkable to his neighbour because the latter has missed the one little point which is the basis of the deduction. The same may be said, my dear fellow, for the effect of some of these little sketches of yours, which is entirely meretricious, depending as it does upon your retaining in your own hands some factors in the problem which are never imparted to the reader. Now, at present I am in the position of these same readers, for I hold in this hand several threads of one of the strangest cases which ever perplexed a man's brain, and yet I lack the one or two which are needful to complete my theory. But I'll have them, Watson, I'll have them! ('The Crooked Man', *Memoirs*)

236

(The passage is quoted by Macherey in the discussion of the characteristic structure of narrative 1978, p. 35.)

The project also requires the maximum degree of 'realism' – verisimilitude, plausibility. In the interest of science, no hint of the fantastic or the implausible is permitted to remain once the disclosure is complete. This is why even their own existence as writing is so frequently discussed within the texts. The stories are alluded to as Watson's 'little sketches', his 'memoirs'. They resemble fictions because of Watson's unscientific weakness for story-telling:

> I must admit, Watson, that you have some power of selection which atones for much I deplore in your narrative. Your fatal habit of looking at everything from the point of a story instead of as a scientific exercise has ruined what might have been an instructive and even classical series of demonstrations. ('The Abbey Grange', *Return*)

In other words, the fiction itself accounts even for its own fictionality, and the text thus appears wholly transparent. The success with which the Sherlock Holmes stories achieve an illusion of reality is repeatedly demonstrated. In their foreword to *The Sherlock Holmes Companion* (1962), Michael and Mollie Hardwick comment on their own recurrent illusion 'that we were dealing with a figure of real life rather than of fiction. How vital Holmes appears, compared with many people of one's own acquaintance'.

De Waal's bibliography of Sherlock Holmes lists 25 'Sherlockian' periodicals apparently largely devoted to conjectures, based on the 'evidence' of the stories, concerning matters only hinted at in the texts – Holmes's education, his income and his romantic and sexual adventures. According to *The Times* in December 1967, letters to Sherlock Holmes were then still commonly addressed to 221B Baker Street, many of them asking for the detective's help.

Nonetheless, these stories, whose overt project is total explicitness, total verisimilitude in the interests of a plea for scientificity, are haunted by shadowy, mysterious and often silent women. Their silence repeatedly conceals their sexuality, investing it with a dark and magical quality which is beyond the reach of scientific knowledge. In 'The Greek Interpreter' (*Memoirs*), Sophie Kratides has run away with a man. Although she is the pivot of the plot she appears only briefly: 'I could not see her clearly enough to know more than that she was tall and graceful, with black hair and clad in some sort of loose white gown'. Connotatively the white gown marks her as still virginal and her flight as the result of romance rather than desire. At the same time the dim light surrounds her with shadow, the unknown. 'The Crooked Man' concerns Mrs Barclay, whose husband is found dead on the day of her meeting with her lover of many years before. Mrs Barclay is now insensible, 'temporarily insane' since the night of the murder and therefore unable to speak. In 'The Dancing Men' (*Return*) Mrs Elsie Cubitt, once engaged to a criminal, longs to speak but cannot bring herself to break her silence. By the time Holmes arrives, she is unconscious, and she remains so for the rest of the story. Ironically, the narrative concerns the breaking of the code which enables her lover to communicate with her. Elsie's only contribution to the correspondence is the word, 'Never'. The precise nature of their relationship is left mysterious, constructed of contrary suggestions. Holmes says she feared and hated him: the lover claims, 'She had been engaged to me, and she would have married me, I believe, if I had taken over another profession'. When her husband moves to shoot the man whose coded messages are the source of a 'terror' which is 'wearing her away', Elsie restrains him with compulsive strength. On the question of her motives, the text is characteristically elusive. Her husband recounts the story:

I was angry with my wife that night for having held me back when I might have caught the skulking rascal. She said she feared that I might come to harm. For an instant it had crossed my mind that what she really feared was that *he* might come to harm, for I could not doubt that she knew who this man was and what he meant by those strange signals. But there is a tone in my wife's voice, Mr Holmes, and a look in her eyes which forbid doubt, and I am sure that it was indeed my own safety that was in her mind.

After her husband's death, Elsie remains a widow, faithful to his memory, and devoting her life to the care of the poor, apparently expiating something unspecified, perhaps an act or a state of feeling, remote or recent.

'The Dancing Men' is 'about' Holmes's method of breaking the cipher. Its project is to dispel any magic from the deciphering process. Elsie's silence is in the interest of the story since she knows the code. But she also 'knows' her feelings towards her former lover. Contained in the completed and fully disclosed story of the decipherment is another uncompleted and undisclosed narrative which is more than merely peripheral to the text as a whole. Elsie's past is central and causal. As a result, the text with its project of dispelling mystery is haunted by the mysterious state of mind of a woman who is unable to speak.

The classic realist text had not yet developed a way of signifying women's sexuality except in a metaphoric or symbolic mode whose presence disrupts the realist surface. Joyce and Lawrence were beginning to experiment at this time with modes of sexual signification but in order to do so they largely abandoned the codes of realism. So much is readily apparent. What is more significant, however, is that the presentation of so many women in the Sherlock Holmes stories as shadowy, mysterious and magical figures precisely contradicts the project of explicitness, transgresses the values of the texts, and in doing so throws into relief the poverty of the contemporary concept of science. These stories, pleas for a total explicitness about the world, are unable to explain an area which nonetheless they cannot ignore. The version of science which the texts present would constitute a clear challenge to ideology: the interpretation of all areas of life, physical, social and psychological, is to be subject to rational scrutiny and the requirements of coherent theorization. Confronted, however, by an area in which ideology itself is uncertain, the Sherlock Holmes stories display the limits of their own project and are compelled to manifest the inadequacy of a bourgeois scientificity which, working within the constraints of ideology, is thus unable to challenge it.

Perhaps the most interesting case, since it introduces an additional area of shadow, is 'The Second Stain' (*Return*), which concerns two letters Lady Hilda Trelawney Hope does speak. She has written before her marriage 'an indiscreet letter . . . a foolish letter, a letter of an impulsive, loving girl'. Had her husband read the letter his confidence in her would have been for ever destroyed. Her husband is nonetheless presented as entirely sympathetic, and here again we encounter the familiar contradiction between a husband's supposed reaction, accepted as just, and the reaction offered to the reader by the text. In return for her original letter, Lady Hilda gives her blackmailer a letter from 'a certain foreign potentate' stolen from the dispatch box of her husband, the European Secretary of State. This political letter is symbolically parallel to the first sexual one. Its contents are equally elusive but it too is 'indiscreet', 'hot-headed'; certain phrases in it are 'provocative'. Its publication would produce 'a most dangerous state of feeling' in the nation. Lady Hilda's innocent folly is the cause of theft: she knows nothing of politics and was not in a position to understand the consequences of her action. Holmes ensures the restoration of the political letter and both secrets are preserved.

Here the text is symmetrically elusive concerning both sexuality and politics. Watson, as is so often the case where these areas are concerned, begins the story by apologising for his own reticence and vagueness. In the political instance what becomes clear as a result of the uncertainty of the text is the contradictory nature of the requirements of verisimilutude in fiction. The potentate's identity and the nature of his indiscretion cannot be named without involving on the part of the reader either disbelief (the introduction of a patently fictional country would be dangerous to the project of verisimilitude) or belief (dangerous to the text's status as fiction, entertainment, also quite possibly politically dangerous). The scientific project of the texts require that they deal in 'facts', but their nature as fiction forbids the introduction of facts.

The classic realist text installs itself in the space between fact and illusion through the presentation of a simulated reality which is plausible but *not real*. In this lies its power as myth. It is because fiction does not normally deal with 'politics' except in the form of history or satire, that it is ostensibly innocent and therefore ideologically effective. But in its evasion of the real also lies its weakness as 'realism'. Through their transgression of their own values of explicitness and verisimilitude, the Sherlock Holmes stories contain within themselves an implicit critique of their limited nature as characteristic examples of classic realism. They thus offer the reader through the process of deconstruction a form of knowledge, not about 'life' or 'the world', but about the nature of fiction itself.

Thus in adopting the form of classic realism, the only appropriate literary mode, positivism is compelled to display its own limitations. Offered as science, it reveals itself to a deconstructive reading as ideology at the very moment that classic realism, offered as verisimilitude, reveals itself as fiction. In claiming to make explicit and *understandable* what appears mysterious, these texts offer evidence of the tendency of positivism to push to the margins of experience whatever it cannot explain or understand. In the Sherlock Holmes stories classic realism ironically tells a truth, though not the truth about the world which is the project of classic realism. The truth the stories tell is the truth about ideology, the truth which ideology represses, its own existence as ideology itself.

Reference

Macherey, Pierre, (1978) *A Theory of Literary Production*, trans. Geoffrey Wall (London: Routledge and Kegan Paul).

BIBLIOGRAPHY

Argenot, M. (1979), 'The Absent Paradigm: An Introduction to the Semiotics of Science Fiction', *Science Fiction Studies*, 6, 9–18.

Batsleer, J. (1982), 'Pulp in the Pink', *Spare Rib*, 109.

Batsleer, J., Davies, T. and Weedon, C. (eds) (1985), *Rewriting English: Cultural Politics of Gender and Class*, London and New York: Methuen.

Benjamin, W. (n.d.), 'The Storyteller', in *Illuminations*, (1968), New York: Harcourt Brace Jovanovich.

Bennett, T. (1981), 'Marxism and Popular Fiction', *Literature and History*, 7, No. 2.

Bennett, T. and Woollacott, J. (1987), *Bond and Beyond: The Political Career of a Popular Hero*, London: Macmillan.

Bloom, C., Docherty, B., Gibb, J. and Shand, K. (eds) (1988), *Nineteenth Century Suspense: From Poe to Conan Doyle*, London: Macmillan.

Bloom, C. (ed.), (1993), *Creepers: British Horror and Fantasy in the Twentieth Century*, London: Pluto.

Bromley, R. (1978), 'Natural Boundaries: The Social Function of Popular Fiction', *Red Letters*, 7.

Bromley, R. (1981), 'The Gentry, Bourgeois Hegemony and Popular Fiction: Rebecca and Rogue Male', *Literature and History*, 7 (2), 166–183.

Burgin, V., Donald, J. and Kaplan, C. (eds) (1986), *Formations of Fantasy*, London: Methuen.

Cannadine, D. (1979), 'James Bond and the Decline of England', *Encounter*, 53, (3).

Carr, H. (ed.), (1989), *From 'My Guy' to Sci-Fi: Genre and Women's Writing in the Postmodern World*, London: Pandora.

Carroll, N. (1990), *The Philosophy of Horror or Paradoxes of the Heart*, London: Routledge.

Cawelti, J.G. (1969) 'The Concept of Formula in the Study of Popular Literature', *Journal of Popular Culture*, 3.

Cawelti, J.G. (1976), *Adventure, Mystery and Romance*, Chicago: University of Chicago Press.

Cawelti, J.G. (n.d.), *The Six-Gun Mystique*, Bowling Green, Ohio: Bowling Green University Popular Press.

Chandler, R. (1950), 'The Simple Art of Murder', in *Pearls are a Nuisance*, London: Hamish Hamilton.

Clover, C. (1992), *Men, Women and Chain Saws: Gender in the Modern Horror Film*, London: BFI.

Constable, A. (1985), 'Crime for Social Change', *Red Letters*, 18, 12–22.

Cook, D. (1985), 'Yes, Virginia, There's Always Been Women's Science Fiction ... Feminist, Even', in *Contrary Modes: Proceedings of the World Science Fiction Conference*, Melbourne: Ebony.

Cranny-Francis, A. (1988), 'Gender and Genre: Feminist Rewritings of Detective Fiction', *Women's Studies International Forum*, 2, 1, 69–84.

Cranny-Francis, A. (1990), *Feminist Fiction*, Cambridge: Polity.

Creed, B. (1993), *The Monstrous-Feminine: Film, Feminism and Psychoanalysis*, London: Routledge.

Demtrakopoulos, S. (1977), 'Feminism, Sex Role Exchanges, and Other Subliminal Fantasies in Bram Stoker's *Dracula*', *Frontiers* 2, 3, 104–13.

Denning, M. (1987), *Cover Stories: Narrative and Ideology in the British Spy Thriller*, London: Routledge.

Dixon, B. (1977), *Catching Them Young 2: Political Ideas in Children's Fiction*, London: Pluto.

Eagleton, T. (1983), *Literary Theory: An Introduction*, Oxford: Blackwell.

Eco, U. (1977), *The Bond Affair*, London: Macdonald.

English Studies Group, Centre for Contemporary Cultural Studies, University of Birmingham (1978–9), 'Recent Developments in English Studies at the Centre', in Hall, S., Hobson, D., Lowe, A. and Willis, P. (1980) *Culture, Media, Language*, London: Hutchinson.

Fiedler, L. (1975), 'Towards a Definition of Popular Literature', in Bigsby, C. (ed.), *Superculture: American Popular Culture and Europe* (1975), Bowling Green, Ohio: Bowling Green University Press.

Fokkema, D. and Kunne-Ibsch, E. (1977), *Theories of Literature in the Twentieth Century*, London: Hurst.

Franklin, S., Lury, J. and Stacey, J. (eds), (1991), *Off-Centre: Feminism and Cultural Studies*, London and New York: Harper Collins.

Frazer, E. (1987), 'Teenage Girls Reading *Jackie*', *Media, Culture and Society*, 9, 407–25.

Freund, E. (1987), *The Return of the Reader*, London: Routledge.

Gray, A. (1987), 'Reading the Audience', *Screen*, 28, (3).

Green, M. (1980), *Dreams of Adventure, Dreams of Empire*, London: Routledge.

Griffith, P. (1987) *Literary Theory and English Teaching*, Milton Keynes: Open University Press.

Grixti, J. (1989), *Terrors of Uncertainty: The Cultural Contexts of Horror Fiction*, London: Routledge.

Hall, S. and Whannel, P. (1964), *The Popular Arts*, London: Hutchinson.

Hamilton, C.S. (1987), *Western and Hard-Boiled Detective Fiction in America*, London: Macmillan.

Harper, S. (1983), 'History with Frills: "Costume" Fiction in World War II', *Red Letters*, **14**, 14–23.

Hoggart, P. (1981), 'The Commercial Literature of School Children', *Media, Culture and Society*, 3, 367–87.

Humm, P., Stigant, P. and Widdowson, P. (eds) (1986), *Popular Fictions: Essays in Literature and History*, London: Methuen.

Jackson, R. (1981), *Fantasy: The Literature of Subversion*, London: Methuen.

Kaplan, C. (1986), 'An Unsuitable Genre for a Feminist?' *Womens Review*, 8, 18–29.

King, S. (1981), *Danse Macabre: The Anatomy of Horror*, London: Macdonald.

Knight, S. (1980), *Form and Ideology in Crime Fiction*, London: Macmillan.

Knight, S. (1981), 'The Case of the Great Detective', *Meanjin*, **40**, (2), 175–85.

Kristeva, J. (1980), *The Powers of Horror: An Essay on Abjection*, New York: Columbia University Press.

Kwasniewski, E. (1987), 'Thrilling Structures? Science Fiction from the Early "Amazing" and Detective Fiction', *Foundation*, **38**, 23–30.

Leavis, Q.D. (1932), *Fiction and the Reading Public*, London: Chatto & Windus.

Leavis, Q.D. (1937). 'The Case of Dorothy Sayers', *Scrutiny*, **6** (3), 334–40.

Light, A. (1984) '"Returning to Manderley": Romance Fiction, Female Sexuality and Class', *Feminist Review*, **16**, 17–25.

Light, A. (1989), 'Young Bess: Historical Novels and Growing Up', *Feminist Review*, 33.

Light, A. (1991), *Forever England: Femininity, Literature and Conservatism between the Wars*, London: Routledge.

Longhurst, D. (1989), *Gender, Genre and Narrative Pleasure*, London: Unwin Hyman.

McRobbie, A. (1978), '*Jackie*: An Ideology of Adolescent Femininity', Stencilled Occasional Paper, Womens Series SP No.53, Birmingham: Centre for Contemporary Cultural Studies.

Margolies, D. (1983), 'Mills and Boon: Guilt without Sex', *Red Letters*, **14**, 5–13.

Modleski, T. (1984), *Loving with a Vengeance: Mass-produced Fantasies for Women*, London: Methuen.

Modleski, T. (1986), *Studies in Entertainment: Critical Approaches to Mass Culture*, Bloomington: Indiana University Press.

Moylan, T. (1986), *Demand the Impossible: Science Fiction and the Utopian Imagination*, New York: Methuen.

Neale, S. (1980), *Genre*, London: BFI.

O'Flinn, P. (1983), 'Production and Reproduction: The Case of *Frankenstein*', *Literature and History*, **9**, (2), 194–213.

Palmer, J. (1973), 'Thrillers: The Deviant behind the Consensus', in Taylor, I. and Taylor, L. (eds) *Politics and Deviance*, Harmondsworth: Penguin.

Palmer, J. (1978), *Thrillers: Genesis and Structure of a Popular Genre*, London: Edward Arnold.

Palmer, J. (1991), *Potboilers*, London: Routledge.

Parrinder, P. (ed.) (1979), *Science Fiction: A Critical Guide*, London: Longman.

Parrinder, P. (1980), *Science Fiction: Its Criticism and Teaching*, London: Methuen.

Pawling, C. (ed.) (1984), *Popular Fiction and Social Change*, London: Macmillan.

Porter, D. (1981), *The Pursuit of Crime: Art and Ideology in Detective Fiction*, New Haven: Yale University Press.

Propp, V. (1928), *Morphology of the Folk Tale*, Austin: University of Texas Press.

Radford, J. (ed.) (1986), *The Progress of Romance: The Politics of Popular Fiction*, London: Routledge.

Radstone, S. (ed.), (1989), *Sweet Dreams . . . Sexuality, Gender and Popular Fiction*, London: Lawrence and Wishart.

Radway, J. (1984), *Reading the Romance*, Chapel Hill, North Carolina: University of North Carolina Press.

Rollin, R. (1975), 'Against Evaluation: The Role of the Critic of Popular Culture', *Journal of Popular Culture*, 9, 355–65.

Rose, M. (ed.), (1976), *Science Fiction: A Collection of Critical Essays*, Englewood Cliffs, New Jersey: Prentice-Hall.

Suvin, D. (1979), *Metamorphoses of Science Fiction: On the Poetics and History of a Literary Genre*, New Haven: Yale University Press.

Taylor, H. (1989), *Scarlet's Women: 'Gone with the Wind' and its Female Fans*, London: Virago.

Todorov, T. (1973), *The Fantastic: A Structural Approach to a Literary Genre* (tr. R. Howard), Cleveland: Case Western Reserve University Press.

Todorov, T. (1988), 'The Typology of Detective Fiction', in Lodge, D. (ed.), *Modern Criticism and Theory: A Reader*, White Plains, NY: Longman.

Tudor, A. (1989), *Monsters and Mad Scientists: A Cultural History of the Horror Movies*, Oxford: Blackwell.

Walker, D. (1973), 'Notes towards a Literary Criticism of the Western', *Journal of Popular Culture*, 7, (3), 728–41.

Walkerdine, V. (1990), *Schoolgirl Fictions*, London: Verso.

Widdowson, P. (ed.), (1982), *Re-reading English*, London: Methuen.

Williams, R. (1961), *The Long Revolution*, London: Chatto & Windus.

Williamson, J. (1981–2), 'How Does Girl Number Twenty Understand Ideology?' *Screen Education*, 40.

Winks, R. (ed.), (1988), *Detective Fiction: A Collection of Critical Essays*, Vermont: Foul Play Press.

Women's Study Group, Centre for Contemporary Cultural Studies, University of Birmingham (1978), *Women Take Issue*, London: Hutchinson.

Wood, R. (1984), 'The Modern American Horror Film', in Grant, B.K., *Planks of Reason*, Metuchen, NJ: Scarecrow Press.

Worpole, K. (1983), *Dockers and Detectives*, London: Verso.

Worpole, K. (1984), *Reading by Numbers: Contemporary Publishing and Popular Fiction*, London: Comedia.

Wright, W. (1975), *Sixguns and Society: A Structural Study of the Western*, California: University of California Press.

Zizek, S. (1991), *An Introduction to Jacques Lacan through Popular Culture*, London and Cambridge, MA: MIT Press.

INDEX

abject, the 165–6, 204–5
adolescence 215–17, 226–36
Adorno, T.W. 43–8, 59–66
Althusser, L. 126, 128, 140–2, 146
Amazing Stories 96–100
anthropological approach 36
anxiety 152–3, 162
archaic mother 199, 202
Aristotle, 'catharsis' 12, 65, 100

Barthes, R. 79–85, 91, 115, 132–4, 134–6, 140
Batsleer, J. 217–22
Beethoven 60–1
Benjamin, W. 52–5, 139
Bennett, T. 143–51
Bergonzi, B. 115
bliss, text of 134–6
Blyton, E. 167–9
book clubs 7–8
bourgeoisie 9–11
Brecht, B. 139
Bromley, L. 123–9

Carroll, N. 182–8
Cartland, B. 217–22
castration complex 158, 159, 160, 199, 205
Cavelti, J.G. 71–5, 92–6
children's fiction 167–9
Christie, A. 209–11
Clover, C. 192–8
conformity 47–8, 166–7
convention 71–2
criticism and critics 13–18, 36, 133–4, 137, 236–9
cultural pessimism 36–9, 43–8, 49–52
cultural studies 137–42

Dadoun, R. 202–4
definitions of popular fiction 2, 9–13
democratization of culture 46–7
Derrida, J. 149
detective fiction 56–9, 87–91, 96–100, 146, 211–14, 233–6
discourse register 229–31
distribution 7–8
Dixon, B. 167–9
double, the 156–7, 164–6, 196
Doyle, A.C.
 Sherlock Holmes stories 236–9
Dracula 199–200

dreams 162

Eagleton, T. 137, 149
Eco, U. 101–9
economics of popular fiction 7–8, 43–8, 49–50
ecstatics 12–13
effects of popular forms 36–9, 47–8, 50–2, 59, 166–8
emotional reinforcement 96–100
English Studies Group 121–2
escape 52, 63–4, 217–18
evaluation 13–17, 36–9, 47–8, 56–9, 71–3, 144–5
evil eye 157

father complex 154–5
father, primal/dead 154
fear 152
fear of death 157, 165, 203–4
feminism 204–8, 211–14, 214–18, 219–22
fetishism 160–62, 202–4, 204–8, 211–14
Fiedler, L.A. 9–13
final girl 193, 195
Fleming, Ian
 Bond novels 82–5, 101–9, 169–74
folk tale 75–8
formula 42–3, 71–5, 216–19
Frankenstein 18–31
Freud, S. 152–62

game/play 73–4, 94–5, 105–7
gangster films 87
gaze, the 198–9
gender 192–8, 212–14, 223–33
genre 72–3, 87–91
Goldmann, L.
 homology of structures 138–9
Gramsci, A.
 common sense 121–2, 123–8
 concept of hegemony 121–2, 123–8, 150–1, 212–14
 naturalisation 124
Grixti, J. 180–1

Hall, S. 49–52, 137–43
hero (of thrillers) 168–74
high/low culture 1–5, 9–13, 36–9, 43–8, 50–1, 59–66
historical context 18–30, 39–43, 175–8
horror/fantasy/gothic 11–12, 18–31, 88, 166–7, 180–1, 182–8, 189–92, 192–8, 202–4, 204–8

identification (b
ideology 18   0, 106–7, 134–6,
    121–2.
    174.
    domi

                         oe,
                     premature burial
    r   –31   production and reproduction 6–8, 18–31,
imit   123–8, 129–32, 139–40
innov .ior   2   Propp, V. 75–8
interpellati   120   pseudo-individualization 62–3
interpretati . 14–18, 129–32, 133–4   publishing 5–9
inter-textuality 140, 147–8

                            Rank, O. 164–6
Jackie 215–17, 226–36   readers and response 15–18, 36–9, **63–5**,
James, P.D. 209–12   96–100, 133–4, 139, 147–8, **212–14**,
Jameson, F. 176–8   219–23, 223–32
jouissance 136, 198   realism 50, 85, 140
                                'classic realist' text 233–6
                            reassurance 63, 91, 95–6, 166–8, **178–80**
Kaplan, C. 211–14   reductionism 145–6
Kristeva, J. 140–2, 166–7   repetition 75–8, 101–11
Kwasniewski, E. 96–100   repression 157
                            resistance (to the study of popular forms) 1–5
                            ritual 95–6
Leavis, F.R. 137   Rollin, R.B. 13–18
Leavis, Q.D. 36–9, 56–9   romance 92–4, 125–8, 175–8, **217–22**,
Light, A. 222–6   222–6, 226–32
Literature 1–5, 143–51
look, the 204–5
Lukacs, G. 138–9, 145–6   sales statistics 5–8
                            Sayers, D. 56–9
                            Science 21–30, 233–6
Macherey, P. 129–32, 141, 234   science fiction 96–100, 176–9
manipulation (of readers, audiences) 43–8,   silences, omissions, absences **125–8, 129–32**
    49–50   Silverman, K. 208–11
Marxism 137–43, 143–51   storytelling 52–5
mass society 33–5   subject (of ideology) 89–91, 120, 212
Medusa 160   suspense 73–5, 90–1, 96–100
Mills and Boon 123–4, 221   standardization 45–8, 50, 59–63
monstrous feminine, the 202–5   structure of feeling 39–43, 121, 138
Moylan, T. 176–9
music 59–66   thrillers 101–9, 170–6
musicals and melodrama 88–9 Todorov, T. 81, 91
myth 72–5, 92   totemism 153–6
                            traditional tales (folk and fairy tales) 54–5,
                                75–8, 83–4, 108
narrative
    closure 126, 222   uncanny 152, 156–9, 165, 198–201, 208
    functions 82–5   Utopia 176–9
    meaning 86–7
    oppositions 101–4, 170–4, 176–7   vampire 200
    process 87–91, 233–6
    resolution 41–3, 73–5, 94–6, 216   Westerns 86–7, 92–6
    social function 52–5, 65, 73–5, 79–80,   Whannel, P. 49–52
        86–7, 89–91, 92–6   Williams, R. 39–43, 121, 137–9
Neale, S. 87–91   Wood, R. 189–92
                            Worpole, K. 5–9
O'Flinn, P. 18–31   Wright, W. 86–7
oppositional text 175–8